THE CONSTITUTION IN FLUX

Philip Norton

Basil Blackwell

OTHER WORKS BY THE SAME AUTHOR

The Commons in Perspective (1981)
Dissension in the House of Commons 1974–1979 (1980)
Conservative Dissidents (1978)
Dissension in the House of Commons 1945–74 (1975)
Conservatives and Conservatism (with Arthur Aughey, 1981)

© Philip Norton, 1982

First published 1982
Reprinted 1983
by Martin Robertson & Company Ltd

This edition published 1984
Reprinted 1986

Basil Blackwell Publisher Ltd
108 Cowley Road, Oxford OX4 1JF, UK

Basil Blackwell Inc.
432 Park Avenue South, Suite 1505,
New York, NY 10016, USA

British Library Cataloguing in Publication Data

Norton, Philip
    The Constitution in flux.
    1. Great Britain − Constitutional history
    2. Great Britain − Politics and government − 1964–
    I. Title
    342.41′029   JN216

ISBN 0-631-14155-3 Pbk

Printed and bound in Great Britain by Billing and Sons, Worcester

Contents

Contents

Preface

This short work has what I trust is a modest aim. It seeks to provide sixth-formers and undergraduates – as well as others with an interest in British politics – with an introductory text on constitutional issues that have come on to the agenda of political debate in Britain in recent years. It assumes a basic familiarity with British politics and by its nature is a supplementary text to those set for introductory courses on British Government and Politics.

That there is a need for such a work appears clear. Despite occasional works on particular issues in British politics, there is a dearth of texts providing introductions to groups of issues. The need for a work on constitutional issues is particularly strong. In a debate in the House of Commons in 1981, the Home Office Minister, Timothy Raison, recalled that in 1964 he had written a book about politics.

When I read it not so long ago [he said] it struck me that it contained virtually no discussion on constitutional problems. . . . It was written at a time when, by and large, we did not regard our constitution as something about which we should be having second thoughts. . . . Over the past decade many issues have come to the fore. . . . These issues include the future of the other place [the House of Lords], referendums, devolution, the European Community and our accession to it, a Bill of Rights, electoral reform and what I might call extra-parliamentary forces. (*HC Deb*. 2, c. 1260.)

Indeed, recent years have been remarkable for the number of issues of constitutional significance that have been the subject of political debate; remarkable given the previous absence of such debate. It is perhaps not surprising that no student text has yet appeared which devotes its pages exclusively to such issues. This work attempts to fill that gap.

By its nature, such a work suffers from a number of limitations. It seeks to cover issues which are ever-changing. No sooner has a chapter been written than an event has occurred that dates it. Given this, it is important to record that the book covers no events beyond the end of 1981. In order to produce a work which is not too long, chapters have not only had to be kept to reasonable lengths but a degree of selectivity has had to be exercised in determining their number. I have eschewed attempts to be comprehensive. A number of subjects that would fall under the rubric of the book's title have been excluded, based on my assessment of their significance in terms of constitutional import and the debate surrounding them. An attempt at comprehensive coverage would have necessitated consideration of a wide range of topics, some of which are of some constitutional importance but little debated, and others which might be subsumed under the heading of constitutional minutiae. The dividing line between the decision to include a topic and to exclude another is a thin one. In any future edition it may well be the case that changed circumstances justify inclusion of a chapter on the powers of the Crown; the existing chapter on the machinery of government (a marginal candidate for inclusion in this issue) may well be eligible for exclusion.

Each chapter constitutes in essence a short and as far as possible self-contained essay. The disparate nature of the subjects covered militates against a rigid common framework for each chapter. Nonetheless, the aim in each is the same: to provide a brief background to the issue and to sketch the arguments involved in the contemporary debate. In Part II the subjects covered lend themselves to a clear division between the arguments for and against. I have sought in each case to provide a balanced summary. Though conscious of my own bias (my views on the position and future role of the House of Commons will be obvious and I favour, as no doubt will be apparent, the Traditionalist view delineated in the conclusion) I have endeavoured to present, as clearly as possible, the essentials of the arguments advanced by both proponents and opponents of constitutional change. Each chapter constitutes a synthesis of existing material. This work makes no claim to present original material. Any claim to originality must lie in the form of its compilation.

In the writing of this book I have incurred a number of obligations. My thanks must go to Michael Hay of Martin Robertson. The book is the result of discussions between the two of us in 1980. In the compilation of the work he has provided support and encouragement, and he and Martin Robertson have displayed their usual efficiency in seeing the work through to publication. For reading and commenting upon the whole or part of the manuscript I am most grateful to Dr Howard

Elcock of the Polytechnic of Newcastle-Upon-Tyne; J.R. Carby-Hall of the Department of Law, Hull University; and Ed Page and Jim Marsh of the Department of Politics, Hull University. For help with typing, over and above the call of duty, my many thanks go to Mrs Catherine Davies and Mrs Enid Tracy. Various of my thoughts on the subject have been developed as a result of talks I have given on the subject of constitutional change and in less formal discussions with students and others. My appreciation is owing to all those who participated in such discussions.

The reaction of my own students to what I have written will come as a matter of course. I would be pleased to receive comments from any other interested readers. As usual, responsibility for what follows rests solely with me.

PHILIP NORTON
Department of Politics
University of Hull
January 1982

Introduction
The British Constitution: an anatomical sketch

If one were to approach a stranger in the street and ask 'what are the essential characteristics of the British Constitution?' and 'what issues of constitutional importance have come on to the agenda of political debate in recent years?' the response would likely be a dismissive and rather rude one. In the case of most individuals this would probably reflect a lack of knowledge of, and interest in, politics. To the busy housewife concerned with getting in the weekly groceries there is no time to waste on such questions. To the young unemployed black in Liverpool the questions are incomprehensible. These reactions in themselves are of some importance in a discussion on the British Constitution, and ones to which we shall return.

If one were to ask the same questions of those with some interest in the subject, such as students of politics and practising politicians (the categories are not mutually exclusive), one might at least expect answers. If one were lucky, the answer to the first question might consist of identifying the constitution as being 'unwritten', flexible and evolutionary, with possibly some reference to the principle of parliamentary sovereignty. The response to the second question would likely be to emphasise one or two of several issues that have become the subject of debate in recent years: for example, devolution, a Bill of Rights or electoral reform. What would be surprising, or rather disappointing, about the responses would probably be their lack of sophistication and comprehensiveness. They would reflect a lack of confidence in and unfamiliarity with discussing the constitution in broad conceptual terms. The language of constitutional debate is somewhat alien to undergraduate classes in politics and to debates on the floor of the House of Commons. Students of politics are rarely invited to address themselves to the topic of the constitution as such. Indeed, it would be rare for such students to know much if anything, let alone care, about matters of constitutional law or jurisprudence. The reasons for the inability to discuss institutional and political changes within the context of their wider constitutional implications we shall consider shortly. It is an inability which afflicts the politician as much as the student. When a backbench MP introduced a motion for debate under the title of 'The British Constitution' in April 1981 the debate was notable on two counts. First, the fact that it was held at all. Second, the nature of the debate: it centred upon, or rather veered erratically between, disparate constitutional issues.[1] Some Members expressed support for electoral reform. Others argued the case for a Bill of Rights. The mover of the motion, Conservative MP John Stokes, argued the case for supporting existing institutions such as the Church of England and the House of Lords (again, two categories that are not mutually exclusive). With the exception of one contribution from a constitutional lawyer,[2] there was little attempt to define or talk in conceptual terms about the constitution.

In response to the two questions posed, it appears likely that few respondents would be able to provide clear and considered answers. There are few works in the literature that would help them to do so. No text designed specifically for student use has appeared recently with a title such as *Current Political Issues*, let alone *Contemporary Constitutional Issues*.[3] By contrast, textbooks with 'British Government' in the title, or some variation, have come tumbling off the printing presses.[4] Constitutional issues, given that they affect the structures of government and their relationship with one another, do gain a mention to a greater or lesser (often lesser) extent in the traditional texts. However, they rarely constitute the focus of such works and, indeed, they may not be identified as issues of constitutional significance.

As a result of the appearance of Nevil Johnson's sophisticated discourse *In Search of the Constitution*[5] and various articles from the pen of Gillian Peele[6] (as well as the incisive and more long-standing works of Geoffrey Marshall),[7] there is some movement designed to increase awareness of and indulgence in the language of constitutional debate. This volume seeks to further that process. Unlike Nevil Johnson, we do not seek to offer a diagnosis and a prescription; this work will lack both the originality and the sophistication displayed by *In Search of the Constitution*. Unlike the standard works on constitutional law, our focus is not the answer to the first question posited above. Rather, we seek to tread the path on which Johnson's Oxford colleague, Gillian Peele, has set out. The focus of the work is the second question stated earlier. We seek to identify and explain the constitutional issues that have come on to the agenda of political debate in recent years. We do so for what we hope is the benefit of the student of politics, the sixth-former and the undergraduate, who wishes to advance beyond the confines of the more traditional texts with which he or she is confronted.

In order to address ourselves to the second question — 'what issues of constitutional importance have come on to the political agenda in recent years?' — we must preface our consideration with an answer to the first one: 'what are the essential characteristics of the British Constitution?' As any good student knows, one must logically begin by defining one's terms. As the debate in the House of Commons in April 1981 demonstrated, failure to do so can lead to confused and dis-jointed thinking. However, it is insufficient to stipulate a definition of a constitution and then proceed immediately to a consideration of contemporary debate on matters such as a Bill of Rights. To understand the significance of the issues to be discussed, it is important not only that we define what we mean by a constitution but also clarify the form in which it is expressed, the sources from which it is derived, the method by which it may be changed, its essential constituents, the political environment in which it exists and the nature of the political authority on which the institutions it stipulates are based, as well as some consideration of the nature of constitutional debate. Many of these points are often overlooked or sometimes confused with one another.

DEFINITION

There is no agreed definition of a constitution. Sir Kenneth Wheare and Professor Hood Phillips, among others, drew a useful distinction between a broad, abstract definition and a narrower, concrete definition.[8] In the abstract sense it is 'the system of laws, customs and conventions which define the composition and powers of organs of the state, and regulate the relations of the various state organs to one another and to the private citizen'.[9] In the concrete sense it is the document in which the most important laws establishing the structure and principles of govern-ment are embodied.

The broad, abstract definition has been in use longer than the narrow, concrete one, though the latter is now more commonly used. We propose to use the term in the abstract sense. To define 'constitution' in the narrow sense of a particular document is too limiting and, in the context of Britain, extremely unhelpful. As a document, it can more appropriately be considered as a form in which the constitution is expressed rather than as a definition of the term itself.

FORMS IN WHICH A CONSTITUTION MAY BE EXPRESSED

There are various forms in which a constitution may be expressed. The most common terms employed are those of 'written' and 'unwritten'. The United Kingdom is often described as having an unwritten constitution. A constitution is said to be 'written' when the most important constitutional laws are specially enacted and put into one formal document.[10] In that concrete sense the UK does not have a written constitution. However, such terminology is extremely unhelpful and somewhat misleading.

There is no formal document which is designated as 'The Constitution of the United Kingdom'. However, as various writers have pointed out, there is a great deal of statute law that could properly be called constitutional law. Much of that statute law treats fundamental political institutions in the same way that a written constitution does.

The early laws dealing with the rights and liberties of English (and, by later extension, of British) subjects are akin to the sentiments and contents of the Preambles and Bills of Right to be found in formal documentary constitutions. There are statutes that deal with the formation of the United Kingdom; there are statutes that provide for the limitation of the power of the Sovereign ... other statutes deal with the House of Lords, the House of Commons and Parliament as a whole, with the Established Church, with the Judiciary, with the Armed Forces, with local and devolved government, with citizenship and with emergency powers.[11]

As Leslie Wolf-Phillips points out, 'this surely makes absurd the use of the term "unwritten" in respect to British constitutional arrangements'.[12] If one wished to talk in terms of a written or unwritten constitution, then Britain may be said to have one that is 'part written'.

One other distinction sometimes drawn to make the point that the UK constitution is not drawn up in one formal document, whereas many others are, is that between 'codified' and 'uncodified' constitutions. There may be said to be degrees of codification. Some written, i.e. single-document, constitutions stipulate only basic or skeletal provision for the structure and operation of government, others stipulate the most detailed of provisions. In the USA, for example, there is a marked contrast between the federal constitution and many of the constitutions of the individual states: some of the latter run to more than 100,000 words. The UK (hereafter Britain) does not have its constitutional provisions codified in one precise charter. Hence it is deemed to have an 'uncodified' constitution.

This may seem to be labouring a simple point. Britain does not have its most important laws establishing the structure and principles of government codified in one solemn document. Nonetheless, it does have such laws. Some but not all of them are expressed in formal documents. Hence, the British Constitution may be described as being, in form, part written but uncodified.

SOURCES FROM WHICH IT IS DERIVED

The sources from which the British Constitution is derived may be subsumed under four headings: statute law, common law, conventions, and works of authority. Judicial decisions are sometimes listed as a separate source as is the law and custom of Parliament: however, both may be included under the heading of common law.

Statute law

Statute law comprises Acts of Parliament and subordinate legislation made under the authority of the parent Act. Of the sources listed, it is the most important, both in quantitative and qualitative terms. It is the main source for the 'part written' element of the constitution. Numerous Acts have been passed which, given our definition of a constitution, quite clearly merit the nomenclature of constitutional law. In terms of measures which 'define the composition and powers of organs of the state, and regulate the relations of the various state organs to one another', the most obvious and important include the Bill of Rights of 1689, the Act of Settlement of 1701, the Act of Union with Scotland of 1706, the Parliament Acts of 1911 and 1949, the Northern Ireland (Temporary Provisions) Act of 1972 and the European Communities Act of the same year. Some of these have a rather unusual status: the Bill of Rights was passed by the so-called Convention Parliament but is deemed to have the force of statute, and the Union with Scotland Act was based on a treaty negotiated by the English and Scottish Parliaments. The significance of the European Communities Act we will consider in detail later (ch. 8). Measures which 'regulate the relations of the

various state organs . . . to the private citizen' include the Bill of Rights
of 1689 (again), the Act of Settlement of 1701 (again), the Habeas
Corpus Act of 1679, the Public Order Act of 1936 and the Administration of Justice Act 1960. In quantitative terms these constitute but the
tip of an extremely large iceberg. Each year various measures which are
of constitutional import reach the statute books.

Common law

Common law as a source of constitutional law has declined quantitatively
as it has been variously replaced by statute law. Nonetheless it remains
an important source. Under this general rubric come the rules of custom
(now partly modified by statute) which provide such fundamental
principles as parliamentary sovereignty, and which determine what
constitutes an Act of Parliament, as well as the royal prerogative. The
principle of parliamentary sovereignty we shall consider in detail
shortly. The royal prerogative constitutes 'the gradually diminishing
residuum of customary authority, privilege and immunity, recognised
at common law as belonging to the Crown, and the Crown alone'.[13] It
is diminishing because much prerogative power has been and continues
to be replaced by statute law. Nonetheless, the prerogative power still
encompasses such matters as the appointment of ministers, the making
of treaties, the power of pardon, the dissolution of Parliament, the
declaration of a state of war, and the dispensing of honours. It remains
important especially but not exclusively in the conduct of foreign
affairs. Its usage is determined largely by convention.

Under this heading we may include also judicial decisions. Much
constitutional law is or has been shaped by decisions of the courts in
particular cases. Such cases arise in the ordinary course of litigation,
and will be found most often in the decisions of the Queen's Bench
Division (which has special jurisdiction in proceedings for habeas corpus,
certiorari, prohibition and mandamus), the Court of Appeal, the House of
Lords on appeal therefrom, the Court of Justice of the European Communities in respect of EC legislation, and the Judicial Committee of the
Privy Council in appeals from British overseas territories.[14] Given the
absence of a comprehensive charter of individual rights, common law and
judicial pronouncements have proved especially important in the sphere
of civil liberties. The limitations imposed upon judicial interpretation by
the principles of parliamentary sovereignty we shall consider later.

The law and custom of Parliament comprise the rules relating to the functions, procedure, privileges and immunities of each House of Parliament. They derive mainly from resolutions of each House and informal understandings or practices. In small part, they are embodied in statute law and judicial decisions, such as the Parliamentary Privilege Act of 1770 and *Stockdale v. Hansard* (1839). Most, though, are outwith the purview of statutes and the courts as the internal proceedings of both Houses are not cognisable by the courts.

Conventions

Conventions constitute probably the most discussed and least definable source of the constitution. The most useful definition of conventions is that posited by Marshall and Moodie:

> By the conventions of the Constitution . . . we mean certain rules of constitutional behaviour which are considered to be binding by and upon those who operate the Constitution, but which are not enforced by the law courts (although the courts may recognise their existence), nor by the presiding officers in the Houses of Parliament.[15]

They are basically 'rules', accepted as such by those at whom they are directed, and accepted in order to ensure that the formal provisions of the constitution are adapted to prevailing conditions and, for all intents and purposes, to ensure that the constitution works. They are, if you like, the oil in the machinery of the constitution. They are not formally binding — there are no official means of enforcement — but derive their strength from the perception that they are legitimate in terms of prevailing constitutional norms and that to break them would, to maintain our analogy, result in the rusting of the constitutional machine.

Given that perceptions differ and that there is no clearly defined or readily observable point at which a desirable principle becomes a convention of the constitution, it is not surprising that there is a not insignificant grey area as to what is and what is not a convention. Some conventions are strong and well-recognised. For instance, it is a convention that the Sovereign assents to measures passed by both Houses of Parliament. Though there is no doubt that Her Majesty has the legal right to deny her consent, to do so would offend current constitutional norms and would create a political crisis deeply damaging to the position of the monarch. Likewise, the convention that a government denied a vote of confidence by the House of Commons must seek a dissolution or tender its resignation (there is no convention dictating which of these alternative courses to pursue). There were fears expressed by some Conservative politicians that the Labour Government denied a vote of confidence on 28 March 1979 would not adhere to the convention, but for it not to have done so would have made its position politically untenable.

The obvious grey area is where a desirable principle is deemed to be a convention by some commentators but not by others. For example, is it a convention of the constitution that the Foreign Secretary should sit in the House of Commons? Labour politicians appear to believe (or rather hope) that it is. Conservative politicians, by contrast, do not and Prime Ministers Macmillan and Thatcher appeared to have little doubt when appointing Foreign Secretaries from the peerage. What influences perceptions as to what should be accepted as a convention is the *effect* that not abiding by it would have. The appointment of a Foreign Secretary who sits in the House of Lords may create political difficulties for the government (as may some of the measures it introduces which are of little constitutional import) but it does not make its position politically untenable by virtue of undermining or significantly altering the structure and distribution of authority within the constitution.[16] For the Queen to refuse assent to a measure would have that effect. Mrs Thatcher appointing Lord Carrington as Foreign Secretary does not.

Works of authority

The last source of the constitution comprises works of authority, which have persuasive authority only. Given the diffuse nature of the constitution, such works tend to be consulted more in the sphere of constitutional law than in the other branches of English law.[17] They may be referred to on abstruse questions of constitutional law in court or within Parliament in the determination of parliamentary privilege. What constitutes a 'work of authority' is rarely defined. Some books are treated as such by reason of scholarship and age. Various early works are given special weight by virtue of the absence of statutes or other written sources. The statements of their writers are presumed to be evidence of judicial decisions that have been lost, and are therefore accepted if not contrary to reason.[18] However, more recent works have been called in aid by those seeking to delineate the constitution. The reason for this is that statute law and judicial decisions are, as we have seen, only partial sources in defining the constitution and there is no formal or defined procedure for determining conventions. To discover conventions and sketch the outlines of the constitution, reference has to be made to works written by scholars of the constitution. Important nineteenth-century authorities were A.V. Dicey and John Austin. Twentieth-century works often cited are those by Sir Ivor Jennings, Professor Hood Phillips, E.C.S. Wade, and Sir Kenneth Weare. The most important single influence has almost certainly been Dicey. In terms of the law and custom of Parliament, the most authoritative work on parliamentary proceedings and privilege — for all intents and purposes treated as definitive by the Speaker and the clerks of the House — is *Erskine May*,[19] 'the parliamentary bible'.

THE METHOD BY WHICH IT MAY BE CHANGED

The method by which a constitution may be formally amended is often categorised in terms of 'flexible' or 'inflexible'. An inflexible (or, in Bryce's term, 'rigid') constitution is one which stipulates extraordinary procedures for amendment. A flexible constitution is one that requires no special procedure for amendment; in other words it can be amended by the same procedures as for non-constitutional law. It would appear common for written, i.e. single-document, constitutions to have special procedures for amending their provisions; in such cases, the document and its provisions are generally referred to as being entrenched. The US Constitution is inflexible inasmuch as an amendment to it requires the assent of a two-thirds majority in both Houses of Congress (or approval by a convention called on application by the legislatures of two-thirds of the states) and ratification by the legislatures (or by conventions) in three-quarters of the states.[20] In the case of some constitutions, certain provisions are deemed to be unalterable.[21] Britain, by contrast, has a flexible constitution. The provisions of the constitution are not entrenched. Statute law which merits the nomenclature of constitutional law can be amended (and, indeed, repealed) in the same way as all other statute law. Common law can be modified or replaced by statute law and there are no special provisions governing the determination or amending of conventions or, for that matter, assertions advanced by works of authority.

Employed in a neutral sense, the terms flexible and inflexible have a certain utility. There are various qualifications that must nevertheless be recorded. There are clearly degrees of flexibility: a constitution which can be amended by a prescribed extraordinary majority of the legislative body may be considered to be less inflexible, at least formally, than one requiring an extraordinary majority in the legislature and ratification by referendum or by state assemblies. This point is not too important for the purposes of considering the British Constitution. More relevant is the fact that formal limitations are not necessarily good guides to the actual flexibility of a constitution. As the late Professor de Smith aptly observed, a constitution containing a cumbersome procedure for its own amendment may in fact be very flexible if there is no effective opposition to the party in power;[22] it may also be subject to amendment in effect by judicial interpretation in those countries (such as the USA) in which the power of constitutional interpretation is vested in the courts. Conversely, a flexible constitution may remain unamended because of strong attachment to its provisions on the part of the majority of the legislative body and/or the populace, or because, as was apparently the case in Ceylon (when it existed under that name), a volatile multi-party system ensured that governments were preoccupied with sustaining their own position, usually successfully, with little time to devote to the niceties of constitutional debate.[23]

Though the British Constitution is flexible, there are certain provisions which any government would be extremely hesitant even to contemplate seeking approval for their removal or amendment. Whereas a government may seek to amend the relationship of organs of the state to the individual citizen by introducing measures dealing with public order or the declaration of emergencies, it is extremely unlikely – to put it mildly – that a government would seek the enactment of an Act removing the vote from women or one abolishing the monarchy. In short, the British Constitution formally is a flexible one, but one has to go beyond the formal position in order to ascertain the likelihood of the amendment of its provisions. In practice, some may be deemed more (or less) vulnerable to amendment than others.

ITS ESSENTIAL CONSTITUENTS

There is no one document which details definitely the essential constituents, the basic principles, of the British Constitution. To ascertain those features one has to fall back on works of authority, works which it must be recalled are persuasive only. The most influential work of the past century has been Dicey's *An Introduction to the Study of the Law of the Constitution*. First published in 1885,[24] it usually comprises the starting point for any consideration of the basic principles of the Constitution.

Dicey asserted that the two pillars of the Constitution were parliamentary sovereignty and the rule of law. The principle of parliamentary sovereignty, he declared, 'means neither more nor less than this, namely, that Parliament . . . has, under the English constitution, the right to make or unmake any law whatever; and, further, that no person or body is recognised by the law of England as having a right to override or set aside the legislation of Parliament'.[25] Parliament, he reminded his readers, comprised the Queen, the House of Commons and the House of Lords acting together — the 'Queen-in-Parliament'. An Act of Parliament would be obeyed by the courts, and no other body could make a rule which overrode an Act and could be enforced by the courts. He contended that the principle was 'fully recognised by the law of England', citing in aid the assertions of Sir Edward Coke as reported in Blackstone's *Commentaries.*[26]

The principle itself finds no expression in statute or any formal constitutional enactment. It exists in common law, but enjoys a special status. Despite the assertions of Coke, parliamentary sovereignty was not accepted without question prior to the latter half of the seventeenth century.[27] It became established as a judicial rule as a consequence of the Glorious Revolution of 1688 and subsequent Bill of Rights, the product of an alliance between Parliament and common lawyers, and the intimidation of judges by the Commons. Its underpinnings are not only legal but also political and historical: it is now too late to challenge the principle and judicial obedience to it constitutes 'the ultimate political fact upon which the whole system of legislation hangs'.[28] No statute can confer the power of parliamentary sovereignty, for that would be to confer the very power which is being acted upon. It is therefore considered to be unique. 'It may indeed be called the one fundamental law of the British Constitution.'[29]

Various consequences of the principle of parliamentary sovereignty can be and have been noted. One precept derived from it, worthy of mention at this point, is that Parliament cannot bind its successors. (Given the very concept of parliamentary sovereignty, this assertion may appear to be paradoxical and to avoid this problem it is sometimes expressed in another way, 'Parliament is not bound by its predecessors'.)[30] This precept has been queried by various authorities, particularly on the basis of the Acts of Union, various Acts granting independence to a number of countries, and the 1972 European Communities Act. Are such Acts repealable by Parliament? The most persuasive authority is probably Professor Hood Phillips. Repeal of an Act, he asserted, would be recognised by the courts of the UK and its dependencies and enforced by those courts in relations to persons and property which are or which come within their jurisdiction. 'Thus if Parliament purported to revoke the independence of Uganda, this would affect the legal status of citizens of Uganda in this country.'[31] It may be asserted that it would be a nonsense for Parliament to pass such an Act but that does not affect its formal power to do so. The removal of this power could be achieved by a change of attitude on the part of the courts or possibly by Parliament extinguishing itself, after surrendering its powers to a new written constitution with entrenched provisions and judicial review, 'a constitution limiting the powers of the new legislature and to which the new legislature would owe its existence'.[32] We shall consider in later chapters the contemporary arguments in favour of such changes. For the moment it is sufficient to assert that the precept 'Parliament is not bound by its predecessors' remains extant and is accepted by the courts.

'Despite recent criticisms', as E.C.S. Wade observed, 'it is still true to-day as a proposition of law of the United Kingdom to say that Parliament has the right to make or unmake any law whatever. Nor can any court within the United Kingdom set aside the provisions of an Act of Parliament.'[33] To understand the contemporary British Constitution, this assertion of parliamentary sovereignty, while valid, requires further comment. Various points and caveats have to be entered. Political developments of the nineteenth and twentieth centuries, while not affecting the formal power of Parliament to enact any measure and the courts' inability to set aside any such measure, have modified significantly the distribution of power within the triumvirate of the Queen-in-Parliament. Some of these developments have found expression in statute; others have been embodied in conventions. As features of the contemporary constitution they may be identified as: election (of the House of Commons) by adult suffrage; a limited 'constitutional' monarchy; Cabinet government; and the dominance of the House of Commons in the decision-making process of the Queen-in-Parliament.

The nineteenth century witnessed the transfer from a form of traditional authority, to use the language of Max Weber, to one of rational–legal authority. Pressure from artisans and the non-landed middle class, coupled with a degree of political opportunism, resulted in the principle of some form of limited democracy via the ballot box being conceded; by the end of the century this had been extended to adult male suffrage. The twentieth century has witnessed the further extension of the franchise, as the principle of adult female suffrage has been conceded as has the lowering of the age of majority to 18 years. These changes have been embodied in statute.[34] They have been accompanied by related measures. The period from 1883 to 1885 witnessed the passage of a number of significant Acts. 'These equalised the borough and county franchises, adopted single-member electoral districts of roughly equal size as the norm, limited the amount candidates might spend on elections, and introduced new and more stringent prohibitions against corrupt practices.'[35] These measures were reinforced and amended by later Acts. With the passage of the Representation of the People Act of 1949 (which abolished university seats and plural voting), the principle of 'one person, one vote' was finally deemed, for all intents and purposes, to have been conceded.[36] Whether the Benthamite principle of 'one man, one vote, one value' has been achieved is a matter of current controversy and one to which we shall return in a later chapter.

The conceding of the principle of election by popular vote raised fundamental questions about the concept of parliamentary sovereignty. How can Parliament be sovereign if, in Austin's words, 'the members of the Commons' house are merely trustees for the body by which they are elected and appointed'?[37] To Austin, sovereignty resided 'in the King and the Peers, with the electoral body of the Commons'.[38] Dicey recognised this problem and addressed himself to it. He resolved it by distinguishing between 'political sovereignty', which rested with the electors, and 'legal sovereignty', which continued to rest with Parliament.[39] 'Legal sovereignty' could not be exercised by the electors. The courts would enforce only Acts of Parliament.

The electors can in the long run always enforce their will. But the courts will take no notice of the will of the electors. The judges know nothing about any will of the people except in so far as that will is expressed by an Act of Parliament, and would never suffer the validity of a statute to be questioned on the grounds of its having been passed or being kept alive in opposition to the wishes of the electors.[40]

This distinction has given rise to an important semantic argument. If one accepts that sovereignty is indivisible, how can one have two distinct bodies (the electorate and Parliament) each exercising sovereignty? Several constitutional scholars have sought to resolve this problem by referring instead to parliamentary 'supremacy', though this hardly solves the problem. Some dictionaries treat the two words as synonymous. There is no satisfactory solution to the problem. Given the common usage of the term 'parliamentary sovereignty' it may prove convenient to retain it, though recognising it for what it is, a specific legal concept.

The position of the monarch was restrained as a result of the struggles of the sixteenth and seventeenth centuries, culminating in the Glorious Revolution and the Bill of Rights of 1689. The king retained prerogative powers under common law but could no longer pass laws or levy taxes without the consent of Parliament. 'The supremacy lay in Parliament, but national policy was determined by the king subject to certain controlling powers of Parliament.'[41] As a result of the king's increasing dependence upon his ministers, especially in the eighteenth century, and the achievement of an adult male suffrage in the nineteenth, national policy came to be determined by the Cabinet. The relationship between the monarch, ministers and Parliament was modified by convention. The monarch's powers now are exercised on the advice of ministers or by ministers in the Queen's name (Her Majesty's choice of ministers being governed by the advice of the Prime Minister); ministers remain responsible legally to the Queen for their actions, but by convention are responsible to Parliament. 'They defend their conduct there, and continuance in office depends on retaining the confidence of the Commons.'[42] The Cabinet is, by convention, at the hub of government: it has no formal powers but it is deemed to be responsible for the final determination of policy to be submitted to Parliament, for the supreme control of the national executive in accordance with the policy prescribed by Parliament, and for the continuous co-ordination and delimitation of the interests of the several Departments of State.[43] From the development of Cabinet government flowed a number of new or reinforced conventions: ministers sit in Parliament (predominantly, by convention, the House of Commons), the Cabinet is bound by the principle of collective ministerial responsibility, and the government tenders its resignation or requests a dissolution in the event of being denied a vote of confidence by the House of Commons. The developments of the nineteenth century ensured that, politically, the Cabinet dominated the House of Commons through a party majority, a majority prepared to support it regularly in the division lobbies. However, the very same developments ensured that the Commons became the dominant of the two chambers in Parliament. With the growth of a mass suffrage, with the emergence of the 'political sovereignty' of the electorate, the House of Lords could not maintain a claim to be politically co-equal with the Commons. It fought to maintain its formal power but its diminished status was to find embodiment in statute in the Parliament Acts of 1911 and 1949.[44] The various powers as exercised by the elements of the Queen-in-Parliament and the relationship between them we shall have cause to explore in later chapters.

The other pillar of the British Constitution identified by Dicey was 'the rule of law'. The concept is in some respects similar to that of 'democracy': almost everyone appears to favour it but cannot agree upon what it means. (Indeed, the concepts may have similar roots: reference to the rule of law is to be found in Aristotle.)[45] Dicey himself contended that it encompassed 'at least three distinct though kindred conceptions'. First, 'that no man is punishable or can be lawfully made to suffer in body or goods except for a distinct breach of law established in the ordinary legal manner before the ordinary courts of the land'. Second, 'no man is above the law, [and] . . . every man, whatever be his rank or condition, is subject to the ordinary law of the realm and amenable to the jurisdiction of the ordinary tribunals'. Third, 'the general principles of the constitution (as for example the right to personal liberty, or the right of public meeting) are . . . the result of judicial decisions determining the rights of private persons in particular cases brought before the courts'.[46] The extent to which these 'kindred conceptions' hold good today is far from agreed. Some authorities regard Dicey as still relevant,[47] others tend to be dismissive. S.A. de Smith, for example, referred to Dicey's views as idiosyncratic ideas which no longer warranted detailed analysis.[48] Dicey has been criticised on various grounds. His first point, as he defined it, precluded the exercise of 'wide, arbitrary, or discretionary powers of constraint'.[49] This has been criticised on the grounds that it constituted a principle of political action, not a juridical principle governing the actual distribution of powers;[50] Dicey's Whiggishness led him to view with disfavour the possibility of government vested with significant powers of regulation. Today, many discretionary powers are vested in officials and public bodies, as indeed many were at the time that Dicey wrote. His second point has been variously questioned. In so far as it may be said to mean that all persons have equal rights and duties before the law, it is of doubtful value: local authorities, ministers, police officers and others have many powers that the ordinary citizen has not got.[51] In the sense that Dicey apparently meant it, that it 'excludes any exemption of officials or others from the duty of obedience to the law which governs other citizens',[52] then various exceptions may be recorded: certain immunities are enjoyed by judges, ambassadors and, in particular respects, the Crown. Trade unions also enjoy a special position in law. Jennings believed that Dicey meant only that an official committing a tort would be liable for it in the ordinary civil courts, and contended that 'it is a small point upon which to base a doctrine called by the magnificent name of "rule of law", particularly when it is generally used in a very different sense'.[53] Dicey's third point has been queried because it is not clear why it should be considered 'kindred' to the first two points, and because certain rights have been enacted in or modified by statute. The Bill of Rights, for example, prescribes that 'excessive bail ought not to be required nor excessive fines imposed nor cruel and unusual punishment inflicted'; the Public Order Act 1936 restricts the freedom to assemble and to march. It has also been criticised as a statement of the obvious (in as much as rights being part of the ordinary law is a necessary consequence of an uncodified constitution) and as the expression of the nineteenth-century liberal obsession with the liberty of the individual. This catalogue of criticisms and qualifications is not exhaustive. It is sufficient, though, to substantiate the point that Dicey's definition of the rule of law does not enjoy the universal assent of other authorities.

Even if one were to accept Dicey's conception of the rule of law, it would not be logically compatible with the concept of parliamentary sovereignty. Parliament, if it wished, could confer arbitrary powers on government. It could limit or remove some of the rights 'determined' by judicial decisions. Dicey himself recognised that 'the two principles which pervade the whole of the English constitution may appear to stand in opposition to each other, or to be at best only counterbalancing forces',[54] and sought to reconcile the two. The sovereignty of Parliament favoured the supremacy of the law of the land, he wrote, because (a) the commands of Parliament could be uttered only through the combined action of its three constituent parts 'and must, therefore, always take the shape of formal and deliberate legislation',[55] and (b) 'the English Parliament as such has never, except at periods of revolution, exercised direct executive power or appointed the officials of the executive government'.[56] Furthermore, the supremacy of the law necessitated the exercise of parliamentary sovereignty. 'The rigidity of the law constantly hampers . . . the action of the executive, and from the hard-and-fast rules of strict law, as interpreted by the judges, the government can escape only by obtaining from Parliament the discretionary authority which is denied to the Crown by the law of the land.'[57] In other words, the rule of law prevented government from exercising arbitrary powers; if government required such powers, it could acquire them only through Parliament (Parliament itself has never sought to exercise executive powers) and the grant of them could be given only after deliberation and approval by the constituent elements of the Queen-in-Parliament. This interpretation constitutes a blend of the descriptive and the prescriptive and clearly reflects the liberal view of the relationship of government to the individual: that individual freedom is best assured by limited government and a separation of powers. It does not overcome the truth of the assertion that under the principle of parliamentary sovereignty Parliament could, if it wished, enact measures which are contrary to what Dicey defined as the rule of law.

We are thus left with a principle to which authorities on the constitution assent, but one which enjoys no agreed definition and which, on most definitions, is not logically compatible with the principle of parliamentary sovereignty. (It is not incompatible when defined as power derived from law, but that is hardly a useful definition; on that basis, as Jennings noted, 'all civilised states possess it'.)[58] The problem of definition is not one confined to Britain. Various attempts to find an internationally accepted definition have been made. As the secretary of one international colloquium observed, 'the rule of law is an expression of an endeavour to give reality to something which is not readily expressable'.[59] Some authorities subscribe to definitions posited by international bodies, such as the International Commission of Jurists' Declaration of Delhi,[60] while others stipulate their own definition. Most views of what is encompassed by the rule of law appear to share some common ground: that the term implies certain substantive and procedural rights, that government must be subject to the law, and the judiciary must be independent. One is still left with the problem of determining what the substantive and procedural rights are, how they are to be protected, and how the independence of the judiciary can be guaranteed. Some, indeed many, scholars — as well as the British Government — subscribe to the basic rights embodied in certain international conventions, but the doctrine of parliamentary sovereignty prevents their entrenchment as a form of higher law. The same problem is faced by those wishing to entrench the independence of the courts. For many, parliamentary sovereignty constitutes not an encouragement to the rule of law but rather an impediment to its attainment.

Apart from the twin and potentially contradictory pillars of parliamentary sovereignty and the rule of law, are there any other features of the British Constitution that can usefully be identified? Again, there is no definitive guide. Some of the features identified by certain writers are incorporated within or closely allied with the two principles just identified. A belief in certain substantive rights, such as freedom of speech, is encompassed by the rubric of the rule of law. So too is the independence of the judiciary. Britain does not enjoy a formal separation of personnel and powers between the executive, legislature and judiciary comparable to that which exists, for example, in the USA. Nonetheless, judicial independence has largely been achieved. This has been the result partly of statute, common law, parliamentary rules and acceptance by government that the rule of law requires abstention from interference with the conduct of litigation. Judges of superior courts cannot be removed except for misbehaviour in office, and their salaries are fixed by statute in order to avoid annual debate. A superior court judge enjoys immunity from civil proceedings for anything said or done while acting in a judicial capacity; a judge of an inferior court is immune also if acting within his jurisdiction. By custom, questions are not asked in either House of Parliament about the conduct of courts in particular cases.[61] It remains the case, though, that judges are appointed by the Crown on the advice of the Lord Chancellor (a member of the Cabinet), that the structure, size and jurisdiction of the courts can be and are determined by statute and Parliament can (and on occasion does) pass legislation to reverse a court's interpretation of a particular measure.[62]

Another central characteristic of the constitution is that the state is a unitary and not a federal or confederal one. The UK is a union of England, Wales, Scotland and Northern Ireland, as provided by statute.[63] Were the UK to become a federal state, then Parliament would cease to be omnicompetent and the courts would likely (though not necessarily) enjoy a new position in the political process. This point, as we shall see, is relevant to the discussion on the possible devolution of powers to elected assemblies in Scotland and Wales.

Included on occasion in lists delineating the main features of the constitution is the fact that the Civil Service is impartial. By that is meant that civil servants enjoy tenure in employment and serve successive governments without political favour: governments come and governments go, but the Civil Service endures and provides administrative continuity. The recruitment and administration of the civil service is carried out under prerogative powers. Control is exercised via Orders in Council, Treasury Minutes and circulars, though provision for superannuation has been made by statute. Civil servants are disqualified by statute from election to the House of Commons,[64] and by internal regulation various categories of civil servants are barred from engaging in, or allowed only restricted involvement in, political activity. The relationship between civil servants and Parliament is governed by the convention of ministerial responsibility.

There are various other constituents of the constitution that could be identified under this section, but the foregoing constitute the most central and certainly the most important for the purposes of our later considerations.

THE POLITICAL ENVIRONMENT AND THE BASIS OF AUTHORITY

Constitutions, unlike the Ten Commandments, are not fashioned out of stone, God-given and immutable, though some of their supporters may believe them so to be. As John Stuart Mill conceded, they 'are the work of men. . . . Men did not wake up on a summer morning and find them sprung up.'[65] To gain some understanding of why a particular constitution was devised, the way in which it is applied, received and amended, and pressures (if any) for its modification or replacement, one has to consider the political environment in which it was created and nurtured and how that environment has changed since. Americans sometimes view the US Constitution as being 'in fact imperfect man's most perfect rendering of what Blackstone saluted as "the eternal immutable laws of good and evil, to which the creator himself in all his dispensations conforms: and which he has enabled human reason to discover, so far as they are necessary for the conduct of human actions" ',[66] their holding such a view being central to an appreciation of the status and effect of the constitution in American political life.

However, other more mundane influences have been seen to be at work in the document's compilation and content. The framers of the constitution met in Philadelphia in 1787 to discuss constitutional change because of what James Madison entitled the 'vices of the political system' under the existing Articles of Confederation.[67] The framers' deliberations have been identified as having been influenced by what might be termed Lockean values (as well as the writings of Montesquieu), by reactions to recent experiences and, in Charles Beard's analysis, by a desire to protect the economic interests of large planters, merchants and financiers against those of small farmers and the artisans of the cities.[68] Though one cannot prove why the members of the Constitutional Convention acted in the way that they did (since why men act and why men say and believe they act are not the same, and the former can never be proved), the evidence in support of the contention that their deliberations did not take place independently of the contemporary political environment is more than sufficiently plausible to merit acceptance.

Similarly with British experience. An understanding of the constitution is possible only with an appreciation of British history, of the events producing the signing of the Magna Carta, the departure of James II and the promulgation of the Bill of Rights, the industrial revolution and the pressure from the rising middle class for the vote, and of the absence since the seventeenth century of a revolution entailing the sweeping away of the existing constitution. As we have touched upon briefly already, the Bill of Rights of 1689 can be seen as the product of the struggle between Parliament and the Crown, the former winning and asserting by statute the new relationship between the two. An alliance between Parliament and common lawyers helped produce 'the very keystone of the law of the constitution', parliamentary sovereignty.[69]

Indeed, an awareness of contemporary political circumstance is made especially important in the British context given the absence of an uncodified constitutiton. The dividing line between what constitutes the constitution and what does not is far from clear. The divide between the formal constitutional structure and changing political circumstance is bridged by convention, but as we have seen the point at which a desirable principle becomes a constitutional convention is not easy to determine. The point was well put by G.H.L. LeMay in his study of the constitution in the Victorian era: 'The conventions of the constitution . . . have meaning only when they are looked at against a background of continuous political change. It is very difficult to say with certainty what they were at any particular moment. Above all, they cannot be understood "with the politics left out".'[70]

One cannot understand the workings of the constitution 'with the politics left out'. As constitutional lawyers themselves have variously conceded, what may be formally possible under the constitution may not be politically possible to achieve. As long as a government maintains a parliamentary majority there are no legal limits to what it may do. 'The only restraints', as Bernard Crick noted, 'are political. Governments are restrained by what they think the country will stand for come the general election, and they adhere to things like general elections because they *prefer* (whether out of ethics, habit or prudence, or all three) to settle disputes politically rather than despotically and

coercively.'[71] Before introducing measures, ministers normally consult
with interested bodies. They will rarely introduce measures which they
know or believe to be unenforceable. Some political constraints
eventually find embodiment in conventions. Others do not. Some
appear to hover somewhere in between. Jennings sought to elevate the
doctrine of 'the mandate' — 'fundamental changes of policy must not
be effected unless they have been an issue at a general election'[72] — to
the status of a convention[73] but this has found little favour elsewhere
and hardly accords with modern practice.[74] The practice of government
to consult interested parties prior to drafting measures also appears to
be in or approaching a constitutional haze.

One must have recourse to the attitudes of politicians and the
populace and to the effectiveness and efficiency (or otherwise) of the
organs of government in order to analyse the endurance of a constitution. 'The constitution is what people with polticial influence (thus
including the organised electorate) accept as a proper way of reaching
political decisions.'[75] That acceptance is contingent, not certain. In an
important article highly germane to this point Richard Rose has pointed
out that government rests on political authority.[76] Political authority
'concerns persisting and pervasive relationships between governors and
governed', and it has two elements: effectiveness and consent. 'An
organisation that cannot effectively influence the society around it is
not a government. A government that acts without the consent of the
governed is not government as we like to think of it in the Western
world today.'[77] To be effective a government has to be able to organise
the complex maze of institutions that constitute the modern state and to
raise and allocate resources to meet its commitments to public policy.
It is also important that it maintain consent. As Rose states, the two are
inter-related, for the success of any public policy requires the co-
operation of affected citizens.[78]

The importance of consent and its relationship to government
effectiveness was recognised and aptly stated by John Stuart Mill. To
work, he said, political machinery required not just the acquiescence
but the active participation of ordinary men. This implied three conditions: the people for whom the form of government was intended had
to be willing to accept it; they had to be willing and able to do what
was necessary to keep it standing; 'and they must be willing and able to
do what it requires of them to enable it to fulfil its purposes'.[79] 'The
word "do" is to be understood as including forbearances as well as acts.
They must be capable of fulfilling the conditions of action, and the

conditions of self-restraint, which are necessary either for keeping the established polity in existence, or for enabling it to achieve its ends, its conduciveness to which forms its recommendation.'[80] As Rose noted, the ideal government is a fully legitimate authority, enjoying both the consent of citizens and effectiveness in action. 'A repudiated regime, without effectiveness of consent can be consigned to the ranks of historical has beens.'[81] If government *qua* government (we are not here talking about individual governments) cannot secure the wants of citizens, then those citizens may start to look elsewhere. They may look to other bodies in society, in which case the governmental structure stipulated by the constitution appears irrelevant, or they may seek a new form of government, in which case the existing constitution is reformulated or replaced.

Rose contended that there were four points in the policy process at which it was particularly relevant to look for trends that could alter political authority. The first was where resources were not adequate to meet commitments. The second was where the growth of institutions of government, in terms of number and activity, produced a complexity conducive to a diminution rather than an increase in efficiency and effectiveness. The third was where outputs of government in conflict with the values of a significant fraction of society could result in the diminution of consent. The fourth was where outputs of government could stimulate indifference rather than compliance and hence again produce a diminution of consent.[82] These points are important for a consideration of political authority and the challenges to it in Britain in recent years.

THE NATURE OF CONSTITUTIONAL DEBATE AND THE CHALLENGES OF THE 1970s

The nature of constitutional debate varies from country to country. Constitutions differ, both in terms of form and content. The political authority enjoyed by the organs of government prescribed by those constitutions differs from polity to polity. In certain continental countries there is a problem in maintaining consent and a traditional and conscious emphasis on maintaining internal security. In the Anglo–American world political legitimacy is or usually has been taken for granted and so there is little institutional focus concentrating publicity upon the defence of political authority. 'Most politicians worry about relatively trivial matters, like questions in the House of Commons or headlines in tomorrow's newspaper. An individual Cabinet minister concentrates upon the problems of his department, not upon the authority upon which the whole of government rests.'[83]

Indeed, in Britain, constitutional debate is notable for its paucity. A number of reasons for this may be identified. The absence of a codified, single-document constitution has meant that the dividing line between what constitutes the constitution and what does not has been a somewhat blurred one. It is difficult to engage in debate on constitutional issues *qua constitutional* issues when one is not sure what is encompassed by that rubric. History has proved important. Since the seventeenth century there has been no need, or at least no perceived need, to think of the constitution in broad conceptual terms. The Constitutional Settlement of 1688, modified and consolidated by the Act of Union, preceded the enactment of the first 'written' constitution, the US Constitution, in 1787. The existing constitution has not been overthrown or repudiated, so Britain has not felt the need to emulate new nations in drawing up a single-document constitution. The part-written, uncodified constitution has tended to be taken for granted. This has encouraged and in turn been fed by a belief in the moral superiority of that constitution. 'We Englishmen are Very Proud of our Constitution, Sir', declared Mr Podsnap in Charles Dickens' *Our Mutual Friend*. 'It was Bestowed Upon Us by Providence. No Other Country is so Favoured as This Country.'[84] Such attitudes were not and are not confined to fictional characters. George III described the constitution as 'the most perfect of human formations'.[85] In the nineteenth century, 'it was commonplace, among commentators, to eulogise the English constitution for its antiquity and its continuity'.[86] Positive connotations clearly attached to descriptions of it as 'a living organism in a condition of perpetual growth and change',[87] as 'flexible' and 'dynamic'. It created an equipoise between the governors (legal sovereignty) and the electors (popular sovereignty) and between the constituent parts of the Queen-in-Parliament. In so doing it embodied the traditional nineteenth-century belief in 'balance', a belief shared by such diverse figures as John Stuart Mill and the Marquis of Salisbury.[88] That balance soon disappeared in practice as a result of the changes of that century,[89] but the manner of the changes was deemed to reflect the versatility of the constitution. The formal position remained, but conventions and certain changes in statute law helped to adapt it to the changed circumstances. As Walter Bagehot expressed it, 'an ancient and ever-altering constitution is like an old man who still wears with attached fondness clothes in the fashion of his youth: what you see of him is the same; what you do not see is wholly altered'.[90] Reverence for this ancient and ever-altering constitution was not confined to the nineteenth century. It has continued into the twentieth and continues to find expression in various places. In 1967 one foreign observer referred in affectionate terms to the organic and flexible nature of the constitution and its 'proven usefulness and practicality'.[91] In the debate on the constitution in the House of Commons in April 1981, MP John Stokes drew attention to 'the uniqueness of the British Constitution, which is not readily susceptible to analysis on continental models', and declared that, distinguished from other constitutions, 'our consitution is the envy of the world'.[92]

Given the general acceptance of the value of the constitution, there seemed little point in discussing it (other than to laud its merits). Where change was deemed to be necessary it took place incrementally. There was little to disturb or question the constitution as a constitution. On the whole, political authority could be, and was, taken for granted. Consent, at least in England, was forthcoming. The reason most often advanced for this has been the homogeneity and the social deference of the English, especially deference by the working class. Deference, that is where one person defers to another because the latter has or is presumed to have certain qualities (knowledge, wealth, rank or social competence, for example), was a feature of English society recognised in the last century by various writers, though a number — such as Mill — bemoaned its demise as a consequence of industrialisation. Others have identified it as continuing in the twentieth century. It has often been seen as connected with 'strong' government: that is, Britain has experienced strong government with a deferential, in effect a passive, citizenry. This thesis has been subject to a cogent critique by Dennis Kavanagh. In an incisive article he queried not only the assumption about strong government being a feature of British political life, but also threw doubt on the deference thesis.[93] The essence of his argument was that consent, far from being the product of deference, was the consequence of comparatively high levels of political participation and a widespread sense of political competence. This sense of political competence was derived from the perceived responsiveness of the political system. Where citizens felt that they were meaningful participants in the political process, trust and deference followed.[94] But that trust and deference was and is conditional. It appears to be conditional on the effectiveness of government. So long as the citizen believes he or she can influence government, and government proves capable of delivering the goods, consent is maintained.

For much of the last century and for much of this, government was capable of raising and allocating resources to meet its commitments of public policy. Although there is some dispute among economists and economic historians as to whether Britain has been in a period of relative economic decline since about 1890,[95] the annual rate of growth in the first six or seven decades of this century was usually if not always sufficient for government to fulfil its commitments. Serious problems were encountered as a result of the depression of the 1930s, but the country enjoyed a period of apparent economic prosperity in the 1950s and, to a lesser extent, the 1960s. Growth rates remained low relative to other advanced countries, but the 1950s were seen by most Britons as 'an age of prosperity and achievement'.[96] In 1954 *The Economist* could comment: 'The miracle has happened ... full employment without inflation'.[97] Labour followed by Conservative Governments were able to provide and sustain a national health service and full employment. 'Much more was expected of Governments than before 1914 or indeed 1939. But equally, Governments were now in a much better position to deliver the goods.'[98] So long as government continued to produce the goods, consent for the political system was maintained.

This was to change to some extent in the 1960s and much more so in the 1970s. With the advantage of hindsight, the roots of Britain's economic malaise can be seen to pre-date this period. Nonetheless, it was at this time that Britain began to experience severe economic problems. By 1973 Britain had the lowest growth rate of the major industrialised Western nations. After the Yom Kippur war and the price rise in oil which was to have disastrous consequences for Western economies, the output growth in manufacturing from 1973 to 1978 was −0.9 per cent, again the worst figure for the major industrialised nations of the West.[99] By 1977 the annual rate of growth of the Gross Domestic Product (GDP) was zero per cent, unemployment had risen to 7.6 per cent of the work force, and consumer prices (annual rate) had risen by 15.9 per cent.[100] With a decline in the growth rate the Government found it difficult to meet the costs of its public policies. 'In the 1970s, Western economies have grown more slowly than before ... while the cost of public policy has continued to rise as before. Every major Western government now faces the risk that the growing costs of public policy may consume all the dividends of economic growth, and then some.'[101] The position is exacerbated, according to some commentators, when governments seek support by escalating public expectations. For Samuel Brittan this is one of 'the economic contradictions of democracy'.[102] The failure of government to meet these expectations results in what has been termed 'overload', and 'overloading the political economy immediately threatens a loss of effectiveness and efficiency'.[103] Consent is threatened by the government's difficulty in maintaining effectiveness. In its attempts to meet its commitments, government may employ policies which encounter a lack of co-operation. 'It is far easier to encourage participation in programmes dispensing cash benefits, such as pensions, than in programmes that impose costs upon those involved, such as a wage freeze.'[104] In the 1970s governments encountered difficulty in mobilising support for precisely such policies as wage freezes and wage restraint. Questions of consent surfaced when the trade unions challenged particular legislation, in this instance the 1971 Industrial Relations Act. Indeed, as Gillian Peele observed, the trade unions denied or appeared to deny the legitimacy of the Act, 'and it often seemed that the unions denied also the general right of Parliament to pass legislation to regulate industrial relations'.[105] Failure to produce the goods in terms of a reduction in the rate of inflation and the number of unemployed appeared also to stimulate dissent or civic indifference. And civic indifference 'can be as debilitating to government effectiveness (and far less risky on the part of individuals) as resort to organised or unorganised protest'.[106] Inflation is one indicator of civic indifference. 'Inflation reflects a determination by organised workers and business firms to raise money earnings by their own actions, indifference to government exhortations to restrain wage and price increases. Economic groups will not voluntarily comply with the exhortations of political managers of the economy when they have no confidence that their exhortations will be effective.'[107] As Rose notes, rising rates of inflation in the 1970s suggested that indifference may be growing.[108] Growing indifference to established political institutions may also be reflected in a decline in voter turnout at elections and in greater volatility in electoral behaviour, as well as a more general and pervasive indifference to politics. The percentage of the electorate actually bothering to vote showed a decline in the 1966 and subsequent general elections: since 1964 turnout has never reached the level of 80 per cent of those eligible to vote.[109] There has also been a relative desertion of the two main parties,[110] more voters than before supporting parties which (significantly) are critics of the existing political framework and favour major constitutional change. There would appear to be a wider indifference towards the political organs of the state and their operation. Even in the heady days of the *Civic Culture*, Almond and Verba reported that 31 per cent of men and 48 per cent of women in their British sample were 'low scorers' in following politics and political campaigns.[111] More recently, in *Politics in England*, Rose has estimated that less than 20 per cent of the adult population take a 'great deal of interest' in politics.[112] Indifference would seem now to be more acute among unemployed youths in Britain's inner cities. When the Environment Secretary, Michael Heseltine, visited Liverpool in the wake of the riots there in July 1981 he asked a group of disaffected young people whether they had been in touch with their councillors. The reply was: 'What's a councillor?'[113] A survey of young people in one Liverpool district found that '85 per cent of those interviewed had no political convictions at all; many were vehement in their indifference to politics'.[114] The riots in Liverpool Toxteth and other inner city areas in the summer of 1981 revealed that the problem of consent among a fraction of the population had spread beyond the level of passive indifference.

What, then, are the implications for the constitution of these developments? When Britain enters a period of economic travail, when government has difficulty in maintaining effectiveness and/or consent, there is a tendency to look to constitutional change as a palliative or a means of dealing with the problem, of producing a system capable of being effective and maintaining consent. In this there is nothing new. During the depression in the 1930s the political structure came in for severe and some withering criticism, with various schemes for constitutional reform being advanced. The position was recognised by Stanley Baldwin. Speaking in Coventry in 1930 he observed that people were impatient and that a current of discontent was running through England, and though 'I do not think that it is likely to boil up and submerge the parliamentary institutions with which we are familiar', he did not consider it surprising that social ideals and administrative methods had been challenged as never before.[115] 'There is bound to be unrest when more questions are being put that statesmen can answer. . . . Within the House of Commons itself there is a growing sense of the need for overhauling the ship of State.'[116] Various proposals for overhauling the ship of state were proposed. Winston Churchill advocated the creation of an Economic Sub-Parliament to address the economic problems faced by the nation. Beatrice Webb proposed a Social Parliament co-existing with a Political one (an idea first aired by the Webbs in 1920), and the idea of a form of Industrial Parliament was also aired.[117] Proposals for devolving powers to regional or (in Scotland and Wales) national assemblies were also voiced, as were more concrete schemes for electoral reform.[118] They were to disappear from the political agenda in the latter half of the 1930s as other matters began to occupy the attention of the government and of the country.

Criticism of the constitution, or perhaps more accurately discrete criticisms of elements of the constitutional structure, and proposals for reform were to be a feature also of the 1970s as well now as the 1980s. As one observer noted in 1977: 'In the early 1930s the volume of criticism of the constitution was as large as it is today. Then, as now, there was a failure of the political economy.'[119] The observer added perceptively: 'Those who work the system have failed by too wide a margin to match by their effects the expectations maintained by the public. When things go as badly as that, blame is not confined to those who work the system, it implicates the system itself.'[120] As a response to a decline in effectiveness on the part of government and problems in maintaining consent, a number of proposals for constitutional reform, among other types of reform, were advanced. The reforms proposed were many and varied. Constitutional reform became a marked feature of political discourse.

What, then, were the issues and the changes affecting the constitution that could be identified in the 1970s and which remain on the agenda of political debate in the 1980s? For convenience they may be grouped under two simple headings. The first encompasses proposed or actual reforms of the existing formal framework, that is as stipulated (in most cases by convention) by the constitution: the executive, the Houses of Commons and Lords, the Crown, the judiciary and the civil service. As we shall see, critics have ascribed some of Britain's ills in part to the operation of one or more of these bodies and, as a result, seek some radical modification of their behaviour through structural reform. For example, as we have mentioned, there are those who believe that the political authority of government is undermined as a result of overloading the political economy and that this overloading is exacerbated by government stimulating rising expectations by promising too much. This stimulation is made possible by what is termed the system of 'adversary politics' in Britain, a system that is not only not discouraged, but is actually facilitated by the structure and behaviour of the contemporary House of Commons. The reform proposed is one external to the House itself (that is, reform of the electoral system) but is designed to have a significant impact on the composition and behaviour of the House.

There are those who contend that Parliament is not helping maintain consent for the parliamentary system of government, acting as a 'support' of the political system being seen by some political scientists as one of Parliament's primary functions. In the case of the Commons this is in part attributed to the first-past-the-post system of parliamentary elections, the problems of which were highlighted by the results of the general elections of the 1970s, and in the case of the Lords to its predominant hereditary composition. Fears have been expressed that Parliament has not been able to sustain citizens' beliefs that they do have an influence on the political process, a point of tremendous significance if one accepts Dennis Kavanagh's analysis of the basis of consent. Possible remedies have been put forward, including structural and behavioural changes in the Commons and (again) electoral reform and radical reform or even total replacement of the House of Lords. For example, John Mackintosh recommended that the Upper House be reconstructed as a functional chamber (shades of Churchill's Economic Sub-Parliament) with most of its members nominated by trade unions, industry, and other sectional groups.[121] These various analyses and proposals, the arguments for as well as against, we shall consider in detail later. Our consideration of these various challenges to the existing institutions will constitute Part I of this volume.

We shall then address ourselves to proposals that would provide, or have provided, what may appropriately be called new dimensions to the constitution. Given declining resources with which to meet policy needs, successive governments in the 1960s sought to reach new commercial markets, as well as establish a new political role for the country, via membership of the European Economic Community. Applications for membership by the Macmillan and Wilson Governments were not successful. Success was achieved by the Heath Government, the Treaty of Accession being signed and the European Communities Act passed in 1972. As a result of membership and the provisions of the 1972 Act, the British Constitution underwent modification: legislation emanating from the European Communities was deemed to have precedence (in the event of conflicting provisions) over legislation passed by the Westminister Parliament, and competence for determining cases of conflict was vested in the courts. We shall explore these points later.

In order to maintain political authority, successive governments took actions which many observers viewed as impinging upon rights that had previously been considered inviolable by government. For example, the Labour Government of 1974–9 sought to maintain the support of the trade unions by passing legislation favoured by the Trades Union Congress. Measures which favoured such things as closed shops in industry were seen by various jurists and politicians as constituting an infringement of individual liberty. They criticised the existing constitution for making possible the relatively easy passage of such measures, executive dominance of the legislature and the doctrine of parliamentary sovereignty combining to ensure such an outcome. The favoured solution to prevent such infringements was the introduction and enactment of a Bill of Rights, preferably one with entrenched provisions. What was envisaged was a Bill of Rights on the American model, prescribing fundamental rights, rather than a repeat of the English model of 1689, which dealt with the relationship between Crown and Parliament. Implementation of a Bill of Rights with entrenched provisions would put an end to parliamentary sovereignty. Advocates of a Bill of Rights contend that by so doing it would protect that other essential constituent of the constitution, the rule of law.

British Governments have encountered problems in maintaining consent in Scotland, Wales and Northern Ireland. In the case of Scotland and Wales the Callaghan Government proposed a scheme of devolution, certain powers to be devolved to elected assemblies in Edinburgh and Cardiff. Though devolution was not achieved it is an issue which remains on the political agenda and is one with significant constitutional implications. The position in Northern Ireland is peculiar to that province. The problem of consent is derived from the existence of mutually exclusive and ingrained attitudes on the part of the citizens of Northern Ireland. Following the suspension of the Stormont Parliament in 1972, the problem for successive British Governments has been one of trying to achieve a constitutional settlement in the province that will prove acceptable to both Protestant and Catholic communities.

In order to obtain popular consent for the renegotiated terms of membership of the European Communities in 1975, and to obtain assent from the electors of Scotland and Wales for the provisions of the Scotland and Wales Acts in 1979, the 1974–9 Labour Government resorted to the constitutionally novel device of referendums (in both cases because of dissent within its own ranks); earlier, a referendum to ascertain that a majority within the province wished to remain within the UK was resorted to in the case of Northern Ireland. We shall consider these various proposals and actual constitutional modifications, along with the issue of electoral reform, in Part II.

Finally, we shall try to give some intellectual coherence to the debate on constitutional reform by identifying various approaches to the subject. The task is not a simple or straightforward one. The reforms proposed were and are many and varied. Britain lacks a history of discussing the constitution in conceptual terms: 'the vocabulary of British political debate is not characterised by constitutional concepts and ideas with fairly firm and familiar meanings'.[122] The criticisms of the 1930s were not sustained for a period sufficient to endow the debate with such concepts and ideas 'with fairly firm and familiar meanings'. Hence a tendency in the 1970s and 1980s, as in the 1930s, for analyses of the problem and proposals for its remedy by means of constitutional change to appear to be disparate and rather confused.

Nonetheless, debate on the constitution and its constituent elements did not and does not take place in a vacuum. The stands taken by different participants in constitutional debate have been shaped and informed by existing political attitudes. Politicians and their supporters have some conception, well defined or otherwise, as to the type of society which they would like to see. If the society cannot be created by working through the existing constitutional structure, then they begin to look to a structure through which it can be achieved. Given that politicians differ as to the type of society they prefer, they not surprisingly disagree as to the constitutional changes they wish to see carried through. An analysis of the differing political attitudes leads to the outlines emerging of different but coherent attitudes to constitutional reform.

There are six principal approaches to constitutional reform which we propose to identify: High Tory, Socialist, Marxist, Group (or functionalist), liberal, and Traditionalist. Each will be explored in the concluding chapter. The exploration will, of necessity, be tentative. Given the unfamiliarity with constitutional debate in this country, the application of these approaches in practice, that is in terms of stipulating specific reforms or, more importantly, a constitutional blueprint, has not yet been well developed. Furthermore, the approaches themselves are not necessarily mutually exclusive, nor do they correlate precisely with the existing political parties. Nor are they comprehensive in stipulating a clear stand on each and every one of the issues covered in this volume. Nonetheless, they enjoy characteristics sufficient to justify their delineation. They have enjoyed the advocacy in one form or another of leading figures in constitutional debate in recent years. Furthermore, the more these approaches are delineated and advanced, the greater the likelihood of more mature and sophisticated constitutional debate. This volume thus seeks to identify the broad contours of the debate as well as to inform the debate itself.

NOTES

1 *HC Deb.*, 6th series, vol. 2, cols 1213—77.
2 Sir Derek Walker-Smith, who essentially identified the characteristics of the constitution mentioned above ('unwritten', 'flexible', etc.). *HC Deb.*, 2, c. 1224—8.
3 The last politics student text with 'Constitution' in the title appears to have been Peter Bromhead's *Britain's Developing Constitution* (Allen & Unwin, 1974).
4 See the review by H.M. Drucker, 'The Good Teacher's Guide to British Government Textbooks', *Parliamentary Affairs*, 34 (2), Spring 1981, pp. 234—8.
5 Pergamon Press, 1977. Methuen University Paperback ed., 1980.
6 See, for example, 'The Developing Constitution', in C. Cook and J. Ramsden (eds), *Trends in British Politics since 1945* (Macmillan, 1978), pp. 1—27; 'Change, Decay and the British Constitution', *Hull Papers in Politics No. 1* (Hull University Politics Department, 1978); and chapter 1 in M. Beloff and G. Peele, *The Government of the United Kingdom* (Weidenfeld & Nicolson, 1980).
7 See especially G. Marshall, *Constitutional Theory* (Oxford University Press, 1971).
8 K.C. Wheare, *Modern Constitutions*, 2nd edn (Oxford University Press, 1966), p. 102. O. Hood Phillips, *Constitutional and Administrative Law*, 6th ed. (Sweet & Maxwell, 1978), pp. 5—6.
9 Hood Phillips, *op. cit.*, p. 5.
10 See *ibid.*, p. 6.
11 Leslie Wolf-Phillips, *Constitutions of Modern States* (Praeger, 1968), p. xi.
12 *Ibid.*
13 S.A. de Smith, *Constitutional and Administrative Law* (Penguin, 1971), p. 45.
14 Hood Phillips, *op. cit.*, pp. 23—4.
15 G. Marshall and G. Moodie, *Some Problems of the Constitution*, 4th revised edn (Hutchinson, 1967), p. 26.
16 See the discussion in Marshall and Moodie, *op. cit.*, ch. 2, especially pp. 34—5.
17 de Smith, *op. cit.*, p. 47.
18 Hood Phillips, *op. cit.*, p. 25. Among the most important early sources of constitutional law are Fitzherbert's *Abridgment*

(1516), Brooke's *Abridgment* (1568), Coke's *Institutes of the Law of England* (1628—44), Hale's *History of the Pleas of the Crown* (1736), Hawkins' *Pleas of the Crown* (1716), Foster's *Crown Cases* (1762) and, probably the best known but considered the least authoritative of these works on points of detail, Blackstone's *Commentaries on the Laws of England* (1765).

19 First published 1844. The lastest edition is Sir David Lidderdale (ed.), *Erkine May's Treatise on the Law, Privileges, Proceedings and Usage of Parliament*, 19th ed. (Butterworths, 1976).

20 *Constitution of the United States*, Article V. In practice, all amendments have been on the proposal of two-third majorities in Congress; a convention has never been employed.

21 For example, in the case of West Germany and also Cyprus. See also Wolf-Phillips, *op. cit.*, pp. xv—xvii.

22 de Smith, *op. cit.*, p. 19.

23 *Ibid.*

24 The latest edition is the tenth, with an introduction by E.C.S. Wade (Macmillan, 1959), which has been reprinted at least nine times.

25 *An Introduction to the Study of the Law of the Constitution*, 10th ed. (Macmillan, 1959), pp. 39—40.

26 Dicey, *op. cit.*, p. 41.

27 Indeed, Jennings asserted that 'the notion that Coke supported the sovereignty of Parliament is a rank delusion'. Sir Ivor Jennings, *The Law and the Constitution*, 5th ed. (University of London Press, 1959), p. 159.

28 H.W.R. Wade, 'The basis of legal sovereignty', *Common Law Journal*, 1955, quoted by E.C.S. Wade in his introduction to Dicey, *op. cit.*, p. lvi.

29 Hood Phillips, *op. cit.*, p. 46.

30 *Ibid.*, pp. 63—4. See also the comments of de Smith, *op. cit.*, p. 76.

31 Hood Phillips, *op. cit.*, 5th ed. (1973), p. 63.

32 *Ibid.*, p. 76.

33 Wade, introduction to Dicey, *op. cit.*, p. xxxv.

34 Representation of the People Acts 1832, 1867, 1884, 1918, 1928, 1948 and 1969.

35 H.J. Hanham, *Elections and Party Mangement*, 3rd ed. (Harvester Press, 1978), p. xii.

36 A small number of persons, apart from minors, are still ineligible to vote (peers, certain felons, certified lunatics and those who have failed to register).

37 J. Austin, *Jurisprudence*, 4th edn (1879), quoted in Dicey, *op. cit.*, pp. 74—5.

38 *Ibid.*, p. 75.

39 *Ibid.*, pp. 75—6.

40 *Ibid.*, pp. 73—4.

41 Jennings, *op. cit.*, p. 18.

42   Hood Phillips, *op. cit.*, 6th edn, p. 28.
43   As delineated by *The Report of the Machinery of Government Committee* (1918) as variously quoted.
44   See P. Norton, *The Commons in Perspective* (Martin Robertson, 1981), pp. 20–2.
45   Aristotle, *Politics*, III, 16.
46   Dicey, *op. cit.*, pp. 188, 193 and 195, also pp. 202–3.
47   See, e.g. E.C.S. Wade and Godfrey Phillips, *Constitutional Law*, 8th edn (by Wade and A.W. Bradley) (Longman, 1970), ch. 5.
48   de Smith, *op. cit.*, pp. 39–40.
49   Dicey, *op. cit.*, p. 188.
50   Jennings, *op. cit.*, appendix, p. 308.
51   Hood Phillips, *op. cit.*, p. 37.
52   Dicey, *op. cit.*, pp. 202–3.
53   Jennings, *op. cit.*, p. 312.
54   Dicey, *op. cit.*, p. 406.
55   *Ibid.*, p. 407.
56   *Ibid.*, p. 408.
57   *Ibid.*, p. 411.
58   Jennings, *op. cit.*, p. 311.
59   J.A. Jolowicz, quoted in E.C.S. Wade, introduction to Dicey, *op. cit.*, p. cix.
60   See Hood Phillips, *op. cit.*, pp. 17–18.
61   *Erskine May*, p. 333.
62   As, e.g. the 1972 Northern Ireland Act, introduced and rushed through both Houses in a matter of hours in order to reverse a ruling in the High Court in Northern Ireland, and the 1980 Employment Act, which reversed the holding in Express Newspapers v. McShane [1980] 1 AllER 65 (H.L.).
63   Laws in Wales Act 1536, Union with Scotland Act 1706, Union with Ireland Act 1800, and the Government of Ireland Act 1920.
64   See Wade and Phillips, *op. cit.*, pp. 111–12.
65   J.S. Mill, *Representative Government* (Everyman Library, 1968 ed.), p. 177.
66   Clinton Rossiter, prefatory note to E.S. Corwin, *The 'Higher Law' Background of American Constitutional Law* (Cornell University Press, 1979 ed.), p. vi.
67   J.M. Burns, *The Deadlock of Democracy* (John Calder, 1964), p. 9.
68   See Charles Beard, *An Economic Interpretation of the Constitution* (Macmillan, 1913).
69   Dicey, *op. cit.*, p. 70.
70   G.H. LeMay, *The Victorian Constitution* (Duckworth, 1979), p. 21.
71   Bernard Crick, *The Reform of Parliament*, revised 2nd ed. (Weidenfeld & Nicolson, 1970), p. 16; see generally ch. 2.
72   Jennings, *op. cit.*, p. 176.

73 Sir Ivor Jennings, *Cabinet Government* (Cambridge University Press, 1936) and re-asserted in *The Law and the Constitution*, pp. 176–9.

74 See A.H. Birch, *Representative and Responsible Government* (Allen & Unwin, 1964), pp. 116–22, and Cecil S. Emden, *The People and the Constitution*, 2nd edn (Oxford University Press, 1956). Emden conceded that the principle of 'the people's mandate' (though clearly favouring it himself) is 'still indeterminate and its scope controvertible', p. 315. The assertion appears to remain valid today.

75 Crick, *op. cit.*, p. 28.

76 Richard Rose, 'Ungovernability: Is there Fire Behind the Smoke?' *Political Studies*, 27 (3), September 1979, pp. 351–70.

77 *Ibid.*, p. 353.

78 *Ibid.*, p. 354.

79 J.S. Mill, *op. cit.*, p. 177.

80 *Ibid.*

81 Rose, *loc. cit.*, pp. 354–5.

82 *Ibid.*, p. 356.

83 *Ibid.*, p. 355.

84 Quoted in Sydney D. Bailey, *British Parliamentary Democracy*, revised 2nd ed. (Harrap, 1962), p. 1.

85 Quoted in Dicey, *op. cit.*, p. 2.

86 LeMay, *op. cit.*, p. 4.

87 Sidney Low, *Governance of England* (1904), quoted in Marshall and Moodie, *op. cit.*, p. 18.

88 See Michael Pinto-Duschinsky, *The Political Thought of Lord Salisbury 1854–68* (Constable, 1967), pp. 111–18.

89 See above and, e.g., Sir Llewellyn Woodward, *The Age of Reform 1815–1870*, 2nd ed. (Oxford University Press, 1962), and James B. Conacher (ed.), *The Emergence of British Parliamentary Democracy in the Nineteenth Century* (Wiley, 1971).

90 Walter Bagehot, *The English Constitution* (first published 1867; Fontana ed., 1963), p. 59.

91 Karl Loewenstein, *British Cabinet Government* (Oxford University Press, 1967), p. 6; see generally pp. 4–8.

92 *HC Deb.*, 2, c. 1213.

93 D. Kavanagh, 'The Deferential English: A Comparative Critique', *Government and Opposition*, 6 (6), 1971, pp. 333–60, as reproduced in R. Rose (ed.), *Studies in British Politics*, 3rd ed. (Macmillan, 1976), pp. 58–83.

94 Kavanagh, *loc. cit.*, p. 77.

95 See, e.g., S. Blank, 'Britain's Economic Problems: Lies and Damn Lies', and R. Marris, 'Britain's Relative Economic Decline: a Reply to Stephen Blank', both in I. Kramnick (ed.), *Is Britain Dying?* (Cornell University Press, 1979), pp. 66–88 and 89–94 respectively.

96 V. Bogdanor and R. Skidelsky (eds), *The Age of Affluence*

1951–64 (Macmillan, 1970), p. 7.

97 Cited in Bogdanor and Skidelsky, *op. cit.*, p. 8.

98 Peter Openheimer, 'Muddling Through: The Economy 1951–64', in Bogdanor and Skidelsky, *op. cit.*, p. 117.

99 See Table 1 in chapter 1 in H.J. Elcock (ed.), *What Sort of Society?* (Martin Robertson, 1982).

100 See Table 2.1 in Alan Peacock, 'The British Economy and its Problems', in William B, Gwyn and R. Rose (eds), *Britain: Progress and Decline* (Macmillan, 1980), p. 28.

101 Rose, *loc. cit.*, p. 358.

102 Samuel Brittan, *The Economic Consequences of Democracy* (Temple Smith, 1977).

103 Rose, *loc. cit.*, p. 358. See also Anthony King, 'The Problem of Overload', in A. King (ed.), *Why is Britain Becoming Harder to Govern?* (BBC, 1976), pp. 8–30.

104 Rose, *loc. cit.*, p. 354.

105 G. Peele, 'The Developing Constitution', *loc. cit.*, p. 9.

106 Rose, *loc. cit.*, p. 354.

107 *Ibid.*, p. 367. It may also be reflected in the rise of what Ralph Miliband has termed 'desubordination'. R. Miliband, 'A State of Desubordination', in Kramnick, *op. cit.*

108 *Ibid.*, p. 367.

109 See S.E. Finer, *The Changing British Party System 1945–1979* (American Enterprise Institute, 1980), p. 58.

110 *Ibid.*, pp. 60–1.

111 Gabriel A. Almond and Sidney Verba, *The Civic Culture* (Princeton University Press, 1963), p. 393.

112 R. Rose, *Politics in England*, 3rd ed. (Little, Brown, 1980), Table VI.2, p. 177.

113 Recollected from a recording of the scene on an ITN 'News at Ten' programme.

114 F.F. Ridley, 'View from a Disaster Area: Unemployed Youth in Merseyside', in B. Crick (ed.), *Unemployment* (Methuen, 1981), p. 26.

115 Stanley Baldwin, *This Torch of Freedom*, 4th ed. (Hodder & Stoughton, 1937), pp. 49–50.

116 *Ibid.*, p. 50.

117 See Hansard Society, *Parliamentary Reform 1933–60*, revised 2nd ed. (Cassell, 1967), pp. 32–5.

118 See *ibid.*, chs 1–2.

119 T.J.O. Hickey, 'Constitution Under Mounting Attack', *The Times* (Jubilee Britain Supplement), 5 January 1977, p. 1.

120 *Ibid.*

121 Cited in Gwyn, *op. cit.*, p. 7.

122 M. Beloff and G. Peele, *The Government of the United Kingdom* (Weidenfeld & Nicolson, 1980), p. 10.

PART I

CHALLENGES TO THE EXISTING FRAMEWORK

Two points, both negative, can be made about the reforms advocated and the changes made to the constitutional framework during the past decade: they were neither neat nor comprehensive in scope. As we have seen, criticisms of the existing structure and proposals for change were disparate, debated in a language unfamiliar to the British political ear, and buffeted by the political interests of affected parties. Diagnoses as well as prescriptions varied.[1]

At the end of the 1960s it looked as if there might be a structured and considered review of the constitutional framework: the Wilson Government established the Commission on the Constitution as well as the Fulton Committee on the Civil Service; the incoming Heath Government embarked upon a rational restructuring of the machinery of Government. However, such ventures failed to live up to expectations: a majority of the members of the Commission on the Constitution limited their remit to the question of devolution (and even the devolution proposals of the 1970s were to come to grief); the more significant of the Fulton Committee's recommendations were largely to be circumvented by the machinations of the Civil Service; and the changes in the structure of Government departments were in part undone by subsequent economic pressures (the energy crisis of 1974) and by political whims. Other issues of constitutional import came on to a crowded political agenda: a Bill of Rights, electoral reform, reform or abolition of the House of Lords (a recurring topic), entry into the European Communities, and a new constitutional framework for Northern Ireland, each given some impetus by differing events during the course of the decade. By the end of the 1970s the constitutional landscape and the debate surrounding it was arguably more blurred and confused than at the beginning. According to one analysis,

a picture has emerged: in the 1970s constitutional changes and attempts
at change were debated and enacted in a hurried, messy and partisan
way as reactions to events . . . the changes have been achieved piecemeal with little preparation or prior public debate. . . . This haphazard
approach has served only to make the constitutional confusion worse
while the opportunity for popular involvement has been irregular and
inadequate, thus increasing the feeling of alienation.[2]

Of the reforms advocated some would entail reform of the constituent
parts of the existing constitutional framework and the relationships
between those parts. Others would introduce what we, echoing others,
have called 'new dimensions' to the constitution. These latter innovations would have significant implications for the existing elements of
the constitutional structure, in some cases deliberately so, in others not.
For clarity, we are looking at the constituent parts of the existing
framework before considering the proposed or already implemented
new dimensions. Nonetheless, they are variously interrelated and in
most cases inseparable. These relationships we shall try to explicate.

During the course of the past few years all constituent parts of the
constitutional structure have been the subject of change or pressure
for radical surgery, though some more so than others. Mr Tony Benn
revived the debate on the powers of the Prime Minister and advocated
innovative limitations to those powers. The central twin constitutional
conventions of collective and individual ministerial responsibility,
governing the relationship between government, Civil Service and
Parliament, were both undermined with pressure for the former to be
further modified. Government departments and policy-making
machinery underwent restructuring, though largely ceasing to be a topic
of debate in the latter half of the 1970s. The Civil Service remained the
subject of sustained criticism and limited reform. The House of Commons
was the object of several reform proposals as well as itself experiencing
internal behavioural and structural changes. The House of Lords remained, as it has done throughout the century, the target of multi-
farious proposals for its reformulation or removal, the Labour Party
becoming committed to its abolition. The judiciary was encouraged,
both from within and outside its own ranks, to assert itself against the
growing powers of the executive and in some cases to repudiate the self-
imposed doctrine of parliamentary sovereignty. Reform or abolition of
one of these constituents of the constitutional structure would have
important and often critical implications for the remaining parts and
the relationship between them. So too, as we have mentioned, would

the new dimensions proposed. Let us consider these constituent parts in turn, the debate surrounding them, and the relationship of this debate to the other proposed or actual constitutional changes as well as vice versa. The nature of the debate, as the foregoing implies, precludes a neat and consistent format.

NOTES

1   See, for example, the contributions to A. King (ed.), *Why is Britain Becoming Harder to Govern?* (BBC, 1976).
2   *A New Constitutional Settlement* (Liberal Publications Department, c. 1980), p. 9.

1

Prime Ministerial Government
An absolute premiership?

My argument can be simply summarised. The wide range of powers at present exercised by a British Prime Minister, both in that capacity and as Party Leader, are now so great as to encroach upon the legitimate rights of the electorate, undermine the essential role of Parliament, usurp some of the functions of collective Cabinet decision-making and neutralise much of the influence deriving from the internal democracy of the Labour Party. In short, the present centralisation of power into the hands of one person has gone too far and amounts to a system of personal rule in the very heart of our parliamentary democracy.[1]

So spoke Mr Tony Benn in 1979 in reviving an argument not new to British politics; that surrounding the power of the Prime Minister. Mr Benn not only revived the argument, he also elevated it to a new plane. Whereas previous writers with one or two exceptions had largely been content to identify the development of what they termed 'Prime Ministerial Government', Mr Benn proffered suggestions as to how such a form of government could be brought to an end. He wanted, he said, to transform an 'Absolute Premiership' into a 'Constitutional Premiership'. Such a change 'would involve making some fundamental changes . . . comparable to those made, over the years, when the Crown was transformed from an absolute monarchy to a constitutional monarch'.[2] By his actions as well as his words, Mr Benn ensured that the issue became one of political debate.

Debate on the topic of prime ministerial power is itself not new. It was a feature of academic writings in the 1960s, writer—politicians such as Richard Crossman, Humphry Berkeley and (in a somewhat more studied and qualified manner) John Mackintosh arguing the existence of prime ministerial government,[3] with others such as Patrick Gordon Walker, G.W. Jones and A.H. Brown refuting their claim.[4] It remained a topic of some discussion in the 1970s in large part because of the actions of Prime Ministers themselves. Mr Heath attracted much adverse comment, including from many of his backbenchers, as to his high-handed manner of leadership.[5] Certain members of the Wilson and Callaghan Cabinets, primarily Mr Benn, felt themselves by-passed and out-manoeuvred as a result of prime ministerial (and civil service) actions. The focus of attention in the Conservative Government returned in May 1979 was clearly the Prime Minister, Mrs Thatcher. She adopted a positive and somewhat abrasive approach to leadership, leaving ministers and civil servants in no doubt as to what she expected of them.

The power of the office, and the perceived increase in the powers of the office during the course of this century, have not been ignored by those works which address themselves to current problems in the British polity. Mr Benn is not alone, at least not altogether so, in his analysis. However, such works have tended to view the power of the Prime Minister within the context of a general increase in executive power. The thesis advanced by Lord Hailsham, for example, is that power within the parliamentary system has become more concentrated in the government, that within government power has become more concentrated in the Cabinet, and that within the Cabinet power has become more concentrated in the Prime Minister.[6] Nonetheless, his Lordship made it clear that 'I have never been one of those who believe that the development of the office of Prime Minister has been in the direction of presidential government on the French or American models',[7] and his prescription − a written constitution and a Bill of Rights − is one designed to limit government as such, not specifically the Prime Minister.

Whereas criticism of the growth of executive power and advocacy of an entrenched Bill of Rights have tended to emanate from Conservative and Liberal politicians, renewed criticism of the powers of the Prime Minister (often coupled with censure of a growth in civil service power) and advocacy of measures very different to a Bill of Rights have tended to come from politicians on the Left. This distinction was not exclusive when Labour was in office, a number of Conservatives favouring removal of the Prime Minister's power to recommend dissolution,[8] but was nonetheless significant. The person doing most to return discussion of prime ministerial power as such to the political agenda was and is Mr Benn. As a Labour Cabinet minister he sought to circumvent or limit a number of the Prime Minister's powers, receiving a number of warnings from Mr Wilson and then Mr Callaghan for so doing.[9] More recently in his speeches and writings he has argued the case for a 'Constitutional Premiership'. In this he has been supported by a number of his political allies, including his former Parliamentary Private Secretary, Brian Sedgemore.[10] Mr Benn's main pronouncement on the subject came in a speech at Bristol in July 1979, later revised and published in the journal *Parliamentary Affairs*.[11] His opening declaration is reproduced here at the head of this section.

Mr Benn's argument is distinctive in three respects. First, in terms of the problem of political authority in the 1970s (as outlined in our opening chapter) he is clearly concerned with consent. The concentration of power 'at the top of the tree', he contends, denies a sense of responsibility to electors. Secrecy and the failure to consult results in the public, the House of Commons and sometimes even the Cabinet being presented with decisions they cannot change. They are left out of the process. And being left out may result in people going outside Parliament to seek the social, economic and industrial change they seek. Parliamentary democracy itself could be undermined.[12] Mr Benn makes it clear that he favours strong government, especially to protect the country from extra-parliamentary forces such as multi-national corporations and the EEC, but such government must be accountable and based on consent. 'Strong leadership there must be, but it must be open, collective, and accountable, and must learn to exercise its necessary powers by persuasion and, above all, through the development of a Constitutional Premiership.'[13] In his emphasis on consent he echoes Richard Crossman who in 1963 alluded to traditional deference and the fact that there were signs of 'popular protest against the growing ineffectiveness of Parliament and the oligarchic tendencies inherent in our modern two-party machine politics'.[14] Second, Mr Benn considers the role of the Prime Minister in its wider political context, though drawing out in particular (in line with Crossman's analysis) the interrelationship of the Premier's position as Prime Minister and as party leader. He is concerned especially with the position in the Labour Party, where he contends the principle of intra-party democracy has been undermined by the conventions of the constitution and where the party leader has been able to use his position either as Prime Minister or as Leader of the Opposition (that is, the alternative Prime Minister) to achieve a position of almost unquestioned dominance. Third, unlike Crossman who merely expressed in a few sentences his 'hope and belief' that the British people would throw off their deferential attitude and assert what he called grass-roots democracy, Mr Benn's analysis is as much prescriptive and descriptive. Much of the debate of the 1960s revolved around the question of whether or not prime ministerial government existed. With the exception of Humphry Berkeley,[15] those engaged in the debate did not address themselves to the question of 'If prime ministerial government does exist, what if anything should one do about it?' On the grounds that he believes it does exist and creates tensions for the political system by undermining consent, Mr Benn prescribes a number of specific remedies. These comprise a number of disparate reforms with constitutional implications.

In terms of his analysis of prime ministerial power, Mr Benn identifies the power to appoint and dismiss as the Prime Minister's most potent weapon. This power, 'without any constitutional need for approval by Parliament or the Party is the most decisive for it is by its use, or threat of use, that all the other powers . . . fall into the hands of the Prime Minister alone'.[16] By the exercise of the power to advise the monarch on the use of the prerogative to create peers and confer other honours, again without any element of effective accountability, the Prime Minister enjoys a considerable power of patronage. In addition, the Prime Minister expects to be consulted on the appointment of all chairmen of nationalised industries and Royal Commissions and can appoint permanent secretaries, ambassadors, chiefs of staff and the heads of the security services. Also, he or she can have an influence over the names of all those put forward for the 31 public boards (as listed in 1977) or the 252 fringe boards recorded in the Civil Service Department Record (1978). Given that there are at least two or three hopefuls for every honour or post available, the Premier can exercise considerable influence over those who crave advancement or elevation. Indeed, Mr Benn estimated that 'the seven post-war Prime Ministers [1945 to 1976] extended their influence over between 5,000 and 7,000 would-be ministers, lords, knights and chairmen'.[17] The premier's power of patronage was deemed to be astounding. 'The scale of it all is breathtaking and no medieval monarch could compare with it, either in numbers or in importance.'[18]

The second most important power enjoyed by the Prime Minister was identified as 'his complete personal control of the conduct of Government business as it is carried out by ministers and officials.'[19] By his supervision of the agenda of the Cabinet, the circulation of papers and the flow of information (to the outside as well as within government), as well as his power to appoint Cabinet committees, the Prime Minister can ensure that policies which he favours are brought forward. 'To this extent the conduct of government business can be said to reflect a personal and autocratic, rather than a collective and democratic, spirit.'[20] Furthermore, the Premier enjoys the power to use the prerogative to secure the adherence of the UK to treaties which bind Parliament without any requirement for formal ratification; he enjoys special responsibilities for the conduct of the armed forces through the Defence Secretary; he can advise and normally expect to secure a dissolution of Parliament; and he can terminate the life of the whole Government by simply tendering his resignation to the sovereign. He does not have to consult the Cabinet before requesting a dissolution or resigning, 'but his real power flows from his ability to threaten to resign or to dissolve Parliament if the Cabinet will not support him. Thus votes of confidence, even within the Cabinet, can achieve results when persuasion may have failed.'[21] In exercising his powers, the Prime Minister is able to exclude not only the Cabinet but also the House of Commons collectively as well as his parliamentary party, his party generally and the electorate.

How then is this exercise of prime ministerial power to be restricted? Mr Benn recommends a number of measures. His main proposal is to limit the Premier's constitutional powers through party reform. He advocates a major departure with the election when Labour is in office of Cabinet ministers by the Parliamentary Labour Party and the approval by the PLP of the allocation of portfolios before they are submitted to the Queen. As a result, 'There would be a real sharing of power that would greatly strengthen the role of the Government's supporters, without diminishing in any way the power of the House of Commons as a whole over the government thus constructed, in that it could still overthrow the government if a majority was available for the purpose.'[22] Such a reform has been supported by a number of Mr Benn's allies, including Hugh Jenkins and Brian Sedgemore. In *The Secret Constitution*, Mr Sedgemore argues that the consequence of election would be that 'ministers would see their constituency as being in Parliament, not in 10 Downing Street, and they might be inclined to respond more to the arguments of the elected representatives of the people, within the context of Cabinet government'.[23] Mr Benn advocates a greater role generally for the PLP. He would like it to be the final authority on all matters concerning the day-to-day working of the party in the Commons, within the framework of policy decided by the Party Conference. Placing more emphasis upon the PLP, a body unknown to the constitution, would redress the imbalance between party leader and the MPs in the parliamentary party and in so doing, so the argument goes, would help redress the balance between the

Prime Minister and the other elements of the constitution.[24] Of the formal changes which he advocates, the most important are abolition of the House of Lords, thus ending the Prime Minister's power to recommend the creation of peers; a Freedom of Information Act conferring statutory right of access to government except in a clearly defined number of cases, thus helping obviate secrecy in government which works to the Prime Minister's advantage; the return to Parliament of law-making powers granted to the European Communities under the royal prerogative and by section 2 of the 1972 European Communities Act; a further development of the Select Committee system in the Commons; and a parliamentary confirmation of major public appointments. Interestingly, Mr Benn is silent, at least on this occasion, on a reform advanced by a number of Conservatives. Having identified the Prime Minister's power to advise a dissolution, he makes no recommendation that it be removed. Brian Sedgemore does address himself to this point and recommends that the power to advise dissolution be retained (as preferable to fixed-term Parliaments) but with the decision being taken collectively by the Cabinet, not the Prime Minister. 'The future of the Government is too important a busines to rely on the strength or weaknesses of one man.'[25] Sedgemore also advocates that ministers exercise more independent control over their civil servants.

Given what might appropriately be termed the Benn analysis and prescriptions, are there any criticisms that might be or have been offered? In terms of his analysis of the Prime Minister's powers, Mr Benn is open to many of the charges levelled against Richard Crossman's thesis in the 1960s. In particular, in his emphasis on the power to appoint and dismiss ministers, he can be and has been criticised for failing to give due weight to the political constraints which operate. Working within the convention that ministers must normally be drawn from the Commons and the Lords (and, by convention, predominantly the former), the Prime Minister does not in practice have free rein in his or her appointments. He will be constrained by factors of Members' experience and past record, constituency representation (a Secretary of State for Scotland who does not sit for a Scottish seat would be considered politically intolerable for example), and what Richard Rose has termed representativeness in relation to political factions and tendencies as well as social origins.[26]

Just as an individual may combine within himself several attributes, so too a Prime Minister will combine within a Cabinet people with a mixture of attributes. If he cannot find individuals who are simultaneously representative, loyal and competent, then he must appoint some individuals primarily for their competence, some for their representativeness and some for their personal loyalty.[27]

A Labour Prime Minister may be considered to operate under even greater constraints than a Conservative one. Social representativeness is given some weight,[28] as is, more importantly, a need to bring in Members from, and enjoying support within, the various factional elements of the parliamentary party. Furthermore, in opposition the members of the Parliamentary Committee are elected by the PLP. Though the leader distributes portfolios and may invite others, not members of the Parliamentary Committee, to join the Front Bench, it nonetheless acts as a limitation not only on his powers in Opposition but also when and if he comes to form a Government: he cannot and does not disregard those who have had Front Bench experience. The standing of some Members within the parliamentary party may be such as to ensure not only that they are invited to join the Cabinet but that they are given some choice as to which office they take. (The same applies to the Conservative side: for example, Mr Heath could hardly have denied Sir Alec Douglas-Home the Foreign Secretaryship in 1970 any more than Mrs Thatcher could have denied the Home Secretaryship to Mr Whitelaw in 1979.) Perhaps the most evident limitation on the Prime Minister's choice is where he appoints to the Cabinet someone whom it is well known that he would prefer to exclude. As Philip Canning has pointed out, perhaps the best recent example of such an appointee was none other than Mr Benn himself.[29]

Likewise with the power of dismissal. A Prime Minister, whatever his or her personal wishes, cannot easily dismiss a senior colleague who enjoys significant support on the back benches. The most celebrated use of the power of dismissal occurred on 13 July 1962 when Harold Macmillan dismissed seven senior ministers. However, that event proved a salutary lesson to Mr Macmillan's successors. For one thing, it did not achieve its desired result ('the whole episode did little to enhance Macmillan's reputation; and it failed to produce either a settling effect upon the Parliamentary party or a look of renewed vitality for the public')[30], and for another, more importantly, it was significant that it involved none of the Cabinet ministers considered a serious contender for the succession. As A.H. Brown noted: 'Macmillan dismissed no potential Prime Ministers and sacked his friends rather than prospective rivals'.[31] In recent years, dismissals from the Cabinet have been notable for their rarity. The most celebrated recent example of a minister remaining in the Cabinet despite an apparent desire by the Prime Minister to be rid of him was again none other than Mr Benn.

All this is not to say that the power to appoint and dismiss is not a very powerful weapon in the Prime Minister's armoury: it is. It can well be contended that by retaining it, a Premier is able to influence those who want office, by his selection of ministers he or she can indicate policy preferences, and by the use of Cabinet re-shuffles can subtly or none-too-subtly reduce a minister's influence (as with Harold Wilson's transfer of Mr Benn from Industry to Energy Secretary in 1975); the paucity of dismissals could be construed as a sign of strength rather than weakness.[32] Nonetheless, the power should not be overestimated. It is subject to various constraints. This was illustrated during Mr Benn's service in Labour Governments. It is apparent in the current Conservative Government. Mrs Thatcher has been able to exercise some discretion in removing and re-shuffling certain ministers, but a number enjoy such support that they are considered to be near-irremovable.

Similar limitations apply in the distribution of patronage. Here Mr Benn weakens his case, paradoxically, by his emphasis on the number of posts over which a Prime Minister can exert influence. As a President of the United States knows to his cost, the more posts one can or is expected to fill by patronage, the more difficult and onerous the job becomes. A stage is reached at which it becomes a chore rather than a useful exercise of power. In most instances a Prime Minister will accept the advice offered by others. As for the criticism of the Prime Minister's control of Cabinet business, again various constraints are at work. A Prime Minister can rarely withstand pressure from senior ministers for a matter to be discussed in Cabinet. A Prime Minister is not guaranteed that he or she will get his or her way in Cabinet or in Cabinet committees. Cabinet committees can serve to strengthen the position of their chairmen, not just the Prime Minister,[33] such committees constituting what Gordon Walker characterised as 'partial Cabinets', serving to facilitate the business of the full Cabinet.[34] In Cabinet a Prime Minister can be, and 'on a fair number of occasions' has been, overruled. At the end of the day, the Cabinet can insist and get its way against the premier. 'A Prime Minister who habitually ignored the Cabinet, who behaved as if Prime Ministerial government was a reality, such a Prime Minister would rapidly come to grief.'[35] Again, the Cabinet of Mrs Thatcher illustrates some of the limitations. In her first year of office Mrs Thatcher was unable to persuade the Cabinet to go as far as she would like it to on the issue of trade union reform, and also found herself in a minority in the Overseas Policy and Defence Committee.[36]

Standing at the apex of government and the Civil Service, with limited time and resources, the Prime Minister's role is sometimes seen as being as much one of co-ordinator as it is leader.[37] Even those who look to the Prime Minister for leadership may not always receive it. When Harold Wilson took a vote in Cabinet (something rarely done) and the result was a tie, he asked 'What shall I do?' 'Be a Prime Minister' muttered none other than Richard Crossman. As Crossman himself conceded, how far a Prime Minister can go in getting his way in summing up Cabinet discussions rests largely upon his discretion and 'his estimate of how far he can take his colleagues with him'.[38] The powers that a Prime Minister can exercise make the holder of the office far more than first among equals (or *primus inter pares*, to use the much-repeated term) within the Cabinet and there can be little doubt that in combination those powers create in the office an extremely powerful political position, but the constraints that can and do operate upon the exercise of those powers are such as to throw doubt on the assertion that Britain enjoys an 'Absolute Premiership'.

If one were to accept Mr Benn's analysis, what of the prescription? Perhaps the most important point to be made is that most of the changes advocated would not impinge directly, and certainly not exclusively, upon the powers of the Prime Minister. The extension of the select committee system, as implemented in 1979, is neither a radical constitutional innovation nor a direct limitation upon the exercise of prime ministerial power. Effective select committees may serve to subject government to greater scrutiny and parliamentary influence, but would limit the Prime Minister only through limiting government as such. Such a reform would not affect significantly the most important prime ministerial powers identified by Mr Benn. The same could be said of most of his other recommendations. Abolition of the House of Lords would admittedly remove a source of patronage but this in itself is not of outstanding significance, especially given the number of peerages created on the recommendation of others. In any event, no study has yet been made of the effect on the Prime Minister's powers of an overburdened House of Commons produced by the absence of a second chamber. The only reform advocated by Mr Benn that would affect directly and significantly the powers of the Prime Minister is the election of Labour Cabinet ministers by the PLP and the approval by the PLP of ministerial portfolios before submission to the Queen.

This would be a major innovation, though the election of ministers would to some extent constitute a logical extension of current PLP practices in Opposition. The point at issue here is not whether such a change would reduce significantly the power enjoyed by the Prime Minister – clearly it would – but whether or not it should be implemented.

Those who do not accept the thesis of prime ministerial government would consider it unnecessary. There are those who consider it undesirable. Harold Wilson, echoing Clement Attlee, has condemned it on grounds of being unworkable. 'It is not a task that can be done by a group, or a selection committee.'[39] In Attlee's words: 'It's quite possible that someone with particular technical qualifications may get left out because he doesn't happen to be the popular man. I don't believe in that at all. You must have confidence in the man in charge. If he hasn't got that confidence, he's not fit to be Prime Minister.'[40] Some would argue that the choice of ministers should rest with the Prime Minister given that general elections are in effect contests between the party leaders, and the electorate knows who the Prime Minister will be when a party is returned to power. Others would and do oppose election by the PLP on what might be termed grounds of suspicion: the fact that Mr Benn and his political allies advocate it makes it suspect in the eyes of a number of his critics. There is also what might be termed the 'thin end of the wedge' argument: that once election of ministers by the PLP is conceded, the next step (as with the election of the party leader) is to extend the electorate to include the extra-parliamentary party. Such a move would raise considerable constitutional and political problems, and in terms of consent it could be argued would constitute a negative rather than a positive move, threatening to alienate those excluded (i.e. all those who are not Labour Party activists). Those who accept this thesis advanced by Mr Benn would, by contrast, consider election to be a welcome move: it would get at the heart of the Prime Minister's power, would remove the effects flowing from favouritism and encourage greater independence and responsiveness to the parliamentary party on the part of ambitious politicians.

Whether such a change comes about is extremely problematic. Its implementation would, of course, be confined to the Labour side of the House. In terms of internal party organisation the Conservative Party attaches little weight to the mechanistic counting of heads and invests considerable authority in the leader *qua* leader in terms both of personnel selection and policy determination.[41] That is unlikely to change given the ethos of the Conservative Party. Whether or not the change is implemented on the Labour side is far from certain. It has the support of Mr Benn and a section of the PLP and, one surmises, much wider support within the Labour Party itself. Its success or otherwise will likely depend upon the outcome of the current factional struggle within the Labour Party, upon the outcome of the next general election and whether, in the event of an incoming Labour Government, the Prime Minister would feel bound to abide by the decision. The change, it should be remembered, is one internal to the Labour Party: the formal constitutional position, the Prime Minister tendering advice to the sovereign as to the appointment of ministers, would remain unchanged. There would thus be no constitutional limitations upon the Prime Minister in recommending his own choices; the limitations would be those imposed by the parliamentary party. Whether or not, basking in the wake of an election victory, the PLP would seek to force its will on the Premier remains to be seen. When an attempt was made to foist certain ministers on Clement Attlee in 1945, it failed. Mr Attlee accepted the King's commission to form the government and got on with the job. The erection of delineated hurdles by the party would doubtless constitute a greater obstacle to the exercise of such unbridled power.

Of the other changes advocated by Mr Benn, the Commons now has a new select committee system. We shall consider this in more detail in a later chapter; for the moment, we may note that it came about on the initiative of MPs other than Mr Benn. The passage of a Freedom of Information Act remains a distinct possibility; it enjoys support on both sides of the House and successive governments have given vocal and some limited if grudging support to such a measure. As we have noted, though, neither reform would limit directly the powers of the Prime Minister. Abolition of the House of Lords is a proposal approved by the Labour Party conference and is a possibility in the event of the return of a Labour Government; whether or not it would achieve a high place in such a Government's list of priorities remains to be seen. The most significant political change achieved recently, one advocated by Mr Benn, has been the widening of the franchise for the election of the Labour Party leader. This developed into a highly contentious issue and is one which we shall touch upon later. It need not detain us for the moment as it concerns the way in which the party chooses its leader, not the exercise or extent of his powers when Prime Minister. What has been significant about the Prime Minister's powers has been the extent of the debate about them rather than any substantive change.

To summarise, it can be said that in terms of the measures he advocates, Mr Benn has addressed himself to the problem of prime ministerial power in his recommendation for the election of ministers by the PLP. Other than that, there appears to be a divide between his analysis and his prescription, indeed something of a contradiction. He favours explicitly 'strong government', with collective not prime ministerial leadership, but favours reforms which would limit government rather than specifically or directly the Prime Minister. His advocacy of a reformed select committee structure in the House of Commons reflects his unawareness of the failings of the parliamentary reformers of the 1960s. The reformers failed because they pursued two incompatible aims, 'strengthening the House of Commons without detracting from the power of government'.[42] On the basis of his analysis Mr Benn has at least left himself open to charges of inconsistency and incompatibility in his line of argument. That is not to say that he may not be right in his analysis, nor that the reforms which he champions may not be desirable in themselves, but the latter do not appear to be necessary or sufficient to meet the faults identified with the former.

NOTES

1   Tony Benn, 'The Case for a Constitutional Premiership', *Parliamentary Affairs*, 33 (1), Winter 1980, p. 7.
2   *Ibid.*
3   R.H.S. Crossman, introduction to Walter Bagehot, *The English Constitution* (Fontana ed., 1963); Humphry Berkeley, *The Power of the Prime Minister* (Allen & Unwin, 1968); and John Mackintosh, *The British Cabinet*, 3rd ed. (Stevens, 1977), the first edition being published in 1962; see also the second edition published in 1968, pp. 610–27.
4   Patrick Gordon Walker, *The Cabinet*, rev. ed. (Fontana, 1972); G.W. Jones, 'The Prime Minister's Powers', *Parliamentary Affairs*, 18, 1965, pp. 167–85; and A.H. Brown, 'Prime Ministerial Power (Part II)', *Public Law*, Summer 1968, pp. 96–118. See also D.N. Chester, 'Who Governs Britain?' *Parliamentary Affairs*, 15, 1962, pp. 519–27, and Anthony King (ed.) *The British Prime Minister* (Macmillan, 1969).
5   See Philip Norton, *Conservative Dissidents* (Temple Smith, 1978), especially ch. 9.
6   See Lord Hailsham, *Elective Dictatorship* (BBC, 1976).
7   Lord Hailsham, *The Dilemma of Democracy* (Collins, 1978), p. 204.

8   Also, a number of Labour MPs, such as John Ryman, are in favour of a Bill of Rights.

9   Mr Benn was warned especially for what were viewed as breaches of the convention of collective responsibility and on occasion asked to give assurances that there would be no repetition of such offences. See below.

10   Brian Sedgemore, *The Secret Constitution* (Hodder & Stoughton, 1980), especially ch. 2. See also Ken Coates, *Democracy in the Labour Party* (Spokesman, 1977), ch. IV.

11   33 (1), Winter 1980, pp. 7–22, see above n. 1. See also Coates, *op. cit.*, pp. 49–51.

12   See Benn, *loc. cit.*

13   *Ibid.*, pp. 21–2.

14   Richard Crossman, intro. to Walter Bagehot, *The English Constitution* (Fontana, 1963 ed.), p. 57.

15   Berkeley, *op. cit., passim.*

16   Benn, *loc. cit.*, p. 12.

17   *Ibid.*, p. 12.

18   *Ibid.*, p. 12.

19   *Ibid.*, p. 13.

20   *Ibid.*, p. 13.

21   *Ibid.*, p. 14.

22   *Ibid.*, p. 20.

23   Sedgemore, *op. cit.*, p. 85.

24   Benn, *loc. cit.*, pp. 20–1.

25   Sedgemore, *op. cit.*, p. 87.

26   Richard Rose, 'The Making of Cabinet Ministers', in V. Herman and J. Alt (eds), *Cabinet Studies: A Reader* (Macmillan, 1975), p. 6.

27   *Ibid.*, p. 8.

28   *Ibid.*, pp. 6–7.

29   P.J. Canning, letter to the *Guardian*, 18 July 1979.

30   Nigel Fisher, *Iain Macleod* (Andre Deutsch, 1973), p. 221.

31   A.H. Brown, *loc. cit.*, p. 117.

32   See the letter from John Attenborough, *Guardian*, 20 July 1979; also Norton, *op. cit.*, p. 231.

33   A.H. Brown, *loc. cit.*, p. 97.

34   Gordon Walker, *op. cit.*, pp. 87–91.

35   *Ibid.*, p. 96.

36   See Adam Raphael, 'At the Court of Queen Maggie', *Observer* 7 October 1979. (Some shift in the balance of forces on the committee took place when John Nott replaced Francis Pym as Defence Secretary.)

37   See, e.g. G.W. Jones, 'The Prime Minister's Aides', *Hull Papers in Politics No. 6* (Hull University Politics Department, 1980).

38   Richard Crossman, *Inside View* (Jonathan Cape, 1972), p. 51.

39   Harold Wilson, *The Governance of Britain* (Weidenfeld & Nicolson/ Michael Joseph, 1976), p. 28.

40   Interview with Francis Williams, in King (ed.), *op. cit.*, p. 74.
41   See P. Norton and A. Aughey, *Conservatives and Conservatism* (Temple Smith, 1981), chs 6 and 7.
42   S.A. Walkland, 'The Politics of Parliamentary Reform', *Parliamentary Affairs*, 29 (2), 1976, p. 192.

2

Ministerial Responsibility

Twin – but incompatible – conventions?

The relationships between the executive, Parliament and the Civil Service are governed primarily by the constitutional conventions of individual and collective ministerial responsibility.[1] In terms of definition and application neither convention is precise, and the two are not necessarily harmonious with one another. The convention of individual ministerial responsibility has in various respects been a rather weak one for some time; that of collective responsibility has been weakened especially during the course of the past 10–15 years. Both have been the subject of recent dispute.

MINISTERIAL RESPONSIBILITY

The convention of individual responsibility is best described as a rather limp one. There is no agreed definition of it and, in so far as it is understood to involve culpability for actions of officials within a department, tends to be more honoured in its breach than in its practice. The most common definition, rather a general and near-tautological one, is 'that each departmental Minister is responsible to Parliament for the work of his Department. That includes the way its money is spent, and all aspects of its performance.'[2] The problem lies in trying to translate this convention into practice. What is meant by 'responsibility'? As Marshall and Moodie noted, the word itself has a range of nuances.[3] It may attribute action to the author, indicate a relationship or division of function, or designate blame or praise. To substitute 'accountability' or 'answerability' does not really take us much further. The same problem arises.

Under the convention, a minister is clearly expected to 'answer' to Parliament for the work of his department. That is, he regularly appears in the House to answer Members' questions about his department and matters that fall within its jurisdiction. In any debate on the policy of a particular department, the ministers from that department are the ones who are expected to open and wind up the debate by explaining, justifying and defending that policy. Similarly, when a department sponsors legislation, the minister is the one who brings in the Bill and both explains and defends its provisions during its various legislative stages. In this way, ministers may be said to be 'answerable' or 'responsible' to Parliament. Understood in this sense the convention may be seen to be a useful one: it provides the House of Commons with one of its own number to answer questions for each department and to do so in plenary session (Cabinet members in the United States are questioned only before committees of Congress, Congress itself being a body to which they are outsiders) and it provides a coherent structure through which the work of departments and officials can be explained; it is usually easier for Members to ask a minister for information on disparate points than to track down the various individual officials who have dealt with them and ask them for the information. Nonetheless, even in this sense the convention has been subject to various modifications as a result of recent experience.

The convention becomes more complex when one considers responsibility in the sense of the attribution of action to the author and the allocation of blame or praise. Not only is a minister expected to appear to answer questions about his department, but he is deemed also to be 'responsible' — the person to 'carry the can', as S.A. Smith put it — for his own actions and those of his officials. If he or his officials make errors of judgement, engage in unbecoming conduct or maladministration, then the minister is expected to shoulder the blame. The convention is interpreted as making the minister culpable. In practice it is not as simple as it may sound. The meaning will vary according to context. The least ambiguous instance of culpability occurs in cases where a minister himself is at fault, having engaged in behaviour which is generally accepted to be scandalous or contrary to norms of accepted procedure. In such cases, ministers would be expected to resign. The most recent examples are those of John Profumo in 1962, who resigned after admitting lying to the House about his relationship with Christine Keeler, and Lords Lambton and Jellicoe in 1973, both resigning because of their admitted association with prostitutes. Greater difficulties arise over what may be termed policy culpability. If a minister initiates and is personally identified with a particular policy, and that policy fails or is unacceptable to the Government or the House, then he is deemed to be culpable and is expected to resign. In practice, if the policy fails and/or is unpopular, but the Prime Minister and Cabinet are prepared to stand by it, the convention of collective responsibility provides the minister with a shield. Only in the unusual circumstances of his colleagues' failure to stand behind him will a minister feel compelled to resign, and even then that may not be necessary if he is prepared to accept the new policy substituted for his own. The convention as it applies to policy culpability is thus essentially a weak one. It is undermined by the principle, or rather the effect, of collective responsibility and by the lack of political will on the part of the House of Commons to enforce sanctions against an erring minister.

Even more problems arise when this aspect of the convention is considered in terms of the actions of officials. The convention stipulates that the minister heads his department. The House of Commons can deal with a department formally only through and with the approval of a minister. From the Government's point of view this is valuable in that it denies officials an alternative political master. In practice, when applied to the actions of officials, the convention raises serious problems. For some time it has been recognised that departments are large bodies with a great many decisions being made, of necessity, by officials at all levels, decisions made in the minister's name but of which he can have no knowledge.[4] If a civil servant makes a serious mistake can the minister be expected to resign because of it? He did not make the mistake, but he is 'responsible' for that which is done in his name. In practice there is no clear answer to the question. Some attempts have been made to distinguish between, on the one hand, acts carried out in accordance with a minister's wishes, or of which the minister could reasonably have been expected to have some knowledge, and those which might be attributable to defective supervision on the part of the minister, and, on the other hand, actions which may have been dishonest, carried out against the minister's instructions, or indulged in for reasons of perversity or stupidity, or which were at such a level that the minister could not possibly have known of them. In the former case, the minister would be expected to resign. In the latter case, the minister would probably be expected to answer questions in the House, explain what had happened, and announce the taking of corrective action. Sir Thomas Dugdale resigned as Agriculture Minister in 1954 in the celebrated case of Crichel Down, but his resignation was very much the exception to the rule. Even in instances where ministers may be deemed to have some knowledge of officials' actions, they may — the paucity of resignations suggests they do — decline to resign; colleagues' loyalty, and a desire to avoid political embarrassment, again provide a protective shield.

From the foregoing it is possible to draw out that the strongest sense of the convention is that in which it determines who is responsible for what, rather than who is responsible to whom. The importance of the convention in this sense has been congently argued by Nevil Johnson. 'The enduring effect of the doctrine of ministerial responsibility has been over the past century or so that powers have been vested in ministers and on a relentlessly increasing scale.'[5] The convention has helped determine the formal locus of decision-making and is thus at the heart of British Government. Even in this sense it has been subject to some minor blurring or modification. Various decision-making powers have been statutorily vested in persons other than ministers.

Thus, the convention may be seen as already a weak one in practice. It has been weakened further in recent years. It has also become a point of some controversy. Various observers have attributed its further weakening to the growth of departments and less anonymity on the part of officials. The controversy surrounds the extent to which the convention serves to benefit civil servants rather than their political masters.

Government departments are large, decision-making bodies. Every day a great many decisions have to be made at all levels of which a minister, as we have mentioned, can have no knowledge. It is difficult, indeed impossible, for the minister to know everything that is going on within his department. The convention may vest the minister with 'responsibility' for his department: achieving effective control of what goes on within the department is another matter. This problem has been exacerbated by the growth of departments and by the creation, primarily in the early 1970s, of 'super-departments'. As Lord Crowther-Hunt and Peter Kellner pointed out, in 1900 there were 50,000 civil servants controlled by about 60 ministers. Today there are some 700,000 civil servants with just over 100 ministers. The creation of the giant Department of the Environment resulted in a department of 38,000 officials, nearly 100 of them at under-secretary level and above, but with four ministers. The authors contended that this imbalance 'must in itself have the natural tendency to tilt the balance of Whitehall power more in favour of civil servants and away from ministers'.[6]

The convention, as Smith and Stanyer observed, 'needs to be further amended to take account of a growing willingness to identify civil servants as responsible for certain decisions when mistakes are made –

to name and blame'.[7] In part this may be attributed to the creation and activities of the Parliamentary Commissioner for Administration, the Ombudsman. By the very nature of his work he has to go behind the official facade to investigate cases of alleged maladministration. Nonetheless, the Attorney-General made it clear in 1968 that 'only in exceptional cases' should blame be attached to an individual civil servant; the convention of ministerial responsibility dictated that an official who contributed to a collective decision of a department should remain anonymous.[8] The principle of anonymity has been undermined by bodies other than the PCA. Officials were identified or identifiable following the investigation by the Comptroller and Auditor-General in 1964 which revealed overpayment by the Ministry of Aviation to Ferranti Ltd for work on defence contracts. In 1972 the most celebrated case occurred. A tribunal of enquiry was established to investigate the collapse of the Vehicle and General Insurance Company and the failure of the Department of Trade (later the Department of Trade and Industry) to exercise its statutory powers of control and supervision in respect of the company. The tribunal named an under-secretary and two assistant secretaries as responsible for the failure to deal with the risk of the company's insolvency before 1971. It reported that the under-secretary's conduct fell below the standard which could reasonably be expected of an official in that position and constituted negligence. The constitutional implications of this case have been touched upon by A.W. Bradley:

While the tribunal may have correctly described the facts which they had found, did this resolve the question of political responsibility to Parliament? If so, what is left of the principle that a minister takes the praise for the successes of his department and the blame for its failures? It is today a fiction that all decisions are taken by ministers. But unless some responsibility is borne by ministers for senior officials, the entire bureaucratic structure will have broken free of democratic control.[9]

The anonymity of civil servants has been further reduced by parliamentary activity. Though officials appearing before Commons' select committees do so in the name of their ministers, they do at least present themselves physically before the committees. The greater assertiveness of the committees created in 1979 may result not only in more officials appearing before them but also in the line between official explanation and personal comment becoming blurred. Permanent secretaries will also normally appear before the Public Accounts Committee in their capacities as accounting officers. Also, the expansion of departments and responsibilities has encouraged a practice which to some extent circumvents the answerability of ministers to MPs for actions taken within their departments. In large departments such as the Department of Health and Social Security, a great many decisions which affect individuals are taken every day in local offices. In cases where problems arise and a complaint is made to an MP, the MP often takes up the matter with the local office. Officials look into the complaint and reply direct to the Member. The central department and the minister are not involved. Though this may be deemed to undermine the convention, it is a practice that is encouraged by ministers themselves. Indeed, so many letters are received from MPs by ministers in the Department of Health and Social Security that at the end of 1980 the Secretary of State for the Social Services wrote to MPs suggesting that where possible they write in the first instance to the appropriate local office rather than to a minister.[10] At this parochial level anonymity is not considered to be possible or even desirable.

The anonymity of civil servants is a corollary of the convention of ministerial responsibility. Decisions are taken in the minister's name. Officials are answerable to him for their recommendations and actions, and not to outsiders. There are those who contend that, given their size, permanence and experience, as well as the effects of recent events, civil servants are often the effective policy-makers within a department. This point we shall consider in detail later. Critics contend that the convention provides a protective screen behind which officials can hide. Their actions can be questioned only through the minister and he will normally be reliant upon the brief supplied by his officials. There are some observers, as the foregoing quote from Bradley indicates, who would regard public identification of officials responsible for particular decisions as likely to lead to a breakdown of the formal control exercised by ministers. Conversely, there are those who argue that 'so long as Parliament does not attempt to impose sanctions and discipline directly on civil servants that it judges to be at fault, less anonymity should only mean less secrecy, a development which would be widely welcomed'.[11]

Various proposals have been advanced by those who take a critical view of the position of civil servants in relation to ministers. Some would have the effect of strengthening the convention: for example, giving a minister more direct powers over the hiring and firing of his permanent secretary. Other proposals, sometimes emanating from the same people, would have the effect of weakening it: most notable in this category is the recommendation for a Freedom of Information Act.

These we shall consider later in looking specifically at the Civil Service. For the moment it is sufficient to note that the constitutional convention of individual ministerial responsibility is in many respects a weak one, has been further weakened in recent years, but remains central to an understanding of the relationship between ministers and civil servants, and indeed between Parliament and civil servants. Its effect in terms of these relationships is a point of considerable contention.

COLLECTIVE RESPONSIBILITY

The convention of collective ministerial responsibility 'implies that all Cabinet Ministers assume responsibility for Cabinet decisions and actions taken to implement those decisions'.[12] Once a decision is reached the Cabinet stands united before the House and the country. The instance of William Pitt the Younger managing to secure the dismissal of Lord Chancellor Thurlow in 1792 for disagreeing publicly with a government measure is seen as the beginning of the enforcement of some form of collective responsibility.[13] It developed as a convention between then and 1832, the need for it being reinforced by the developments of the nineteenth century: as party developed and aggregated the wishes of voters, so Cabinet unity provided some cohesion to government (encouraged by the attacks of the opponent party) and provided a body that could be identified as that responsible for government policy. As it has developed, the convention has two well-known elements: a minister who refuses to accept a decision of the Cabinet must resign; and the government must resign or request a dissolution if defeated on a vote of confidence in the House of Commons. Both are adhered to, the latter more stringently than the former, and both have been subject to debate and modification as a consequence of political pressures in recent years.

A minister is bound by the convention to accept the decisions of the Cabinet and to defend them publicly. A corollary of the convention is deemed to be one of secrecy. Ministers may not reveal what has gone on in Cabinet meetings. A failure to accept publicly a decision requires the resignation of the minister. If it is not forthcoming, the Prime Minister would be expected to require his resignation. In a limited instance this part of the convention may be said to have been strengthened or rather extended recently; in more important respects it has been undermined and weakened.

Although the convention applies formally to members of the Cabinet, it has been extended in practice to incorporate all ministers. Junior

ministers are required, on pain of dismissal, to support Cabinet decisions
even though they themselves may have had no voice in the discussions
that produced them. In the 1970s, the ambit of the convention was
deemed by some Prime Ministers to encompass also the unpaid and un-
official parliamentary private secretaries (PPSs). Whereas previously
PPSs voting against the Government in the Commons' division lobbies
were occasionally warned for their behaviour, Prime Ministers Wilson
and Callaghan on occasion required ministers to dismiss their PPSs for
casting dissenting votes.[14] This attempt to extend *de facto* the convention was of advantage to the Prime Minister in that it constituted an
attempt to shore-up and extend the so-called (in this instance, inaptly
so) 'payroll vote' in the Commons.

More seriously, the convention has been undermined by various
developments. The secrecy surrounding Cabinet discussions was torn
aside with the publication of Richard Crossman's *The Diaries of a
Cabinet Minister*, in which he reproduced his notes of what went on in
Cabinet.[15] An attempt to prevent publication failed in the Court of
Appeal. Lord Widgery, the Lord Chief Justice, said that Cabinet proceedings were confidential and subject to legal protection, but only to
the extent analogous to that provided to financial or marital confidences.
What constituted impropriety in this area was a question for the courts
to determine on the merits of the case: mere breach of the convention
was not in itself a matter for judicial intervention.[16] In response, Mr
Wilson established a committee under Lord Radcliffe to consider
ministerial memoirs: it recommended a 15-year embargo on publication
of material if likely to injure foreign relations, the confidental relations
on which the system of government is based, or if covered by national
security requirements. Mr Wilson, though, was able only to announce
that these limitations should be accepted as an obligation of honour.

Further publication of notes made in Cabinet took place in 1980
with the appearance on the bookstalls of Barbara Castle's diaries
covering her years as Social Services Secretary.[17] In the preface to her
book Mrs Castle touched upon an important point in seeking to justify
her actions: 'Sitting round the Cabinet table at No. 10', she wrote, 'I
often used to think that the people outside would feel far less alienated
and hostile if they only knew the sort of problems with which some
twenty honest men and women and true were struggling to deal to the
best of their ability.'[18] Thus, she sought to equate her opposition to
Cabinet secrecy with the issue of political authority. Whether or not
publication of Cabinet discussions would have the effect she envisages

is, at least on the evidence of reaction to the Crossman diaries, doubtful. It would seem likely, though, that other former Cabinet Ministers will follow suit in putting pen to paper.

The convention was undermined not only by revelations of what went on in Cabinet, but also by ministers managing to convey their disagreement with Cabinet decisions. Previously, private post-decision disagreement had been tolerated, even when leaked. The late 1960s and the 1970s witnessed several instances of what amounted to semi-public and in some cases public dissent. In 1969 James Callaghan, then Home Secretary, opposed the Cabinet's decision to proceed with an Industrial Relations Bill based on the White Paper *In Place of Strife*. His opposition to it effectively became public as a result of a speech to the Parliamentary Labour Party and his voting against the government's policy at a meeting of the party's National Executive Committee. Though one source contended that the restrictions imposed by the convention could hardly be considered to apply to private PLP meetings,[19] the proceedings of such meetings are frequently leaked to journalists and Mr Callaghan was too experienced a politician not to know what effect his actions would have. The Prime Minister, Harold Wilson, responded by reminding the Cabinet that acceptance of collective responsibility must transcend all other considerations and loyalties: 'in every action, speech and vote, a minister must act as a minister. Any minister not able to accept that doctrine must resign.'[20] Despite his known opposition, Mr Callaghan nonetheless remained in the Cabinet, in part because the Prime Minister would have found it politically damaging to remove him and in part because the Home Secretary himself was not prepared to force the issue and resign.[21]

Differences within the Cabinet over decisions that ministers felt themselves forced to take as a result of Britain's worsening economic situation further threatened the convention in the Labour Government of 1974–9. (Mr Heath had encountered no problems in ensuring acceptance of the convention during the 1970–4 Government.)[22] In 1974 Mr Wilson wrote to three ministers who sat on the party's National Executive Committee and had voted in a manner inconsistent with the convention of collective responsibility: he reminded them of the convention and required of them an unqualified assurance that they accepted the convention and would comply with its requirements and the rules that flow from it. Failure to provide such an assurance would be construed as a decision 'that you do not wish to continue as a member of this administration'.[23] 'After some little difficulty, satisfactory assurances were received.'[24] Nonetheless, further problems ensued. For the rest of the Parliament, Tony Benn managed to convey his disagreement with various aspects of government policy while remaining throughout a member of the Cabinet.[25] In 1976 one Cabinet minister actually abstained from voting on the second reading of the Scotland and Wales Bill, doing so without encountering even a rebuke from the Prime Minister.[26] And on two occasions the convention was actually suspended. The Labour Party was badly divided on the issue of Britain's membership of the European Communities and in order to maintain some semblance of unity the party committed itself to renegotiate the terms of membership and to submit the renegotiated terms to a referendum, itself a constitutional novelty. So divided was the Cabinet on the renegotiated terms that Mr Wilson decided to suspend the convention in order to allow Cabinet ministers to oppose publicly the Cabinet's decision in the public debate on the referendum and to vote against it in the House. 'Ironically', as Brian Sedgemore noted, 'it was Harold Wilson who did more than anyone to make a nonsense of the doctrine of collective Cabinet responsibility.'[27] The only occasion in the past 50 years when the convention had been suspended was in 1932 when Liberal members of the Cabinet were permitted to dissent on the issue of tariff protection. Mr Wilson cited that occasion as a 'sound' precedent.[28] The precedent was added to in 1977 when Mr Callaghan suspended the convention to allow ministers to vote against the second reading of the European Assembly Elections Bill.[29] His action was motivated by the need to avoid a serious party rift while introducing the measure as a condition of the pact he had negotiated with the Liberal Party. When questioned about the application of the convention, Mr Callaghan replied blithely 'I certainly think that doctrine should apply', adding 'except in cases where I announce that it does not'.[30]

The increasing tendency for ministers to intimate in public their disagreement with Cabinet decisions was not brought to an end with the return of a Conservative Government in 1979. Various Cabinet ministers were known to disagree with certain aspects of the Government's economic policy and they managed to convey their disagreement to those outside the Cabinet by means of leaks and what might be termed coded messages. In August 1981 one Cabinet minister, the Leader of the House Francis Pym, effectively disagreed publicly with the Chancellor in his assessment of whether or not the recession had ended. Though not disagreeing directly with a Cabinet decision, disaccord with the Chancellor's economic strategy could be considered to be implicit in the speech. The Prime Minister, Mrs Thatcher, was reported to be furious with Mr Pym (as well as with Party Chairman, Lord Thorneycroft, not a minister, for a message to party workers couched in similar terms to Mr Pym's speech), as much for upsetting party unity as for any alleged breach of the convention. Mr Pym's standing within the Parliamentary Party was considered sufficiently strong to withstand the possibility of his dismissal. On various occasions a number of ministers (including on one occasion Mrs Thatcher herself) transgressed by indicating their disagreement with their colleagues on certain issues.[31] The contrast between the Cabinet of Mr Heath and that of Mrs Thatcher was a notable one.

The convention of collective ministerial responsibility has thus been weakened and on two occasions suspended. Given the political tensions existing within both main parties, a further weakening may take place. As we observed in our discussion of conventions in the introduction, they are observed largely as a result of the effects they are considered likely to have if not adhered to. In the 1970s they were suspended on two occasions largely because it was deemed less difficult politically to depart from them than it was to try to enforce them.[32] Similar perceptions may apply in the future, especially in the event of the return of a Labour Government.

There are those who would welcome a further relaxation of the convention. Though most politicians accept that it has some value, a number dispute the need for its rigid application. Brian Sedgemore, for example, has conceded that 'the doctrine is not without virtue. But no doctrine can ever be absolute.'[33] He along with Barbara Castle and Tony Benn argues the case for more open government. Mrs Castle, as we have seen, has sought to justify this in terms of political authority, citizens being less likely to be cynical if that which they know to happen in Cabinet is admitted publicly. Mr Sedgemore makes a similar point:

At its most basic ministers who oppose policies from a sense of deep conviction cannot be expected to endure a permanent lie in their public and private lives. Ministers can be expected to support each other in public without having to suggest that that which they publicly know is not true is true. The public today are aware that the major political parties are coalitions and that few big Cabinet decisions will be taken unanimously.[34]

The argument, in short, is that public trust is likely to flow from more openess. This line is taken generally by those who favour a Freedom of Information Act. Nonetheless, this view is by no means a unanimous one.

John Mackintosh has pointed out the demerits of such a change, the most important in this context being that

the sight of ministers dragging their feet or of open disagreement in a Cabinet followed by no resignation, does add to the public's cynicism about politicians; it does confirm the suspicion that politicians are willing to go along with almost anything rather than give up the prestige, the excitement, the sense of power and the emoluments of office.[35]

Certainly, serious public divisions within its ranks may help generate a poor political image for the Government and give the impression that it is not only divided but unsure of what to do. Knowledge of Cabinet divisions on economic policy may also serve to generate hesitancy and indecision on the part of industrialists, financiers and others. As knowledge of growing disquiet among Cabinet ministers on the Government's economic strategy grew in 1981, fears (or hopes) increased that there might be a reversal in policy. A united Cabinet is viewed as a strong Cabinet, even if that unity is artificially imposed. Furthermore, there is the danger, as Donald Shell noted, 'that ministers will cease arguing their views out thoroughly with one another, but instead will just acquiesce in decisions from which they may dissociate themselves publicly. In this way the responsibility of government would diminish and its policies become more fragmented.'[36] Shell nonetheless concedes that where there is an argument in Cabinet, the presentation of different views publicly by the protagonists might do more to enhance respect for government and acceptance of its decisions. As he implies, the argument is not a cut-and-dried one.

Though it is hardly likely that the convention will be dispensed with, the pressures and events of the 1970s, the existing pressures within both parties and the argument advanced for its modification suggest that in future it will be difficult to ensure rigid adherence to it. In 1972, in his book *The Cabinet*, former Cabinet minister Patrick Gordon Walker suggested that the convention was able to work only because ministers could indulge in leaks to the press. Since then, much water has flowed under the bridge. To those who adhere strongly to the view that the convention is desirable, reversion to the occasional leak would now seem extremely palatable. Political circumstance would seem to preclude that. This element of the convention is likely to be subordinated where deemed necessary to the requirements of party unity in the event of serious internal divisions and to a Prime Minister's inability to dismiss a rebellious but politically well-entrenched minister.

The convention of collective responsibility, as we have said, has another element as well: namely, that a Government defeated on a vote of confidence is required to resign or request a dissolution. The Cabinet is collectively responsible to the House of Commons for its actions and its political, as opposed to its legal, authority to govern rests upon it maintaining the confidence of the House. If that confidence is denied it, the Prime Minister is expected to submit the resignation of the Government to the monarch or else request a dissolution. This element of the convention is a strong one and has been adhered to ever since the precedent was set in 1841. In the nineteenth century the decision to resign or request a dissolution tended to be taken by the Cabinet. In the twentieth, the decision has, since Lloyd George's premiership, been taken by the Prime Minister,[37] though usually after consulting senior colleagues.[38] No clear practice has developed as to which option (resignation or advising a dissolution) the Premier should pursue.

Not only is this element of the convention a strong one in terms of adherence to it, it was for much of this century believed by many MPs to extend beyond confidence votes. The belief developed in the latter half of the nineteenth century and was carried over into this, that any serious Government defeat necessitated the Government's resignation. Variants on this theme found expression in a number of politicians' speeches and in some texts. One view taken was that any defeat required the Government either to seek its reversal or else resign or request a dissolution.[39] Other sources appeared to imply, albeit not always clearly, that the Government should resign or request a dissolution, with no provision for attempting to reverse a defeat.[40] A third more limited view was that resignation or dissolution was required in the event of defeat on a major issue only, 'on a matter of major economic strategy, a matter central to the historic power of the House of Commons over the Executive'.[41] Such views were still being expressed in the 1970s. In 1971 Sir Philip de Zulueta asserted that a three-line whip was 'a formality which warns supporters of the administration that the government will resign if the vote in question goes against them',[42] while Lisanne Radice wrote as late as 1977 that, even in committee, 'the fiction is maintained that every vote is a vote of confidence'.[43]

For Members of Parliament, sustaining the Government in office became equated with sustaining the Government in every division. MPs on the Government side of the House normally voted in the Government division lobby because they wanted to: they supported the Government's aims and were normally in agreement with the measure they were being asked to support. On those occasions when they disagreed with a Government proposal, they nonetheless felt constrained to vote for it; failure to do so, they believed, could result in a defeat for the Government and hence bring it down. This belief was widely held and clearly influenced Members' behaviour. It was reinforced by the general scarcity of defeats in the division lobbies.

In the Parliaments of the 1970s these various views as to the extension of the convention to all votes in the Commons were to be dispelled. The period was notable for the number of defeats experienced by successive Governments. The fact that the minority governments of the decade suffered a number of defeats might be considered not surprising, but the earliest defeats were those experienced by a Government with a clear working majority. The Heath Government of 1970—4 suffered no less than six defeats. Disquiet within the Parliamentary Conservative Party over a number of measures that the government introduced, many of them associated with the Prime Minister, and the manner of Mr Heath's leadership, among other factors, combined to produce a divided and volatile parliamentary party.[44] The strength of dissident feeling resulted eventually in the Government losing its majority on six occasions, three times on three-line whips, the most important defeat being that on the immigration rules in November 1972.[45] The subsequent minority Labour Government in the short 1974 Parliament suffered seventeen defeats and the Labour Government of 1974—9 no less than 42 defeats: of these 23 were the consequence of cross-voting by its own backbenchers and 19 the result of opposition parties combining against a minority government.[46] These latter defeats included one on an explicit vote of confidence, on 28 March 1979, and Mr Callaghan advised the Queen to dissolve Parliament.

These defeats were important not for reflecting any deviation from the convention but rather for helping ensure a greater realisation of what the convention entailed. The belief that a defeat on any important issue necessitated resignation or a dissolution may be described as a constitutional myth: it was based on no authoritative source nor upon any consistent practice of behaviour. The Governments of the 1970s responded to the various defeats in line with precedent. The defeats and the response to them served to reveal what was and has been since the 1840s the constitutional 'reality'. There are essentially three types of defeat, each entailing a different response: a defeat on a vote of confidence, in response to which the Government is required either to resign or request a dissolution; a defeat on an item central to Government policy but not made one of confidence, in response to which the Government may either seek a vote of confidence from the House *or* resign or request a dissolution; and a defeat on any matter not central to Government policy, in response to which the Government need only consider whether or not to seek its reversal at a later stage.[47] This delineation was well made by Stanley Baldwin as Prime Minister in 1936.[48] The determination as to whether a defeat falls under the second or third heading usually rests with the Government, though the Opposition always has the option of itself forcing a vote of confidence should the Government not do so.

These different types of defeat were experienced by the Governments of Messrs Heath, Wilson and Callaghan, and the response in each case was in line with the foregoing. On the one occasion that the Government was defeated on a vote of confidence the Prime Minister advised a dissolution. The Government sought or was forced to seek votes of confidence following defeats on items central to Government policy, for example on the Expenditure White Paper in March 1976. On all other defeats (the overwhelming majority), it contented itself with considering whether or not to seek later reversals. In most cases the Government accepted the will of the House.

The popular view that in the 1970s there was a deviation from past practice in terms of the Government's response[49] is incorrect. What changed was not the basis of the Government's response but the number of defeats. Whereas previous defeats had been few and far between (eleven in the period from 1945 to 1970), and did not impact themselves on Members' consciousness, the defeats of the 1970s were too numerous to be ignored. There was an increasing though by no means universal realisation of what was entailed by the convention of collective responsibility. It was far more limited in scope than had generally been realised. This in turn had significant political implications. Members began to be aware that by defeating a government proposal they were not necessarily raising wider constitutional considerations. These implications we shall consider later: for the House of Commons they were to be of some considerable import.

NOTES

1 This section draws heavily though by no means exclusively on Philip Norton, *The Commons in Perspective* (Martin Robertson, 1981), pp. 147–54.

2 Charles Morris, Minister for the Civil Service, in a debate on the Civil Service, *HC Deb.*, c. 1356. (Even the reference to the way money is spent could be contested on the grounds that permanent secretaries are normally the accounting officers in the department.)

3 Geoffrey Marshall and Graeme Moodie, *Some Problems of the Constitution*, rev. 4th ed. (Hutchinson, 1967), p. 58.

4 See, e.g. Shirley Williams, 'The Decision Makers, in *Policy and Practice: The Experience of Government* (Royal Institute of Public Administration, 1980), pp. 81–2.

5 N. Johnson, *In Search of the Constitution* (Methuen, 1980), p. 84.

6 Peter Kellner and Lord Crowther-Hunt, *The Civil Servants* (Macdonald Futura, 1980), p. 220.

7 Brian C. Smith and Jeffrey Stanyer, *Administering Britain* (Martin Robertson, 1980 ed.), p. 184.

8 E.C.S. Wade and G. Godfrey Phillips, *Constitutional and Administrative Law*, 9th ed. by A.W. Bradley (Longman, 1977), p. 107.

9 *Ibid.*, p. 108.

10 Philip Norton, 'Dear Minister . . . The importance of MP-to-Minister correspondence', *Parliamentary Affairs*, 35 (1), Winter 1982, pp. 62 and 67.

11 Smith and Stanyer, *op. cit.*, p. 185.

12 S.A. de Smith, *Constitutional and Administrative Law* (Penguin, 1971), p. 176.

13 Lord Blake, *The Office of Prime Minister* (OUP, 1975), pp. 30–1.

14 See John P. Mackintosh, *The British Cabinet*, 3rd ed. (Stevens, 1977), pp. 531–2. Also B. Sedgemore, *The Secret Constitution* (Hodder & Stoughton, 1980), ch. 9.

15 Hamish Hamilton/Jonathan Cape, vol. 1 (1975), vol 2 (1976), vol. 3 (1977).

16 Gillian Peele, 'The Developing Constitution', in C. Cook and J. Ramsden (eds), *Trends in British Politics since 1945* (Macmillan, 1978), p. 19.

17 Barbara Castle, *The Castle Diaries 1974–76* (Weidenfeld & Nicolson, 1980).

18 *Ibid.*, Preface.

19 Peter Bromhead, *Britain's Developing Constitution* (Allen & Unwin, 1974), p. 56.

20 Harold Wilson, *A Personal Record: The Labour Government 1964–1970* (Weidenfeld & Nicolson, 1971), p. 640. See also p. 627.

21 See Richard Crossman, *Diaries*, vol. 3, pp. 439 and 480.

22 Largely because he had a fairly quiescent Cabinet. See P. Norton, *Conservative Dissidents* (Temple Smith, 1978), pp. 37–8 and 231.
23 Harold Wilson, *The Governance of Britain* (Weidenfeld & Nicolson/ Michael Joseph, 1976), p. 193.
24 *Ibid.*, p. 192. See also Castle, *op. cit.*, p. 206.
25 For a short time he was 'effectively, if temporarily sacked' by Mr Callaghan for his actions following the Cabinet's approval of the Lib–Lab Pact. See Sedgemore, *op. cit.*, p. 74. See also Mackintosh, *op. cit.*, pp. 532–3.
26 Reg Prentice. Mr Prentice's disaffection from the Government and his party was such that he resigned from the Cabinet shortly afterwards, later leaving the party altogether and crossing the floor of the House.
27 Sedgemore, *op. cit.*, p. 75.
28 See Wilson, *Governance of Britain*, p. 196.
29 P. Norton, *Dissension in the House of Commons 1974–1979* (Oxford University Press, 1980), pp. 263–5.
30 *HC Deb.*, 933, c 552.
31 Donald Shell, 'The British Constitution in 1980', *Parliamentary Affairs*, 34 (2), Spring 1981, p. 159.
32 This point is well made by Bradley, *op. cit.*, p. 102.
33 Sedgemore, *op. cit.*, p. 75.
34 Sedgemore, *op. cit.*, p. 75.
35 Mackintosh, *op. cit.*, pp. 535–6.
36 Shell, *loc. cit.*, p. 160.
37 Hans Daalder, *Cabinet Reform in Britain 1914–1963* (Oxford University Press, 1964), p. 247.
38 Wilson, *The Governance of Britain*, pp. 37–8.
39 See Graeme Moodie, *The Government of Great Britain* (Methuen, 1964), p. 100.
40 See, e.g., J. Harvey and L. Bather, *The British Constitution* (Macmillan, 1965), p. 234.
41 Mrs Thatcher, *HC Deb.*, 907, c 642–3 (1976).
42 Letter to *The Times*, 13 July 1971.
43 *Reforming the House of Commons* (Fabian Tract 448, 1977), p. 4.
44 See P. Norton, *Conservative Dissidents* (Temple Smith, 1978).
45 See P. Norton, 'Intra-Party Dissent in the House of Commons: A Case Study. The Immigration Rules 1972', *Parliamentary Affairs*, 29 (4), Autumn 1976, pp. 404–20.
46 See P. Norton, *Dissension in the House of Commons 1974–1979*, appendix.
47 See P. Norton, 'Government Defeats in the House of Commons: Myth and Reality', *Public Law*, Winter 1978, pp. 360–78.
48 *HC Deb.*, 310, c 2445.
49 See, e.g., Grant Jordan, 'The Committee Stage of the Scotland and Wales Bill (1976–77)', *The Waverley Papers: Occasional Paper No. 1* (University of Edinburgh, 1979), p. 38.

3

The Machinery of Government
Constitutional change or managerial tinkering?

The increase in government intervention in the social, industrial and
economic life of the country, especially after the Second World War,
placed a greater burden than hitherto on government in terms of the
number of decisions to be taken. The more demands made of government, the more time it was forced to devote to responding to outside
pressures. Whereas in the nineteenth century the Cabinet often found
itself with little to do, for part of the twentieth century it found
itself with too much to do. The number of decisions that had to be
made was such as to preclude considered debate. As a result, many of
the more important matters requiring determination at Cabinet level
were in effect hived off to Cabinet committees; the post-war years have
witnessed a proliferation of such committees. Other decisions were left
to the individual departments. Indeed, looked at in terms of decision-
making capacity, one could make a case almost for the existence of
'ministerial' as opposed to 'prime ministerial' government. Legal powers
of decision-making are vested in ministers, not in the Cabinet or in the
Prime Minister, the most tangible and lasting impact of the convention
of ministerial responsibility. Very few matters are taken by ministers to
the Cabinet. Two former Education Ministers, Lord Boyle and Anthony
Crosland, both stated that 'the individual Minister of Education rather
than the Cabinet is the focal point of political initiatives and decisions
in education'.[1] Crosland himself only took two matters concerning
education policy to the Cabinet.[2] The greater complexity of issues has
enhanced the likelihood of Cabinet deferring to departmental ministers
on intricate and detailed matters, especially where the minister has
conferred beforehand with the Prime Minister and senior colleagues.
Some ministers, enjoying the confidence of the Prime Minister and/or a
large part of the parliamentary party, may create almost independent
empires within the labyrinth of Whitehall departments. In practice,
though, the thesis of ministerial government is open to serious challenge.

In decision-making, ministers are subject to many constraints. One, ironically, is the sheer number of decisions to be made. The number is such that many, indeed the overwhelming majority, are made in the minister's name by officials. Only the more important matters percolate upwards to find their way into the minister's red despatch box. Even then, the minister's time and resources are limited and he has to rely upon the advice of his advisers. They are permanent and full-time: the minister is likely to be in the post but a relatively short time and there are many other demands on his time: he has to attend Cabinet, deal with parliamentary and constituency matters, and since 1973, attend meetings of EC ministers in Brussels and elsewhere. The relationship of civil servants to ministers we shall consider in more detail shortly. The range as well as the size of departments is a further limitation: one issue may be the responsibility of several departments. This both denies the opportunity to an individual minister to decide the issue and, given that officials tend to dominate inter-departmental negotiations, strengthens the position of civil servants. The growth of quasi-autonomous public bodies has served also to put certain decisions in the hands of others, often beyond the reach of a minister. The 1970s also witnessed a greater willingness on the part of the courts to determine whether or not ministers were acting within their statutory powers.

In terms of the relationship between ministers and civil servants, a number of critics contend that the civil servants wielded too much influence and were the effective decision-makers; this view we shall consider in our analysis of the Civil Service. In terms of the relationship between ministers and the citizen, the view has been taken by some that the balance weighed too heavily in favour of the former, permitting arbitrary and unfair decisions; among those apparently sharing such an opinion, and doing something about it, was a number of judges. This we shall explore further in our section on the judiciary.

Apart from the activities of officials and judges, one important development in the late 1960s and 1970s affecting the position of ministers, certain ministers in particular, was the reorganisation, at least in part, of the machinery of government. This took the form of the amalgamation of certain departments and the creation of new bodies and procedures to co-ordinate and assess policy and its implementation.

The amalgamation of certain departments took place in the 1960s; for example, the Defence Department was created in 1964, encompassing the three service departments and part of the Ministry of Supply, and the Foreign and Commonwealth Office emerged in 1968 from an amalgamation of the Foreign Office and the Commonwealth Office (the latter a product of the merging of the Commonwealth Relations Office and the Colonial Office in 1966). The most important changes were to take place in the 1970s. The return of a Conservative Government in 1970 brought into office a Prime Minister who was keenly interested in improving efficiency, of industry and of government, and was wedded to managerial techniques and a problem-solving approach. A review was undertaken of the organisation of the structure and policy-making procedures within central government and the Government's recommendations embodied in a White Paper *The Reorganisation of Central Government* within four months of coming to office.[3] It aimed by its own delineation to achieve 'a new style of government'.

In the White Paper it was asserted that government had been attempting to do too much.

This has placed an excessive burden on industry, and on the people of the country as a whole, and has also overloaded the government machinery itself. Public administration and management in central government has stood up to these strains, but the weakness has shown itself in the apparatus of policy formulation and in the quality of many government decisions over the past 25 years.[4]

The Government sought to remedy this situation by improving the quality of policy formulation and decision-making in government, by improving the framework within which public policy was formulated by matching the field of responsibility in Government departments to coherent fields of policy and administration, and by ensuring that the government machine responded and adapted itself to new policies and programmes as they emerged. The fulfilment of these aims was geared to enhancing the authority of government, not only in terms of efficiency in allocating resources to meet policy needs, but also in terms of consent.

The fulfilment of these aims will improve the efficiency of government [declared the White Paper]. This does not mean an increase in State power, nor any sacrifice of humanity and compassion in public administration. Indeed, the systematic formulation of policy and the presentation to Ministers of defined options for decision provides them with the opportunity for greater openness in government, and more responsiveness to the needs and wishes of the community and of individuals — in short, a new and better balance between the individual and the modern State.[5]

The measures taken to achieve these aims comprised essentially the creation of the 'super-departments' of Trade and Industry and the Environment, as well as some reorganisation in terms of other departments; the formation of the Central Policy Review Staff, colloquially known as the 'Think Tank'; and the introduction of Programme Analysis and Review (PAR). The Department of Trade and Industry (DTI) incorporated the Board of Trade, the Ministry of Technology and the Ministry of Power. The Department of the Environment took in the former ministries of Housing and Local Government, Transport, and Public Buildings and Works. The amalgamation was designed to reduce the need for interdepartmental compromise, to enable a single strategy to be proposed and implemented within one department, to create the capacity to manage larger resource-consuming programmes, and more direct identification to the community at large of ministers responsible for defined functions. For example, land planning had previously spanned the responsibilities of the ministries that now formed the Environment Department. 'In the new D.o.E.', as Edward Heath explained it, 'there would be one section dealing with land planning. This prevents duplication, prevents friction and saves on staff.'[6] The Central Policy Review Staff was brought into being in order to review the Government's overall strategy in applying its programme, to undertake particular study projects and to play a part in the Public Expenditure Survey exercise. Programme Analysis and Review was designed to provide an in-depth investigation of policies within individual departments to ensure that the best means were being employed to achieve the desired end, the analysis being carried out by civil servants and a number of outside participants, usually businessmen.

What has been the effect of these changes, and what debate has taken place, on government and the relationship between its constituent parts? Of the 'super-departments', only the Department of the Environment has survived, at least in name. As a consequence of the oil crisis of 1973/4, Mr Heath hived off part of the DTI to create the Department of Energy. Under the subsequent Labour Government, the DTI was broken up into the departments of Trade, Industry, and Prices and Consumer Affairs, and Transport broke free of the DoE to regain its status as a separate department. As a consequence, though large departments remain they are not quite the super, rational departments planned by Mr Heath. As a result, some of the advantages – or, in some eyes, disadvantages – of merged departments have been lost.

It was assumed by some, including Mr Heath, that the creation of such large departments would help strengthen both the Cabinet and individual ministers. By reducing the number of departments it was possible to reduce the size of the Cabinet; at the same time it ensured that the situation of having some ministers heading departments but not in Cabinet, thus causing offence to the departments' attentive publics, could be avoided. Both these points were appreciated by Mr Heath himself[7] and by one of the officials most closely associated with government reorganisation, Sir Richard Clarke.[8] The dismemberment of the departments in the latter half of the 1970s effectively prevented the 'killing of two birds with one stone' that Mr Heath believed was possible.

The view that the merging of departments would strengthen the minister at the head of the new department was voiced strongly by G.W. Jones.

Wielding immense statutory powers over a huge range of functions, and supported by a vast administrative apparatus, each Secretary of State has more influence than a Cabinet Minister in the past. Decisions which might once have had to be settled in inter-departmental committees can be taken inside the department where the Secretary of State's voice is decisive. The Ministers beneath him have no statutory powers of their own and are clearly his junior Ministers unable to appeal outside the deparment against his view.[9]

Similar fears were shared implicitly by Mr Heath and by the authors of the 1970 White Paper; they expressed the need for ministers to ensure that important decisions were not immune from collective discussion.[10] As we have noted earlier, though, a contrary view was taken by Lord Crowther-Hunt, a former junior minister, and Peter Kellner. They argued that creating such large departments would increase the power of the civil servants in decision-making rather than ministers: four ministers in the DoE would hardly be expected to ensure effective control of a department of 38,000 officials.[11] Supporting their view is the fact, recognised by Mr Heath, that bodies dealing with departments expect to be able to deal with the Secretary of State, the man at the top, and not one of his junior ministers. As Mr Heath himself expressed it,

it is still very difficult to persuade people that a Minister who is just under the Secretary of State has, in fact, got a sphere of his own, and makes decisions of his own, and that when that is done that is the end of the matter. They still will try to get to the Secretary of State and overload the man at the top with the burden.[12]

A minister with a crowded diary, one organised for him by his officials, is not in the best position to maintain effective supervision of the empire under his nominal control. It is thus an arguable point as to whether or not the renewed proliferation of departments in the years since 1973 has increased or weakened the effective powers of individual ministers.

As for the CPRS and the PAR exercise, the former initially appeared to fulfil the functions stipulated for it, though encouraging a wary attitude by civil servants. It was, reported one source, 'regarded with suspicion by the departments, the Treasury and the Cabinet Office'.[13] It was also to be criticised for coming within what Frank Stacey aptly termed 'the penumbra of Cabinet secrecy'.[14] Though it appears to have had some influence under the Heath Government, possibly influencing Government attitudes on energy and on methods for combating inflation,[15] it appeared to lose ground with a change of chairman and with the change of Prime Ministers in 1974. The relationship between the new chairman, Sir Kenneth Berrill, and Mr Wilson was not as strong as had been that between Lord Rothschild and Mr Heath. Within No. 10 Downing Street a separate and independent Policy Unit was created to provide more party-orientated advice on short-term policy. Within the Think Tank its work focused on specific studies (about forty being undertaken in the first 7 or 8 years of its existence), occupying about half of its time, with most of the rest of its time being taken up with collective briefings for Ministers. Since 1974 it has been accused of falling increasingly under the influence of officials. Though half its members are brought in from outside the Civil Service, they no longer carry the weight of the independent and well-connected individuals recruited (somewhat idiosyncratically apparently) by Lord Rothschild. In the opinion of Lord Crowther-Hunt, it is now often brought in at a high level by officials themselves in order to bring added weight to Civil Service recommendations.[16]

As for Programme Analysis and Review, from the beginning it departed from many of its original aims. Instead of establishing an independent base, run by a detached group of analysts, it ended up under the wing of the Treasury, 'run by the same old faces', and differed little from other analyses which had been going on for some years.[17] PARs were not systematic and they became just another weapon in the

Whitehall battle for a share of the government cake. Departments used studies merely as opportunities to lay claim to extra resources. The increase in the number of departments also tended to make the system unmanageable and in any event, according to one analysis, the whole exercise ran counter to the interests and operation of the existing decision-making process; policy-making was largely a process of minimising conflict between competing groups or trying to get an issue off the political agenda, not one of problem-solving, the assumption on which the whole process of rationalisation was based.[18] In November 1979 PAR was phased out.

By the end of the 1970s, what had started out as a bold exercise to reorganise the structure and policy-making processes of British government to achieve greater efficiency in policy-making and more open government had failed to meet expectations. The CPRS and PAR exercises came up against vested interests and were largely turned to the advantage of those interests, more so the latter than the former. The reorganisation of departments achieved some lasting advantages, especially in terms of functional responsibilities, but the grand design plotted by Mr Heath and his advisers fell under the weight of unforeseen external pressures (the oil crisis), doubts about the ability of individual politicians to control such bodies, and what Mr Heath castigated as the whims of his successors.[19] The attempt by such changes to achieve 'a new and better balance between the individual and the State' was to say the least of it over-optimistic and, with the benefit of hindsight, naively so. The changes that have endured may have helped produce a clearer and less unwieldy method of policy-making, but they have not achieved the paradigmatic change in British government envisaged by Mr Heath. By the latter half of the decade, reorganisation of the machinery of government was not a topic achieving priority among the issues on the agenda of political debate. The focus of attention shifted instead to devolution.

LOCAL GOVERNMENT AND THE NATIONAL HEALTH SERVICE

The 1970s witnessed also the reorganisation of local government and the National Health Service. The changes themselves need not detain us. As Gillian Peele noted, such changes 'had some potential constitutional significance but they were primarily seen as attempts to secure greater efficiency, often in accordance with tenets of management theory, within the framework of the existing set of values and assumptions about the institution's role'.[20] (The same, of course, could be said of the reform of central government machinery, but as we have seen it was justified in terms of an attempt to achieve a change in the relationship between the individual and the State.) Nonetheless, such changes are worthy of comment not so much because of their intent but because of some of the consequences flowing from their effects. Neither reorganisation achieved its desired aim. In terms of local government, as Anthony King noted, 'things are not working out quite as expected'.[21] The new streamlined system proved administratively more costly than the old. Perhaps more importantly, far from having the effect of being responsive to the needs of citizens, the new structure appeared to generate confusion and cynicism. The new tiered system of local government left individuals no clearer than before as to what authority was responsible for what. In many areas resentment was felt and expressed at the emasculation of the old borough councils, almost reduced to constituting the 'dignified' element of local government, and at the creation and composition of the new counties. The exigencies of economic policy have resulted in intervention by central government in local policy and budgetary planning, resulting in a number of cases in serious central–local government conflict. The importance of this for our purposes is that such change had not reduced and may even have encouraged discontent with the existing political structure. Civic indifference may be reflected in the tendency of certain social groupings to ignore local authority and to create their own 'action' or 'defence' committees.

Perhaps less noticeably, civic indifference may have been generated or at least not discouraged by the reorganisation of the Health Service. In introducing the NHS Reorganisation Bill in 1973, the Social Services Secretary, Sir Keith Joseph, made it clear that the emphasis was to be on effectiveness rather than consent. Despite some attempt at modification by the subsequent government, it was clear that the new structure created problems of accountability. In 1980, a study of Area Health Authorities found that they had achieved near-autonomous status.[22] The same year the Government announced that they were to be phased out.

If the reaction to such reorganisation was confined to pressing for change to the new structure, it would not be of concern to us. However, in so far as the failings of the new structures encourage or do not discourage cynical attitudes towards government and a lack of trust, then they are relevant. 'The real failure of both the super ministries and the enlarged counties', declared Norman St John-Stevas in 1976, 'has been their failure to inspire confidence.'[23] He was but one of many who contended that that confidence could be inspired only by radical constitutional change. 'Government', declared Mr St John-Stevas, 'must now respond to public wishes and devise policies to combat this remoteness. Devolution is an urgent need, not only to oil the wheels of government and to present a more human aspect, but, above all, to recreate confidence in [the] governmental process.'[24]

NOTES

1   *The Politics of Education: Edward Boyle and Anthony Crosland in Conversation with Maurice Kogan* (Penguin, 1971), p. 38.
2   *Ibid.*
3   *The Reorganisation of Central Government*, Cmnd. 4506 (HMSO, Oct. 1970).
4   *Ibid.*, p. 3.
5   *Ibid.*, p. 3.
6   Edward Heath and Anthony Barker, 'Heath on Whitehall Reform', *Parliamentary Affairs*, 31 (4), Autumn 1978, p. 373.
7   Heath and Barker, *loc. cit.*, p. 376.
8   Sir Richard Clarke, 'The Machinery of Government', in W. Thornhill (ed.), *The Modernization of British Government* (Pitman, 1975), p. 92.
9   G.W. Jones, 'Development of the Cabinet', in Thornhill, *op. cit.*, p. 43.
10 *The Reorganisation of Central Government*, p. 5; Heath and Barker, *loc. cit.*, p. 375.
11 Crowther-Hunt and Kellner, *The Civil Servants* (Macdonald Futura, 1980), p. 220.
12 Heath and Barker, *loc. cit.*, p. 374.
13 B.C. Smith, *Policy Making in British Government* (Martin Robertson, 1976), p. 140.
14 F. Stacey, *British Government 1966–75* (Oxford University Press, 1975), p. 94.
15 Stacey, *op. cit.*, p. 91.
16 Lord Crowther-Hunt, 'Whitehall – The Balance of Power', *The Listener*, 6 Jan. 1977, p. 11.
17 Hugh Heclo and Aaron Wildavsky, *The Private Government of Public Money* (Macmillan, 1974), pp. 280–1.
18 J.J. Richardson and A.G. Jordan, *Governing under Pressure* (Martin Robertson, 1979), pp. 37–9.
19 Heath and Barker, *op. cit.*, p. 389.

20 Gillian Peele, 'The Developing Constitution', in C. Cook and J. Ramsden (eds) *Trends in British Politics Since 1945* (Macmillan, 1978), p. 9.
21 A. King, 'The Problem of Overload', in King, *Why is Britain Becoming Harder to Govern?* (BBC, 1976), p. 9.
22 H.J. Elcock and S. Hayward, *The Buck Stops Where? Accountability and Control in the National Health Service* (University of Hull Institute for Health Studies, 1980).
23 Norman St John-Stevas, 'The Disappearing Consensus', in King, *op. cit.*, p. 71.
24 *Ibid.*, pp. 71–2.

4

The Civil Service

Masters or servants? Which is which?

For many years the British Civil Service was regarded, as Herman Finer described it, as 'rightly the envy of the world'. It was perceived as a well-oiled machine, manned by public servants of integrity, and serving loyally successive governments of whatever political persuasion. It was taken as a model of what a Civil Service should be. However, starting at the end of the 1950s and throughout the 1960s and the 1970s, it came in for serious and sustained criticism.[1] That criticism centred on two independent but related points. The first covered what might be termed the quality of the Civil Service: it was censured for being socially exclusive in recruitment, outdated in structure, and misguided in its philosophy. It was argued that a body dominated by public school and Oxbridge-educated men, working with an essentially nineteenth-century structure, and adhering to a philosophy of the generalist or 'all-rounder', was inadequate to deal with the highly complex problems and technology of the latter half of the twentieth century. Pressure for change led to the establishment of the Fulton Committee, which reported in 1968.[2] The second line of criticism dealt with the relationship between civil servants and ministers (and, through ministers, Parliament). It was argued that whereas constitutional convention stipulated that ministers headed departments, with civil servants serving to advise them and execute their instructions, the reality was that it was officials who dominated the relationship and were the effective decision-makers in government. It is with this latter argument that we are primarily concerned. Nonetheless, the former remains pertinent and, as we shall see, can be looked at within the context of minister–Civil Service relations, especially in the 1970s.

Criticism of the position of civil servants in relation to their ministers has been most marked in the past decade or so. The most vocal and sustained criticism has emanated from a number of Labour politicians, some of them former ministers and one a former civil servant himself.

Among ex-ministers drawing on their experiences to find fault with the role of officials in decision-making have been Richard Crossman, Tony Benn, Michael Meacher, Lord Crowther-Hunt and Alex Lyon.[3] Other Labour activists drawing on somewhat different experiences have been Brian Sedgemore, a former civil servant,[4] and Joe Haines, who served as Harold Wilson's press secretary.[5] They have not been alone in expressing their misgivings. Journalists such as Chapman Pincher, academics on the political right such as Sir Max (now Lord) Beloff, and Conservatives such as Sir Ian Gilmour and even Mrs Thatcher herself have given voice to critical views. For example, in the days before he became a minister, Ian Gilmour expressed the opinion that 'only about one Minister in three runs his department'[6] and in 1980 Mrs Thatcher was reported to be so highly critical of the influence wielded by officials over both ministers and the choice of where expenditure cuts were to fall that *The Economist* went so far as to refer to her 'bitter disaffection from the Whitehall ethos'.[7]

The main thrust of the criticism has been that civil servants wield too great an influence in decision-making, being able to ensure in many cases that ministers decide what they, the officials, want them to decide (or, if not, that such decisions are effectively circumvented), their influence deriving from certain instutional factors, reinforced by more recent developments of the 1970s. The factors giving civil servants the balance of advantage in their relations with ministers have been identified as those of size, permanence, expertise, co-ordination, anonymity, the control of information and, in large measure, control of ministers' diaries. More recent developments reinforcing this balance of advantage have been the creation of the Central Policy Review Staff, British membership of the European Communities and the selective implementation of the recommendations of the Fulton Committee. The argument is that civil servants enjoy now an even stronger position than ever before in the determination of ministerial decisions.

The Civil Service is a large body comprising over 700,000 people.[8] This is important in the context of ministers' knowing (or not knowing) what is going on within their departments rather than in terms of policy-making. It is the size of the body of civil servants of Principal level and above (the old Administrative Class of the Civil Service) occupying the senior positions in Whitehall departments that is important in the influencing of ministers' decisions. (Indeed, below this level, many civil servants are critical of their lack of input into policy discussions.) In the larger departments such as Environment the number of officials at under-secretary rank and above is sometimes more than fifty. This numerical superiority might rank only as a minor advantage if ministers served in a full-time and permanent capacity. They do not. Their officials do.

Ministers come and go at a rate that some might describe as rapid. Between 1944 and 1976, there were nineteen Ministers of Education. Lord Crowther-Hunt served as a junior minister in the department for 15 months, his immediate predecessor served 6 months, and the four before that an average of 17 months each. Crowther-Hunt was faced with a permanent secretary who had been there 6 years and, like most of the deputy secretaries, had spent most of his career in the same department.[9] There is little time for a minister to get to know a department and to get to grips with its problems. While in office, he is limited in the amount of time he can devote to decision-making. He has other significant demands made of his time: parliamentary debates, constituency commitments, official visits and meetings of Cabinet and Cabinet committees. The less time he has to consider questions requiring his determination, the more dependent he becomes upon his officials.

A minister's knowledge of the subject covered by his department may be slight. He cannot hope to match the administrative expertise of his officials or their experience of negotiations with groups that have contact with and make demands of the department. What time he has to devote to the department and decison-making is influenced and largely shaped by his officials.[10] His diary is largely controlled by his private secretary; the material that is put before him is largely controlled by the permanent secretary. He will usually lack the time and alternative sources of informed research with which to question let alone dispute the options and the advice laid before him. (One permanent secretary once told Harold Macmillan apparently that it would be 'unconstitutional' for the minister to seek advice from anyone but his permanent secretary.) A minister is denied access to the papers of his predecessors. Upon taking office, he is supplied with a briefing document prepared by his officials. This, coupled with the foregoing, ensures that civil servants can largely determine the content of the minister's political agenda. As Lord Armstrong, former head of the Civil Service, once conceded: 'The biggest and most pervasive influence is in setting the framework within which questions of policy are raised. It would have been enormously difficult for any minister to change the framework, and to that extent we had great power.'[11]

For a minister who does reach a decision at variance with the strongly-held views of his department, there are various ways which his officials may seek to obtain its reversal. One way is to wait for a change in ministers. The new minister may prove more amenable to the advice offered him and work within the framework of the brief supplied to him.[12] Briefs may thus be used to re-fight lost battles. Another way is to brief officials in other departments to ensure that their ministers are primed to oppose the minister's decision.[13] There is close contact between senior civil servants in Whitehall, both officially and unofficially. For every committee of ministers there is an equivalent committee of officials. Senior civil servants are usually members of the same Whitehall clubs. A Cabinet minister may arrive at Cabinet to find that other ministers, briefed by their officials, are hostile to his proposal. A third way is to leak something to the press as a means of undermining a minister's credibility or policy. In 1975, for instance, an accounting officer minute sent by Sir Peter Carey to his minister, Tony Benn, was leaked. The aim was to suggest that Mr Benn's support for industrial co-operatives was somehow improper.

It is thus not difficult to see how officials may determine the framework within which a minister decides matters and influence the decisions which he reaches. In this, they are aided by the anonymity which, as we have seen, is a corollary of the convention of ministerial responsibility. This anonymity is reinforced by the provisions of the Official Secrets Act which encompasses most official documents. If officials do wield undue influence over a minister, it cannot easily be detected by outsiders. Officials are shielded by anonymity and their documents protected from outside scrutiny.

To these various factors have been added three developments of recent years which, it has been argued, have further strengthened the position of civil servants in relation to their ministers. One, probably the most important, is British membership of the European Communities. This has had the effect of increasing substantially the burden of ministers' work. Major policy questions now have to be considered in the context of Europe and this entails regular visits to Brussels and consultations with one's continental colleagues.[14] Furthermore, the harmonisation of a whole range of national policies made necessary by EC membership has meant that there has to be much preparatory discussion between British civil servants and their European counterparts, both in Brussels and in the capitals of the other member states. A busy minister, arriving for a meeting of the Council of Ministers, is briefed, sometimes at the last minute, by his officials: it is obviously difficult for him to challenge their advice.[15] 'I have little doubt', wrote Lord Crowther-Hunt, 'that any detailed study there would show that UK ministers generally are more dependent on the assessment and advice of their civil servants in policy matters they have to decide in Brussels than in purely domestic policy-making in London.'[16] The same point has variously been made by Mr Benn.

A second development has been the creation of the Central Policy Review Staff. Although created for the purpose of evaluating policies in terms of long-term objectives and for providing the Cabinet with alternative advice and options to those being put forward by departments, both Lord Crowther-Hunt and Mr Benn have argued that it has now become a weapon in the armoury of officials. They contend that it is now brought in at a high level by senior civil servants to bring added weight to bear in support of official recommendations.[17] If a minister reaches a decision not favoured by his officials, the CPRS now constitutes a body through which the latter can channel their alternative views.[18]

The third development, perhaps surprisingly, has been the implementation of some of the recommendations of the Fulton Committee. Established to consider what we earlier referred to as the quality of the Civil Service in terms of its recruitment, organisation and philosophy, it recommended a number of changes designed to produce a more open and efficient Civil Service, one geared to meeting the challenges of a highly complex society. It was recognised by the Committee that many of its recommendations would strengthen the position of civil servants in the process of governmental decision-making. It therefore made a number of recommendations designed to act as a counterbalance. In terms of implementation, the outcome has not been what the members of the Committee wanted. 'Those Fulton recommendations which have been adopted are all those which strengthen the power and position of the traditional administrative class while those which have not been adopted are the ones which would have produced countervailing pressures.'[19] The Civil Service and in particular the head of the service, Sir William Armstrong, managed to effectively avoid or render ineffective those proposals which threatened their structure and recruitment: the service remains Oxbridge-based in personnel and recruitment and senior administrators continue to see themselves as administrators geared to offering policy advice rather than as managers, contrary to the hopes and recommendations of Fulton.[20] Proposals for planning units within each department, manned by comparatively young people,

were seen as a threat and implemented in such a way as to ensure that
the intentions of the Fulton Committee were never realised. Ministers
were thus denied an alternative source of policy advice. Officials also
effectively ignored or worked around the 38 policy advisers brought in
by some Labour ministers in 1974. 'The real difficulty', as one member
of an official committee set up to 'implement' the Fulton proposals
put it, 'is that you are trying to solve a problem with people who are
themselves part of the problem'.[21]

Proposals that strengthened the position of civil servants were, by
contrast, put into effect. The recommendation that representatives of
departments should be in a majority on Civil Service selection boards
was readily accepted. The proposal that the Prime Minister be aided in
the selection of senior appointments by a committee consisting of
permanent secretaries, scientists and other specialists, and one or two
distinguished people from outside the service, was carried into effect, at
least inasmuch as it concerned senior officials; the committee comprises
no-one else. The recommendation for a Civil Service College was
implemented, but the proposal for its governing body to comprise civil
servants and people from outside the service was limited so that only
civil servants formed the governing body; since its creation, the College
has been limited in its activities, geared to the Civil Service concept of
administration rather than that of management and research. As the
Eleventh Report from the Expenditure Committee (1977) revealed, the
intentions of the Fulton Committee have not been achieved.

It can thus be contended that civil servants are in an extremely
strong position should they wish to influence minister's decision-
making. Tony Benn and Joe Haines, among others, have given examples
of cases where officials have sought to use that position to achieve a
particular outcome. Mr Benn, in particular, complained of officials
keeping from him information which he should have been given. For
example, as Energy Secretary he had not been told that the Atomic
Energy Authority knew there had been a major nuclear disaster in the
Soviet Union in the 1950s, nor had he been told about the high-jacking
of a shipload of uranium which had taken place in 1968 or about leaks
of toxic waste material at the Windscale processing plant.[22] 'The Civil
Service', as Shirley Williams suggested, 'is good at losing things'.[23] (The
reference is to information, not toxic waste.) The most serious case
instanced by Mr Benn was on the question of what type of nuclear
reactor Britain should opt for in the 1980s: the British Advanced Gas-
Cooled Reactor (AGR) or the American Pressurised Water Reactor

(PWR). Mr Benn favoured the former, his officials favoured the latter and told him so. Mr Benn decided to draw up a paper for Cabinet advocating the AGR system but ran into a reluctance on the part of his permanent officials to help him in this task. The CPRS then became involved and put in a paper to the Cabinet, some CPRS members even going so far as to ring the offices of other ministers to enlist their support for the PWR.[24] On this occasion Mr Benn won the battle but lost the war. The Cabinet went along with his proposal, but a new government returned in 1979 provided the Civil Service with an opportunity to re-fight the battle: in December 1979 the government announced a major increase in the nuclear programme, including the PWRs.

In such cases there is little to suggest that civil servants seek to achieve partisan political decisions. Though the 'Whitehall mandarins' did appear somewhat worried and alarmed at the prospect of Mr Benn occupying a minister's chair, they do not constitute a cohesive Conservative- or a cohesive Labour-oriented body. Rather they might be accused of considering themselves to be non-, or rather anti-party political in their approach, believing it their duty to steer politicians towards what Sir Anthony Part referred to as 'the common ground'.[25] (This is, of course, a highly political approach but that is not how civil servants see it.) 'Senior civil servants', reported Richard Norton-Taylor, 'say that both the Conservative and the Labour parties are really coalitions — suggesting that in this right-of-centre consensus Whitehall represents a democratic majority and thereby gives its actions and advice an unquestionable legitimacy.'[26] This attitude, derived from and reinforced by officials' backgrounds and experience, may and does apparently lead to a somewhat aloof and self-confident approach, civil servants appearing to see themselves as guardians of some elusive but enduring national interest rather in the manner that the Turkish military views itself as the defender of the principles of Ataturk. The only difference is that the Civil Service prefers to work behind the screen of anonymity.

The view that civil servants can and do seek to use their positions to determine ministers' decisions, and hence undermine or rather reverse the relationship between ministers and civil servants posited by constitutional convention, is not one that enjoys universal assent. Various former ministers and other observers have contended that the reality matches the constitutional expectation. Some ministers have argued that in office they have been very much in charge of their departments, their officials serving to carry out loyally and effectively their decisions. Taking part in a radio discussion, Peter Walker said

In preparing legislation it is the Minister who is very much in command. For example, the major legislation I was responsible for on the environment [in the Heath Government] was very much legislation that I decided on in Opposition and which I went to the Department and told the Department I wanted legislation achieving the following objectives.[27]

Bruce Headey's research of the Civil Service revealed that officials looked for a minister who was capable of taking a decision as well as defending the department in Cabinet, in the Commons and in the country.[28] Once a minister had 'taken a view', they could carry it out. One thing they did not like was an indecisive minister. Though it is an arguable point as to whether this strengthens ministers or their officials, civil servants spend much time analysing election manifestos and feel bound to try to find ways of helping ministers to carry out manifesto promises.[29] Though Mr Benn has suggested that an analysis of the briefing document presented to new ministers would provide a better guide to policies implemented in recent years than would an analysis of manifestos, it is instructive to note that post-war Governments have usually achieved implementation of most if not almost all of their election promises once in office. Indeed, Lord Hailsham has contended that the Civil Service has proved perhaps too effective in carrying out measures that a Government has promised to implement. He concedes that by the selection and presentation of materials, officials can limit a minister's choice, but that he sees as no bad thing and something that is marginal compared to their carrying out of a minister's wishes.

The Civil Service [he declared] is an evil at present, not because of its vices, but because of its virtues, not because it is not impartial, but because it adds to the power of the elective dictators, according impartially its skills, its disciplines, its expertise to the organized minority in power so that it becomes less possible to unseat them.[30]

In short, the Civil Service adheres faithfully and effectively, perhaps too much so, to the relationship stipulated by the convention of ministerial responsibility.

The view that the Civil Service is a monolithic entity has also been variously challenged, including by former Foreign Secretary David Owen.[31] The individuals making up the service differ in their own perceptions of what is in the national interest ('If I had my way', one senior civil servant told Norton-Taylor, 'I would nationalise merchant banks', another that he would like to tear up the Treaty of Rome);[32] so too do the departments themselves. What officials in one ministry believe to be in the national interest (which will often coincide with the department's interests) does not necessarily coincide with the views of their colleagues in another department. 'Divide and rule' is a tactic that can be employed against officials as well as by them.

The argument, then, is not a one-sided one. Nor is it necessarily an argument of extremes. It is possible to contend that officials are in a position to exert great pressure on a minister to reach a particular decision and on occasion do so, but that on the whole they seek diligently and honestly to carry out the wishes of their minister. The extent to which officials will or will not enjoy a certain mastery over their minister's decisions will vary from minister to minister, depending upon the minister himself, his permanent secretary and other senior officials, the ethos of the department (the Environment Department has a reputation for being fairly open, the Home Office one for being secretive) and the political conditions then prevailing. Civil servants, as we have mentioned, like a minister who can make decisions and who can defend his department. A minister who loses out in expenditure cuts or some other Cabinet decision loses face within his department. One who effectively fights for his department will be in a strong position.

PROPOSALS FOR REFORM

Various proposals have emanted from those who have criticised the Civil Service in recent years, most such proposals stemming from perceived weaknesses in the application of the convention of ministerial responsibility. Some reformers have concentrated upon the relationship between officials and ministers, seeking to strengthen the position of the latter. Some have concentrated upon the House of Commons as the vehicle for scrutinising via ministers the work of departments and as a possible vehicle for strengthening ministers. Others have concentrated upon the effect of anonymity and secrecy entailed by the convention and the implications of that for officials' decisions concerning individuals, decisions of which ministers can have no knowledge. The reforms proposed can be categorised under three headings: those focusing upon ministers, those focusing upon the House of Commons, and those concentrating upon individuals. As we mentioned earlier, the effect of some of these would be to strengthen the convention, others to weaken it.

A number of changes have been proposed by those who wish to strengthen the position of ministers in their dealings with civil servants. The two most important are those to give ministers power to dismiss their own permanent secretaries and the appointment of a body of policy advisers, drawn from outside the Civil Service, to provide each minister with an alternative source of advice to that presented by officials. On rare occasions a minister has sought to influence the removal of his permanent secretary, sometimes successfully, other times not; permanent secretaries apparently threatened to resign *en masse* if Barbara Castle achieved her aim of removing her permanent secretary when she was Transport Minister. To vest in a minister formal power to dismiss the permanent secretary would hardly be incompatible with the doctrine of ministerial responsibility; quite the reverse. However, it would raise the possibility of permanent secretaries becoming too closely attached to or associated with particular ministers. It is also unlikely to come about. It is improbable that the Prime Minister will wish to dispense with his or her power to approve such appointments. There are also obvious obstacles in the way of ministers appointing their own political advisers or advisory bodies similar to the French *cabinets*, a proposal advocated by John Silkin and Charles Morris.[33] As the experience of the 1974–9 Parliament showed, the Civil Service can effectively ignore or work round political advisers. Also, a number of Labour ministers proved none too keen to have such advisers. Conservative ministers have not taken to the idea. The main proponent of their appointment has again tended to be Mr Benn; he has admitted that he favours the widest possible use of political appointees, be they MPs of laymen.[34] None of these points denies the merits or the case for such appointments, but they do point to the obvious obstacles that have to be overcome for such a change to be effective.

Reform proposals focusing upon the House of Commons have tended to emphasise the need for effective Select Committees in order to achieve effective scrutiny of Civil Service actions. Such proposals are not new, but they received their most authoritative support from the Expenditure Committee in its report on the Civil Service in 1977 and from the Select Committee on Procedure the following year. The main proposals contained in the latter's report were implemented in 1979.[35] The work of such committees affects the convention of ministerial responsibility in two ways. On the one hand it weakens the anonymity of civil servants. Officials appear before Select Committees on behalf of their ministers (the exceptions are permanent secretaries appearing before the Public Accounts Committee in their capacities as accounting officers), but nonetheless by their presence they make themselves known to MPs. There is the danger that by appearing they may be led into expressing their own opinions and seek to justify their own positions rather than that of their minister; that, though, would be a sign of weakness on their part, indicating their inability to persuade the minister on the point. On the other hand the Committees could help strengthen the position of ministers in relation to their officials. Ministers can use the reports of Select Committees as alternative sources of advice and, to some extent, information (though much of the information obtained by the committees comes from the departments themselves) and may use them to bolster a decision taken against Civil Service advice. It has been argued that the work of the committees can strengthen ministers especially when allied with what goes on on the Floor of the House of Commons. A combination of effective committees and an assertive House could result in the House taking decisions ostensibly against Government advice but in reality in line with what the minister wants but has been unable to achieve.[36] The ability to say to his officials 'The House won't have this' is an important weapon in a minister's armoury,[37] the more so given the incidence of Government defeats in the Commons' division lobbies in the 1970s.[38]

The third category of proposals concentrate upon the anonymity and secrecy which are a corollary of the convention. Civil servants have to make a great many decisions every day, not only policy decisions of one sort or another but also decisions in cases affecting individual citizens. This is especially so in departments which handle a tremendous amount of casework: the DHSS and the Home Office are obvious examples. Unless a case is taken up by an MP there is little likelihood of it ever reaching a minister. In most cases there is no reason why it should. The convention of ministerial responsibility operates nonetheless, and provides a protective screen behind which civil servants may reach their decisions. Even where the Parliamentary Commissioner for Administration investigates cases of alleged maladministration it is not usual for those involved to be named and at the end of the day the formal remedy for any maladministration revealed rests with the minister.

It has been argued that the application of the convention hides or can serve to hide mistakes and can contribute to complacent and insensitive decisions, officials not having to make public the material on which they based their decisions. Secrecy serves also to breed suspicion. This is important in terms of consent. Not knowing why or how decisions are taken, and whether or not they are actually taken by ministers or unelected officials, does nothing to instil trust in government.[39] Such trust, it is argued, can be achieved by 'open government'. The reforms posited to achieve this end are the enactment of a Freedom of Information Act and a revision of the Official Secrets Act.

In 1972 the Franks Committee recommended that it should no longer be an offence for a civil servant to communicate information about his work unless it fell into certain closely specified categories (for example, if it was classified information concerning defence, foreign affairs, or currency; or if it was likely to impede law-enforcement); successive governments have committed themselves to reforming the Official Secrets Act, a commitment as yet unfulfilled. (The latest attempt, a Protection of Information Bill introduced by the Conservative Government in 1979, was withdrawn when it was realised that it would have prevented publication of the book which had just led to the identification of spy Anthony Blunt.) Various attempts to go further and seek passage of a Freedom of Information Bill have been made, in particular by Liberal MP Clement Freud. The main intent of such moves is to provide public access to official documents, save in clearly specified cases. Such legislation now exists in the USA, Sweden, Denmark and Norway, and it is argued strongly that! Britain should follow suit. The Fulton Committee observed that 'the public interest would be better served if there were a greater amount of openness'[40] and advocates of a Freedom of Information Bill argue that such a measure would produce that openness. Greater awareness of what is done, and why, would contribute to greater trust in government as well as support for decisions taken.

Those opposed to public access to official documents argue that it would undermine the convention of ministerial responsibility, would inhibit officials in tendering advice to ministers, and would cost too much to implement. Neither of the first two consequences necessarily flow from allowing access to public documents. Where such access reveals maladministration the convention is not undermined if the remedy remains in the hands of the minister. The frank interchange of views between officials and ministers is not jeopardised by the publication of the evidence and analyses on which decisions are reached. The question of cost raises no constitutional implications and is one that must be treated with caution; there is a growing tendency to use it as an excuse for not answering parliamentary questions. In itself it is not an argument that denies the merits of the case for public access.

On balance, the weight of argument tends to favour the case of the reformers. ' "Open decisions openly arrived at" can only improve the quality of decision making in government. . . . After all, a proposal that cannot stand up to public criticism can hardly be of much value.'[41] Those who wish to maintain the present position have a case in contending that public access to documents might encourage civil servants to commit less to paper than before, but given the size and responsibilities of the Civil Service that might be difficult to achieve and marginal in its effect.

Finally, it is pertinent to record that these various reforms are not mutually exclusive. Quite the reverse. There is no reason why anyone wishing to ensure a more accountable Civil Service, encourage greater trust in government and maintain the principle of ministerial responsibility should not advocate all the foregoing proposals. Indeed, as we have seen, Mr Benn, among others, has done so. Though he has tended to be in the forefront in arguing the case for ministers to have their own political advisers, support for Select Committees and a Freedom of Information Bill is drawn from both sides of the House of Commons. The new Select Committee structure was achieved in 1979. As we have mentioned earlier, passage of a Freedom of Information Bill remains a distinct possibility. Like the Select Committee reform, it may have to be enacted as a result of pressure from the House of Commons and against the advice of ministers – and their civil servants.

NOTES

1   The earliest criticism was Dr (now Lord) Balogh in his essay in *The Establishment* in 1959, Professor Brian Chapman in *British Government Observed* (Allen & Unwin, 1963), Peter Shore in *Entitled to Know* (MacGibbon & Kee, 1966) and Max Nicholson in *The System* (Hodder & Stoughton, 1967).

2   *Report of the Committee on the Civil Service* (Cmnd. 3638), (HMSO, 1968).

3   See, e.g. Richard Crossman, *The Diaries of a Cabinet Minister* (Hamilton/Cape, vol I, 1975; vol. II, 1976; vol. III, 1977); Tony Benn, 'Manifestos and Mandarins', in *Policy in Practice* (Royal Institute of Public Administration, 1980), pp. 57–78; Lord Crowther-Hunt and Peter Kellner, *The Civil Servants* (Macdonald

Futura, 1980); and Michael Meacher, 'Civil Service: the Men who Block the Corridors of Power', *Most*, 21 October 1979.

4   *The Secret Constitution* (Hodder & Stoughton, 1980); also his alternative first chapter to *The Eleventh Report from the Expenditure Committee* (HC 535, 1977).

5   *The Politics of Power*, revised ed. (Coronet, 1977).

6   *The Body Politic*, rev. ed. (Hutchinson, 1971), p. 201.

7   *The Economist*, 9 Feb, 1980.

8   What constitutes a Civil Service is not always easy to define. Rather like elephants, they are difficult to describe but you know one when you see one. The usual definition of civil servants is: 'Servants of the Crown, other than holders of political or judicial offices, who are employed in a civil capacity and whose remuneration is paid wholly and directly out of moneys voted by Parliament'.

9   Lord Crowther-Hunt, 'Whitehall – Just Passing Through', *Listener*, 16 Dec. 1976, p. 773.

10   See Crossman's remarks, *Diaries of a Cabinet Minister*, vol. I, pp. 21–2.

11   Quoted in M. Meacher, *loc. cit.*, p. 22.

12   See Tony Benn, 'The Mandarins in Modern Britain', *Guardian*, 4 Feb. 1980.

13   See, e.g., David Owen, *Face the Future* (Oxford University Press, 1981 ed.), p. 137.

14   Lord Crowther-Hunt, 'The Case for Civil Service Power', *Listener*, 13 Jan. 1977.

15   *Ibid.*

16   *Ibid.*

17   Lord Crowther-Hunt, 'Whitehall – The Balance of Power', *Listener*, 6 Jan. 1977, p. 10.

18   Mr Benn, interviewed on the Granada TV Programme, 'World in Action', 7 Jan. 1980.

19   Crowther-Hunt, 'The Case for Civil Service Power', *loc. cit.*

20   See John Garrett, *Managing the Civil Service* (Heinemann, 1980); on this, I have also found valuable Christopher S. Shore, 'Recruitment and Training in the Civil Service', Third-year undergraduate dissertation, University of Hull Politics Dept., 1981.

21   Quoted in Bruce Page and Isabel Hilton, 'The "reformers" who made sure nothing changed', *Daily Express*, 6 Apr. 1977, p. 11.

22   'World in Action', 7 Jan. 1980, reported in the *Daily Telegraph*, 8 Jan. 1980. See also Sedgemore, *The Secret Constitution*.

23   Speaking on Newsweek, BBC2, 5 Dec. 1980, reported in *The Times*, 5 Dec. 1980.

24   'World in Action', 7 Jan. 1980.

25   Speaking on BBC2 Newsweek, quoted in *The Times*, 5 Dec. 1980.

26   Richard Norton-Taylor, 'Civil But Not Service', *Guardian*, 12 Oct. 1976.

27   Speaking on BBC Radio 3 programme, 'The Parliamentary Process: Politicians and Bureaucrats', broadcast 26 Feb. 1976.
28   Bruce Headey, 'Cabinet Ministers and Senior Civil Servants', in V. Herman and J. Alt (eds), *Cabinet Studies: A Reader* (Macmillan, 1975), pp. 131–5.
29   See the comments in J. Mackintosh, B. Lapping and N. Percy, *Inside British Politics* (Granada and Political Broadcasting 8, Granada TV, 1977), pp. 20–1.
30   Lord Hailsham, *The Dilemma of Democracy* (Collins, 1978), p. 161.
31   Owen, *op. cit.*, pp. 137–8.
32   Richard Norton-Taylor, 'The Dedicated Servants of Two Masters', *Guardian,* 11 Oct. 1976.
33   See 'New-style Aides for Labour Ministers?', *Tribune*, 10 July 1981, p. 6. Also Owen, *op. cit.*, pp. 147–9.
34   Tony Benn to Philip Canning. P.J. Canning ' "Yes, Minister!" A Study of the Whitehall Power Game', unpublished third-year undergraduate dissertation, Hull University Politics Department, 1980, p. 28.
35   See Philip Norton, *The Commons in Perspective* (Martin Robertson, 1981), pp. 132–7, and R.L. Borthwick, 'Up-dating on Parliament: Recent Changes in House of Commons Committees', *Teaching Politics*, 9 (3), Sept. 1980, pp. 228–41.
36   Norton, *Commons in Perspective*, pp. 159–60.
37   Also, the claim that 'the parliamentary party – or one of its committees – will not stand for this'.
38   See Philip Norton, *Dissension in the House of Commons 1974–1979* (Oxford University Press, 1980), especially pp. 461–2. See also the comments of Owen, *op. cit.*, p. 161.
39   See the comments of Owen, *op. cit.*, p. 136.
40   Report of the Committee on the Civil Service, *op. cit.*, para. 277.
41   Canning, *op. cit.*, p. 28.

5

The House of Commons

Changes within, threats from without

By convention, Parliament consists of the Queen, the House of Lords and the House of Commons with parliamentary sovereignty residing in the collective entity. The events of the nineteenth century ensured that the Commons became the dominant element of that triumvirate. The monarch was relegated by convention to form one of what Bagehot called the 'dignified' parts of the Constitution. The House of Lords was relectant to follow suit but was forced eventually to accept its limited political role by the Parliament Acts of 1911 and 1949. The House of Commons became the body which made the authoritative decisions on behalf of the electoral body, the other two elements of Parliament then concurring in those decisions (exceptions to this we shall consider later). Paradoxically, the very developments which made the Commons the dominant element of Parliament – the rise of a mass electorate and the demands of the new electors – were to serve also to shift the point of decision-making from the House to other bodies. Of the functions of the House identified by Bagehot, it lost its two most important: 'the elective function' (choosing the government), which it lost to the electorate, and its function of legislation, which effectively passed to the Cabinet. Party served as the conduit for this transfer. Contact with the new electors could only be made through highly organised political parties and the support of the voters obtained through promising the passage of measures salient to their interests; such passage was possible only by the presence in the House of Commons of a party majority. The initiative for promising measures passed to the party leaderships; election success resulted in the party leader becoming Prime Minister and his lieutenants serving in the Cabinet. The Cabinet depended upon the support of a majority in the House; party ensured that the majority was usually forthcoming. Having voted for a party and a programme, as John Mackintosh noted, both the electors and those MPs in tune with the time expected that Parliament would enact the programme. 'The task of the House of Commons became one of supporting the Cabinet chosen at the polls and passing its legislation. . . . By the 1900s, the Cabinet dominated British government.'[1] Within the Commons, the most obvious consequences were cohesive party voting in the division lobbies and a timetable revised to favour government business. In terms of the Commons' relationship with that part of it which formed the Government, the House adopted or rather was forced to adopt what Michael Mezey has aptly termed a 'reactive' role.[2] The government initiated measures, the House of Commons and other elements of Parliament approved them.

With the growing but not immediate realisation that the House of Commons had lost its functions of election and legislation, there developed some doubts as to the role of the House in the new political environment. Clearly it remained important in that the legislative out-puts of Parliament remained binding and that the House gave its assent to measures on behalf of the politically supreme electorate. But what else? The Government remained dependent upon the confidence of the House, but as long as a party majority was returned at an election that majority was assured. What other functions did the House have, and what was its relationship now with government? There was and is no definitive answer. As A.W. Bradley observed: 'the responsibility of Government to Parliament is a political relationship. As such, it is not a matter of precise definition and lawyers must resist the temptation to lay down rules for it.'[3] The conventions of collective and individual ministerial responsibility came largely to govern that relationship, but as we have seen they are far from problem-free. Even if one takes the heart of the conventions as being the requirement of being 'accountable' to the House, how is that accountability to be achieved? Lacking any formal delineation the functions of the House have been left to politicians themselves, in their behaviour, and political scientists, in their writings, to determine.

To try to accommodate the formal position of the House to the changed circumstances, one model that was developed and became widely accepted was that sometimes described as the 'Westminster model' of government. Under this model it was posited that the initiative for measures rested with government, the House of Commons then subjecting those measures to sustained scrutiny and debate, and having done so, approving them on behalf of the electorate it was returned to represent; the measures approved by Parliament were then applied, their legitimacy being accepted by citizens on the grounds that such measures had the approval of their elected representatives.[4] The important functions of the House thus became those of scrutiny and legitimisation, the exercise of them constituting an important support of the political system. This model incorporated the role played by parties: the Opposition was deemed to be the main element in Parliament which ensured that government was subject to scrutiny; the government majority ensured that measures received assent. Hence a somewhat idealised model, government being able to ensure passage of its measures but only after considered debate. It was a popular model both at home and abroad.[5] However, it was to come in for critical evaluation and in some cases rejection in the 1930s, again in the 1960s and more especially in the 1970s.

The model came in for criticism on the grounds that it did not match what was actually happening. The House of Commons may be expected to fulfil the function of scrutiny but to what extent did it do so? How could it be fulfilled given the information and resources at the disposal of government and the knowledge that at the end of the day the government controlled not only the parliamentary timetable but also the outcome of votes? Was not the government free to ignore MPs if it wished to, knowing that it would get its way? Many reached the conclusion that the answer to this question was in the affirmative. Cohesion was a notable feature of the Commons' division lobbies. Governments rarely amended or withdrew measures as a result of what happened on the Floor of the House. There was a growing view that the balance in the relationship between the House and that part of it which formed the Government had tipped not merely in favour of government but too much so, and that the Westminster model served not to illuminate but to mask this relationship. The result has been that various proposals have been forthcoming in an attempt to rectify this perceived imbalance. Such proposals have been a notable feature of political debate at certain times rather than others, and the aims of the reformers have varied, some seeking reform that would ensure that reality matched the Westminster model, others wanting changes that could give the Commons an even stronger role than that posited by the model, and some seeking to by-pass the Commons altogether as a vehicle for restraining government. Since Bernard Crick wrote *The Reform of Parliament*, parliamentary reform has been a topic of contemporary debate.

As we mentioned briefly in the Introduction, Parliament experienced a period of weighty criticism in the 1930s. In the critical review of national institutions engendered by the nation's poor economic health, Parliament was found wanting. In his book *How Britain is Governed*, Professor Ramsay Muir declared that the Cabinet was omnipotent; by subjecting Parliament to its power, it had 'atrophied' control on behalf of the nation by the latter's elected representatives.[6] In his evidence to the Select Committee on Procedure in 1931, he expressed the opinion that there was no country in north-western Europe 'in which the control exercised by Parliament over the Government – over legislation, taxation, and administration – is more shadowy or unreal than it is in Britain'. 'The fact of the matter', declared Lloyd George appearing before the same committee, 'is that the House of Commons has no real effective and continuous control over the actions of the Executive.'[7] Among prescriptions offered were radical ones such as Winston Churchill's Economic Sub-Parliament and Beatrice Webb's Social Parliament; a more limited but somewhat more popular proposal was the greater use of select committees within the House. The most radical change that came closest to being implemented, one that would have had a profound effect (or potentially so) upon the House, was the alternative vote in general elections; the minority Labour Government introduced such a measure in January 1931 in order to fulfil a promise to the Liberals. It failed to pass the Lords and went no further: it was overtaken by the government crisis and general election of 1931. Other proposals failed to find favour with Government or for that matter with many MPs; the Select Committee on Procedure concluded that the procedure of the House 'was sufficiently flexible to meet all the demands made upon it'.[8] Reform literature was less in evidence in the latter half of the decade and the nation's attention turned to more pressing international matters.

The House of Commons emerged from the Second World War with its reputation enhanced and post-war calls for parliamentary reform were offset by an evaluation of the reforms achieved by the Attlee Government and the prosperity of the 1950s as giving some credence to the Westminster model.[9] The country appeared to be faring well so there was little motivation to question the operation of the political system. Not until the end of the decade and more especially in the 1960s did the House witness deep and critical scrutiny. In line with other institutions, the House was again found wanting. Reform literature began to proliferate, with the writing of Professor Crick in the van.[10] The reformers of the 1960s generally adhered to the Westminster model and sought changes in parliamentary procedure that would restore the

Commons to the position posited by the model. They advocated the more extensive use of select committees to scrutinise government departments and sectors of government responsibility (the Select Committee on Nationalised Industries being used as the basis on which to build), as well as more streamlined procedures and better pay and facilities for Members.

Many of the changes advocated saw the light of day in the latter half of the 1960s, primarily during Richard Crossman's tenure as Leader of the House of Commons. The most important development was the greater use of select committees.[11] Further changes were carried through in the early 1970s, most notably the creation of the Expenditure Committee. However, by the mid-1970s it was apparent that the reforms had failed to achieve as much as the reformers had hoped, a fact appreciated by many of the reformers themselves. There had been no realignment in the relationship between the House and Government. As Bernard Crick observed of the Crossman reforms, 'while they may have gone a long way to "streamlining" the passage of legislation, they have gone only a short distance towards increasing the power of the House to scrutinise and call to account administration or to increase its critical effectiveness in debate'.[12] If there was to be a change in the relationship between the House and the executive, a longer step was needed.

That the 'Crossman reforms' did not achieve what their proponents wanted is not surprising. With the benefit of hindsight it is apparent that they were too limited in their conception and their supporters adopted a somewhat contradictory approach in seeking their implementation. They adhered to the 'strong' single-party model of government and sought in consequence to pursue two incompatible aims, 'strengthening the House of Commons without detracting from the power of government'.[13] The onus for change was put on the Government. As the Crossman *Diaries* helped to reveal, Ministers and their officials were none too keen on establishing bodies designed to keep their work under critical review.[14] In the words of S.A. Walkland, 'it seemed . . . inconceivable that any single-party Government, secure in its voting strength on the floor of the House, would allow any significant scope to powerful investigatory agencies of the type that were being proposed'.[15] If such reforms were to come about, it would have to be by another route.

The perceived failure of the limited reforms encouraged advocacy of more radical changes. Pressure for such changes built up during the

1970s as the country's economic health worsened (especially after 1973) and received some impetus as a result of developments deemed to undermine even further the role of the House of Commons in the political process. British membership of the European Communities was seen as challenging both the formal powers of the House as well as the functions ascribed to it by various authorities. By virtue of the provisions of the 1972 European Communities Act, EC legislation was to take precedence over municipal, i.e. Westminster legislation; cases of dispute were to be resolved by the courts as matters of law. These provisions raised serious questions as to the position of the cornerstone of the constitution, parliamentary sovereignty. They served also to give the constitution a new judicial dimension, disputes being dealt with as legal rather than political questions, to be resolved by the courts and not by Parliament. British membership served also to rob Parliament of its 'legitimising' function in respect of EC legislation, such legitimisation being deemed to have been given in advance under the terms of the 1972 Act. On matters within the competence of the EC, Parliament also lost its representative function in 1979 with the introduction of direct elections to the European Parliament.[16]

The function of legitimisation, of giving assent to measures, was undermined also as a result of the use of referendums. They were employed on the issue of Britain's continued membership of the EC and in Scotland and Wales on the issue of devolution, on both occasions employed as a means of averting serious dissent within the ranks of the Labour Party. Their employment carried serious implications. 'The implication . . . was that majorities in the House of Commons did not confer sufficient authority or legitimacy to a decision when this was of the utmost importance.'[17] Many viewed the referendums of the 1970s as creating precedents to be built upon. Various calls have since been made for referendums on the issues of capital punishment and electoral reform and when in Opposition Mrs Thatcher wondered aloud about the possibility of using them as a counterweight to trade union influence. Once the principle is conceded that Parliament lacks the authority to grant legitimacy to major measures on behalf of the voters, then its most long-standing function is called into question. This drift towards what John Mackintosh termed a plebiscitary approach to decision-making we shall consider in more detail later. For the moment it is sufficient to record that it was seen as weakening still further the position of the House of Commons.

Also seen as challenging the position of the House in the discussion and determination of national questions was the increasing tendency for government to consult with outside interests and to effectively bring them into the policy-making process. This was marked especially in the case of government consultation with the Confederation of British Industry and, especially so during the 1974–9 Labour Government, the Trades Union Congress. To this list, one may also add the International Monetary Fund. Government was seen as devoting more of its resources to achieving the assent of such groups to its measures than it was to achieving the assent of Parliament; the former had sanctions which they were willing to employ, the latter had a sanction which it was not willing, or was believed not to be willing, to employ. A perceived consequence of this was for the locus of decision-making to be shifted even further away from the floor of the House of Commons.

These developments, coupled with the apparent failure of the parliamentary reforms of the 1960s and early 1970s, a worsening economic climate and indecisive election results in 1974, encouraged on the part of many observers a critical reassessment of Parliament's ills. The result was a number of disparate prescriptions, differing in their views as to what the role of the House of Commons should be in the future and differing as to the remedies necessary to achieve the desired result. The existing House of Commons retained its defenders, but the debate of recent years has been notable for the number of new and radical approaches to parliamentary reform jockeying for acceptance. The debate remains current.

APPROACHES TO REFORM

Proposals for reform of the House of Commons which have come on to the political agenda in recent years, most especially since the mid-1970s, can be categorised under five broad headings. These headings we have identified in more detail in *The Commons in Perspective*.[18] As we shall see, two of them encompass topics we shall be exploring in depth later (a Bill of Rights and electoral reform); another is based on opposition to, rather than advocacy of, change. The approaches may be briefly identified as follows.

Internal reform

This approach continues the line of argument adopted by the reformers of the 1960s. It seeks to restore the Commons to the position posited by the Westminster model, doing so through the implementation of procedural reforms. The emphasis is on the use of procedure that will permit scrutiny of Government, scrutiny that will produce more information and hence more informed debate. Through scrutiny and debate, the House can serve to keep the Government alert to public opinion. The approach is thus one geared to consent: by keeping the Government responsive to what Bernard Crick called 'the underlying currents and the more important drifts of public opinion', and being seen to do so, the House would be performing its role as a support of the political system.

This approach was, as we have mentioned, criticised for being too limited in its conception. Its main advocates in the 1960s were in the main committed Labour Party supporters who favoured strong government. As a result they were unwilling or unable to accept an approach that would result in a diminution of government power and appeared not to comprehend that an effective House of Commons could not be attained without such a diminution. This failing was compounded by placing the onus for change on the Government of the day. Ministers and their officials, as we have said, tend not to be too keen on the creation of bodies designed to keep their work under critical review. This was borne out by Ministers' reactions to the new select committees.[19] It is thus not surprising that the changes in the 1960s failed to meet expectations. So long as the advocates of internal reform continued to press for reform without giving thought to how their reforms were to be achieved and without accepting that it was not what Americans would call a non-zero sum game (that is, one could not increase the power of the Commons in dealing with government without reducing the power of the latter) then they were for that very reason likely to be ineffective.

Anti-reform

The anti-reform categorisation encompasses a somewhat unwieldy collection of opponents of reform. The most important analyses falling within this category appeared at the same time as those of the internal reformers and in part were a response to the work of Professor Crick and his like-minded associates. The outstanding work was that of Ronald Butt, whose book *The Power of Parliament* was first published in 1967. Mr Butt adhered in essence to the Westminster model of government. Where he differed from the internal reformers was in his argument that the House actually fulfilled the role posited by the model, and that since the advent of party always had done. He contended that the role of the House was to keep the Government responsive to the wishes of the people and that it did this through party. There was give-and-take between the parties in the House and if the Government went too far its own backbenchers would put a warning shot across its bows. The role of the House, as posited by the Westminster model, was essentially a reactive one; as Butt pointed out, the House had never shared in the government of the country. By reacting, though, it served to set the limits within which government could operate and it retained the ultimate sanction over government: it could turn it out. By keeping government responsive or within the limits of what was acceptable to the electors, the House served to maintain the authority of both itself and government.

Mr Butt's analysis was to be criticised for drawing too optimistic a conclusion from limited data. The instances of the House influencing Government decisions cited in his work (i.e. pre-1967) was relatively few. While emphasising the importance of party he fails to give due weight to the limitations it imposed upon Members. Though Government occasionally made concessions to backbenchers for the sake of party harmony, there were no instances of the Government being forced to modify or withdraw measures which the House found unacceptable. On those occasions where the Government decided to go ahead with measures despite backbench opposition it always achieved their passage. Realisation of this fact raised questions about the ability of the House to sustain the support of citizens, and it led to pressure for change.

A somewhat different approach was that proffered by Henry Fairlie in *The Life of Politics*. Published in 1968, the book took a very limited view of the Commons' role. The argument was that power had passed via party to the electors and it was they who exercised a check upon government. Between elections the Government was strong, controlling the time and business of the House. MPs were largely amateurs, there to play the 'game of politics'. Their functions were those of supporting their party, choosing their leaders and providing the personnel of government. 'Electors ask no more than that, between elections, the MP should be the servant of the government, or alternative government, which he was returned to the House of Commons to support.'[20] All this appeared to attract Mr Fairlie's approval.

The Fairlie analysis was criticised on the ground that the electors wanted far more than MPs who were party fodder. Indeed, the fact that MPs were seen as lobby fodder undermined the authority of the House and led to pressure for reform. Placing the onus on the electorate to keep the Government in check via elections may also be considered too blunt an approach for ensuring that Government remains responsive and indeed sensitive to the wishes of electors. In between elections, how is Government activity to be scrutinised and its actions debated and highlighted? The news media and interest groups subject Government to some scrutiny but do so in the interests of their members or to sell newspapers. Absent the House of Commons, the busy elector has no-one in a position to act on his behalf and in his interests in dealing with Government. Electors thus look to the House of Commons to provide far more than Mr Fairlie contends they do.

Such approaches opposed to reform appeared to lose ground in the 1970s, though they have continued to be championed by parliamentarians such as Michael Foot and Enoch Powell. Both these MPs adhere to the Westminster model of government and continue to attach great importance to the Floor of the House as the place for debating the actions of government. The House, declared Mr Foot, 'is a place where we can hear how intelligent, formidable and considerable are the arguments of one's critics or opponents in other parties or in one's own party',[21] such debate having a 'very considerable effect on what Governments dare to propose and what Governments are capable of getting through'.[22] Despite advocacy of such views from two of what by general consent are the best debaters in the House, they failed to carry their colleagues with them when they opposed the recommendations of the 1978 Report of the Procedure Committee; indeed, Mr Powell even decided to acquiesce in their implementation.[23]

Under this rubric of 'anti-reform' is also included what has been termed the 'irrelevancy' approach. This incoporates those who believe power to make important decisions has now shifted to an array of extra-parliamentary bodies and that institutions such as Parliament are largely irrelevant; reforming such institutions will not affect the power wielded by such bodies.[24] The more people who come to share this belief, the more the Commons' role as a support of the political system is undermined. If Parliament is seen not to be an influence on government or on those bodies making decisions that affect citizens' lives and well-being, individuals may feel alienated, deprived of the feeling that they are able to play a part in the political system. The House of Commons is the only body which represents individuals *qua* individuals.

Perceptions of its irrelevancy thus have serious implications for the whole political system.

A related approach, which is not so much an anti- as a non-reform approach is that posited by Marxists. This need not concern us too much as it has not been central to debate on the House of Commons. The approach itself is an analysis rather than a prescription. Parliament is seen as relevant to an analysis of capitalist society, constituting a body through which the state elite exercises its power.[25] Pressure for reform is important in that it reflects the crisis of capitalist society. Bob Jessop has presented a sophisticated critique, contending that corporatist and parliamentary institutions constitute what he calls a 'contradictory unity', with parliamentary institutions being displaced by corporatist institutions as the dominant state apparatus.[26] The crisis faced by British government derives from the system of production and reforms of government, the civil service or Parliament will not remove the problems created by that system. 'The problems will not go away. On the contrary, as the crisis deepens, the problems of governing Britain will grow even larger.'[27]

These analyses have been criticised on the grounds that they take too pessimistic a view and fail to take into account recent data that suggest Parliaments can and do have some influence on decision-making. Dr Jessop's analysis could be interpreted by some as the basis on which to argue even more strongly than hitherto that the Commons *should* play an ever greater role in decision-making in order to counter the influence of corporatist pressures. The Marxist view that the basic problem is one of production raises questions somewhat beyond the scope of our immediate concern. If one accepts the Marxist analysis then reforming of the House of Commons does appear largely irrelevant, except as a symptom of the crisis of capitalism. If one does not accept it, then it is possible to consider reform as a way of achieving a meaningful role for the House of Commons in the political system.

Apart from these approaches, the three most recent — all having come on to the political agenda with some effect in the past few years — are those advocating electoral reform, a Bill of Rights, and what has been called (with 'engaging immodesty' as one reviewer put it) the 'Norton view'. The first two advocate reforms which are external to the House and as such posit fundamental reform in terms of the existing Constitution, the latter advocates change which is internal to the House and which blends the Westminster model with the House's formal constitutional powers.

External reform through a new electoral system

Advocacy of a new electoral system based on the principle of proportional representation has been indulged in by Liberals and others for some time. It was advanced on the grounds of fairness: the principle of 'one man, one vote' should be extended to 'one man, one vote, one value', a principle not realised by the existing first-past-the-post electoral system. Realisation of this point could serve to undermine the authority of the House and of the government, no post-war government having been returned to office without an absolute majority of the votes cast. This point we shall consider later in the section on electoral reform.

Advocacy of electoral reform received a boost in the mid-1970s as a result of the general elections of 1974 — a minority government being returned to office with less than 40 per cent of the votes cast — and by the formulation of what was termed the 'Adversary Politics' thesis. This thesis addressed itself to the question of political authority in the 1970s but did so from the perspective of effectiveness as well as consent. The argument was that the adversary system produced competition between parties, one party being returned at a general election and proceeding to undo the work of its predecessor, pursuing policies categorised by S.E. Finer as politically 'off-centre'.[28] There was thus perceived to be a problem of consent — Government pursuing policies not consistent with the centre ground of British politics, and a problem of effectiveness — governments being inconsistent in their allocation of resources. The remedy was seen to be electoral reform. A system based on proportional representation would (on current voting behaviour) deny any one party a majority of seats, so forcing an alliance between parties of the centre. The consequence would be a centre-coalition capable of ensuring continuity of policy given the unlikelihood of its defeat in subsequent elections. Political authority would be enhanced also by virtue of the fact that government would be the product of the majority's wishes, or at least some aggregate thereof, and the position of the Commons' enhanced by the fact that MPs would be less tied to party. Again, these points we shall consider in some detail later.

This approach was criticised on various grounds and was opposed by both the Conservative and Labour Parties, the two main beneficiaries of the existing system. The analysis was criticised on the grounds that it misrepresented what happened in British politics, policies not being reversed as often as the reformers believed, and confused the common ground of British politics with the ideological centre ground. Further-more, the results posited were also challenged. It was argued that far from increasing consent, the centre-coalition government might under-mine it: a permanent centre-coalition government continuously in power could alienate far more displaced voters (those voting for parties who never formed all or part of government) than hitherto, and would likely pursue policies that were a compromise between the parties to the coalition and upon which electors had not had an opportunity to pass judgement. It was also noted that the reformers appeared to be advocating two potentially incompatible aims: policy continuity and a more independent House of Commons.[29]

Advocacy of electoral reform gained ground in the wake of the two 1974 elections, though this proved insufficient to influence Commons' votes on the subject.[30] It appeared to lose some ground following the 1979 general election but then gained strength with the emergence of the Social Democratic Party in 1981. Both the Social Democrats and the Liberals favoured electoral reform and the forming of the SDP–Liberal alliance with some significant electoral support made the prospect of such a reform possibly less distant than hitherto.

External reform through a Bill of Rights

Whereas those advocating electoral reform posited a positive role for the House of Commons in the decision-making process, another school of thought developed which sought to restrict Parliament and indeed to restrict the fundamental principle of the constitution, parliamentary sovereignty. This school of thought, in constitutional terms the most radical of those we are considering, advocated an entrenched Bill of Rights. This school of thought was concerned not so much with the effectiveness of government but with its effectively almost unlimited powers. Party ensured that government could get its measures passed and in responding to the pressures and demands of interested groups in order to maintain their support government was increasingly impinging upon the rights of the individual. Parliament had proved powerless to prevent such encroachment. The answer was thus deemed to lie outside Parliament with the introduction of a Bill of Rights, its guardians being the independent courts and not party-orientated MPs. Perhaps not surprisingly, those associated with this line of argument have included a number of prominent jurists such as Lords Hailsham and Scarman and various Conservative politicians who favour limited government. The advocacy of such a measure appeared to reach something of a peak in the period of Labour Government between 1974 and 1979 and appears to have lost ground since.

We shall consider the case for and against a Bill of Rights in detail in a later section. For the moment, we may note that opponents of such a measure argued that it was impossible to achieve, both in form and content. No machinery existed for entrenchment and such a move would destroy the concept of parliamentary sovereignty. Also, there was precious little agreement on what would be included in such a document. Nor was it something designed to strengthen the House of Commons. To the contrary, it sought to by-pass Parliament and put certain rights beyond its easy reach. It was thus not an approach that sought to change the relationship between the House and the executive, but sought instead to limit both.

The 'Norton view'

The final approach, one which draws upon the utilisation of existing constitutional powers rather than a reformulation of the constitutional framework, is that associated with this author, the 'Norton view'. This view emphasises the importance of attitudes within the Commons and the powers available already as the basis on which the Commons might more effectively subject the government to scrutiny and influence. The importance of this view is that it draws on recent parliamentary behaviour, employing a recognition of what *is* as the basis for bringing about what *ought* to be.

The Norton view rejects the approaches previously identified, largely for the reasons given. It contends that the Commons can achieve a change in the relationship between it and that part of it which forms the government and that, to some degree, it has begun to do so already. The powers for the House to achieve this change exist: the power to defeat the government in the division lobbies, in other words to deny legitimisation to a government measure. What has been lacking has been a willingness to utilise this power: the political will has been lacking. MPs have been unwilling to employ the basic power at their disposal partly because when in office, they want their side to succeed and because they have felt themselves constrained by the belief that a government defeat would endanger the government's existence, and by fears of what may happen to them at the hands of their whips or constituency associations if they were to vote against their own side.

The 1970s were to witness the undermining of these various assumptions. The environment created by the economic poor health of the country and the response of government to it helped contribute to a feeling of unease within the House; successive governments indulged in policy changes which many government supporters viewed as not altogether compatible with party philosophy. This became most marked during the Conservative Government of Mr Heath. The combination of measures for which he was considered to be responsible (notably the U-turns on industrial policy and the economy in 1972), the way in which he insisted measures were forced through the House, and his general manner of leadership generated resentment within the ranks of the parliamentary Conservative Party.[31] This resentment found expression not only in a marked increase in dissent within the party's ranks but also contributed to six government defeats, a number of Conservative MPs on each occasion entering a whipped Opposition lobby. Three of these defeats were on three-line whips. The Government did not resign, it did not even contemplate asking the House for a vote of confidence. The whips did not take any action against any of the Members responsible for engineering the defeats (for the very good reason there was nothing they could do)[32] and no Conservative MP was denied re-adoption by his constituency association because of his parliamentary behaviour. The constraints presumed to operate on Members began to appear akin to the Emperor's clothes.[33] Members themselves began to appreciate this and its implications. As one Member commented in the wake of the government defeat on the immigration rules in 1972, once one had defeated the government a first time it was much easier to do it a second time.[34]

The defeats of the 1970–4 Parliament, a Parliament in which the Government had a clear working majority ('a parliamentary majority at just the level of modesty once thought most likely to ensure solidarity and so . . . policy-making effectiveness'),[35] were then added to by the defeats experienced by the minority Labour Government in the short 1974 Parliament: a total of seventeen in the 6-month Parliament. The Labour Government returned at the October 1974 election was vulnerable to defeats as a result of some of its own Members cross-voting and (after April 1976 when it formally lost its overall majority) to opposition parties combining against it. Its vulnerability was exploited from both sources. The Government suffered a total of 42 defeats, 23 attributable to Labour MPs voting in the Opposition lobby and 19 to opposition parties combining in the 'No' lobby. The defeats themselves were on important issues – the Government's devolution proposals (the defeats being a necessary but not sufficient condition to ensure that devolution failed), the Budget (reducing the standard rate of income tax), the Dock Work Regulation Bill (effectively emasculating the measure), the so-called Green Pound (devalued by more than the Government proposed) and the Government's policy of imposing sanctions against firms breaking its 5 per cent pay limit, amongst others.[36] These defeats were but the tip of an iceberg, over 100 defeats being imposed in Standing Committee.[37]

The 7-year period from April 1972 to April 1979 witnessed a total of 65 Government defeats on the floor of the House of Commons. To find a similar number in a 7-year period one has to go back to the 1860s. The House of Commons in the 1970s was thus exercising its basic power in a way it had not done before in the twentieth century. This in itself was clearly important. However, a growing realisation of what could be achieved by Members' actions led to an attitudinal change within the House, a change that could produce more lasting and tangible reforms. This change in attitude was well described by Labour MP George Cunningham who was responsible for engineering a number of Government defeats:

Just as the habit of blind obedience can grow, so can a habit of thinking and voting for oneself on occasions. . . . The interesting thing is that, as the period advanced, it became easier to approach colleagues asking them to look at an argument and consider supporting a move against a specific Government proposal. Slowly, enough Members came to take a mild degree of voting independence for granted. They ceased to believe that the Government in the end must know best and they enjoyed the use of the power the electorate had given them.[38]

This new attitude was not confined to the 1974–9 Parliament. It carried over into the current Parliament. By the end of 1981 there had been at least nine occasions on which the Conservative Government had withdrawn or modified measures under threat of defeat. Equally important, the new Parliament witnessed a significant structural change, one made possible by this change in attitude.

In 1978 the select committee on procedure recommended a new comprehensive framework of select committees to ensure scrutiny of the various departments of State. Initially, it looked as if the committee's report would go undebated and generally ignored by the Government, rather in the manner of previous reports. However,

Members were no longer content to leave the onus for change on government. Pressure from Members built up on both sides of the House and forced the Leader of the House, Michael Foot, to concede a debate on the recommendations. In the debate Mr Foot was forced to concede that a vote should take place on the proposals. The 1979 general election then intervened, the vote on the recommendations taking place in the new Parliament in June 1979. A combination of backbench pressure (which had just manifested itself in no uncertain terms on the question of MPs' pay) and a sympathetic Leader of the House, Norman St John-Stevas, resulted in the proposals going through Cabinet despite the fact that a majority of ministers were ill-disposed towards them. The House approved the new select committees by 248 votes to 12.[39] In less than 2 years the new committees have established themselves as far more effective scrutineers of government than their predecessors and, though major problems remain, have clearly achieved some of the intentions of their creators — that is, the generality of MPs rather than government. An attitudinal change has thus made possible effective structural change.

The Norton view contends that if the House of Commons is to go further to ensure a more balanced relationship with the executive, then these developments show the way to go.

Members can, if they wish, build on the precedents set in the 1970s. In so doing, they can move towards a more effective scrutiny of government and to acting more often as a counterweight to the executive power. That they should do so appears to be in little doubt. The developments of the past decade reveal that they can do so. There is no need for radical prescriptions divorced from experience.[40]

And the more MPs are seen to be performing the functions expected of them, the greater the authority of the House of Commons.

NOTES

1   *The British Cabinet*, 2nd ed. (Methuen, 1968), p. 174.
2   Michael L. Mezey, *Comparative Legislatures* (Duke University Press, 1979).
3   E.C.S. Wade and G. Godfrey Phillips, *Constitutional and Administrative Law*, 9th ed. by A.W. Bradley (Longman, 1977). p. 97.
4   See Philip Norton, 'The US Congress in Comparative Perspective: The British Parliament', Paper presented at the American Political Science Association Conference, New York, September 1981.

5 See Norton, *loc. cit.*, and Leon D. Epstein, 'What Happened to the British Party Model?', *American Political Science Review*, 74 (1), March 1980.

6 Cited in Hansard Society, *Parliamentary Reform 1933–60*, rev. 2nd ed. (Cassell, 1967), p. 132.

7 Quoted in G. LeMay, *British Government 1914–63* (Methuen, 1964), p. 163.

8 Quoted in Ivor Jennings, *Parliamentary Reform* (Victor Gollancz, 1934). p. 170.

9 See Epstein, *loc. cit.*

10 See Philip Norton, *The Commons in Perspective* (Martin Robertson, 1981), pp. 203–4.

11 See *ibid.*, pp. 204–7.

12 Crick, *The Reform of Parliament*, rev. 2nd ed. (Weidenfeld & Nicolson, 1970), p. 230.

13 S.A. Walkland, 'The Politics of Parliamentary Reform', *Parliamentary Affairs*, 29 (2), 1976, p. 192.

14 See also David Owen, *Face the Future* (Oxford University Press, 1981 ed.), p. 160.

15 Walkland, *loc. cit.*, p. 192.

16 See Philip Norton, 'The House of Commons and the Constitution: The Challenges of the 1970s', *Parliamentary Affairs*, 34 (3), Summer 1981, p. 258.

17 John Mackintosh, 'Attitudes to the Representative Role of Parliament', in J.P. Mackintosh (ed.), *People and Parliament* (Saxon House, 1978), p. 3.

18 Norton, *op. cit.*, ch. 9.

19 See *ibid.*, p. 222.

20 Fairlie, *The Life of Politics* (Methuen, 1968), p. 253.

21 *HC Deb,.* 909, c. 915.

22 *First Report from the Select Committee on Procedure 1977–8*, vol. 2: Minutes of Evidence (HC 588-2), p. 64.

23 See Norton, *The Commons in Perspective.*, pp. 217–18.

24 *Ibid.*, p. 218.

25 See Ralph Miliband, *The State in Capitalist Society* (Quartet, 1973), especially pp. 49–50 and 148–9.

26 Bob Jessop, 'Capitalism and Democracy: The Best Possible Shell?', in G. Littlejohn (ed.), *Power and the State* (Croom Helm, 1978), pp. 10–51, especially pp. 44–5.

27 David Coates, 'Politicians and the Sorcerer: the Problems of Governing with Capitalism in Crisis', in A. King (ed.), *Why is Britain Becoming Harder to Govern?* (BBC, 1976), p. 55.

28 S.E. Finer, *Adversary Politics and Electoral Reform* (Wigram, 1975), p. 13.

29 Norton, *The Commons in Perspective*, p. 224.

30 See P. Norton, *Dissension in the House of Commons 1974–1979* (Oxford University Press, 1980), p. 479 and footnote 164.

31 P. Norton, *Conservative Dissidents* (Temple Smith, 1978), ch. 9.

32 Norton, *Conservative Dissidents*, ch. 6.
33 See P. Norton, 'The Changing Face of the British House of Commons in the 1970s', *Legislative Studies Quarterly*, Vol. 3, August 1980, pp. 333–57.
34 Conservative MP (now a Cabinet Minister) to author. See also Philip Norton, 'Intra-Party Dissent in the House of Commons: A Case Study. The Immigration Rules 1972', *Parliamentary Affairs*, 29 (4), Autumn 1976, pp. 404–20.
35 Leon D. Epstein, 'What Happened to the British Party Model?', *American Political Science Review*, 74 (1), March 1980, p. 19.
36 See Norton, *Dissension in the House of Commons 1974–1979*, appendix.
37 See John Schwarz, 'Exploring a New Role in Policy-making: The British House of Commons in the 1970s', *American Political Science Review*, 74 (1), March 1980.
38 Book review, *The Parliamentarian*, July 1980, pp. 192–3.
39 *HC Deb.*, 969, c. 247–50.
40 P. Norton, The House of Commons and the Constitution: The Challenge of the 1970s', *Parliamentary Affairs*, 34 (3), Summer 1981, p. 270.

6

The House of Lords

The four R's

One element of the constitutional framework of Britain that is no stranger to having its role and future questioned is the House of Lords. 'On summer evenings and winter afternoons, when they have nothing else to do, people discuss how to reform the House of Lords', wrote Janet Morgan. 'Schemes are taken out of cupboards and drawers and dusted off; speeches are composed, pamphlets written, letters sent to the newspapers. From time to time, the whole country becomes excited.'[1] Such has been the case now for well over 100 years.

By convention, the House of Lords constitutes part of the triumvirate of the Queen-in-Parliament. Prior to 1911 the House was formally co-equal in powers with the House of Commons, though the latter had achieved some priority in financial matters. (As early as 1407 Henry IV had affirmed the position of the Commons as the exclusive originator of taxation.) The position of the House and the exercise of its powers became a point of contention in the nineteenth century. The authority of the House was traditional and could be accommodated in a rational—legal system only through its acceptance of being subordinate to the chamber which was elected by 'the people'. However, 'the people' granted the vote by the Reform Act of 1832 were not numerous and the Lords could still, on occasion, cause problems. Prior to Peel's second ministry, the Lords tended, in Greville's words, 'to bowl down [Whig] Bills like ninepins'.[2] The Reform Act of 1867 largely removed the remaining authority if not the formal powers of the Lords. Nonetheless, a permanent Conservative majority in the House provided unwilling to acquiesce in the passage of major items of Liberal legislation and in 1884 refused to pass the Franchise Bill until a scheme of redistribution was also introduced. This was followed in 1893 by rejection of the Home Rule Bill. Further use of its power to negate measures emanating from the Lower House occurred with the return of the Liberal Government of 1906. Bills on education, licensing, plural voting, Scottish smallholdings, and land valuation were all rejected. So too was the Budget in 1909. The Budget rejection provided the motivation for action on the part of the Government and, after two general elections, the Parliament Bill of 1911 was introduced and passed, the Lords acquiescing in its passage under threat of being swamped by a mass of new Liberal peers. Under the provisions of the Act, a Bill certified by the Speaker as a Money Bill was to receive the Royal Assent 1 month after leaving the Commons, whether approved by the Lords or not. Non-money bills could be delayed by the House for only two successive sessions, such bills being enacted if passed by the Commons again in the succeeding session. The only power of veto retained was that over bills to prolong the life of a Parliament, provisional order bills, and delegated legislation. The delaying power over non-money bills was reduced by a further session by the 1949 Parliament Act, itself passed under the provisions of the 1911 Act. As John Mackintosh expressed it, 'the whole experience of this struggle forced the Lords to appreciate and be content with the position to which they had been relegated when Cabinets became dependent first on the House of Commons and then on the electorate'.[3]

Further reforms were to follow, most notably the Life Peerages Act of 1958 and the Peerages Act of 1963. The former measure empowered the Crown to create life peers and peeresses. The latter enabled hereditary peers to disclaim their titles as well as admitting peeresses in their own right to the House. In terms of reforms proposed, though, such measures were the tip of an iceberg. Since the latter half of the nineteenth century, schemes to reform the Lords have been commonplace. Various proposals for life peers had been put forward, including in 1888 by the Government. Lords reform was the subject of debate and legislative proposals in both Houses, and following the Lords' rejection of the Home Rule Bill a radical MP introduced a motion calling for 'such alterations in the relations of the two Houses of Parliament as will effect a remedy to this state of things'.[4] Suggestions for reform came from far and wide, including from such diverse figures as the Marquess of Salisbury, Walter Bagehot and John Stuart Mill, with Bagehot worrying that it might never be reformed at all. Nor did the passage of the 1911 Act put an end to such proposals. The Act was widely regarded as a temporary measure, and since then *Hansard* and parliamentary papers have been littered with debates, bills and proposals for further reform.[5] Reform of the Lords was mentioned in the King's Speeches of 1920, 1921 and 1922, was the subject of discussion by Cabinet committees and was embodied in various Government proposals and Private Members' Bills, none of which was passed.[6]

Apart from the 1958 and 1963 Acts, the most recent sustained attempt at reform was the Parliament (No. 2) Bill in 1969. It proposed a two-tier House with voting members (life peers) and non-voting members (existing hereditary peers), and with a 6-month delaying power over non-financial legislation. Though receiving a substantial majority on second reading, the bill ran into opposition from backbenchers on both sides of the House.[7] A number of Labour Members led by Michael Foot felt that it did not go far enough; a number of Conservatives led by Enoch Powell were of the opinion that it went too far. The result was what amounted to a sustained filibuster, the Government not always having one-hundred supporters present to carry closure motions. Though no vote was actually lost, the Government found its parliamentary time being eaten away and decided not to proceed with the Bill.

The experience of the 1969 Bill discouraged subsequent governments from tackling the issue. Nonetheless, reform of the House of Lords remained a subject of debate. As a constitutional issue, it became one of several under discussion. The fact that it was one of several and was itself a rather well-worn topic meant that it might not occupy the same attention as hitherto, and hence might escape radical surgery. However, fears on the part of Socialists that an unreformed House of Lords might act as a brake on reforming Socialist legislation, and worries on the part of Conservatives that such attitudes might lead to the abolition of the Upper House, thus robbing the constitution of one of its essential balancing elements, led to a variety of reform proposals. Many in the Labour Party favoured abolishing the Lords altogether and the Labour Party Conference supported such a move. Many in the Conservative Party favoured some reform, either along the lines of the 1969 Bill or a new House based on election. Reform of the Lords also appeared in the designs of those who wanted sweeping changes in the constitution as a whole.

As debate on constitutional issues developed in the latter half of the 1970s, it became apparent that the views being expressed on reform of the House of Lords could be categorised under four headings, 'the four R's' — retain as it is, reform, replace or remove altogether. Let us consider each briefly.

RETAIN

The House of Lords and its hereditary composition has always had its defenders. They claim that the House does a useful job, especially as a revising chamber, as a forum for debating issues ignored by the Commons, and as the initiator of non-contentious legislation. (These three functions were listed by the Bryce Report in 1918 along with a fourth: 'the inter-position of so much delay (and no more) in the passing of a Bill into law as may be needed to enable the opinion of the nation to be adequately expressed upon it'.) The hereditary principle is defended on the grounds that it provides a measure of independence. Hereditary peers, declared one MP, 'are trained for the job from youth upwards, and they are truly independent, being answerable to no constituents'.[8] Lord Boyd-Carpenter has also drawn attention to a practical benefit: a number of peers inherit their titles when young, so providing a number of young peers capable of doing much of the routine work of the House.[9] In favour of the House as it is now composed, it is argued that the intro-duction of life peers has not only added to the active membership of the House but also has enabled experts in many fields to be ennobled. (Including many, such as trade union leaders, who object to the heredi-tary principle.) The ability of peers to attend as they wish, free of the dictates of party, produces informed debates.

It is a rare experience [wrote one Lord] to attend a debate in the House of Lords, on any subject from hare-coursing to nuclear strategy, in which there is not at least one participant who can legitimately be regarded as a leading authority on the subject. It is also unusual to hear in the House of Lords any of the sterile and often offensive party political bickering which characterizes all too much of the proceedings in the elected Chamber.[10]

As for those who object to the party imbalance in the House, the Conservatives having a permanent majority, it is pointed out that in terms of regular attenders the Conservative majority is small (a ratio of 1.2 to 1 in terms of Conservative to Labour and Liberal votes). Further-more, such party categorisation is deemed as not terribly relevant given that peers are free to vote as they wish and sometimes do so. Votes, in any event, are not numerous. Finally, and perhaps ironically, the Lords can produce a broader spread of backgrounds and opinions than can the Commons. As Janet Morgan observed, the Lords takes all sorts into its embrace. Perhaps two of its most striking features are the large numbers it contains of scientists and engineers and of women. There are in the Lords more physicists, biologists, doctors, chemists, engineers of all types than grace the Commons benches. There are 53 women Peers, compared with 10 [*sic*] women Members of the Commons. These two groups, added to the Bishops and Law Lords, alone make the Upper House an unusual part of a Parliament.[11]

It is also the only House in recent years to have boasted a Communist member (Lord Milford) and indeed independent members, the cross-benchers.

Perhaps the most spirited defence of the existing House was put forward by Norman St John-Stevas in the 1968 debate on the Government's White Paper for Lords Reform.

The case for the House of Lords [he said] is not theoretical because politics is not an exercise in logic but in life. The case for the Lords is an eminently practical one. First, it is an assembly which works — it is not perfect — tolerably well and, secondly, any Second Chamber that is thought up *a priori* is likely to be much worse. If one required proof of that general proposition, the White Paper provides it. No nation has been able to construct in theory a satisfactory second chamber . . . . We, by accident of history, have the good fortune to have inherited a special second chamber, based partly on the principle of heredity and partly on the principle of life peerages, and it works reasonably satisfactorily. I appeal to the Government once again, in the words of Lord Melbourne, to accept that the case has been overwhelmingly made out for the situation to be left as it is.[12]

The case for retaining the House of Lords as it is has been variously refuted. The thrust of the argument against it centres not on the functions or efficiency of the House — it is deemed to do a reasonable job as a revising chamber and as a scrutineer (via its committees) of EC legislation — but on its composition. Hereditary membership is considered to be anachronistic in a political system based on the principle of democracy, with 'political sovereignty' having been conceded to the people. 'In this day and age', declared George Cunningham, 'no one, whether in other countries or in this country, would say that as a matter of conscious choice it is desirable that we should give a voice and a vote on legislation to a person merely because he is the son of his father. . . . There is no justification for that.'[13] It is argued by those who wish to have a second chamber that can act as a counterweight to the Commons that the hereditary element prevents the Lords from fulfilling such a function. Recognising that it has the formal power to delay a Government measure but not the political authority to do so, the House refrains from clashing too much with the government of the day. The fear is that were it to do so, its remaining powers would be removed. Government defeats in the Lords are rare (the exceptions making the news by virtue of the fact that they are exceptional) and it is extremely rare for the House to insist upon an amendment if rejected by the Commons.[14] Under an agreement reached between the two sides in the 1945–50 Parliament, the House does not divide on the second reading of any measure promised in the winning party's election manifesto.[15] The result is a dog that dare not bite for fear of losing its teeth. What to defenders of the existing House is its strength is to critics its major weakness.

REFORM

Those who oppose the hereditary principle but wish to retain a second chamber, either as a revising chamber or as a potential brake on the Commons or both, have a choice between advocating reform of the existing House or its replacement by a different body. Those who prefer to reform the existing House rather than replace it altogether largely do so because replacement would likely entail election, and an elected House could challenge the authority and powers of the Commons – a recipe for stalemate. Also, the existing House has shown itself capable of performing its functions reasonably well. If the problem of composition could be resolved without a fundamental reformulation of the House's functions and powers the result would be a House doing a useful job and acceptable (if not wildly so) to contemporary thinking on the position of a second chamber.

Such a reform was attempted by the Parliament (No. 2) Bill in 1969. It sought to reform the existing House of Lords rather than replace it with a different body. Its two-tier proposal enabled the right of hereditary peers to vote on legislation to be removed while still allowing them to offer the benefit of their advice in debate and in committees. Only existing hereditary peers would be entitled to non-voting status, their successors not being entitled to seats in the House. Hence, the hereditary element would slowly be removed. Under the provisions of the bill, the government of the day would be provided with a working majority and the powers would be amended, but not drastically (a 6-month delaying power on legislation and the power to return subordinate legislation for reconsideration). The result, according to the White Paper that preceded the Bill, would be a move in the direction of ensuring that the Upper House played a role 'complementary to but not rivalling that of the Commons'. It was envisaged that closer co-operation between the two Houses and a review of the Lords' functions would follow once the changes were implemented.

Though the 1969 Bill failed to get beyond committee stage, the changes embodied in it have retained the support of a number of politicians. Though conceding that the functions would need to be discussed and agreed before any reform of the Upper House took place, Lord Chalfont has contended that 'given what appears to be the present consensus regarding the functions of a Second Chamber in a modern parliamentary democracy, the proposals contained in the 1968 White Paper and the Parliament (No. 2) Bill seem to be eminently practical and constructive'.[16] What essentially amounted to a variation on the 1969 Bill was proposed by a Working Party of Labour Peers in 1980: they favoured the two-tier proposal, with 250 voting peers being chosen from life peers and peers of first creation, the House to have a 6-month delaying power.[17]

Despite this residual support for the provisions of the 1969 Bill, the debate on the Lords now tends to revolve around more radical proposals. The reform proposed by the Wilson Government was subject to various criticisms. Some of these were directed at specific provisions of the 1969 Bill, such as those concerning attendance requirements and the age limit. The primary argument against the measure was that it would not solve the basic problem of political authority. Membership by virtue of birth and, in some cases, by nomination of the Prime Minister, was to be replaced solely by nomination by the Prime Minister. After each election the Prime Minister would be able to create new peers to ensure a majority of at least 10 per cent over opposition parties. As the majority report in the Report by the Constitutional Reform Committee of the Society of Conservative Lawyers opined:

we very much doubt whether the public will have any more affection for a House of Lords composed of life peers than for one largely composed of hereditary peers, and without positive support we see no prospect of the House of Lords regaining, let alone retaining, greater powers or even of remaining long in existence. . . . We cannot see that a House of Lords largely dominated by creations of recent Prime Ministers is likely to gain much public regard.[18]

As a result, the reformed House would, like its predecessor, lack the authority and probably the political will to act as an effective safeguard. Indeed, its lack of authority and a government plurality made possible by the 1969 Bill would probably result in a House carrying even less political weight than before. It would lack the mystique and the deference associated with the peerage and would create the invidious position of having voting and non-voting members. The government of the day would likely find the new Chamber no greater restraint than the existing House of Lords.

REPLACE

The proposal that the existing House of Lords should be replaced altogether by a new body, preferably with a different name (Senate appearing popular), has gained strength in recent years. There is no one common scheme suggested: some writers have advocated a second chamber based on appointment by regional bodies or interest groups, others have advocated an elected chamber, and some have suggested a 'mixed' scheme.

The appointed second chamber, or one indirectly elected, has tended to find favour with various supporters of devolution and corporatism. In 1973 the minority report of the Royal Commission on the Constitution recommended that the Upper House should be reconstituted so as to include 150 extra members drawn from the Scottish, Welsh and English Assemblies that it proposed.[19] It was envisaged that the House would act as 'a countervailing force against the centralising tendencies of the United Kingdom Government'.[20] However, it suggested no change in the existing powers of the House and would retain life peers as members and probably hereditary peers as well; hence, not as radical a proposal as at first it might appear. A more thoroughgoing reform would be for the House to comprise only representatives of regional Assemblies. Dr David Owen, parliamentary leader of the Social Democrats, has revived the case for the 1973 minority report,[21] and it is likely that similar ideas will be aired and given more support if the prospect of some form of devolution gains ground in the near future.

The proposal for the Upper House to comprise representatives of interest groups such as the TUC and the CBI has also been put forward. As we mentioned in the introduction, John Mackintosh recommended that the House be reconstructed as a functional chamber with most of its members nominated by trade unions, industry and other sectional groups.[22] The idea of a functional chamber is itself not new. In the 1930s Winston Churchill recommended an Economic Sub-Parliament, comprising 40 MPs, 20 peers and 60 others – businessmen, trade union representatives and economic experts. A group of Conservative MPs who produced a pamphlet on Commons reform in 1963, *Change or Decay*, also favoured some element of functional representation, albeit in relation to Commons' committees.[23] The reformulation of the Lords to comprise *ex officio* representatives of functional groups would kill two birds with one stone: reforming the Upper House and providing interest groups with a formal position in the political process. In the current debate on the Lords' future, some Conservatives have also embraced an element of functional representation as a means of strengthening the existing House, as a supplement to, rather than a replacement for, the existing membership.[24] The argument for functional representation is that it would increase support for the political system by incorporating within it representatives of those bodies upon which government is dependent for advice, co-operation and consent. Whereas the Commons is based upon the representation of individuals, the Upper House would balance it with the representation of functional groups.

The other main scheme proposed for replacing the current House is for a Senate with an elected membership. The most detailed proposals for such a reform have emanated from two Conservative groups, the Conservative Review Committee chaired by Lord Home and the Constitutional Reform Committee of the Society of Conservative Lawyers. Both groups reported in 1978 and made similar recommendations.[25] The Home Committee advocated what it terms a 'mixed chamber' of up to 402 members, two-thirds chosen by election, the remainder appointed by the Crown on the advice of the Prime Minister, but with the latter under a duty to consult a special Committee of Privy Councillors. The element of appointment would allow a measure of continuity, one enhanced by initially allowing life peers and 50 hereditary peers to remain as members. 'The merit of this particular scheme for a mixed composition is that it seeks to combine the enhanced legitimacy and hence more defensible composition of a directly elected House with an element of continuity with the historic House of Lords'.[26] It was also admitted that such a mixed composition would likely make it more attractive to Conservative opinion than a wholly-elected House. The purpose of the reform would be to create a House 'with very strong moral authority [which] could be expected to provide an effective constitutional check'[27] on the Commons. There were dangers inherent in having a Lower House based on the principle of 'mandated majority government' with no safeguard to prevent it encroaching upon the liberties of the individual. The proposed new House would provide such a safeguard. The report recommended that the elected members be chosen by a system of proportional representation and that the House should have power to delay legislation similar to that provided under the terms of the 1911 and not the 1949 Parliament Act.

The report of the Conservative Lawyers' Constitutional Reform Committee went somewhat further in recommending a wholly-elected House. It considered non-elected members should not be allowed to be voting members and the presence of non-voting members would weaken the authority of the House in the eyes of the public. It favoured a House comprising 300 members elected at staggered intervals. Like the Home Committee it supported a method of proportional representation. It recommended procedures for resolving disputes between the two Houses and suggested a complicated requirement of 'weighted' majorities in order for the Upper House – the Senate – to reject Supply measures. In reaching its conclusions its reasoning was similar to that of the Home Committee: both wanted an Upper House capable of acting as a constitutional safeguard against excesses on the part of an executive-dominated Commons.

Various objections have been raised to these various proposals for the existing House of Lords to be replaced by a wholly or substantially different House or Senate. The problem associated with representation based on regional assemblies, of course, is that as yet no such assemblies exist. Were they to do so, the proposal would become a viable one. However, the Conservative Lawyers' group contended that in the event of devolution there would be even more reason for having a second chamber elected by constituencies of approximately equal electorates throughout the kingdom; such an elected chamber 'could well prove the sole available instrument for preserving the unity of the United Kingdom'.[28] Arguments employed against an Upper House based on a formal representation of functional groups are basically three in number. First, it would introduce a form of representation that is alien to the prevailing liberal concept of representation.[29] Second, though it might help incorporate important groups into the political process it could undermine support for the House among citizens. The Conservative Lawyers were especially worried about *ex officio* representation for trade unions: 'far from being welcomed by the electorate, any apparent deliberate enhancement of the power and position of trade union leaders would be regarded with grave suspicion'.[30] Third, even if one concedes the principle, it is virtually impossible to achieve in practice. There is the problem of what bodies are to be represented, and how representatives are to serve, for a duration of Parliament or while they hold office in their organisation; furthermore, how can one ensure that members remain 'representative' of their organisation's membership? 'Such a plan is manifestly absurd. It would not only be impossible to organise but, more important, there would be no way of measuring the political affiliations of *ex officio* members and therefore no way of knowing that their decisions would be reasonably acceptable to the majority of the electorate.'[31] It has also been pointed out that such a scheme is unnecessary: trade union leaders, industralists, leading academics and others are often made life peers, serving in an individual capacity, and their organisations already enjoy close and effective links with government.[32] Such a reform would effectively create more problems than it would solve.

The proposal for an elected second chamber has been subjected to various criticisms, some of which the Conservative Review Committee sought to anticipate. One significant objection to election has been that it would endow the House with greater moral authority, approaching or on a par (if wholly elected) with that enjoyed by the House of Commons. Hence it would have a claim to exercise powers similar to those of the Commons. If it were restricted to the limited powers suggested, such as the power of delay provided by the 1911 Act, one would have difficulty encouraging candidates of sufficient calibre to seek election. If given extra powers, indeed even with the modest increase recommended by the Conservative Review Committee, there would be the potential for conflict between the two Houses, hence undermining the traditional Westminster model of British government (see Chapter 5). To some extent the Conservative groups realised these problems though did not deal with them in any comprehensive manner. The Conservative Review Committee conceded that there might be tension between the two Houses, but felt that was one of the problems that had to be accepted; it recommended a Mediation Committee to try to resolve any formal conflicts. The Conservative Lawyers' committee made a similar recommendation. The former group did touch upon the question of candidates by suggesting a form of list system of election, enabling parties to choose eminent people who did not wish to contest elections. However, it did not consider the possibility of an elected second chamber seeking to enlarge its powers. The committee conceded that there might be a case for equality of powers in the case of a wholly-elected chamber, but considered that that would be inconsistent with the traditional position of the Commons and would be undesirable. The Conservative Lawyers' committee proposals on the delaying powers on non-financial legislation were ambiguous.

. A practical problem facing those favouring a system of election based on the principle of proportional representation (PR) is that such a system would be and is unacceptable to most Conservative and Labour politicians. As Hartley and Griffith have observed, the adoption of PR for election to the Upper House could make it more difficult to resist pressures for its adoption for elections to the House of Commons.[33] A more substantive objection has been identified and voiced by Labour politicians. As Baroness Llewellyn-Davies observed, 'Senates are always more conservative than the congress, in every legislature I can think of, and I mean conservative with a small "c" as well as a big one'.[34] A more powerful second chamber, as proposed by the Conservative Review Committee, could act as an effective brake on Labour legislation. Whereas the Commons would sometimes have a Conservative majority and sometimes a Labour one, an Upper Chamber elected on the basis of PR, argued George Cunningham, would always have an anti-Labour majority.[35] That, he said, would be 'severely inimical to the advancement of progressive legislation'.[36] Though a number of Labour politicians accept the need for a second chamber for the purposes of revising legislation and acting as some sort of constitutional long-stop, they are wary of acceding to a chamber that would have a similar outlook to the existing House of Lords and the political authority and will to act upon it.

REMOVE ALTOGETHER

The final approach, one that appears to have gained ground in recent years, is to remove the House of Lords altogether and not bother to put anything in its place. Abolition has been advocated primarily by Labour politicians such as Tony Benn and Lord Wedderburn and has been adopted by the Labour Party Conference. The 1976 Labour Party manifesto stated that the Lords was 'an out-dated institution completely inappropriate to a modern democratic system of Government. It should not therefore continue in its present form.' Abolition was envisaged in a policy document drawn up by the TUC–Labour Party Liaison Committee in 1977. The same year the Labour Conference approved a motion in favour of 'an efficient single-chamber legislating body'. It was apparently only the intervention of the Prime Minister, James Callaghan, that prevented a pledge to abolish the Lords from appearing in the party's 1979 manifesto. The Labour Conference of 1980 reaffirmed its previous decision in favour of abolition and Mr Benn made it clear that he believed abolition should be the first task of an incoming Labour Government.

The main argument in favour of abolition is, not surprisingly, the reverse of why supporters wish to retain a second chamber. It is contended that such a chamber would act as a brake on a reforming Socialist government. The case for doing away with it was put neatly by Lord Wedderburn. 'Either the second chamber is less democratic than the Commons in which case it should not be able to delay legislation', he said, 'or it is just as democratic, when there is no point in having two chambers.'[37] He would hive off the work currently done by the Lords to a reformed and full-time House of Commons. The proposal has also gained support from some Labour activists such as Lord Melchett who would prefer a wholly-elected second chamber but, thinking that impossible to achieve, are prepared to opt for abolition.[38] The overwhelming majorities achieved in support of abolition at the Labour Party Conference, and the prominence given the issue by Mr Benn, have brought the question well to the fore in political debate. The possibility of the demise of the House of Lords is probably greater now than it has been since 1911.

The main argument employed against abolition is that a second chamber is essential as a constitutional safeguard and useful if not necessary on practical grounds. The need for a constitutional safeguard has been stressed by the various Conservative groups to consider the issue and has been reiterated by the present Government. 'In the Government's view', declared Minister of State Timothy Raison, 'a bicameral legislature is an essential element in the British constitution. We are committed to the maintenance of that principle, since it provides safeguards to continued constitutional government in this land.'[39] A second chamber can serve as a long-stop to minority and/or extremist government. The thrust of the argument of the Conservative Review Committee was that a second chamber capable of fulfilling such a function was even more necessary as a result of recent developments, government impinging more and more upon the lives and well-being of individuals and the volatility in electoral behaviour (as well as the capriciousness of the electoral system itself) increasing the risk of the return of a minority government committed to policies of sweeping change. 'All this adds up to the danger of "elective dictatorship".'[40] An effective second chamber was needed to act as a constitutional check. By removing such a body one would be doing violence to the existing constitutional framework.

The practical objection to doing away with the House of Lords is that it would place a heavy burden on the Commons. There is generally recognised to be a need for legislation to be revised after it has emerged from the Commons. Abolitionists such as Lord Wedderburn consider that such a task could be incorporated within the structure of a revised House of Commons, the Commons having a more extensive committee system and comprising full-time MPs. However, there is little sustained research on this point. What research has been done suggests that the burden might be more onerous than is realised by those favouring abolition. Indeed, the main research on the implications for the Commons is that being undertaken by Nicholas Baldwin at the University of Exeter. His initial conclusion is that for the Commons to do the essential work currently done by the Lords 'would not contribute to the better functioning of Parliament, and would prove detrimental to the legislative process as a whole'.[41] Giving the Lords' tasks to the Commons also would not overcome the problem posited by the 'elective dictatorship' thesis: the Commons could hardly act as a constitutional check upon itself.

There is one final point of crucial constitutional significance, one not often recognised other than by constitutional lawyers. By convention, as we have noted, the House of Lords forms part of Parliament. The courts enforce Acts of Parliament under the judicially self-imposed concept of parliamentary sovereignty. If the House of Lords ceased to exist would that put an end to 'Parliament' as understood by the courts? If so, it would jeopardise the concept of parliamentary sovereignty, since the body accepted by the courts as the legitimate exercise of that sovereignty would no longer exist. At the end of the day, whether the courts would take this line or not would depend upon the judges, and as we shall see there are those within the judiciary, encouraged by a number of constitutional lawyers, who would welcome an excuse to do away with the concept of parliamentary sovereignty. Abolition of the Lords would provide that excuse. Ironically, therefore, abolition of the Lords could produce an effect not desired by its proponents, a more active judiciary with powers that in the eyes of many would be a more effective threat to Socialist legislation than the House of Lords.

CONCLUSION

The question of whether or not the House of Lords should be reformed is one that is currently on the agenda of political debate but one upon which there is no agreed view. As Lord Denham once observed, if you put four people in a room and ask for their opinions on reform of the Upper House you get five different responses.[42] A number of right-wing and traditional Conservatives favour retaining the House as it currently exists. They appear to have lost some ground in the recent debate — even Mr St John-Stevas who so eloquently supported the *status quo* in 1969 has since voted for an elected second chamber[43] — but may see their wishes fulfilled, as in 1969, by a failure of their opponents to agree on any change. Other Conservatives appear to favour an elected second chamber as a means of retaining a House capable of acting as a constitutional safeguard. Support for such a reform (especially with the use of PR in the elections) has come from a variety of MPs but is strong especially within the Conservative leadership in the Lords — Lords Carrington,[44] Hailsham[45] and Home (chairman of the Review Committee), as well as Lady Young, are among its most prominent advocates. Three members of the Conservative Review Committee are now ministers. The issue is one being considered (among others) by the Government.[46] The prospect of an unreformed House of Lords being abolished by an incoming Labour administration has helped concentrate the minds of many Conservatives and support for an elected second chamber is now probably greater on the Conservative side of the House than ever before.

However, the prospects of such a change being implemented are not good at the moment. In May 1981 a Conservative backbencher, Sir Brandon Rhys Williams, introduced a 10-minute rule bill to 'provide for the election by proportional representation of certain members of the House of Lords'. Leave to introduce the bill was refused by 137 votes to 61.[47] The bill was supported primarily by Liberals, Social Democrats and a number of Conservatives. It was opposed by an alliance of traditional Conservative and Labour Members very similar to that witnessed in 1969 on the Parliament (No. 2) Bill; again, Messrs Foot and Powell were to be found in the 'No' lobby. Such a bill would obviously stand a greater chance — but not a guarantee — of passage if supported by the Government. Whether or not such support will be forthcoming is problematic. Even if the Government was to resolve its doubts in favour of such a measure, the chances of it achieving the all-party support it would like before proceeding with a bill must be considered to be slim. Probably the greatest likelihood of such a reform being introduced would be in the event of the return of a Liberal/Social Democratic Government. It appears to be one issue upon which the two putative partners are agreed.

On the Labour side, as we have seen, the support for abolishing the Upper House altogether is now strong, though a number of Labour peers appear keen (not surprisingly) to resuscitate the 1969 proposals or something similar. Support for abolition may be stronger in the party as a whole than in the Parliamentary Labour Party. Whether or not a future Labour Government would introduce such a measure – and achieve its passage – is another matter. It would need to ensure cohesion within its own ranks in the Commons and would then need to get it through the House of Lords. Given that the existing House is virtually certain not to pass the bill, Mr Benn has suggested the creation of sufficient new peers to ensure a majority for it. The problem with that is the existing procedure for introducing new peers: unless the House changes its procedure the Parliament would have ended before even a proportion of the necessary number of new peers had been introduced. It is also quite possible that the Government would decide that it had more pressing matters to contend with, such as the state of the economy. In addition, there is the problem of what attitude the courts would take should the House of Lords cease to exist. It is a problem not really addressed by the abolitionists.

An elected Upper House and abolition appear to be the most discussed reforms. Whether or not either is likely to come about is far from certain. Such proposed reforms also tend to figure in broader schemes of constitutional reform, but such schemes are obviously called into doubt if Lords' reform cannot be achieved. It may well be the case that while other elements of the constitution undergo adjustment, the House of Lords continues as before. Or it could prove the only fatal casualty of the contemporary attack on the British constitution.

NOTES

1   Janet Morgan, 'The House of Lords in the 1980s', *The Parliamentarian*, 62 (1), January 1981, p. 18.
2   A.J. Anthony Morris, *Parliamentary Democracy in the Nineteenth Century* (Pergamon, 1967), p. 99.

3   John Mackintosh, *The British Cabinet*, 2nd ed. (Stevens, 1968), p. 223.

4   *HC Deb.*, 294, c. 141–2.

5   See *Select List of Published Material on the House of Lords in Twentieth Century*, House of Lords Factsheet No. 7 (House of Lords Information Office, 1980), pp. 22–30.

6   See *House of Lords Reform: 1850–1970*, House of Lords Factsheet No. 1, 2nd ed. (House of Lords Information Office, 1979), p. 3.

7   See P. Norton, *Dissension in the House of Commons 1945–1974* (Macmillan), 1975), pp. 312–54.

8   John Stokes MP, *HC Deb.*, 6th series, vol. 2, c. 1216. See also the comments of Diana Spearman, *The House of Lords* (The Salisbury Group, 1978), pp. 1–6.

9   Lord Boyd-Carpenter, 'Reform of the House of Lords – Another View', *The Parliamentarian*, 59 (2), April 1978, p. 92. See also Leolin Price and Anthony Lincoln, 'Note of Dissent', in *House of Lords Reform?* Report by the Constitutional Reform of the Society of Conservative Lawyers (Macmillan, 1979), p. 36.

10   Lord Chalfont, 'Reform of the House of Lords', *The Parliamentarian*, 58 (4), 1977, pp. 233–4.

11   Morgan, *loc. cit.*, pp. 10–20.

12   *HC Deb.*, 773, c. 1396.

13   *HC Deb.*, 6th series, vol. 2, c. 1253–4.

14   See Appendix 7 in The Report of the Conservative Review Committee *The House of Lords* (Conservative Central Office, 1978), pp. 52–3.

15   P. Norton, 'The Forgotten Whips: Whips in the House of Lords', *The Parliamentarian*, 57 (2), April 1976, p. 90.

16   Chalfont, *loc. cit.*, p. 239.

17   See Morgan, *loc. cit.*, p. 25.

18   Report by the Constitutional Reform Committee of the Society of Conservative Lawyers, *House of Lords Reform?* (Macmillan, 1978), p. 12.

19   *Report of the Royal Commission on the Constitution* (Cmnd. 5470, 1973), minority report, paras 297–307.

20   *Ibid.*, para. 301.

21   David Owen, *Face The Future* (Oxford University Press, 1981 ed.), pp. 172–6.

22   Cited in William B. Gwyn, 'Jeremiahs and Pragmatists: Perceptions of British Decline', in W.B. Gwyn and R. Rose (eds), *Britain: Progress and Decline* (Macmillan, 1980), p. 7.

23   *Change or Decay* (CPC, 1963).

24   See e.g. Ivor Stanbrook's comments, *HC Deb.*, 6th series, vol. 4. c. 631, and Lord Boyd-Carpenter, *loc. cit.*, p. 93.

25   *The House of Lords*, and *House of Lords Reform?* See also Peter Temple-Morris MP, *Secundus Inter Pares* (Bow Group, 1977).

26   *The House of Lords* p. 30 (para. 54).

27   *Ibid.*, p. 19 (para. 30).
28   *House of Lords Reform?* p. 19.
29   See P. Norton, *The Commons in Perspective* (Martin Robertson, 1981), pp. 52–6, and Birch, *Representative and Responsible Government* (Allen & Unwin, 1964), ch. 5.
30   *House of Lords Reform?* p. 13.
31   Elizabeth Lyon and Anthony Wigram, *Electoral Reform: The House of Lords* (Conservative Action for Electoral Reform, 1977), pp. 66–7.
32   See *ibid.* and *The House of Lords*, p. 27.
33   T.C. Hartley and J.A.G. Griffith, *Government and Law*, 2nd ed. (Weidenfeld & Nicolson, 1981), p. 242.
34   Quoted in Hugh Hebert, 'The Lords under the Microscope', *Guardian*, 1 March 1979.
35   *HC Deb.*, 6th series, vol. 2, c. 1254.
36   *Ibid.*
37   Quoted in Hebert, *loc. cit.*
38   *Ibid.*
39   *HC Deb.*, 6th series, vol. 2, c. 1262.
40   *The House of Lords*, p. 19, para. 29.
41   N.D.J. Baldwin, 'The abolition of the House of Lords: The effect on the House of Commons and the legislative process', Paper presented at the PSA Conference, Hull University, April 1981, p. 27.
42   Speaking to a group of students from Hull University Politics Department, March 1979.
43   See *HC Deb.*, 6th series, vol. 4, c. 631.
44   See Hebert, *loc. cit.*
45   Lord Hailsham, *The Dilemma of Democracy* (Collins, 1978), p. 152.
46   See *HC Deb.*, 6th series, vol. 2, c. 1263.
47   *HC Deb*, 6th series, vol. 4, c. 631–2.

7

The Judiciary

Guardians of our rights? Or a threat?

Works on British politics rarely devote much space or sustained discussion to the role and influence of the judiciary. This is attributable largely to the limitations imposed upon the courts by the principle of parliamentary sovereignty. The principle was established as a judicial rule as a consequence of the Glorious Revolution and subsequent Bill of Rights of 1689, the product of an alliance between Parliament and common lawyers and the intimidation of judges by the House of Commons. Its effect has been to deprive the courts of the power to rule on the 'constitutionality' of legislative acts. It is the vesting of such power that makes the judiciary in other countries such as the United States so important politically: judges have the power to declare an act of the legislature, as well as executive actions, to be unconstitutional. In Britain, judges are limited to the exercise of the power of statutory interpretation as well as applying common law. Even the exercise of statutory interpretation takes place within fairly narrow limits: judges are bound by certain rules of interpretation and by precedent.[1]

In the days when the executive encroached little upon the lives of individuals, there was little need to look to the courts to act as a restraints. When government did begin to acquire and to utilise powers that impinged upon the liberty of the individual, the courts were considered as being in too weak a position to do much about it. True, the courts were able to exercise review of executive actions through the power to declare the discharge of delegated power *ultra vires* or contrary to the common law concept of natural justice, but such powers were rarely employed. In part, this reluctance may have been due to the realisation that the executive dominated the legislature and could thus obtain legitimisation of past or proposed actions and, concomitantly, to a lack of will on the part of judges. They were, and have more recently been, accused of not being too sympathetic to the claims of the individual when pitted against the demands of government.[2] Denied the power to question Acts of Parliament and unwilling to exercise their powers over acts of the executive, few judicial decisions entered the realms of controversy.

This is no longer the case. Beginning in the 1960s the courts have proved more willing to utilise their powers to review executive actions and, more recently, a number of prominent judges have pressed for power via an entrenched Bill of Rights to strike down legislative measures. In so far as they can, some judges have sought to nibble away at the edges of the principle of parliamentary sovereignty, aided in so doing by Britain's obligations under international law and in particular her obligations under the Treaty of Rome. In the study of British politics, much more space must now be devoted to the role of the courts, a role which is far from being free of controversy.

REVIEW OF EXECUTIVE ACTS

The courts have jurisdiction at common law to determine, in any case brought before them, whether the purported exercise of a power is authorised by law. If it is not authorised, either because the alleged power does not exist or its scope is exceeded, the act is *ultra vires* (beyond the powers) and void. If a power is abused or exercised unreasonably, or if the principles of natural justice are not observed, the act is illegal: the courts can declare it void and in some cases may set it aside.[3] Though derived from common law, the power to make an act void on grounds that it is *ultra vires* is a corollary of the principle of parliamentary sovereignty; the courts seek to ensure that powers exercised are within the scope of the relevant Act of Parliament. The common law principle of natural justice is derived from the other pillar of the constitution, adherence to 'the rule of law'. Though parliamentary sovereignty is superior to the rule of law (should the two clash) and statute law superior to common law, the first love of judges is the rule of law, in essence the rule of common law, 'a lawyer's law of universal application' as Lord Scarman called it.[4]

In recent years the courts have appeared to be more assertive in the exercise of their common law power to review executive acts of ministers and administrative authorities. Professor John Griffith has referred to 'the emergence of a period of judicial activism or intervention which began in the early 1960s and has been growing in strength ever since'.[5] (Prior to that time, wrote Michael Beloff, 'the judiciary were clearly on the retreat from the interventionist state'.)[6] The new willingness of the judges to flex their judicial muscles has taken various forms. They have declared certain ministerial decisions to be *ultra vires* and the exercise of executive power in a number of cases has been deemed contrary to the principle of natural justice. In so doing, the judges have started to review in a limited way the substance of decisions as well as the manner in which they were made.

In the 1960s there were four important cases in which the courts adopted what has been termed an activist line in reviewing the exercise of administrative bodies. In 1964 in *Ridge v. Baldwin*, it was held that a police officer who had been dismissed without having been given a hearing by a watch committee had not been validly dismissed. The right to a hearing was deemed to be an essential ingredient of natural justice. Previously, it had been considered that such a right existed where authorities were acting in a judicial or quasi-judicial capacity but not in an administrative capacity. This case extended the right in cases where authorities were acting administratively. In subsequent cases it was held that the allied duty to be fair, to give affected parties the chance to make representations, was imposed upon immigration officers, tax officials and others.[7] In *Anisminic v. Foreign Compensation Commission* in 1968, the courts reviewed a decision of the Foreign Compensation Commission. Under the Foreign Compensation Act of 1950 it was provided that 'the determination by the commission of any application made to them under this Act shall not be called in question by any court of law'. However, the House of Lords reasoned that a decision of the Commission that was beyond its jurisdiction was a nullity and hence not a 'determination' at all. It held that a decision of the Commission based on an error of law going to jurisdiction could be quashed. As Professor Griffith observed, what the decision meant, in effect, was that the courts could set aside the decision of an authorised body if they disagreed with that body's interpretation of the rule which it was required to apply.[8] Parliament responded by passing the Foreign Compensation Act of 1969 which included the provision 'In this section "determination" includes . . . anything which purports to be a determination.'[9]

The remaining two cases, both decided in 1968, dealt with ministerial actions. Prior to that time it was assumed that the Crown had a right to withhold documents in cases in which it was considered that the contents of a document were such that its production would not be in the public interest or if it belonged to a class of documents which, as a class, should be withheld. This view derived largely from the *obiter dictum* of the Lord Chancellor, Lord Simon, in *Duncan v. Cammel, Laird & Co.* in 1947. The importance of the *Duncan* case was that the House of Lords laid down that if a Minister objected to the production of a document in any civil proceedings, that had to be treated by the courts as conclusive. This was overturned in *Conway v. Rimmer*. The Home Secretary, on behalf of the police, objected to the production of reports made during the probationary period of a police constable in a case in which the ex-constable was suing his former superintendent for malicious prosecution. The Home Secretary claimed that the documents fell into a class of documents, the release of which would be contrary to the public interest. In *Conway*, the House of Lords held that the case was not such that the production of the documents would be contrary to the public interest, that the Home Secretary's claim was therefore not conclusive, and that the court might call for the documents and decide after inspecting them whether an order for their production to the other party ought to be made.[10] The effect of the case was thus to transfer to the courts the power to decide whether such documents should be produced. In such cases, 'the interest of the State must be balanced against the rights of the individual. The court held . . . that it is the judge who must make this decision.'[11]

In *Padfield v. Minister of Agriculture, Fisheries and Food*, the House of Lords held that a minister could not employ discretionary powers if their exercise thwarted the object of the Act conferring those powers. Under the Act in question, the Minister of Agriculture could refer complaints against the Milk Marketing Board to a committee of investigation 'if the Minister in any case so directs'. Milk producers from the south-east complained that the prices paid by the Board were too low and asked the minister to refer the matter to a committee of investigation. The minister refused: he felt it was inappropriate for investigation because it raised wider issues, if the committee upheld the complaint he would be expected to make an order to give effect to the committee's recommendations, and he considered that it was a matter best dealt with by the Board itself. A majority of the House of Lords found these reasons insufficient and ordered the minister to set up a committee. In this instance what the court was doing was reviewing the reasons for a minister's decision, a decision which was one of policy.

Lord Scarman subsequently cited the *Padfield* and *Anisminic* cases as

indications that in the commercial and financial fields, where . . . the state has intruded with its administrative agencies, the judges are ready to take the activist line, and intervene if there is no *substantial evidence* to support the administrative or tribunal decision, if the tribunal took into account a factor which they had no right to take into account[12] [my emphasis].

In short, the courts were willing to consider why, and not just how, decisions were made.

The examples of judicial activism were to be added to in the 1970s, most notably in four cases in the period from 1975 to 1977. In each case a ministerial decision was involved. In 1975 the Home Secretary announced his intention to raise the licence fee for a colour television with effect from 1 April. Some licence-holders, in order to avoid the increase, took out new licences at the existing rate before their licences had expired. The Home Secretary had a statutory discretion to revoke television licences and it was announced that he proposed to revoke over-lapping licences unless the increased fee was paid. The case went before the courts, and in *Congreve v. Home Office* the Court of Appeal held that this power to revoke licences could not properly be used to force people who had legally bought licences to pay the extra money. The minister's discretion had to be exercised reasonably. In this case, said Lord Denning, it was being used contrary to the provisions of the Bill of Rights since it constituted an attempt to levy money for the Crown without the authority of Parliament. As in *Padfield*, the court was looking beyond the exercise of a power to the reasons behind the exercising of it. In this instance, the Home Secretary responded by obtaining statutory power to raise licence fees without giving advance notice.

Perhaps the most politically controversial decision was that in the *Tameside* case.[13] In 1976 the newly-elected Conservative council in Tameside announced that it did not propose to implement the plans of its Labour predecessor for five grammar schools to be converted into comprehensive schools and sixth-form colleges. Under section 68 of the 1944 Education Act, the Secretary of State has power to give directions to a local education authority if he or she is satisfied that the authority 'have acted or are proposing to act unreasonably'. Using this section, the Secretary of State gave a direction to the Tameside Council requiring the implementation of the scheme for converting the schools. The case went before the courts. The Divisional Court ordered the Council to comply with the direction, but the Court of Appeal reversed the decision and was upheld by the House of Lords. The case turned on the question of what was meant by acting 'unreasonably'. 'To fall within this expression', said Lord Diplock, 'it must be conduct which no sensible authority acting with due appreciation of its responsibilities would have decided to adopt.'[14] The minister could only give a direction if it could be held that no reasonable local authority would have acted in the way that the Tameside authority acted. Since it could not be so held, the minister had exceeded his powers.

The remaining two cases were important for the court's decisions and the *obiter dicta* of Lord Denning. In *Laker Airways Ltd v. Department of Trade* in 1977, the Court of Appeal held that the 'guidance' given by the Secretary of State to the Civil Aviation Authority was *ultra vires* since it conflicted with the 1971 Civil Aviation Act under which it purported to be given. The minister had given 'guidance' to the Authority to the effect that it should not license more than one British airline to serve the same route, with British Airways as the preferred airline for the route to the USA. The Authority had already granted a licence to Laker Airways to operate its 'Skytrain' service on the USA route and Laker Airways appealed against the minister's decision. In upholding Laker's claim, the Court of Appeal also held that the Government could not use the prerogative in order to nullify the statutory licence already granted. (The Government had claimed that designating airlines for particular routes was within the prerogative as an aspect of international relations and hence could not be reviewed.)[15] In the equally controversial case of *Gouriet v. Union of Post Office Workers*, the courts had to consider whether a private citizen could bring proceedings for a declaration of injunction without the consent of the Attorney-General. The Union of Post Office Workers had decided to call upon its members not to handle mail destined for South Africa. John Gouriet applied to the Attorney-General for consent to bring a relator action against the union, claiming that the union's boycott would be a criminal act under the Post Office Act of 1953. The Attorney-General, Sam Silkin, refused his consent. Mr Gouriet then went to the Court of Appeal to seek an injunction. The Court decided that Mr Gouriet had standing to pursue such an action as a private citizen and issued interlocutory injunctions against the union. The Court's action attracted the headlines because of its departure from previous practice in determining *locus standi* and because of the political line-up of the interested parties: the Union of Post Office Workers and a Labour Attorney-General on one side and Mr Gouriet, supported by the right-wing pressure group The National Association for Freedom, on the other. However, the Court of Appeal was reversed by the House of Lords. The Lords reaffirmed the tradition doctrine: a private person could have standing only if the alleged breach of law infringed a private right of his or would inflict special damage on him: and the refusal by the Attorney-General to give his consent to a relator action is not reviewable by the courts. Mr Gouriet therefore had no right to bring the action. The attempt by Lord Denning and the Court of Appeal to break new judicial ground was thwarted.

The Gouriet case in particular achieved attention because of the views expressed by the Master of the Rolls, Lord Denning. The assertion by the Attorney-General that he was answerable only to Parliament and his refusal to give reasons for his refusal of Mr Gouriet's request was, said his Lordship, 'a direct challenge to the rule of law'. In Lord Denning's opinion, the Attorney-General's discretion to refuse was not absolute or unfettered.

It can be reviewed by the courts. If he takes into account matters which he ought not to take into account, or fails to take into account the matters which he ought to take into account, then his decision can be overridden by the courts. Not directly, but indirectly. If he misdirects himself in coming to his decision, the court can say: 'Very well then. If you do not give your consent, or your reasons, we will hear the complaint of this citizen without it'.[16]

As Bradley observed, his Lordship's reasoning provoked fears among some MPs that the courts were seeking to usurp the functions of Government and Parliament.[17] Though the judicial committee of the House of Lords was to help allay some of those fears, suspicion remained in the minds of many politicians as to the intentions of some of Britain's leading judges.

This suspicion was to be maintained into the new decade with two judicial decisions in 1981. One of them dismayed Conservative ministers, the other enraged Labour politicians. In the first case, a number of London boroughs challenged the decision of the Environment Secretary, Michael Heseltine, to reduce the rate support grant to them under the provisions of the Rate Support Grant (Principles for Multipliers Order) 1980. They challenged his action on four grounds. The High Court on 22 October upheld the challenge on one of these four grounds, namely that the minister failed to listen to representations made late on behalf of the authorities and by so doing had not validly exercised his discretion under sections 48–50 of the Local Government, Planning and Land Act 1980. Mr Heseltine's decision was therefore squashed. The following day Mr Heseltine announced in the Commons that the Government would have to consider carefully the judgement before deciding what its responses would be.[18] Though the minister sought to play down the importance of the case, the Opposition used the occasion to criticise the minister and it was clear that the Government had suffered an embarrasing shock in its attempt to restrict spending by local authorities.[19]

The second case, not involving the Government, proved to be more politically contentious. The London Borough of Bromley challenged the legal right of the Greater London Council to impose a supplementary rate percept to pay for reduced fares on London Transport's bus and underground services, something which had been promised by the ruling Labour group in its election manifesto and which it introduced in October 1981. On 3 November the High Court had found against Bromley. On 10 November the Appeal Court allowed an appeal by Bromley Borough against the judgement and issued a writ of certiorari to quash the precept. The court held that the GLC's action was an abuse of its powers and *ultra vires.*[20] The council had a duty to hold a balance reasonably between the interest of the travelling public and the ratepayers, and that the council had not done. In his opinion, Lord Denning further created controversy by declaring that 'a manifesto issued by a political party in order to get votes was not to be regarded as a gospel. It was not a covenant.'[21] A party returned to power, he said, should consider what it was best to do, and what was practical and fair.

The court's holding and Lord Denning's *obiter dictum* aroused a storm of protest from Labour politicians. Whereas the Prime Minister, Mrs Thatcher, congratulated Bromley Borough on its initiative, Labour MP Alex Lyon accused the court of making political and not judicial decisions.[22] Two days later the Leader of the Opposition, Michael Foot, said that he hoped ministers understood 'that transport policy and the way in which is has been laid down by this Parliament must be protected by this Parliament, and that we cannot have the courts interfering with policy matters of that nature'.[23] Even *The Economist*, not noted for its sympathy with radical causes, had to concede 'Lord Denning's view of the general behaviour of the GLC is hard to interpret as anything but a covert political counterattack against a legally elected, if unpopular, local authority'.[24] His Lordship was demonstrating 'his popular thesis that judges are a higher form of animal than politicians'.[25] It was this thesis and its manifestation that carried the Master of the

Rolls into the political arena, where his thesis was not greeted with universal assent. His penchant for his interpretation of the rule of law was not well received by parliamentarians weaned on, and deriving power from, the concept of parliamentary sovereignty.

The controversy was not stilled when, on 17 December 1981, the House of Lords upheld the judgement of the Appeal Court, the five Law Lords sitting on the case unanimously rejected the appeal of the GLC. In the House of Commons there was a repeat of the exchanges experienced in the wake of Lord Denning's *dictum*. The Prime Minister again congratulated Bromley Council on its initiative, while Labour MP Norman Atkinson described the Lords' judgement as 'an extra-parliamentary political instrument . . . in order to further the politics of the Conservative Party'.[26] The clashes between Conservative and Labour MPs on the issue revealed that, whether it liked it or not, the higher judiciary was not operating free of the political fray.

A NEW JUDICIAL DIMENSION

Although recent years may have witnessed a new assertiveness on the part of the higher judiciary in Britain, the powers exercised in reviewing executive actions have not been new. What is novel is the pressure for the judges to exercise some element of constitutional review. To some extent the potential for this has been realised by British membership of the European Communities and could be reinforced if legislative powers were devolved to elected Assemblies in Scotland and Wales. The most important constitutional innovation that would very likely but not necessarily endow the courts with such power would be an entrenched Bill of Rights. An attitudinal change on the part of the judiciary would ensure a willingness to exercise such power and there is pressure from some constitutional lawyers for the judges to take whatever opportunity they can to put an end to the doctrine of parliamentary sovereignty.

The Treaty of Accession to the European Communities was signed in 1972 and the European Communities Act, giving legal effect to British entry, was enacted the same year. (Britain became a member of the Communities on 1 January 1973.) By passing the 1972 Act, Parliament provided that existing European Communities law would have general and binding applicability in the UK, as would all law promulgated subsequently by the Communities. Section 1(2) of the Act gives the force of law in the UK to 'rights, powers, liabilities, obligations and restrictions from time to time created or arising by or under the Treaties'.

In the event of conflict between the provisions of Communities law and those of a domestic Act of Parliament (known in formal parlance as municipal law), the latter were to prevail. The constitutional implications of this we shall consider in detail later.

Section 3(1) of the Act provides that any dispute as to the interpretation, effect of validity of the Treaties, or of any legislation made under them, is to be treated by British judges as a matter of law. Cases which reach the House of Lords must (under the Rome Treaty) be referred to the Court of Justice of the European Communities for a definitive ruling and requests may be made from lower courts to the European Court for a ruling on the meaning and interpretation of the Treaties. 'In fact', wrote Gillian Peele, 'what the European Communities Act has done is to change the *grundnorm* of our legal system and amend the rules to which the judges will look in their attempt to settle legal disputes. Judges now have to refer to principles which are, in short, superior to parliamentary legislation.'[27] The Act thus created a new role for the British judiciary.

Nonetheless, the importance of this change should not be overstated. Though critics of the 1972 Act argued that it undermined or virtually destroyed the doctrine of parliamentary sovereignty, the doctrine remains extant. Parliament remains able to 'unbind' the measures of its predecessors and can, should it so wish, repeal the 1972 Act. Furthermore, the doctrine ensures that while any European Communities law takes precedence over previously-passed domestic legislation, any new Act of Parliament which runs contrary to EC law will be enforced by the British courts. What the 1972 Act does, in effect, is to provide a rule of interpretation: Parliament is presumed not to intend to legislate contrary to Community law. In the absence of a clear and express statement in an Act of Parliament that it is to override Community law, the courts would regard the Act as being subordinate to Community law.[28] (Cases involving express conflict are notable for their absence.) It is also important to note that Community law does not impinge upon citizens in their private capacities (it can impose monetary penalties under civil proceedings in relation to industrial and commercial activities) and is mainly concerned with customs duties, agriculture, free movement of labour, services and capital; restrictive trade practices; and the regulation of the coal, steel and nuclear energy industries. Most domestic law, such as criminal law, is unaffected.

The role of the courts as arbiter between an Act of Parliament and conflicting measures emanating from another law-making body would

be extended in the event of devolution of legislative powers to elected
Assemblies in Scotland and Wales. In practice, the devolution of such
powers to a Welsh Assembly is an extremely unlikely prospect. Pressure
for such powers to be devolved to a Scottish Assembly, as intended by
the 1978 Scotland Act, continues to be exerted. The role of the courts,
in such an event, would not be an onerous one. Acts of Parliament
would take precedence over any Assembly measures and, under the
provisions of the 1978 Act, the determination of what matters fell
within the legislative competence of the Assembly would be determined
in certain instances by the judicial committee of the Privy Council, in
certain instances (dealing with the EC) by the Secretary of State for
Scotland, and in the remaining instances by Parliament under referral
by the Secretary of State. The importance of such a development for
the courts, albeit limited, would be that it would further their role in
resolving matters that would likely be matters of some political controversy. In the event of a major constitutional upheaval, with the UK
becoming a federal as opposed to a unitary state, then the courts would
assume a central political role: disputes between the constituent parts
of the federation or between a constituent part and the federal government would, absent the stipulation of an alternative method, be resolved
by the judicial process. Such a major constitutional innovation appears
unlikely.

One constitutional innovation that would affect significantly the
role of the courts, one supported by many jurists and politicians, is the
introduction of an entrenched Bill of Rights. Pressure for such a measure
built up in the 1970s and remains on the political agenda. We shall
consider it in detail later. For the moment, it is important to note that
an entrenched Bill of Rights — that is, one making certain stipulated
rights immune to simple-majority amendments by Parliament — would
likely jettison the courts well into the forefront of the political arena. If
Parliament passed a measure that the courts deemed to conflict with
the Bill of Rights, then the judicial bench could strike it down as being
contrary to this 'higher law'. That, at least, would be the presumption.
It is not axiomatic that the courts would enjoy such a power. It is
possible to introduce an entrenched Bill of Rights (indeed, a Constitution) and provide that the power to interpret its provisions be vested in
an authority other than the courts. One argument employed against the
power of constitutional interpretation effectively read into the US
Constitution by the Supreme Court in 1803 (*Marbury v. Madison*) was
that it was for the different branches of government to interpret their

own powers under the Constitution, with any abuse being subject to remedy by the sovereign electorate.[29] Such an argument in Britain would have the effect of nullifying the purpose for which an entrenched Bill of Rights is intended. If Parliament was to decide for itself whether a measure was contrary to the provisions of the Bill of Rights, the courts applying the measure as a matter of law, the higher law document would be no more than a declaratory statement. The whole thrust of the contemporary argument for an entrenched Bill of Rights is that it would protect certain rights from parliamentary infringement, the courts serving as guardians of the measure. This is clear from the writings and speeches of the advocates of such a change. In the 1974 Hamblyn Lecure, Lord Scarman argued for 'a new constitutional settlement that makes use of judicial power to keep within constitutional limits the legislative sovereignty of Parliament'[30] (an ingenious but paradoxical statement, for if legislative sovereignty is constitutionally limited it ceases to be sovereign), the settlement to include a Bill of Rights, a codified law, and 'I would hope . . . a supreme court of the United Kingdom . . . with power to invalidate legislation that was unconstitutional and to restrain anyone — citizen, government, even Parliament itself — from acting unconstitutionally.'[31] The introduction of an entrenched Bill of Rights, as anticipated by its proponents, would put an end to the doctrine of parliamentary sovereignty and concomitantly thrust the judiciary into the political arena, there to defend the liberty of the individual from the encroaching powers of an 'elective dictatorship'.

Some more modest reformers such as Peter Wallington and Jeremy McBride, conscious of the difficulties associated with entrenchment, have advocated the passage of a Bill of Rights as an ordinary legislative measure but with the insertion of a provision that it is to take precedence over subsequent measures unless the latter state expressly that they override the Bill of Rights. In short, the measure would establish a rule of interpretation, akin to that provided by the 1972 European Communities Act and with attendant implications for the courts. It would provide the courts with a further politically sensitive task without dispensing with the doctrine of parliamentary sovereignty.

A further factor that needs to be taken into account is the attitude of judges themselves. Formal changes in the constitution may confer additional duties and powers upon the courts. What the courts make of them will depend largely upon those sitting on the bench. As we have seen, the courts have the power to review executive actions but only in recent years has the power been employed in what may be termed a spurt of judicial activism by the higher echelons of the judiciary. The attitude of judges is important, especially in Britain. The doctrine of parliamentary sovereignty is a legal concept. It is at the heart of the British Constitution. As a legal concept its guardian is the judiciary, not Parliament. The doctrine is upheld so long as the courts accept it. Continuing attachment to the doctrine by the courts may be attributable to a combination of history and practical politics: for nearly three centuries now judges have accepted the concept of parliamentary sovereignty; to suddenly dispense with it would create untold political controversy, a controversy which most judges would prefer to avoid. Nonetheless, recent years have witnessed a willingness on the part of some authorities to nibble away at the edges of the doctrine and to encourage a change in judicial attitudes. Increasingly worried by the powers at the disposal of an 'elective disctatorship' and a tendency to use those powers, a number of lawyers have observed a growing conflict between parliamentary sovereignty and the rule of law: the former provides the government with the means to have its way over the latter. The greater the conflict, the more likely are judges to consider abandoning parliamentary sovereignty in favour of the rule of law. This is reflected in the argument advanced for an entrenched Bill of Rights. Parliamentary sovereignty would be dispensed in favour of certain fundamental rights. However, legislation is not sufficient and, indeed, in certain cases not even a necessary condition to ensure the entrenchment of certain rights and the concomitant abandonment of parliamentary sovereignty. As Professor H.W.R. Wade has congently argued, a necessary and possibly sufficient condition is an attitudinal change on the part of judges. 'It is the minds of the judges which require to be adjusted, and to pass statutes merely telling them to adjust themselves is futile. . . . Always in the end we come back to the ultimate legal reality: an Act of Parliament is valid only if the judges say it is, and only they can say what the rules for its validity are.'[32]

Should an attitudinal change take place among Britain's leading judges, there are various devices that could provide them with an avenue for dispensing with the concept of parliamentary sovereignty. The European Communities Act provides one conduit. The self-imposed restraint of parliamentary sovereignty is the only barrier between the courts and the holding that Community law takes precedence over *any* domestic legislation, whenever enacted. (Cases of conflict between Community and municipal law are rare, though not non-existent.)

Such a case could be used to remove the barrier of parliamentary sovereignty. The provisions of the Act make it clear implicitly that Community law should take precedence over all domestic law and such provisions are in accord with the holding of the Court of the Communities.

Another means, which we have touched upon briefly in a preceding section, would be afforded in the event of the abolition of the House of Lords. An Act passed only by the Queen and the Commons might not be accepted by the courts as constituting on its face an Act of Parliament. Already there is some authority for contending that Acts passed under the provisions of the 1911 and 1949 Parliament Acts are forms of subordinate rather than primary legislation, and Professor Hood Phillips has argued that the 1911 Act, as an enabling Act, cannot itself be amended by subordinate legislation of the Queen and Commons; hence he queries whether the measure called the Parliament Act 1949 bears the character of an Act of Parliament.[33]

Other means for carrying through such a judicial revolution would, of course, be a Bill of Rights. Peter Wallington and Jeremy McBride have suggested that such a bill be enacted without provision that it takes precedence over later legislation (unless expressly overriding the Bill of Rights), with the judges of the House of Lords issuing a practice statement that any legislation not containing an express 'notwithstanding the Bill of Rights' clause would be disallowed in so far as it conflicted with the Bill of Rights.[34] A novel and more radical proposal (in practice if not in form) is that of Professor Wade. He has argued that the necessary change would be wrought by simple amendment of the judicial oath. 'If we should wish to adopt a new form of constitution . . . all that need be done is to put judges under oath to enforce it . . . merely by a change in the judicial oath a new judicial attitude can be created, and that is all that is needed.'[35]

It is unlikely that such a judicial revolution will be practised. Nonetheless, the possibility can no longer be discounted. While the judiciary may not be straining at the leash to dispense with the doctrine of parliamentary sovereignty, a few growls have already been heard. We have witnessed a greater degree of judicial activism in reviewing executive actions and growing speculation as to the need to defend fundamental rights from encroachment by an executive-dominated Parliament. The more the executive appears to be impinging upon rights previously considered inviolable, the greater the likelihood of judicial reaction. There are now various means through which such a reaction may be

chanelled. One can no longer consider possible constitutional developments without taking into account the fact that the power of constitutional interpretation, in one form or another, may be grasped by or
thrust upon the courts. Such an event would put an end to the fundamental princple of the British Constitution, the concept of parliamentary sovereignty.

GUARDIAN OR A THREAT?

Support for a more assertive judiciary and an entrenched Bill of Rights
has been expressed by those who view the courts as guardians of one's
liberties and who favour limited government. Not surprisingly, it has
tended to emanate from judges and constitutional lawyers and from a
variety of Conservative and Liberal politicians (the two categories —
lawyer and politician — are not mutually exclusive). Conservatives tend
to the view that there is too much legislation, especially of the sort that
impinges arbitrarily upon citizens (for example, provisions for compulsory purchase and town planning), such legislation being seen as a
feature of Labour Governments. Whereas law was once 'settled', it is
seen as now becoming part of the political battle. 'The law', wrote Sir
Keith Joseph in 1975, 'is becoming a party-political football. If we are
to save the law from Parliament, and Parliament from itself, we need a
new safeguard.'[36] Labour Governments use their parliamentary majority
to further the interventionist state, and when the courts seek to limit
such encroachments via their existing powers (as in the mid-1970s) they
themselves come under attack from Labour politicians. All the more
need, so the argument goes, to strengthen the courts.

Direct attacks on the judiciary [wrote Lord Hailsham in 1978] almost
unknown when I entered Parliament forty years ago . . . are now
constantly being made, not merely by back benchers, but by ministers
. . . judicial courage, previously required only when the judge was
risking possible offence to an individual monarch or his favourite, is
more and more required when he is inadequately protected by the
government, assailed by back benchers and even ministers, and criticised
by name in the press or the media.[37]

The judges are perceived as guardians of liberty in the face of a
devouring executive. MPs such as John Stokes, and judges such as Lord
Scarman, have imputed to society (Scarman) and 'ordinary men and

women' (Stokes) the desire for judges to defend liberties and their own independence from arbitrary acts of government.[38]

Society wishes to lose neither their independence nor their self-confidence. Society, if I read the movement aright, asks only that they transfer their traditional skills, spirit and attitudes from declaring a law, the basis and nature of which no longer suffices to meet society's needs, to interpreting, and guarding against the abuse of power, a modern, statute-based, and more activist law. Society asks of the judges no more than that they be true to the ideals of Coke and Cromwell.[39]

The defence of traditional liberties, of fundamental rights, is no longer provided adequately by Parliament: the defence must be provided by an entrenched Bill of Rights and by a vigilant judiciary.

Such an argument is not universally accepted. In particular it tends to be rejected by Labour politicians. An entrenched Bill of Rights is viewed (not without justification) as a device to limit the implementation of Socialist measures. The courts are viewed as inherently conservative in outlook and geared more to the preservation of order than to the rights of the individual.

There have been mighty and great statements on individual liberty [declared George Cunningham from the Labour Front Bench in 1981]. But there have been other occasions when the judiciary, down the decades and centuries, has been extremely reactionary with regard to the rights of the public. I should hate to rely upon the appointed judiciary rather than upon the elected members of a legislature for the rights of the people.[40]

(In short, Mr Cunningham was employing a line of argument similar to that used against the US Supreme Court's assumption of its own power to partake of constitutional review.[41]) Similar comments have been made by other Labour supporters.[42]

The most sustained criticism of the judiciary has emanated from John Griffith. In *The Power of the Judiciary*, Professor Griffith argues that the top 30 or so judges (in the Divisional Court, Court of Appeal and House of Lords) have 'by their education and training and pursuit of their professions as barristers, acquired a strikingly homogeneous collection of attitudes, beliefs and principles, which to them represent the public interest'.[43] What is or is not in the public interest is a political question which admits a great variety of answers. To the judges, argues Professor Griffith, the public interest is usually construed to favour law and order and the interests of the State (in times of perceived threat) over the rights of individuals, property rights are upheld more assiduously than personal human rights, and their perception involves usually 'the promotion of certain political views normally associated with the Conservative Party'.[44] The latter is deemed to be reflected in cases involving trade unions, race relations and (overlapping with protection of property rights) the striking down of ministerial decisions in the period from 1975 to 1977.

Though the higher courts may occasionally render invalid a ministerial action, such occasions are rare.

'If . . . we look more broadly and more widely we see that this judicial activity of opposing Governments is a departure from the norm, an aberration, which occurs most infrequently and in very special circumstances. The judiciary is not placed constitutionally in opposition to the Government but, in the overwhelming mass of circumstances, alongside it.[45]

The senior judges, argues Griffith, are part of the few hundred people who form the governing group in Britain and as such are geared to protect the social order from threats to its stability and the existing distribution of political and economic power. In the event of an attempt by government to exercise arbitrary and extensive powers, curtailing individual liberty, it could not be forecast how the judges would react. 'A left-wing attempt would meet with judicial opposition more immediately than a right-wing attempt. And there is little evidence to suggest that the judiciary would be quick to spring to the defence of individual liberty wherever the threat came from.'[46] Rather, suggests Griffith, our freedom depends far more on the willingness of the press, politicians and others to publicise the breach of these freedoms and on the continuing vulnerability of ministers, the Civil Service, the police, other public officials and powerful private interests to accusations that those freedoms are being infringed.[47]

There is thus serious disagreement as to the role and functioning of judges. This disagreement became serious in the 1970s. Such disagreement clearly raises a problem of consent for the political system. If the courts are perceived as not being impartial arbiters, favouring government and the existing order over the rights of the individual, and become what Sir Keith Joseph termed a 'party-political football', then respect for the judicial process is undermined. To some extent, the controversy over the position of the higher judiciary abated somewhat with the return of a Conservative Government in 1979. Nonetheless, it is likely to be revived in the event of the return of a Labour Government, of trade union legislation being passed by the present Conservative Government requiring judicial adjudication, of the enactment of a Bill of Rights (especially with entrenched provisions, should such prove possible), or of the growing assertiveness on the part of senior judges. Membership of the European Communities, and to some limited extent a greater willingness of the Appeal Court and the House of Lords to be more assertive in employing their existing common law powers, have provided already a new judicial dimension to the Constitution. The courts thus have a greater political significance than hitherto: they may have an even greater significance in the future.

NOTES

1. The exception since 1966 is the House of Lords. It is not now bound by its own previous decisions. Judges in lower courts do not altogether have their hands tied: they have the power to distinguish cases.
2. See, e.g., J.A.G. Griffith, *The Politics of the Judiciary* (Manchester University Press, 1977), ch. 9.
3. *O. Hood Phillips' Constitutional and Administrative Law*, 6th ed. by O. Hood Phillips and Paul Jackson (Sweet and Maxwell, (1978), pp. 595–6.
4. Sir Leslie Scarman, *English Law – the New Dimension* (Stevens, 1974), p. 2. See Hood Phillips, *op. cit.*, pp. 597–605, for an explanation of 'natural justice'.
5. Griffith, *op. cit.*, p. 210.
6. Michael Beloff, 'The Silkin Squeeze', *New Society*, 10 February 1977, p. 271.
7. *Ibid.*
8. Griffith, *op. cit.*, p. 124.
9. T.C. Hartley and J.A.G. Griffith, *Government and Law*, 2nd ed. (Weidenfeld & Nicolson, 1981), p. 367.
10. O. Hood Phillips, *op. cit.*, p. 655.
11. Hartley and Griffith, *op. cit.*, p. 322.
12. Scarman, *op. cit.*, p. 49.
13. *Secretary of State for Education and Science v. Tameside Metropolitan Borough Council.*
14. O. Hood Phillips, *op. cit.*, p. 601.
15. See, E.C.S. Wade and Godfrey Phillips, *Constitutional and Administrative Law*, 9th ed. by A.W. Bradley (Longman, 1977), pp. 663–4.
16. Quoted in Griffith, *op. cit.*, pp. 130–1.
17. Bradley, *op. cit.*, p. 664.

18   *HC Deb.*, 10, c. 426.
19   *The Times*, 23 October 1981. *HC Deb.*, 10, c. 426–30.
20   *R. v. The Greater London Council, Ex parte Bromley London Borough Council.*
21   *The Times*, Law Report, 11 November 1981.
22   *HC Deb.*, 12, c. 418.
23   *HC Deb.*, 12, c. 668.
24   *The Economist*, 14 November 1981, p. 19.
25   *Ibid.*
26   See *The Times*, 18 December 1981; *HC Deb.*, 15, c. 447–9, 451–2, 532–97 and 889–929.
27   G. Peele, 'The Developing Constitution', in C. Cook and J. Ramsden (eds), *Trends in British Politics since 1945* (Macmillan, 1978), p. 7. (*Grundnorm* is a specific term with jurisprudential meaning.)
28   See Phillips and Jackson, *op. cit.*, p. 74–80, and Hartley and Griffith, *op. cit.*, pp. 406–7.
29   The most cogent expression of this argument is contained in the dissenting opinion of Justice Gibson, of the Supreme Court of Pennsylvania, in *Eakin v. Raub* (1825). See Harold W. Chase and Craig R. Ducat, *Constitutional Interpretation* (West Publishing Co., 1974), pp. 27–33.
30   Scarman, *op. cit.*, p. 75.
31   *Ibid.*, p. 77.
32   H.W.R. Wade, *Constitutional Fundamentals* (Stevens, 1980), pp. 37 and 39. Note also the comments in S.A. de Smith, *Constitutional and Administrative Law* (Penguin, 1971), pp. 80–1.
33   Hood Phillips and Jackson, *op. cit.*, p. 90. The point is made in earlier editions.
34   P. Wallington and J. McBride, *Civil Liberties and a Bill of Rights* (Cobden Trust, 1976), p. 86. See also de Smith, *op. cit.*, p. 81.
35   H.W.R. Wade, *op. cit.*, pp. 38 and 39.
36   Sir Keith Joseph, *Freedom under the Law* (CPC, 1975), p. 13.
37   Lord Hailsham, *The Dilemma of Democracy* (Collins, 1978), p. 105.
38   See Scarman, *op. cit.*, p. 86, and John Stokes, *HC Deb.*, 6th series, vol. 2, c. 1218.
39   Scarman, *op. cit.*, p. 86.
40   *HC Deb.*, 6th series, vol. 2, c. 1256.
41   See note 29 (*Eakin v. Raub*) above.
42   See, e.g. Joe Jacob, 'Say No to a Bill of Rights', *Tribune*, 6 February 1976, and Robert Kilroy-Silk, MP, 'Wrongs of a Bill of Rights', *Guardian*, 4 February 1977.
43   Griffith, *op. cit.*, p. 193.
44   *Ibid.*, p. 195; see pp. 195–202.
45   *Ibid.*, p. 203.
46   *Ibid.*, p. 208.
47   *Ibid.*, p. 214.

PART II

NEW DIMENSIONS

The past decade has been notable not only for the challenges to the existing constitutional structure but also for the advocacy of innovations which would effectively introduce new dimensions to the British Constitution. The constitutional innovations advocated may be divided into those which have been implemented and those which have not. A further and more analytically fruitful division may be drawn between those which seek to facilitate governmental effectiveness and those which seek to maintain consent. Whereas the years between 1964 and 1974 were what Anthony Barker called the 'years of the managers',[1] a period when the emphasis was on problem-solving and creating a rational and efficient structure for government, the years since have witnessed a greater stress on the need for a reformulated constitutional framework that will serve to maintain the consent of the governed. Indeed, five of the six reforms considered in succeeding chapters fall into this latter category.

From the perspective of constitutional changes that were enacted, the constitutional landscape of the UK in 1980 was notably different from that in 1970; though even more significant was the pressure for further change. At the beginning of the 1970s Britain was outside the European Communities, enjoyed unitary government though with a devolved Parliament at Stormont, employed a first-past-the-post method of election, and lacked experience of national referendums or an entrenched Bill of Rights. By the beginning of the 1980s Britain was a member of the European Communities, Northern Ireland had lost its Parliament (and witnessed briefly an elected Assembly), the UK electorate and subsequently the electorates only of Scotland and Wales had taken part in referendums (as had the electors of Northern Ireland on the issue of the border), attempts had been made to introduce elected Assemblies in Scotland and Wales, attempts had been made to introduce proportional representation for elections (with such a method being used in Northern Ireland for elections to the European Parliament), and a number of prominent jurists and politicians pressed with some vigour for a Bill of Rights. All these issues remain on the political agenda. There are those who argue that Britain should withdraw from the European Communities, and in terms of consent can cite opinion polls favourable to their agrument. Others argue for the wider and more regular use of referendums, for devolution or decentralisation of government, for proportional representation for parliamentary elections, for a Bill of Rights embodying fundamental rights, and for a system of government in Northern Ireland that will enjoy a degree of consensual assent from the two communities in the province.

From the perspective of political authority, all such changes are geared to enhancing consent for government by increasing participation in and effect on government (proportional representation, referendums, devolution) or by limiting government (Bill of Rights); advocates of withdrawal from the EC would contend that that too would have similar effects. The reformers seek to reverse what they perceive to be a growing alienation with a political system which claims to be liberal-democratic yet one in which the majority does not carry the day in elections and where minorities and the rights of the individual are not protected against the whims of a parliamentary majority. In practice the system is seen as neither liberal nor democratic. If constitutional change is not wrought in order to ensure that what is coincides with what is believed (and expected) to be, then political authority will further wane as alienation spreads and becomes more intense. Government will appear increasingly as being either a threat or an irrelevancy and citizens will start to look elsewhere for the satisficing of their needs. Government will be reduced to being ignored or repudiated. 'A repudiated regime', as Richard Rose noted, 'without effectiveness or consent can be consigned to the ranks of historical has beens.'[2] Hence, in order to restore and maintain the consent of the governed, radical surgery is necessary. Well may the reformers cite in aid the words of Edmund Burke: 'A state without the means of change is without the means of its own conservation.' Change is sought in order to conserve.

Yet what the reformers seek to restore — consent — is that which, ironically, they too lack. Of the constitutional reforms implemented or advocated, there is no consensual support for any of them. Electors and/or perhaps more important political elites are divided on each and every one of them. Given the attitudes to constitutional change which we will delineate later (see the Conclusions), this is not surprising. There is no agreement as to the sort of society, and hence constitutional framework, that should exist. Even among those who do agree on the basic tenets of liberal-democracy, there is no agreement that any one modification to the constitution would be necessary or desirable. Hence, the uneven constitutional landscape with which we are faced in the 1980s. Let us now consider its main features.

NOTES

1   Edward Heath and Anthony Barker, 'Heath on Whitehall Reform', *Parliamentary Affairs*, 31 (4), Autumn 1978, p. 364.
2   Richard Rose, 'Ungovernability: Is there Fire behind the Smoke?', *Political Studies*, 27 (3), September 1979, pp. 354—5.

8

The European Communities

Co-operation or incorporation?

The UK became a member of the European Communities (EC) on 1 January 1973. Constitutionally it was a radical move. From the perspective of other West European countries it was also seen as a belated one. Within Britain, attitudes towards membership were divided: they remain so today. Arguments as to the advantages and disadvantages of British membership have centred on constitutional, political and economic issues. Though not occupying as much public attention as when membership was being negotiated or when renegotiated terms were put to a referendum, the issue of Britain's place in the EC remains on the agenda of political debate.

The EC comprises the European Steel and Coal Community (ECSC), the European Atomic Energy Community (Euratom) and the European Economic Community (the EEC): the three were merged in 1967. The ECSC was created in 1951 under the Treaty of Paris: it placed iron, steel and coal production in member countries under a common authority. Though joined by France, Germany, Italy and the Benelux countries, Britain declined to become a member. The Attlee Government found the element of supra-national control to be unacceptable. A motion by Winston Churchill calling for Britain to participate in the Paris talks was defeated in the House of Commons by 20 votes. Among six Conservative MPs who abstained in the division was Enoch Powell.[1] The EEC and Euratom were formed under the Treaty of Rome and came into being on 1 January 1958. The EEC created a 'common market' for goods within the community of member states and Euratom was designed to help develop a civil nuclear industry in Europe. The membership of both bodies comprised the six member countries of the ECSC. Britain declined to sign the Rome Treaty, opting instead for the more limited and solely inter-governmental organisation of the European Free Trade Association (EFTA), established in 1960.

The reasons for Britain declining to join the Communities at their inception have been variously commented upon. In the post-war years Britain was preoccupied with economic and social reconstruction. The countries of western Europe were in a worse shape than Britain and appeared to have little to offer. Britain still saw itself as a world power. A European community thus appeared to have little economic and political appeal. It also lacked a psychological appeal. Britain had stood alone during the war: it had survived invasion and it remained separated by water from the continental mainland. To the French and the Germans, as well as the Italians, the creation of a united Europe was a political imperative. To the British it was a vague aspiration, one tempered by an awareness of the 'foreignness' of those across the English Channel.[2] Despite the favourable but vague soliloquies of Churchill, wariness of a European political community with supra-national control was shared by Conservative as well as Labour politicans: Conservatives still looked to the Empire (and then the Commonwealth); Labour politicians viewed with distrust the creation of an organisation that would likely be anti-Socialist and could act as a brake upon the realisation of Socialist aspirations in Britain. In the post-war years, and throughout the 1950s, a combination of economic prosperity and an unwillingness to share power with continental countries thus helped keep Britain clear of entanglement with the EC. The position was to change in the 1960s.

At the end of the 1950s there was a growing awareness that Britain was facing problems, both political and economic. The country's world role came into question. Britain had lost an Empire and gained a Commonwealth. However, that Commonwealth was not as amenable to British leadership as many Conservatives would have expected, nor was it proving to be the source of trade and materials that was hoped for. The special relationship with the USA was also proving to be not quite so special. Some anti-Americanism still lingered in the Conservative ranks following the decision to abort the Suez operation (on American insistence) in 1956. The relationship was also weakened during Macmillan's premiership – despite close personal links between the Prime Minister and his distant relative, President Kennedy – by the cancellation of the Blue Streak rocket in 1960 and by America paying an increasing amount of attention to the EEC. At a meeting between Macmillan and Kennedy in April 1961, 'it is clear that Kennedy left no doubt in Mr. Macmillan's mind that a British decision to join the Six would be welcome'.[3] The more the EEC began to be considered as a possible solution to Britain's problems, the more the advantages of membership began to be appreciated: the growth rate of EEC countries had been outstripping that of Britain and the Community offered a market of some 180 million people. It also offered the opportunity for Britain to regain a position of leadership and, through the Community, build up the relationship with the USA. The reasons for not joining the EEC no longer carried so much weight as in the immediate post-war years; the advantages of joining began to carry more weight and, increasingly, to occupy the minds of the Prime Minister and his officials. During the latter half of 1960 'a considerable evolution in thinking had taken place within the British Government',[4] and by 1961 there was a willingness to accept the essential features of the Treaty of Rome. On 31 July 1961 Mr Macmillan announced to the Commons that Britain was applying for membership of the European Economic Community. In a subsequent debate, on 2 and 3 August, the Government's decision was approved by 313 votes to 5. An Opposition amendment, stipulating the need for approval by the Commonwealth Prime Ministers' Conference and for conditions of membership to be compatible with Britain's obligations to its EFTA partners, was defeated by 318 votes to 209. More than 20 Conservative MPs abstained from voting.[5]

The 1961 application for membership was vetoed by the French President, General de Gaulle. In 1967 a second application was made, this time by the Labour Government of Harold Wilson.[6] In moving a motion to approve the Government's White Paper on the subject, Mr Wilson said that entry into the EEC would have a profound effect on British industry by creating a new confidence, a new upsurge in investments, and a new concentration on modernisation, on productivity and reduced costs. British entry into the Community would also impart to the Community a new dynamic.[7] The motion was carried by 488 votes to 62. A backbench Conservative amendment regretting the Government's decision was lost by 487 votes to 26.[8] In 1969, formal agreement to open negotiations was reached. In the general election of the following year the Conservative manifesto committed an incoming Conservative Government 'to negotiate, no more no less', though nonetheless making it clear that, if the right terms could be negotiated, 'we believe that it would be in the long-term interest of the British people for Britain to join the European Economic Community'.[9] Negotiations opened on 30 June 1970 and by October 1971 most of the terms for British entry had been agreed. Following a Commons debate on the issue in July 1971 – and what was designated a 'Great Debate' in the country during the summer[10] – the Government recommended entry into the EEC on the terms negotiated.[11] The House of Commons gave its approval in October 1971 in a division which was to prove the most divisive for both parties in that Parliament. Voting was 356 votes to 244 in favour of 'Her Majesty's Government's decision of principle to join the European Communities on the basis of the arrangements which have been negotiated'. Thirty-nine Conservatives voted against the motion and another two abstained; 69 Labour MPs voted for it, a further 20 abstaining from voting.[12]

The Treaty of Accession to the European Communities was signed early in 1972 and the European Communities Bill, to give legal effect to British membership, came up for second reading on 17 February. It was given a second reading by a majority of only eight votes, 309 to 301.[13] Despite having been made a vote of confidence, 15 Conservatives voted against and a further five abstained from voting. In parliamentary terms, the division proved the high-water mark for opposition to the measure. Despite vigorous opposition,[14] the bill completed its remaining stages unamended and was given a third reading on 13 July. On the first day of the following year, Britain became a full member of the EC.

Since joining the EC, two events of constitutional importance have taken place concerning Britain's membership. The first was the referendum of 1975. In order to keep his divided party from tearing itself apart on the issue, Harold Wilson committed the Labour Party to renegotiating the terms of entry and to putting the renegotiated terms to the British people, either at a general election or through the medium of a referendum.[15] When Labour was returned to office in 1974, Foreign Secretary James Callaghan undertook the task of trying to agree some modification in the terms of British membership. On the question of Britain's contribution to the Community budget, the Community agreed to a 'correcting mechanism of a general application'.[16] The Community conceded that New Zealand dairy products should be allowed privileged access to Britain at least until 1980. As for other proposed changes, 'many of the items on Labour's renegotiation agenda either were subsumed under corresponding items on the Community's own agenda or were overtaken by events'.[17] The Community was moving already in the direction Britain wished on the question of co-operation with the developing world. On the common agricultural policy, the rise in world prices for grain and sugar, to a level in excess of that of the EEC, helped allay British fears. The Community was deemed also to have given satisfactory assurances on the issue of regional aid. (When the Community established its new regional fund, it was decided that Britain would be a major beneficiary, second only to Italy.)[18] The renegotiations came to a formal close in March 1975. The Cabinet had decided already to consult the electorate by means of a referendum and agreed subsequently to recommend a 'yes' vote for Britain remaining a member of the EC on the renegotiated terms. The Conservative and Liberal Parties also recommended a 'yes' vote. On 9 April the House of Commons approved the recommendation of the Government to continue Britain's membership by 396 votes to 170. (Though, with a free vote, more Labour MPs actually voted against it than for it.)[19] On 5 June the referendum was held, and 17,378,581 electors voted 'yes' and 8,470,073 voted 'no' to Britain remaining a member of the EC on the renegotiated terms. 'The main lesson of the voting', wrote Butler and Kitzinger, 'is one of uniformity. . . . It was a national argument, a national campaign in the national media, and a national result.'[20] For many, the result was seen as settling the argument once and for all.

The second event of constitutional importance was the direct election of members to the European Parliament in 1979. As a body, the European Parliament has few powers: it can dismiss the EC Commission *en bloc* and it can reject the Community Budget. It bears little resemblance to the Westminster Parliament, though a number of British members did seek to lessen the differences. Initially, members of the Parliament were appointed by the member states, the British members being drawn from MPs and peers. After some delay, the intention to elect Members of the European Parliament (MEPs) was realised, with elections being held throughout the Community in June 1979. All countries bar Britain employed some form of proportional representation, though Denmark used the first-past-the-post system in Greenland, and Britain used PR in Northern Ireland. In the new directly elected Parliament Britain had 81 seats. In the 1979 elections the Conservatives won 60 seats, Labour 17, and the Democratic Unionist, Ulster Unionist, Scottish National, and Social Democratic and Labour Parties one each.[21] Of the MEPs elected only five were Members of the Westminster Parliament. The country having affirmed British membership in 1975, supporters of the EC felt that direct elections would now bring the Community close to electors. 'The importance of direct elections to the European Community', declared Geoffrey Rippon, 'is inestimable. For the first time the election will give ordinary men and women a chance to have a voice in the future of Europe.'[22]

By the latter half of 1979 those who supported Britain's membership of the EC had reason to feel satisfied. Membership of the Communities had been achieved, that membership had been affirmed by popular acclaim in a referendum, Britain's members of the European Parliament had been chosen by popular vote, a government which was more wholehearted in its support of the EC than its predecessor had been returned in the 1979 general election (a month before direct elections), and after 6 years of membership Britain was playing a full role in EC affairs and was now too enmeshed in the Communities to consider withdrawing. For better or worse, Britain was a member of the EC and would remain so.

Not everyone shared this assessment. A number of politicans who had opposed British membership in 1972 continued their opposition, arguing now for British withdrawal. Among their number were some prominent Labour figures, as well as Enoch Powell, sitting now on the Ulster Unionist bench in the Commons. A number of organisations opposed to Britain's continued membership of the EC also remained in existence. The public displayed scepticism or opposition to British membership, despite the referendum result of 1975. 'In 1980', reported Webb and Wybrow in their analysis of Gallup surveys, 'the British public continued to exhibit its established general mood of hostility and scepticism towards the Community.'[23] The enthusiasm of Conservative politicians also began to cool, Mrs Thatcher indulging in a bitter row with EC partners over Britain's contribution to the Community Budget. Other heads of government felt the Prime Minister was demanding too much; Gallup polls revealed that Britons felt she should have been even tougher.[24] The Labour Party, for its part, became committed to a policy of withdrawal. In short, the issue of British membership of the EC became once again an issue of political debate.

THE CASE FOR

The case for British membership of the EC was and is based essentially on political and economic grounds. In addition, supporters of British membership have sought to refute the constitutional objections raised by opponents.

The foremost consideration favouring British membership, at least as far as those primarily responsible for it were concerned, was and is political. Harold Macmillan and Edward Heath both recognised and emphasised the need to create a strong and united Community, one that could provide a coherent force in world affairs and one that could create the stability necessary for economic expansion. The political aim was seen as inextricably linked to the economic. 'If we are to meet the challenge of Communism', Harold Macmillan wrote to President Kennedy, '[we must show] . . . that our modern society — the new form of capitalism — can run in a way that makes the fullest use of our resources and results in a steady expansion of our economic strength.'[25] The linkage, with the primacy of the political goal, was similarly emphasised by Edward Heath in 1977:

Our purpose in creating the new Europe is political; let us never lose sight of that fact. It is to prevent Europe from being destroyed, either from within or without; to create the prosperity which will ensure support for its democratic institutions; to provide the economic growth on which to base its security. The political objectives of the Community have therefore to be achieved by economic means. The recognition of this truth enabled far-sighted men in the early fifties to begin the construction of which we are now a part. It remains the lynch-pin for the future development of the Community.[26]

This emphasis was not confined to the Conservative advocates of membership. In 1967 Prime Minister Harold Wilson declared that 'whatever the economic arguments, the House will realise that . . . the Government's purpose derives, above all, from our recognition that Europe is now faced with the opportunity of a great move forward in political unity and that we can — and indeed must — play our full part in it.'[27] Mr Wilson's statement succinctly pinpointed the extent to which EC membership would provide Britain with a new world role, one based on an economy revitalised by membership.

Together, we can ensure that Europe plays in world affairs the part which the Europe of today is not at present playing [he declared]. For a Europe that fails to put forward its full economic strength will never have the political influence which I believe it could and should exert within the United Nations, within the Western Alliance, and as a means for effecting a lasting detente between East and West; and equally contributing in ever fuller measure to the solution of the world's North-South problem, to the needs of the developing world.[28]

To British leaders, Britain was the ideal catalyst for such a change.

Economically, the EC offered an attractive and dynamic new market. It would provide the advantages of economy of scale and would encourage greater efficiency in British industry through more vigorous competition. Though conceding that there would be costs as well as benefits, the Government in 1971 emphasised that membership would enable Britain to sell more and to produce more. 'As a result, we would

increase our national wealth and so be able to improve our standard of
living as well as meet the cost of entry. Given a minimum increase, by
the end of five years our national income could be some £1,100 million
a year higher.'[29] The Community also offered an alternative to trade
with the Commonwealth which was stagnant, a Commonwealth which
in any event was losing its political appeal as far as Prime Minister
Edward Heath was concerned.[30] By 1981 supporters of membership
could point to the fact that British trade with the EEC the previous
year had produced a positive trade balance of £700 million. Since
British entry in 1973, exports to the Community had increased by 27
per cent a year, compared with a 19 per cent average growth in Britain's
exports to the rest of the world.[31] 'Furthermore, the Community has
offered us a more stable market for our exports; the disruption which
might have been caused by an over-dependence upon politically volatile
markets like Iran does not bear contemplation.'[32] In addition, Britain
was benefiting substantially from the regional fund.

Anticipating objections from opponents, supporters of EC membership have also addressed themselves to the constitutional problems
attendent upon entry. The 'loss of sovereignty' argument was countered
by the observation that the loss or pooling of sovereignty with other
countries was nothing new for Britain – it was inherent in other treaty
alliances – and in practice would strengthen rather than weaken Britain's
position. 'We should beware of clinging to a nominal sovereignty', said
Labour MP Harold Lever in 1971, 'at a cost of losing a real and effective
control over our destiny which we might have co-operatively if we
pooled it.'[33] Nor would the central column of the British Constitution,
parliamentary sovereignty, come tumbling down in consequence of
entry. In 1967 Mr Wilson reminded the Commons that Community law
would derive its force as law in Britain from domestic legislation.

Accession to the Treaties would involve the passing of United Kingdom
legislation. This would be an exercise, of course, of Parliamentary
sovereignty, and it is important to realise that Community law, existing
and future, would derive its force as law in this country from that legislation passed by Parliament.[34]

By the exercise of that same sovereignty, Parliament could repeal the
legislation providing for EC entry. Though the Treaty of Rome was of
indefinite duration, 'it goes without saying', wrote two Conservatives,
'that the Community could not compel a member state to remain within
the Community system against its will'.[35]

Once Britain had entered the EC, supporters of continued membership were able to cite additional arguments for staying in. These were advanced especially in 1975 during the referendum campaign and again more recently in response to the Labour Party's support for withdrawal. The dangers of withdrawal were summarised most cogently by Conservative MP Peter Blaker. Leaving the Communities would result in a loss of the tangible benefits already provided, he wrote. 'Although not yet as extensive as they might be, these benefits are none the less of considerable help to this country.'[36] Withdrawal would also jeopardise exports and industrial growth. EFTA and Commonwealth countries had already diversified trading arrangements and would be unwilling or unable to offer compensating advantages. Britain would be economically isolated, squeezed between the USA, the EC and Japan, and there would be a weakening of Western security. The alternatives to EC membership touted by opponents – such as an Atlantic or new Commonwealth alliance – were no longer seen as viable.

These points carried even greater weight in 1981, when there was even more tangible evidence to support them.[37] Furthermore, there was the financial and administrative burden that would be borne by the sheer act of withdrawal. Prior to 1973, those advocating British membership of the EC were the radicals. After 1973 this nomenclature applied to those calling for withdrawal. The presumed natural conservatism of the British people seemed to militate against pulling out, an attitude that appeared to be confirmed by the referendum result of 1975. The words of Belloc now appeared appropriate: 'Better keep a hold of Nurse, for fear of finding something worse'.

THE CASE AGAINST

Those opposed to British membership sought to refute both the political and economic arguments advanced by EC supporters, while advancing their own argument against, on constitutional grounds. They were, and remain, able also to enlist much public sympathy for their case.

The refutation of the political case for entry was and is tied up with the constitutional argument. Far from the EC providing a vehicle for British leadership, opponents contended that it would make Britain a subservient part of a United States of Europe. Hegemony would be enjoyed by the EC, not by Britain. The eventual effect would be to reduce the independence of the country, with the Westminster Parliament enjoying the status equivalent to some parochial council. The point was put most directly by Conservative MP Neil Marten:

Where does it end up? It ends up quite clearly with a European Parliament — there is one now of course — but it will be strenghtened. . . . It will go on, it will get budgetary power and so on, it will be directly elected and in the end it will vote on a majority vote. It will have a common foreign policy, a common defence policy, common social, money and even now they're talking about a common education policy. So in the end this is what will rule this country and the British Parliament will be reduced, and I do not say that this is exaggeration, it will be reduced to the status of a County Council as we know it. And that, ladies and gentlemen, is for ever.[38]

By 1981 a number of these fears had been realised, with the European Parliament having been directly elected and that Parliament (also in 1979) having rejected the draft Community budget; an attempt by the EC to achieve a common foreign policy had been made in 1974, on the issue of the Middle East and the supply of oil, but had failed rather miserably. Other opponents of EC membership emphasised not the role of the European Parliament but rather that of the EC Commission. Membership was seen as enhancing the power and influence of bureaucrats, both in the EC and in Whitehall (see above, Chapter 4). Opponents were agreed on two points: that the EC would not provide Britain with the opportunity to maintain a position of leadership in world affairs (it was entering the Communities too late for that), but membership would undermine the position of the British Parliament, indeed would put an end to parliamentary sovereignty. This point we shall return to shortly.

    The economic arguments in favour of entry were seen as tenuous; indeed, they are still so viewed. By joining the EC Britain would be jeopardising its trading position with its EFTA and Commonwealth partners, a trading area greater than that offered by the EEC. The possible economic benefits were seen as overly optimistic and, in some respects, rather vague. One body opposed to EC membership, the Open Seas Forum, published various tracts by economists questioning the economic benefits of entry. Peter Oppenheimer drew attention to the fact that Britain's slow growth in the 1950s and 1960s could not be attributed to non-membership of the EEC. EEC countries had enjoyed a higher growth rate, but a number of non-EEC countries such as Sweden and Switzerland had equalled the EEC performance.[39] Furthermore, as

Edward Mishan wrote, 'even if we accepted the view that the Common Market would continue to grow apace, what warrant is there for the view that by the mere process of attaching ourselves to a more rapidly growing body we, too, will grow more rapidly?'[40] For the intangible benefits of entry, Britain was to suffer costs which were far from intangible. The close trading links with Commonwealth countries such as New Zealand would be lost, and Britain would be contributing a large stipulated sum to the Community budget. What many opponents found upsetting was the fact that Britain would be helping subsidise inefficient French farmers through the Common Agricultural Policy. The CAP would also result in higher food prices, given that food would have to be imported from the EEC where prices were then running higher than prevailing world prices. Even the Government conceded this point, though arguing that the effect would be an increase in the cost of living of about ½p in the £ per year.[41] Though by the mid-1970s the argument about food prices had lost much of its force (world prices now exceeding EEC price levels) the contention as to the uncertain benefits of a wider market had not. EC membership may have provided more opportunities for British industry but there was little evidence that those opportunities had been exploited to the extent that the Government had hoped they would be. Indeed, the benefits of this wider market in the 1970s could not compare with those of the 1960s. With the rise in oil prices and a world recession, Britain could not enjoy the same fruits as had the member states in the first decade or so of the Community's existence. To some extent, there was force in the argument that Britain had missed the boat.

Given that the political and economic effects of membership were not what the Government expected, opponents contended that Britain should stay out. The constitutional implications were serious and the claimed political and economic benefits of membership insufficient to outweigh them. The constitutional position consequent to British membership of the EC we have touched upon in earlier sections. In 1972, as Uwe Kitzinger observed:

the constitutional problems were very clearly displayed. The British Parliament had to take over lock, stock and barrel forty-two volumes of legislation passed by Community institutions — whose legitimacy as democratic representatives (even of the citizens of the original Community) seemed obscure. Worse still, Parliament entered into an open ended commitment to incorporate into British law all future Community legislation and make it virtually unamendable by the domestic Parliament.[42]

This was achieved by the 1972 European Communities Act. There was little the Government could do to avoid it. 'The relegation of the Westminster Parliament', as Kitzinger put it, 'in matters where the Community has competence was not so much an unfortunate accidental disadvantage as inherent in the essence of the Community as such, and thus part and parcel of the aim of entry.'[43] Given that the Treaty of Rome existed for an indefinite period, opponents claimed that the net effect was to destroy parliamentary sovereignty. Domestic legislation was 'for ever' in Mr Marten's words, to be subordinate to Community legislation, any conflict to be resolved by judicial, not parliamentary, determination.

Though it can be asserted that this line of argument was not formally correct, inasmuch as Parliament can still repeal the 1972 Act and any Act of Parliament which expressly contradicts EC legislation will be enforced by the British courts (at least according to the prevailing legal wisdom, see above, pp. 143), opponents of EC membership were nonetheless on strong grounds in their contention that Parliament's functions and decision-making capacity would be weakened by EC entry, at least in those limited areas of EC competence. The effect of British membership of the Communities has been that Parliament has effectively handed over a number of functions that traditionally it has fulfilled.[44] The task of scrutinising legislation, prior to giving assent to it has been severely circumscribed. The House has no formal power to determine or withhold consent to any measure agreed upon by the Council of Ministers or the Commission. All it can attempt to do is scrutinise draft legislation proposed to the Council by the Commission and then influence the British Government before the Council meeting at which the Commission's proposals are considered. The House of Commons has modified its procedures in order to facilitate this limited role but has not been altogether successful in achieving it; in many respects the scrutiny provided by the House of Lords is considered more thorough and effective.[45] The giving of assent, of legitimisation, to proposals put before it is the oldest function of Parliament. Under the provisions of the 1972 Act legitimisation is provided in advance to Community law. The provision of the personnel of government is also extremely limited in the context of the EC: the British minister at the Council of Ministers is (since January 1981) but one of ten. Also, to some extent, the function of representation[46] may be said to have been lost in matters of EC competence to the directly elected European Parliament. The overall effect was summarised by David Coombes. 'Where Community business is concerned', he wrote, 'Parliament has to accept certain special limitations.'[47] Though membership of the EC may not have dealt a death blow to parliamentary sovereignty, it nevertheless has had the effect of handing over to the EC, in a limited field, certain of parliament's decision-making powers.

Our final line of attack is based on the question of legitimacy and consent. The legitimacy of EC institutions was, as we have seen, challenged at the time of the debate on British entry in 1971 and 1972. Supporters of British membership felt that legitimacy would be acquired by virtue of direct elections to the European Parliament. Elections, declared Mr Heath, would enable the people of Europe to be directly represented in the Parliament.

It will make it possible for them to lobby personally or in writing to their own European Member of Parliament and to hold him responsible to them for his actions. It will increase the degree of democratic control over the institutions of the Community; on so doing it will also enable the European Assembly to emphasise the common Community interest in our affairs rather than the purely national interests.[48]

Critics could, with some justification, claim that none of these objectives has been achieved. National interests still predominate, both in the Parliament and in the Council of Ministers, and the Parliament has few powers to ensure any effective control, democratic or otherwise, over the other EC institutions. As for the relationship between electors and their MEPs (and, through them, the European Parliament), it can best be described as apathetic, at worst one of hostile indifference. There is little popular interest in the Parliament or its workings. MEPs attract little attention in Britain, either from the media or, it would seem, from constituents. Elections have not generated interest in the Parliament nor increased the degree of popular support for the institution. Gallup polls reveal that most respondents remain hostile to British membership,[49] a hostility that has not been tempered by direct elections. Indeed, since direct elections the number of respondents considering British membership of the EC to be a bad thing has increased.[50] Throughout 1980 well over 70 per cent of those questioned said they would be indifferent or relieved if told that the EC has been scrapped.[51] Whatever else supporters of the EC can claim in its defence, popular support in Britain for the institution is clearly not something that can be included. This, of course, creates wider problems in Britain, given that most political leaders remain supporters of EC membership. There is a clear gulf between the political leadership of the country and the public on this issue. It is a gulf which creates the potential for tension.

What, then, do opponents of Britain's membership of the EC propose if Britain withdraws from that membership? In the 1960s and early 1970s, talk of an Atlantic or new Commonwealth alliance was popular. However, not all opponents took such a line.

Although anti-Marketeers were at times tempted to stray on to their opponents' ground, feeling compelled to suggest alternatives, notably the North Atlantic Free Trade Area, the most effective reply was probably that of Enoch Powell. The alternative to the Common Market was like the alternative to suicide — don't do it.[52]

Britain could survive outside the EEC without creating any structured alternative. This line was taken not only by Enoch Powell but also by one of the leading Labour opponents, Michael Foot. It is an argument which may be deemed to carry even more weight now with EC opponents, given that the proposals for such things as an Atlantic Free Trade Area no longer appear feasible. For opponents, there is little reason to remain in the EC but several weighty reasons justifying withdrawal. If, on their merits, the arguments for withdrawal outweigh those for staying in, then, so the argument goes, a case exists for that course of action without necessarily requiring institutional alternatives to the EC.

CONCLUSIONS

Though not at the forefront of public attention as in 1972 and 1975, and to some extent in 1979 (though turnout in the direct elections was low), the issue of British membership of the EC has remained on the agenda of political debate. It has assumed a somewhat higher profile in the past year or so as a result of the election of an anti-EC Leader of the Labour Party, Michael Foot, as well as by the Labour Party's support for withdrawal, and by Mrs Thatcher's argument with EC partners over the size of Britain's contribution to the Community Budget.

Supporters of continued membership have the advantage of Britain actually being a member. Though not realising their most optimistic ambitions, they could claim that to a limited extent membership has provided political and economic benefits for Britain and that to withdraw would put the country in a dangerously isolated position, both politically and economically. Many would also doubtless argue that in terms of mobilising popular support for the concept of the EC and the European Parliament, the potential of membership has yet to be realised. Opponents of membership would argue that any gains derived from membership have been more than outweighed by the detrimental effect on Britain's traditional law-making processes and that the British public remain opposed to membership.

In terms of Britain actually remaining within or withdrawing from the Communities, supporters of membership are probably justified in assuming that Britain is likely to remain a member for the foreseeable future. Opponents of membership can take some comfort from the fact that not only does popular opinion remain hostile to the EC but the enthusiasm among political leaders has also waned notably in the recent past. The Labour Party favours withdrawal, the Conservative Party remains committed to membership though without exhibiting the zeal witnessed under Mr Heath's leadership, and only the Social Democratic and Liberal Parties remain committed with some fervour to the EC, a commitment out of line apparently with the views of their electoral supporters. It may well be the case that Britain remains a member of the EC for better or worse, with most people in Britain assuming it to be for the worst.

NOTES

1   See Andrew Roth, *Enoch Powell: Tory Tribune* (Macdonald, 1970), pp. 67–8.
2   See Anthony King, *Britain Says Yes* (AEI, 1977), pp. 2–7.
3   Miriam Camps, *Britain and the European Community 1955–1963* (Oxford University Press, 1964), p. 336.
4   *Ibid.*, p. 325.
5   One Labour Member and one Conservative voted against the main motion; they were joined by five independent Labour MPs (two of the latter acting as tellers). The number of Conservative abstainers was put at 29 by *The Times*, 4 Aug. 1961. See Philip Norton, *Dissension in the House of Commons 1945–74* (Macmillan, 1975), pp. 189–90. On this application to join, see especially Robert J. Lieber, *British Politics and European Unity* (University of California Press, 1970).
6   See Uwe Kitzinger, *The Second Try* (Pergamon, 1968).
7   *HC Deb.*, 746, c. 1082.
8   Norton, *op. cit.*, pp. 269–72.
9   F.W.S. Craig (ed.), *British General Election Manifestos 1900–1974* (Macmillan, 1975), p. 342.

10   See Uwe Kitzinger, *Diplomacy and Persuasion* (Thames & Hudson, 1973).

11   See *The United Kingdom and the European Communities* (Cmnd. 4715) (HMSO, 1971).

12   Full details of the voting appear in *The Political Companion*, No 9, Oct.–Dec. 1971. See also Norton, *op. cit.*, pp. 395–8.

13   Norton, *op. cit.*, pp. 404–6.

14   See Philip Norton, *Conservative Dissidents* (Temple Smith, 1978), pp. 64–82.

15   The commitment to a 'fundamental renegotiation of the terms of entry' appeared in the February 1974 manifesto. See David Butler and Uwe Kitzinger, *The 1975 Referendum* (Macmillan, 1976), pp. 26–7.

16   See *ibid.*, p. 39 and pp. 42–3.

17   King, *op. cit.*, p. 75.

18   *Ibid.*, p. 76.

19   See Philip Norton, *Dissension in the House of Commons 1974–1979* (Oxford University Press, 1980), pp. 58–62.

20   Butler and Kitzinger, *op. cit.*, pp. 265 and 272.

21   See F.W.S. Craig and T.T. Mackie (eds), *Europe Votes 1* (Parliamentary Research Services, 1980), pp. 109–41.

22   G. Rippon, MP, in *Conservatives in Europe* (European Conservative Group, n.d.), p. 7.

23   Norman Webb and Robert Wybrow (eds), *The Gallup Report* (Sphere, 1981) p. 76.

24   *Ibid.*, p. 79.

25   Harold Macmillan, *Pointing the Way* (Macmillan, 1971), p. 310.

26   Edward Heath, *Our Community* (Cons. Political Centre, 1977), p. 4.

27   *HC Deb.*, 746, c. 313.

28   *Ibid.*

29   *Britain and Europe: A Short Version of the Government's White Paper* (Issued by HM Govt, July 1971), p. 8.

30   Arthur Aughey, 'Conservative Party Attitudes Towards the Common Market', *Hull Papers in Politics No. 2* (Hull University Politics Department, 1978), p. 11.

31   *Yorkshire Post*, 31 August 1981.

32   Scott Hamilton and Edward Bickham, 'Britain in the European Communities', *Politics Today*, 17 (5 Oct. 1981) (Conservative Research Department, 1981), p. 306.

33   *HC Deb.*, 809, c. 1110.

34   *HC Deb.*, 746, c. 1088–9.

35   Tufton Beamish and Norman St John-Stevas, *Sovereignty: Substance or Shadow* (CPC, 1971), p. 7.

36   Peter Blaker MP, 'Labour's "Renegotiation" Policy: a Conservative View', *The World Today*, Aug. 1974, reprint, pp. 1–8.

37   See Hamilton and Bickham, *loc. cit.*

38   N. Marten, MP on Thames TV programme, 'Europe — The Great Debate', 11 Aug. 1970, transcript (Thames TV, 1970), p. 7.

39   Peter Oppenheimer, 'What Economic Case?', *Common Market Debate No. 4* (Open Seas Forum, 1971), pp. 13—14.

40   Edward Mishan, 'The Economic Fallacies', *Common Market Debate No. 3* (Open Seas Forum, 1971), p. 13.

41   Britain and Europe, (see note 29), p. 10.

42   Kitzinger, *Diplomacy and Persuasion*, p. 32.

43   *Ibid*.

44   See Philip Norton, 'The House of Commons and the Constitution: The Challenges of the 1970s', *Parliamentary Affairs*, 34 (3), 1981, p. 258.

45   See P. Norton, *The Commons in Perspective* (Martin Robertson, 1981), pp. 160—4.

46   *Ibid*., pp. 52—62.

47   D. Coombes, 'Parliament and the European Communities', in S.A. Walkland and M. Ryle (eds), *The Commons in the Seventies* (Fontana, 1977), p. 214.

48   Heath, *Our Community*, pp. 20—21.

49   Webb and Wybrow, *op. cit*., pp. 76—7.

50   *Ibid*., p. 87.

51   *Ibid*., pp. 77—8.

52   Aughey, *op. cit*., p. 16.

9

Devolution

A threat to the UK? Or a reinforcement?

Devolution may be defined as the delegation of central government
powers to subordinate units, these powers being exercised with some
degree of autonomy though with ultimate power remaining with central
government. The definition is somewhat unwieldy and by its very
statement raises a number of problems. As we shall see, these problems
have been reflected in the attempt to apply the concept.

As a political issue, devolution became important especially in the
mid-1970s. In the 1974—9 Parliament, the issue was one of devolving
powers to elected Assemblies in Scotland and Wales. Since 1979 pressure
has increased, especially from some leaders of the Social Democratic
Party, for a more comprehensive scheme of devolution throughout the
UK. The question of devolution has been present also in Northern
Ireland. Though the circumstances of Northern Ireland are deserving of
separate attention (chapter 10), many observers have detected a
common strand in terms of the difficulty of maintaining popular
consent for the existing political framework. The dissensual politics of
Norther Ireland are seen by some to have some limited parallels in other
parts of the UK. Devolution is seen as one of the possible responses to
the problems of declining consent.

DEVOLUTION: SCOTLAND AND WALES

As we observed in the introduction, the UK is a unitary state. Wales and
Ireland were invaded and mostly conquered by Anglo-Norman barons
in the twelfth and thirteenth centuries, though not until 1536 was an
Act of Union with Wales passed. England and Scotland were joined
under the monarchy of James I and united eventually in a treaty of
union under the terms of the Act of Union of 1707. The position in
respect of Ireland is more complex, and will be considered separately.

Though there is general acceptance, at least on the British mainland, of the unitary state of the UK, that acceptance has not been unanimous. Some pressure has always existed for Scotland and (to a lesser extent) Wales to be granted independence or, less radically, for them to enjoy some measure of Home Rule through the devolving of executive and legislative powers. In recent years the vehicles for this pressure have been largely though not exclusively the Scottish National Party in Scotland and Plaid Cymru in Wales. The SNP supports independence for Scotland, though has tended to favour measures for devolution as a means to achieving that end; Plaid Cymru, by constrast, tends to talk in terms of 'freedom' and 'self-government' for Wales, rather than independence.[1] Until the 1960s neither party was considered to be politically significant and 'Home Rule' for Scotland and Wales was not on the agenda of political debate.

This was to change in the latter half of the 1960s and, more especially in the 1970s. Both nationalist parties were able to draw support from rising discontent within their respective countries. The discontent experienced in Scotland was not the same as that experienced in Wales. In Scotland there had been not only economic decline but also rapid social and industrial change. This had produced a new middle class, one that had had its expectations fuelled by the promises of successive Westminster Governments. When those promises were not fulfilled, a significant proportion of this rising middle class began to desert the two major parties in favour of the Scottish National Party.[2] In many respects this is not surprising. 'Movements of support for nationalist objectives since 1945', as Birch noted, 'have coincided with periods of obvious weakness in British economic management'.[3] Reaction against the economic difficulties faced by successive Westminster Governments in the 1960s was thus not altogether unexpected. What gave the SNP a decisive boost, however, was what Birch refers to as the 'eruptive factor', the discovery of North Sea Oil. The SNP was able to make political capital out of the claim that the oil should be considered as Scottish oil and that revenues accruing from its exploitation should accrue to Scotland. A Scottish Government would thus have the economic capacity to fend for itself. Also facilitating a case for devolution, or even independence, was the very existence and growth of the Scottish Office (and, in Wales, the creation of the Welsh Office in 1964): it encouraged people to think of Scotland in terms of an administrative unit.

In Wales, Plaid Cymru exploited not only the economic neglect of the country but also, more importantly, fears of a loss of cultural identity. In this it differed from the SNP. Scotland has little problem in maintaining a separate identity: it retained and retains its own legal system and its own education system (for long considered superior to the English) as well as certain distinctive cultural habits. In Wales, by contrast, there was no such independent infrastructure. The Welsh language was seen as under threat as was Wales itself. The country had witnessed a large influx of workers from across the border, especially in the industrial south, and in recent years experienced the apparently widespread phenomenon of middle-class English families buying second homes, holiday homes, in the principality; this practice, which had the effect of putting properties in certain areas in a price range well beyond the capacity of the average Welsh family, was bitterly resented. In some instances it led to arson attacks on English-owned holiday cottages. Many Welshmen could be forgiven for believing that their culture was being swamped and their heritage, most notably the Welsh language, in danger of disappearing. Such attitudes were most prevalent among the Welsh-speaking dwellers of the rural counties of central Wales. It was such attitudes that Plaid Cymru appealed to. 'Whereas resentment of cultural domination by the English is unimportant in Scotland, it is,' as Birth observed, 'the mainspring of modern Welsh nationalism.'[4] However, the very strength of Plaid Cymru may also be seen as its main weakness. English-speaking Welsh inhabitants were afraid of becoming second-class citizens under a Welsh Government dominated by Welsh-speaking Welshmen. The emphasis of the SNP on economic matters in Scotland gave it an appeal that extended beyond a sense of emotional attachment to Scotland; in Wales, Plaid Cymru, by its very defence of Welsh culture, lacked such an appeal. The Welsh, to again quote Birch, 'are visionary and romantic and essentially hostile to the values associated with an industrial society'.[5] To some extent Plaid Cymru was thus hoisted by its own petard in a way that the SNP was not and has not been. Of the two, the SNP has had the greater electoral success and has tended to be taken more seriously by government than its Welsh counterpart.

Both nationalist parties experienced important if isolated electoral successes in the 1960s. The SNP had achieved the election of one MP for a very brief period, at Motherwell, in 1945; he sat for just 32 days. Otherwise, up until the first half of the 1960s, the major achievement of the SNP and Plaid Cymru was, as Drucker and Brown noted, 'simply to survive'.[6] In 1962 the SNP achieved a good result in the West Lothian bye-election, a result that gave a boost to membership. The breakthrough came in the 1966 Parliament. In July 1966 the Plaid won the bye-election at Carmarthen, taking 39 per cent of the vote, and in November 1967 (after performing well in the by-election at Glasgow Pollock in March) the SNP won the previously safe Labour seat of Hamilton; a Labour majority of 16,576 was transformed into an SNP majority of 1799. The two parties also made notable advances in local government elections as well.

For the Labour Party in particular this was a worrying development. Wales was a Labour stronghold and Scotland had been a country in which the party had made notable advances. The nationalist movement was seen as a threat to the party's electoral fortunes. The Labour Government of Harold Wilson responded by setting up a Royal Commission on the Constitution. Its creation was announced in 1968 and its members appointed in 1969. Its chairman was Lord Crowther; his subsequent sudden death in 1972 led to Lord Kilbrandon succeeding as chairman, and the Commission's Report is popularly known by his name. The Kilbrandon Report was issued in 1973.[7]

Although given wide terms of reference, the Commission decided against a wide-ranging constitutional review, limiting itself instead to a study of the constitutional position of Scotland and Wales. 'The Government had been too polite to say that it was responding to the political pressure of votes for the SNP and Plaid Cymru, but this was the fact of the matter and the Commission's majority decided to acknowledge it.'[8] In its lengthy and somewhat meandering report, the Commission rejected the constitutionally radical proposals for independence (or separatism as the Commission called it) and federalism. It emphasised the need to preserve the essential unity of the UK and argued that there was little demand either for independence or a federal system.[9] Instead it opted for a scheme of devolution. The majority report of the Commission favoured the devolving of legislative, executive and advisory powers over certain enumerated subjects, powers being devolved over more subjects in Scotland than in Wales; for example, power over the control of the police, fire service and administration of justice was to be devolved in Scotland but not in Wales. Such powers were to be devolved to elected Assemblies with the existence of Scottish and Welsh governments responsible to them. The Commission argued that the creation of these Assemblies would do much to encourage participation and alleviate the dissatisfaction felt with the British democratic system. Although it touched upon economic arguments, the thrust of the argument was based upon the problem of maintaining consent. A Memorandum of Dissent by two members, Lord Crowther-Hunt and Professor Alan Peacock, advocated a somewhat more radical approach. The Memorandum argued for devolution for England as well as Scotland and Wales, recommending five regional Assemblies in England, with the Assemblies to have tax-raising powers. Interpreting the Commission's remit in wider terms than their colleagues, the two dissenters also made a number of wide-ranging constitutional proposals.

When the Commission's Report was published, no substantial action was forthcoming in response to it from the Conservative Government of Edward Heath, other than referring the Report for consideration by the Privy Council Office. Although Mr Heath had spoken in favour of the principle of an Assembly for Scotland in 1968 at Perth (known subsequently by some as 'The Declaration of Perth') and had established a committee on the subject under Lord Home, one that reported in favour of an elected Assembly in 1970, there were too many other important items on the political agenda in 1973 for devolution to be given serious consideration. Furthermore, the impetus for it appeared to have died away. The nationalist parties had not been able to sustain their successes of the 1966 Parliament. Plaid Cymru lost Carmarthen and the SNP lost Hamilton in the 1970 general election. The only nationalist returned was the SNP candidate in the Western Isles, and that was believed to have as much to do with the factor of personality as it did the issue of Scotland's constitutional status.

The position changed drastically in 1974. By that time the SNP was beginning to make inroads into the traditional support of the two main parties; North Sea oil had become a salient issue. The SNP had won Glasgow Govan in a by-election in November 1973 and in the February 1974 general election captured a total of seven seats; at the same election Plaid Cymru won two seats. In the October election the SNP increased the number of its seats to eleven, becoming the second party in Scotland in terms of the votes garnered. Although it had won nine of its seats from Conservatives, it took second place in 35 of the 41 Labour-held seats. Both parties thus viewed the challenge from the SNP as a serious one; Labour in particular feared that at the next general election the SNP could become the majority party in Scotland. In Wales, Plaid Cymru managed to increase the number of its seats from two to three.

The response of the new Labour Government to these developments was to publish a White Paper, *Devolution within the United Kingdom: Some Alternatives for Discussion* (as its name suggests, it was more of a

Green than a White Paper in content) in 1974, followed by another, *Our Changing Democracy: Devolution in Scotland and Wales* in 1975. This was modified by another White Paper, *Devolution to Scotland and Wales: Supplementary Statement*, which was published in August 1976. Shortly afterwards the Government introduced a Scotland and Wales Bill in the House of Commons and it received a second reading on 16 December by 292 votes to 247.[10] The bill effectively embodied the proposals outlined in the 1975 and 1976 White Papers. It stipulated the creation of elected Assemblies in Scotland and Wales, each with a fixed term of 4 years, with responsibility for those areas of government responsibility that concerned only the people of Scotland and Wales (e.g. health, land-use, tourism), though with Scotland to have more devolved powers than Wales. Neither Assembly was to have powers of taxation, money being provided by a block grant voted by the Westminster Parliament as well as via local authority taxation and borrowing by local authorities and public corporations.

The bill itself was the subject of divided opinion on both sides of the House. The Opposition officially supported the principle of devolution but found sufficient reasons to find the provisions of the bill objectionable. A substantial number of Labour MPs opposed not only the bill but also the principle of devolution, and seventy of them wrote to the Leader of the House to say that they would not vote for a guillotine motion on the bill.[11] 'At this stage . . . the future of the Bill was entirely unpredictable.'[12] The extent of intra-party dissent was apparent in the period immediately prior to the bill's second reading: on the Conservative side, the Shadow Scottish Secretary Alick Buchanan-Smith, a supporter of devolution, was forced to resign from the Front Bench as a result of the Opposition's decision to vote against, and a few hours before the division the Government announced its support for referendums in Scotland and Wales in an attempt to reduce some of the opposition on the Labour benches. The Government achieved the second reading of the bill, but it encountered a stormy and prolonged Committee stage (taken on the Floor of the House) and the decision was taken to introduce a guillotine motion.[13] The opportunity to defeat the measure indirectly on a procedural motion maximised the opposition on the Labour backbenches, and in the fateful division the Government lost by 312 votes to 283;[14] 22 Labour MPs voted with the Opposition and a further 21 abstained from voting.

The defeat on the guillotine motion effectively killed the bill. Despite a notable lack of support for devolution within its own ranks, the Government was by this time committed to the Lib–Lab Pact and in need of the support of nationalist MPs. It therefore decided to introduce two new bills, a Scotland Bill and a Wales Bill. Although the Scotland Bill provided for the devolution of a substantial number of powers, as originally intended, to a Scottish Assembly, the Wales Bill devolved only power over essentially environmental and social issues. Scotland was to have an executive, whereas Wales was to have executive responsibilities exercised through Assembly committees. The Wales Bill was, as Beloff and Peele noted, a much less far-reaching measure than the Scottish one.[15]

This time the Government was more successful, obtaining passage of both bills. Nonetheless, enactment of the measures was not problem-free. Both were the subject of sustained opposition from MPs on both sides of the House and a number of defeats were imposed on the Government: ten on the Scotland Bill and four on the Wales Bill.[16] Of these, the most important provided that in the referendums in Scotland and Wales, a 'yes' vote in favour of devolution by 40 per cent of eligible voters was necessary; otherwise, the Government was required to lay orders for the repeal of the measure(s). Government attempts to reverse this provision failed.[17]

The referendums were held on 1 March 1979. In Wales 956,330 people (46.9 per cent of the Welsh electorate) voted against the devolution proposals and only 243,048 (11.9 per cent of the electorate) voted in favour. The result in the principality was clearly a decisive one. In Scotland, it was less clear-cut. 1,230,937 electors voted 'yes' to the devolution proposals and 1,153,502 voted 'no'. Though a majority of those going to the polls supported the proposals, the number constituted only 32.85 per cent of eligible electors. The 40 per cent threshold requirement was thus not met. As a consequence the relevant orders for repeal were laid and subsequently approved.

The results of the referendums, coupled with the loss of ten nationalist seats (nine SNP, one Plaid Cymru) in the May general election, and the return of a Conservative Government pushed the issue of devolution out of the limelight of political debate. The new government was not keen to give the matter much priority in its deliberations. In the 1979 Conservative manifesto there was a commitment 'to discussions about the future government of Scotland'.[18] In practice this took the form of inter-party talks (boycotted by the SNP) 'to consider whether the present system of government in Scotland could be improved by changes in the procedure, powers and operational arrangements for dealing with Scottish parliamentary procedure',[19] that is, by improvements in Westminster parliamentary procedure. The outcome was a number of recommendations covering the powers, composition and possible places of meeting of the Commons' Scottish Grand Committee, recommendations approved by the House on 16 June 1981.[20] Thirteen years after the announcement of the Royal Commission on the Constitution, the only changes achieved by devolutionists were the creation of the Scottish and Welsh Development Authorities (under the Scottish and Welsh Offices) and a number of amendments to the Standing Orders of the House of Commons.

DEVOLUTION – THE ARGUMENTS FOR AND AGAINST

The arguments advanced in favour of devolution were essentially twofold. The first was that it would enhance consent for the political system and, by alleviating discontent with government from Westminster, effectively enhance rather than threaten the unity of the UK. The second argument was economic: devolution would result in a government capable of more efficient management. Decisions could be taken quickly and with greater regard for local circumstances. The SNP was particularly active in advancing this latter argument, though it believed more efficient government could and can be achieved by an independent government rather than a subordinate one with devolved powers.

The argument for devolution on the grounds that it would help alleviate discontent with centralised Westminster Government was one of the few clear things to emerge from the Kilbrandon Report. The focus of the Royal Commission's analysis was reflected in the title of Part III of its Report: 'The Present Discontents'. It identified dissatisfaction with government from London on two counts. 'Nearly all of the complaints of substance', it declared, 'spring either from the centralisation of government in London or from the developments in the operation of government which have tended to run counter to the principles of democracy.'[21] The 'weakening of democracy' it identified as the product of fears about the position of government in relation to Parliament, the drift towards government by nominated bodies, and the inadequacy of voting for a parliamentary candidate as an expression of the democratic will. 'More generally, it is felt that government has developed a momentum of its own which seems to leave the people out of account.'[22] Government was viewed as being remote, insufficiently

sensitive to the feelings of people, and as having enlarged its powers at
the expense of individual feedom without providing adequate machinery
for the redress of grievances. 'In relation to these complaints, most
people feel that government should do more to keep in touch with them
and take their views into account.'[23] On centralisation the Report
noted that the concentration of the ever-increasing volume of government business was believed to impose strains upon both Westminster
and Whitehall with the result that congestion and delay were caused and
the quality of decisions taken affected accordingly. Provincial leaders, it
reported, felt that more decisions should be taken in the regions by
people living and working there and possessing a greater knowledge of
the regions' needs and interests.[24] Resentment of centralisation was felt
more in Scotland and Wales than it was in England.[25] To meet both
discontents, the Commission argued for devolution. 'We think that
devolution could do much to reduce the discontent. It would counter
over-centralisation and, to a lesser extent, strengthen democracy.'[26] It
would also preserve the essential political and economic unity of the
UK.

In so far as these two arguments can be subsumed under the headings
of the democratic and the economic arguments, the Labour Government and Plaid Cymru tended to emphasise the former. The SNP was
more active in arguing the latter. On the second reading of the Scotland
Bill Scottish Secretary Bruce Millan declared: 'We propose within the
continuing union, to give the people of Scotland much improved democratic participation in making their own choice on matters which
primarily are of concern to themselves.'[27] Welsh Secretary John Morris
made a similar point in moving the second reading of the Wales Bill.
The bill, he said, was designed to increase democracy and accountability,
'to give people a bigger say in decision-making'.[28] The stress on democracy was notable in a number of supporting speeches. Alick Buchanan-
Smith declared that there was a basic dissatisfaction with the machinery
of government in the unitary state and what was needed more than anything was the dispersal of power. 'What concerns me more than anything
else', he said, 'is the overriding need to reform the institutions of
democracy within this country.'[29] The same emphasis was employed
by Plaid Cymru. It differed from its Scottish counterpart 'in stressing
that the main advantage of self-government would be greater democracy
rather than greater efficiency'.[30]

Though putting forward the case for self-government on grounds of
improving participation, the SNP and others attached to the idea of

greater economic independence for Scotland called attention to the benefits to be derived from such independence. 'The only hope for Scotland', declared the founder-member of the Scottish Labour Party, James Sillars, 'is economic self-management. If we are to achieve a substantial acceleration in our rate of economic growth . . . we shall require an instrument of decision-making and resource allocation which, being Scottish based and obsessed with Scottish priorities, can feel and touch the everyday situation in a way this place never can'.[31] North Sea oil appeared to give this approach an economic viability that it previously lacked.

By helping alleviate discontent with government from London, the Government and the Royal Commission both believed devolution would serve to maintain the unity of the UK. Without such a reform, discontent would swell until the UK was rent asunder, the SNP gaining support until it was the majority party in Scotland and using that position as a mandate for secession. The SNP supported the Government's devolution legislation because they believed that it would have the contrary effect. Conflict between central government and the devolved Assemblies would increase pressure for a greater degree of self-government. The Liberals, who favoured a federal structure, supported the Scotland Bill as an acceptable compromise solution.[32]

The argument against devolution was put most succinctly by Professor Hugh Trevor-Roper.

A cardinal belief of those who oppose the project [he wrote] is that such devolution is not only pointless, in that it will solve no real problems, and harmful, in that it will increase the economic cost of Scottish administration, but also unworkable and can only lead, through inevitable friction, to the ultimate disintegration of the United Kingdom'.[33]

Opponents of devolution could discern little popular support for self-government, be it via independence or devolution. Opinion polls in Scotland demonstrated little support for separation. They generally showed that about 80 per cent of Scottish voters were opposed to the separation of Scotland from the UK.[34] Even at the height of the devolution debate a 1977 Gallup poll in Scotland found that 50 per cent of respondents would only vote for independence if it meant they would be better off materially.[35] The Royal Commission sought to discern some popular desire for devolution on the basis of an attitude survey it commissioned. However, its own data revealed that the sense of dissatisfaction it claimed to discern was not substantial and that people were more interested in having better roads than they were in having a greater say in government.[36] Furthermore, as the Commission itself conceded, though their survey had thrown some light on people's attitudes to devolution, 'there is no clear evidence of what they want'.[37] The lack of overwhelming support for devolution was borne out by the results of the 1979 referendums. Ironically, the large 'no' vote in Scotland was attributed to the SNP and pro-devolutionists losing the economic argument. Voters were not persuaded that they would not be economically disadvantaged by a measure of self-government and voted accordingly. The democratic argument, according to Drucker and Brown, was not put forcefully enough.[38] Having achieved an increase in support in 1974 because of its economic stand, the SNP lost the 1979 debate because of the alleged weakness of that stand. The poor performance of the SNP and Plaid Cymru in the 1979 general election was taken as a further indication that little popular pressure existed for devolution.

Devolution was not only not wanted, so the argument went, its implementation would have a harmful effect. It would add an extra layer of government. Far from simplifying matters, this would add to the complexities and cost of government. Instead of helping Scotland or Wales economically,[39] it would increase the burden on industry at a time when manufacturers had enough problems to cope with. Furthermore, it would likely put an end to the favourable treatment accorded Scotland and Wales by the Westminster Government. This line of argument was advanced most forcefully by leading anti-devolution Labour MP Tam Dalyell:

Although the nationalists like to pretend that Scotland has always received a raw deal compared with the rest of the United Kingdom, Scottish businessmen are fully aware that this is far from true, and that she has, if anything, received preferential treatment from successive Westminster Governments; and they fear that this would no longer be the case once Scotland had her own Assembly.[40]

Scotland and Wales would no longer benefit from discrimination in their favour, and fragmentation of governmental responsibilities would create planning problems for business.

Though devolution was considered likely to end economic discrimination in favour of Scotland and Wales, it was argued that it would result in political discrimination against England. Scotland would have its own elected Assembly under the Government's proposals; so too would Wales. England would not. To add insult to injury, the size of Scottish and Welsh representation at Westminster was not reduced under the provisions of the Scotland and Wales Bills. The Royal Commission had recommended that the number of Scottish and Welsh seats be reduced to take into account the new forms of government acquired, in the same way that Northern Ireland had fewer seats than its population would justify because of the existence (until 1972) of the Stormont Parliament. However, such a reduction would damage the position of the Labour Party and so the Callaghan Government decided against it. The result, stated one Liberal publication, would be that UK citizens resident in England, 'already second class in terms of representation, [would] be third class since they will have no assemblies. Why should any English person be expected to support such treatment?'[41]

Finally, the most important constitutional objection to devolution was that it would lead to the disintegration of the UK. The Scotland Bill, declared Mr Dalyell, would create ' a motorway without exit roads to a separate Scottish state'.[42] Though the Scotland and Wales Bills sought to maintain the constitutionally subordinate status of the proposed Assemblies in relation to the Westminster Government, their position as elected bodies would provide an incentive to seek further powers. The absence of any revenue-raising power would likely prove a source of instability, especially in Scotland. The Westminster Government would be blamed for failure to provide adequate funding to meet Scotland's economic needs and friction between the Government and the Scottish Assembly would fuel pressure for separation. The effect of the Scotland Bill, according to Vernon Bogdanor, would be to establish a quasi-federal form of government,[43] one which many believed would constitute a half-way house to separation. Far from helping maintain the essential unity of the UK, devolution would be the first step in the direction of bringing it to an end. Whereas the SNP welcomed such a development, opponents of devolution did not.

DEVOLUTION: THE CURRENT DEBATE

The results of the referendums and the general election of 1979 served to remove devolution from the forefront of political debate. However, the issue did not disappear. Rather it has returned in a more radical if, for the moment, less prominent form. Pressure for devolution to Scotland and Wales has been superseded by pressure for a federal structure and, only marginally less radical, by the advancing of the case for devolution throughout the UK as a part of a more comprehensive scheme of decentralisation.

The argument for federalism has been variously expressed and has been advanced by the Liberal Party for some time. David Steel refers to the commitment to such a policy stemming from Gladstone's pamphlet of 1886 arguing for a reform of government consistent with the aspirations of the individual nations in Great Britain.[44] A federal system of government would carry the advantages of home rule without the disadvantages associated with separatism and devolution. Adherence to such a view appears to have spread in the wake of the failure of the Scotland and Wales Acts, and has been argued recently by Bernard Burrows and Geoffrey Denton.[45] Federalism, they contend, would be less likely to provide a springboard for separatism than devolution, and would overcome some of the problems associated with the Scotland and Wales Bills.

The case for a more radical scheme of devolution was advanced by Lord Crowther-Hunt and Alan Peacock in their Memorandum of Dissent to the Royal Commission's Report. Whereas the majority of the Commission favoured some form of advisory regional bodies in England, the two dissenters argued the case for five elected regional Assemblies in the country, on a par with those proposed for Scotland and Wales. The minority report recognised the problems associated with recommending Assemblies for Scotland and Wales alone. Dissatisfaction with central government was not confined to Scotland and Wales, but became more pronounced the further north one went. As the experience of the debate over the Scotland and Wales Bill revealed, political leaders in northern England were not keen on a measure that left their region out of account.[46] A comprehensive scheme of devolution would not only be a more equitable solution but by helping obviate the resentment that would otherwise be felt by regions without Assemblies would help maintain the unity of the UK.

More recently, the case for a wider scheme of devolution has been taken up by the Social Democratic Party. The two central and identifiable themes of the new party have emerged as the need for equality and for decentralisation. The case for decentralisation has been variously argued,[47] not least by Dr David Owen in his book *Face the Future*.[48] It has found expression in the party's Statement of Principles.[49] Decisions should rest with the people, not with the State. Power, it is argued, should be devolved to the people in their local communities, not concentrated in the hands of a central bureaucracy. In the industrial sphere, this entails support for small businesses, co-operatives and schemes of worker-participation; in the social sector it entails de-centralisation of the National Health Service; and in government it requires a comprehensive scheme of devolution.

Running through the argument for decentralisation of government, one again finds the democratic and economic arguments that were advanced during the devolution debate of the 1970s. What has changed has not been the argument, but rather the vigour with which it is now advanced (Social Democrats believing in it on grounds of principle rather than expediency) and the more radical conclusions drawn from it. 'The case for decentralising government', wrote Robert Maclennan in a 1981 SDP discussion paper, 'rests, in essence, on the belief that decisions should be taken as closely to the people who are affected by them as possible. People know what they want, perceive what they need and should be free to choose how to attain their ends.'[50] Such a reform would serve also to alleviate pressure on Parliament. 'Parliament', declared Mr Maclennan, 'is overburdened by its somewhat ineffective attempts to scrutinise and control the whole field of public administration.'[51] Returning decision-making to the people would, so the Social Democrats believe, alleviate discontent and encourage responsibility and more effective production. It is an approach with which they are largely in empathy with the Liberals.[52]

Those opposed to decentralisation can call in aid some of the arguments employed in the earlier debate. There is no evidence of over-whelming support for such a radical change. Indeed, even one of the SDP's own discussion papers declares baldly: 'There is little demand in the country for further reform of local government. . . . Clearly, re-organisation should be undertaken only where it can be achieved without much upheaval and where the benefits are obvious.'[53] It can also be argued that it would add an unnecessary and expensive layer to the structure of government. Social Democrats contend that their proposals could be achieved by a reformulation of local government,[54] avoiding an additional tier of government. Critics can point to the re-organisation of local government under the 1972 Local Government Act as evidence of the dangers — and costs — of such a reformulation. Devolution would also add unnecessary burdens to industry, and could lead to ever greater economic imbalances between different regions. The more power is devolved, the greater the difficulty to ensuring an equitable national distribution of resources. (Indeed, the problems of incompatibility between equality and decentralisation are recognised by Social Democrats;[55] Maclennan contends that decentralisation would have to be tempered by 'the need to secure certain standards of provision throughout the country'.[56]) Furthermore, though perhaps now a more dubious argument than when employed in the 1970s, devolution to regional assemblies would create *de facto* a quasi-federal structure of government; one which, with tensions generated by economic inequality between regions, could threaten the essential economic and political unity of the UK.

The debate on the argument for a radical reformulation of the governmental structure of the UK has not yet come to occupy a high place on the agenda of political debate. The more success the Social Democrats enjoy, and the more they formulate precise policies, the more likely it is to enjoy greater attention. Conversely, if the SDP starts to fade as a serious political entity, the debate may subside. It is unlikely to go away (the Liberal Party, not to mention the nationalist parties and elements of the Labour Party — which remains formally committed to devolution — will doubtless see to that); if the Social Democratic/Liberal alliance were to hold the balance of power in a future Parliament it may become part of government policy. However, given the practical difficulties of achieving its implementation and the fact that it does not rank as the primary demand to be made by the alliance in the event of holding the balance of power (Proportional Representation has that honour), it would probably be fair to say that a comprehensive scheme of devolution is unlikely in the near future.

NOTES

1   A.H. Birch, *Political Integration and Disintegration in the British Isles* (Allen & Unwin, 1977), p. 125.

2   H.M. Drucker and Gordon Brown, *The Politics of Nationalism and Devolution* (Longman, 1980), chs 3 and 4. See also W.P. Grant and R.J.C. Reece, 'Welsh and Scottish Nationalism' *Parliamentary Affairs*, 21, 1967–8.

3   Birch, *op. cit.*, p. 107.

4   *Ibid.*, p. 118. See also Denis Balsom, 'The Nature and Distribution of support for Plaid Cymru', *Centre for the Study of Public Policy, Paper No. 36* (University of Strathclyde, 1979).

5   Birch, *op. cit.*, p. 127.

6   Drucker and Brown, *op. cit.*, p. 42.

7   The Royal Commission on the Constitution 1969–1973. Vol. 1: Report. Cmnd. 5460 (HMSO, 1973). Excluding appendices and

supplementary volumes, the Report ran to 490 pages.
8   *Ibid.*, p. 55.
9   See Birch, *op. cit.*, pp. 156–8.
10 *HC Deb.*, 922, c. 1871–6.
11 *The Sunday Times*, 27 June 1976.
12 William Stallard, 'Minority Government and Party Discipline. A Case Study: The Devolution Bills 1976–78', Undergraduate dissertation, Department of Politics, University of Strathclyde, 1979, p. 23.
13 On the intra-party dissent experienced during Committee stage, see Grant Jordan, *The Committe Stage of the Scotland and Wales Bill* (1976–77). The Waverley Papers: Scottish Government Studies (Occasional Paper 1, University of Edinburgh, 1979), and Stallard, *op. cit.*
14 *HC Deb.*, 926, c. 1361–6.
15 Max Beloff and Gillian Peele, *The Government of the United Kingdom* (Weidenfeld & Nicolson, 1980), p. 306.
16 The defeats are listed in P. Norton, *Dissension in the House of Commons 1974–1979* (Oxford University Press, 1980), pp. 492–3.
17 See *HC Deb.*, 944, c. 597–606.
18 *The Conservative Manifesto 1979*, p. 21. See also Michael Keating, 'Scotland in Parliament: Options for Reform', *Centre for the Study of Public Policy, Paper No. 45* (University of Strathclyde, 1979).
19 See *HC Deb.*, 6th series, vol. 6, col. 958.
20 *HC Deb*, vol. 6, cols, 958–97.
21 *Royal Commission on the Constitution*, p. 469.
22 *Ibid.*, p. 330 (para. 1099).
23 *Ibid.*
24 *Ibid.*, p. 329 (para. 1096).
25 *Ibid.*, p. 330 (para. 1101).
26 *Ibid.*, p. 331 (para. 1102).
27 *HC Deb.*, 939, c. 69.
28 *HC Deb.*, 939, c. 358.
29 *HC Deb.*, 939, c. 141.
30 Birch, *op. cit.*, p. 122.
31 *HC Deb.*, 939, c. 134. See also David Simpson, 'Independence: The Economic Issues', in Neil MacCormick, *The Scottish Debate* (Oxford University Press, 1970), pp. 121–31.
32 See the speech of Russell Johnston, *HC Deb.*, 939, c. 105–13.
33 Preface to Tam Dalyell, *Devolution: The End of Britain* (Jonathan Cape, 1977), pp. x–xi.
34 Birch, *op. cit.*, p. 151.
35 Drucker and Brown, *op. cit.*, p. 49.
36 See *ibid.*, pp. 153–4.
37 *Royal Commission on the Constitution*, p. 334 (para. 1112).
38 Drucker and Brown, *op. cit.*, p. 124.

39   The economic benefits to Scotland as part of the Union are out-
      lined in 'Scotland and the Union', *Politics Today*, 20, 14
      November 1977, (Conservative Research Department, 1977).
40   Dalyell, *op. cit.*, p. 183.
41   *The Government's Devolution Plans: A Note of Dissent from the
      U.K. Liberal Party's Machinery of Government Policy Panel
      (1977)*, para. 4, quoted in Bogdanor (see below).
42   *HC Deb.*, 939, c. 126.
43   Vernon Bogdanor, 'Devolution and the Constitution', *Parlia-
      mentary Affairs*, 31 (3), Summer 1978, p. 257. This paragraph
      draws largely on this article.
44   David Steel, 'Federalism', in MacCormick, *op. cit.*, p. 81.
45   *Devolution or Federalism?* (Macmillan, 1980).
46   See Bogdanor, *loc. cit.*, pp. 262–3.
47   See Ian Bradley, *Breaking the Mould?* (Martin Robertson, 1981),
      pp. 130–4.
48   *Face the Future* (Oxford University Press, 1981), ch. 2.
49   *Draft Constitution of the Social Democratic Party* (SDP, 1981),
      p. 1.
50   Robert Maclennan, MP, 'Decentralisation of Government', *SDP
      Discussion Paper 1*, Social Democrats Conference 1981.
51   *Ibid.*
52   See 'A Fresh Start for Britain: Statements and Principles com-
      mended by a joint working party of Liberals and Social Demo-
      crats', (Poland Street Publications Ltd, June 1981).
53   Tyrrell Burgess, 'Local Government and Finance', *SDP Discussion
      Paper 8*, Social Democratic Conference 1981.
54   See Maclennan and Burgess, *op. cit.*
55   See Bradley, *op. cit.*, p. 135.
56   Maclennan, *op. cit.*

10

Northern Ireland

The insoluble problem?

Britain is perceived by some as moving from being a consensual to a dissensual society. However, the problems of maintaining a shaky consensus are as nothing compared to the problems of Northern Ireland. In the province there is no consensus. There never has been. Even now, the consideration of constitutional change is not designed to create a consensus. 'The immediate task of Ulster politicians', as Richard Rose wrote in 1976, 'is not to create consensus where none exists, but to create institutions of civil government that can work without full consensus.'[1] That task appears near insuperable.

The problems of Northern Ireland are alien and impenetrable to the British mind. British politicians are unsure of the constitutional framework they favour for the province. By contrast, Northern Ireland politicians know what framework they want. That, though, is a contribution to and not a solution of the problem. The politicians in the province support mutually exclusive structures. A form of civil government that will work appears unlikely to be achieved by those politicians. Government ministers at Westminster are hesitant to impose it. Northern Ireland remains very much the problem that won't go away.

BACKGROUND[2]

In 1920 the Westminster Parliament passed the Government of Ireland Act. It attempted to provide home rule for Ireland by creating two Parliaments, one for the six northern counties and one for the remaining 26 southern counties. The provisions for the southern counties were not applied because of the conflict within the country. They were superseded by the Treaty of Ireland in 1921 which created the Irish Free State. Ireland was partitioned and the provisions of the 1920 Act were applied in the new province of Northern Ireland. (Often referred to as Ulster, the six counties of Northern Ireland comprise two-thirds of the counties that form the historic region of Ulster.) The province acquired its own Parliament, at Stormont, and a Governor. The Stormont Parliament comprised two Houses, comprising 52 elected members, and an Upper House, the Senate, one with two *ex officio* members (the Mayors of Belfast and Londonderry) and 24 members elected by the Lower House. Members of the Lower House were initially elected by a form of proportional representation but in 1929 this was displaced in favour of the first-past-the-post method. The province returned 12 Members to the Westminister Parliament.

From the Stormont Parliament an executive was formed, and the powers exercised by it were rarely questioned by the Westminster Government. Various powers were devolved under the provisions of the 1920 Act and any dispute as to the allocation of powers between the Stormont and Westminster Governments was referred to the Judicial Committee of the Privy Council. Such disputes rarely arose. British politicians were unwilling to be drawn into the mesh of Irish politics. The result was that the Stormont Government acquired a degree of autonomy that was in part to contribute to its later demise.

The constitutional structure so created was not one that found favour with all the inhabitants of the province. The six counties were formed to create Northern Ireland in response to the demands of the Protestants in the North who felt threatened by the Catholic majority in the South with whom they had little in common. However, though a majority in the new province, they were not the sole inhabitants. They comprised approximately two-thirds of the population; the remaining one-third was Roman Catholic. There was a clear and rigorously maintained divide between the two communities. The divisions ran deep. The Protestant majority was not only separated from the Catholics by reasons of religion but also by culture, education, geography and basic political attitudes. The Protestants were largely derived from Presbyterian Scottish settlers. They considered themselves to be more thrifty and hard-working than Catholics. They considered themselves both superior to and threatened by the untrustworthy Catholic minority. The Protestants were loyal to the Union; the Catholics identified with the South and most, though not all, would like to have been rid of the border. There was thus a basic divide between the two communities. Protestants looked upon Catholics as disloyal; Catholics looked upon the Protestant majority as oppressors. The divide was reinforced by culture and education; children attended schools with a religious affiliation. The Protestant schools generally taught British history, the Catholic emphasised Irish history. Catholic children were also taught the Irish language and played Gaelic games. To Protestants, Gaelic culture became something that belonged to 'the other side'. The two communities were also segregated, Catholics living in one area, Protestants in another. In the so-called 'Plantation towns', such as Ballymena, the Protestants tended to live in and around the centre of the town, the Catholics in the outskirts or beyond the inner town boundaries. In the countryside the Protestants tended to farm in the valleys, the Catholics on the high ground. Within the most segregated areas each community had its own doctors, tradesmen and services. The common ground between the two sides was virtually non-existent: each regarded the other as being gravely in error.

This division was to be reflected in the political structure of the province. It became essentially a state dominated by one party. The Protestants regularly won two-thirds of the seats at Stormont (there was little alternation of seats from one party to the other) and they enjoyed uninterrupted power in government. Given attitudes towards the Union, the Protestants identified themselves – and their religion – with the very existence of Northern Ireland. 'We are', declared Lord Craigavon, 'a Protestant Parliament and a Protestant state.'[3] The attitude towards the province and its constitutional structure was a possessive one. Even the date chosen for a national holiday was 12 July, the date of the anniversary of William of Orange's victory over the forces of James II at the Battle of the Boyne in 1690. The attitude toward the constitution, and the use made of governmental powers, reinforced the divide between the two communities. Catholics found little to support in Northern Ireland's political structure: the constitutional framework favoured the Protestant majority and that majority employed the power of government to discriminate against them, especially in areas such as housing. Unlike blacks in the American South, Catholics had no Bill of Rights or Supreme Court to protect them; and the British Government preferred not to get involved. The Catholic minority was not only unwilling to play the game of Northern Ireland politics, it challenged the legitimacy of the rules of the game. To push the analogy a little further, most Catholics preferred another game, the one being played by their friends in the next field. The game in which they found themselves was not of their choosing.

For nearly 50 years of the province's existence the Protestant politicians employed the powers of government and the police to maintain their dominant position. Despite various acts of violence by nationalist extremists, notably the Irish Republican Army (the IRA) in the 1930s and 1950s, relative peace was maintained. The Catholic population, in a minority and remembering the bloodshed of the early 1920s, adopted a generally withdrawn and bitter but nonetheless non-violent approach.

However, conditions were to change in the 1960s. On the Unionist side divisions appeared as a result of attempts by the new Prime Minister, Terence O'Neill, to seek better relations with Dublin. On the Catholic side the tentative steps taken by the O'Neill Government were viewed as too little and too late. Inspired by the civil rights movement in America, a number of nationalists and radical sympathisers formed in 1967 a Civil Rights Association (CRA), joined in 1968 by a more revolutionary organisation called People's Democracy (PD). The tactic employed by the two groups was to provoke violence by their opponents in the expectation that they, the discriminated-against minority, would win sympathy not only from the Catholic community but also from British and international opinion. 'In the explosive political atmosphere of Northern Ireland this tactic worked brilliantly.'[4] Various demonstrations and marches produced vigorous reaction both by the Royal Ulster Constabulary and by groups of Protestants. Clashes between Catholics and Protestants erupted into civil disorder which the police and their auxiliary forces, the so-called B-Specials, were unable to contain. In August 1969 the British Government, at the request of the Northern Ireland Cabinet, introduced British troops to the province to maintain order, In return, the Government of Harold Wilson demanded certain concessions, notably the phasing out of the B-Specials and the introduction of full civil rights for Roman Catholics.

For the British Government, its involvement in the affairs of Northern Ireland was not a happy one. Its actions encountered criticism from both communities. Though the Government's decision had initially been welcomed by Catholics in the province, the use of troops to support the civilian power — in other words, the Protestant Government and police — and the searching of Catholic areas for arms caches produced a fairly rapid dissipation of that support. A 'shooting war' between the IRA and the British army broke out in February 1971, followed in August by the introduction of internment without trial. Far from lessening violence, internment exacerbated the problem. The detention of IRA leaders resulted in their replacement by more extreme followers and in a significant section of the Catholic community extending its sympathy to the IRA cause. British policy also ran into trouble with Protestant leaders. Responsibility for the province at that time rested with the Home Secretary, and the new Conservative occupant of the office in 1970, Reginald Maudling, was much criticised by Unionist politicians for his failure to take a tougher line in responding to IRA activity.[5] They urged on him the need for stronger security precautions and an end to so-called 'no-go' areas, areas in Catholic communities where security forces did not venture. An attempt by the Northern Ireland Cabinet to persuade the Defence Secretary to put the troops under their political control was rebuffed.

Pressure for further action by the Westminster Government increased in the latter half of 1971 and early 1972. Far from abating, violence in the province was on the increase. In the first 2 months of 1972, 49 people were killed and a further 257 injured as a result of gunshots and bombings. As a result of the deteriorating situation and the stalemate between the two sides the British Government decided to introduce some form of political initiative, 'which it is hoped may prove enough to break the months of deadlock and reduce the violence in the streets'.[6] Part of this initiative entailed the transfer of responsibility for law and order from the Stormont to the Westminster Government. This proposal proved unacceptable to the Government of Northern Ireland. In consequence, the British Government took the step it least wanted to take. On 24 March the Prime Minister, Mr Heath, announced that the Government was left with 'no alternative to assuming full and direct responsibility for the administration of Northern Ireland until a political solution to the problems of the Province can be worked out in consultation with all those concerned'.[7] A bill to transfer executive and legislative powers from Stormont to Westminster was quickly introduced and passed, opposed by Ulster Unionist MPs and a few Conservatives,[8] and a new Northern Ireland Office created under a Secretary of State. Within a matter of days the constitutional framework of Northern Ireland underwent radical surgery.

As announced by Mr Heath, direct rule by Westminster was intended as a temporary expedient and the 1972 Act, the Northern Ireland (Temporary Provisions) Act, had to be renewed annually. According to Reginald Maudling, the starting point for moulding a lasting constitutional settlement was 'that the Westminster pattern of democracy, which suits us well, is not easily exportable'.[9] The solution favoured was nonetheless premised on traditional British assumptions: that individuals are rational and that disputes between them are resolvable by sitting round a table to talk. The approach taken was designed to isolate the men of violence and to bring together the men of reason. This was sought through a constitutional framework that would permit power-sharing between the two communities. The Northern Ireland Secretary, William Whitelaw, convened a conference at Darlington attended by Ulster Unionists, the Northern Ireland Labour Party and the Alliance Party. In March 1973 he published a White Paper (Cmnd. 5259) proposing power-sharing via an Executive drawn from an 80-member Assembly elected by a method of proportional representation. The constitutional framework envisaged by the White Paper was created by the 1973 Northern Ireland Constitution Act. In November Mr Whitelaw was able to announce agreement between the parties involved on the formation of a Northern Ireland Executive. To incorporate what was termed the 'Irish dimension', agreement was also reached between the British Government, the Irish Government and party leaders from Northern Ireland on the creation of a Council of Ireland, with the Irish Government accepting that there could be no change in the status of Northern Ireland without the consent of a majority of the people in the province.

The Government's proposals for power-sharing, as well as the Council of Ireland, badly divided the Unionists in Northern Ireland. The Official Unionists under Brian Faulkner were prepared to support the proposed Assembly; other Unionists such as the Rev. Ian Paisley were vehemently opposed to it. A power-sharing Executive was formed in January 1974. The following month, Unionists opposed to power-sharing won 11 of the 12 Northern Ireland seats in the UK general election. A general strike organised by the Ulster Workers Council virtually brought the province to a standstill. For its part, the British Government proved unwilling to utilise its coercive powers to break the strike. It was, declared a bitter John Hume of the Social Democratic and Labour Party (SDLP), 'one of the most squalid examples of government irresponsibility in our times'.[10] Recognising its weak and vulnerable position, the Executive resigned. It had lasted a total of 4 months.

In July 1974, 2 months after the collapse of the Executive, the British Government published a White Paper proposing that political leaders in Northern Ireland be given the chance to work out a settlement through the medium of an elected Constitutional Convention. The Government made clear its continued commitment to the principle of power-sharing. The Unionist-dominated Constitutional Convention met between May and November 1975 but failed to resolve the deadlock between the Unionists opposed to power-sharing,[11] and the predominantly Catholic SDLP which favoured power-sharing and, in the long term, a united Ireland. The Convention Report followed the proposal of the Unionists for a Stormont-type Cabinet government. The Report was rejected by the British Government. The Convention was reconvened to see if agreement could be reached on some form of power-sharing. It failed and the Convention was dissolved in March 1976.

From 1976 to 1979 the British Government adopted the approach of trying to maintain order while encouraging the people and politicians in the province to reach agreement amongst themselves. Some modest proposals for a non-legislative Assembly were put forward. They were rejected by the Northern Ireland parties. In October 1979 the new Conservative Northern Ireland Secretary, Humphrey Atkins, announced the Government's intention to introduce proposals to transfer some governmental powers to locally elected representatives in Northern Ireland. The following month the Government published a paper proposing a conference of political leaders (hardly a novel proposal) and outlining various options for discussion.[12] The conference met between 7 January and 24 March 1980 but was virtually doomed to fail before it even met. The Official Unionists boycotted the proceedings. At the conference there was disagreement between Ian Paisley's Democratic Unionist Party and the SDLP on the appropriate form of government for the province: the former wanted a Stormont-type majority government, the latter (as well as the Alliance Party) favoured some form of power-sharing.[13] The SDLP also put forward proposals to incorporate the Irish dimension to the problem. The conference failed to reach agreement.

The Government reponded with another paper, reiterating the need for minority involvement in the government of the province. The paper stressed that no system could work without the clear support of the two communities. 'While the Government could create fair and workable institutions', observed Derek Birrell, 'it could not create the will to make the institutions work.'[14] Given the absence of that will, the Government was inclined to maintain direct rule until agreement could be reached. However, pressure for a political initiative built up. The Irish Government and various influential American politicians were keen for action by the British Government. On 2 July 1981 Mr Atkins announced his intention to create an advisory council of some 50 representatives drawn from elected sources: MPs, Members of the European Parliament, councillors and the like. The functions of the council would be to report on the activities of government departments covering the range of matters transferred under the 1973 Constitution Act, to scrutinise proposals for legislation affecting Northern Ireland, and to consider the future government of the province.[15] The proposal was stillborn. The debate itself was overshadowed by a recommendation from former Prime Minister James Callaghan that Northern Ireland develop into a 'broadly independent State',[16] and events were dominated by a continuing hunger strike by IRA prisoners in the Maze prison. The prisoners demanded various concessions, including the re-introduction of 'political status' (introduced by Mr Maudling but abolished by Merlyn Rees). The British Government resisted the prisoners' demands. The IRA exploited the publicity arising from the strike, especially when one of the hunger strikers, Bobby Sands, was elected as MP for Fermanagh and South Tyrone at a by-election in April 1981 following the death of the sitting Member. The death of Mr Sands the following month served to fan anti-British sentiment, including among Irish Americans in the United States. Mr Atkins's proposal was seen by some, like T.E. Utley, as a 'ploy . . . to convince the Americans and other critics that Britain was still trying to do something in Ulster'.[17]

The hunger strike eventually ended, in October 1981, in the face of British Government refusal to concede the prisoners' demands. Nonetheless, the Government was not in a strong position. The hunger strike had increased support for the IRA among the Catholic community (many opposed to IRA violence having voted for Bobby Sands and his successor) while the Protestants were expressing their opposition to meetings held by Mrs Thatcher with Irish Prime Minister Charles Haughey in December 1980 and with his successor, Dr Garret Fitzgerald, in November 1981. At the former meeting the two leaders had agreed to establish joint Anglo–Irish study groups and at the latter agreement was reached on an Anglo–Irish Inter-Governmental Council. The Council was to involve regular meetings between the two governments at ministerial and official levels to discuss 'matters of common concern' and to give 'institutional expression' to the relationship between the Governments.[18] To the Unionists, pursuit of this 'Irish dimension' – which they had consistently opposed – smacked of betrayal by the British Government. Mr Paisley led various demonstrations against the Government's actions. Mr Paisley's deputy, Peter Robinson, MP, made clear the view taken of the Council: 'The intention is to use it as a means of getting us down the Dublin road towards a united Ireland.'[19] In the House of Commons, in a remark noted by journalists but not recorded in *Hansard*, Mr Paisley rose to accuse the Prime Minister, Mrs Thatcher, of being a traitor to Northern Ireland.[20] Unionist feelings were further incensed by the murder of several members of the security forces in the province and by the assassination of Unionist MP Robert Bradford on 14 November. The IRA claimed responsibility for the attacks.

By the end of 1981 the British Government faced a problem that seemed just as intractable as before. The IRA was continuing to mount attacks both in the province and in Britain itself. The Unionists feared a British betrayal. Domestic opinion appeared to be that Northern Ireland was an unfortunate problem, one that most people would apparently prefer to go away. There was no obvious strong public support for maintaining the union. Nonetheless, there was condemnation of the IRA: not only had it killed and maimed in the province (though it had no monopoly of violence) it had been responsible for wanton murder and destruction in various parts of Britain. In 1976 it had been responsible for horrific deaths in pub bombings in Birmingham – an event that motivated the introduction of the Prevention of Terrorism Act – and various bombing campaigns in London and other provincial cities. Splinter groups had been responsible for the assassinations of the Conservative spokesman on Northern Ireland, Airey Neave, in 1979 and of Lord Mountbatten the same year. For many in Britain the desire to leave Northern Ireland to its own devices was tempered by an unwillingness to give in to men of violence.

Given this, what was and is the British Government to do? The situation in Northern Ireland was and remains a complex one. So too are the various options mooted for providing an acceptable constitutional framework for the province. Is it possible to create 'institutions of civil government that can work without full consensus'? The schemes suggested are many and varied.

PROPOSED CONSTITUTIONAL FRAMEWORKS

There are at least nine separate options which have been canvassed, some of which may be further sub-divided. These may be identified briefly as follows.

Direct Rule

One option is to maintain direct rule of the province by the Westminster

Government. 'I have found a great many people in the Province who approve of it', observed Humphrey Atkins in 1981. 'They believe that it has served the Province well and are not at all convinced that it ought to be challenged. I, too, believe that the system has worked well over the past seven years.'[21] Above all, he said, it was generally regarded as 'being fair between one section of the community and another'.[22]

Nonetheless, there are limitations to pursuing such an option, limitations of which Westminster politicians are well aware. The most obvious point has been variously made. As Merlyn Rees put it, 'direct rule can only be temporary'.[23] It is a form of government which places a heavy burden on the Northern Ireland Office, it is based on a military presence, and as Mr Atkins conceded 'there is not enough of a Northern Ireland political input into the governing of the Province'.[24] It also conveys the impression of colonial rule, an impression that does not commend itself to politicians in the province. 'Politically,' as Richard Rose observed, 'the arrangements are unstable, because sooner or later they tend to unite *all* Northern Ireland politicians against rule by a London government that is not accountable to them. . . . In turn, this offers the initiative to paramilitary groups in Ulster to use violence to resolve disagreements.'[25]

Recognition of some of these limitations has led to a number of proposals designed to modify direct rule to make it more acceptable, usually by injecting some elected Northern Ireland elements into the governing process. The proposal for an advisory council comes into this category. An advisory council of nominated members existed for a time when direct rule was first introduced, but it did not work.[26] The idea was variously resuscitated. The Liberal Party manifesto in 1979 proposed an elected Assembly of 15–20 members to 'represent the views of the people of Northern Ireland to the Secretary of State and to advise him accordingly' and 'discuss how a constitutional conference should be set up to consider the means by which a generally acceptable form of Government for the Province could be developed'. The proposal also received some support from some Conservative MPs such as Michael Mates, and in 1981 found favour with the Northern Ireland Secretary. It was argued that an Advisory Council would allow the Secretary of State to be better advised and to consider representations from both sides while a longer-term solution was being sought. It was viewed as permitting gradual change at a time when more radical initiatives seemed unlikely to find sufficient acceptance to be implemented. Nonetheless it was variously criticised, especially by Ulster

Unionist MPs. 'A Northern Ireland Council as an advisory body would be powerless', declared James Kilfedder. 'It would be a talking shop.'[27] And in the words of the late Robert Bradford, 'We shall have a hotch-potch of people discussing the Northern Ireland Constitution Act 1973, with which this House is ill at ease, let alone a group of untutored councillors and nominees.'[28] As he observed, it would not deal with the basic problems of the irreconcilable differences between two conflicting and religious philosophies.[29] Mr Atkins's proposal, as we have noted, was stillborn.

Self-government within the UK

The majority of Official Unionists, as Derek Birrell noted, 'advocate the return of full-scale devolved powers with a majority-based system of government'.[30] In short, they favour a return to something akin to the pre-1972 structure. Though some Unionists have indicated a willingness to consider certain other possibilities, such as full integration with the UK, a return to a parliament at Stormont remains the 'emotional favourite' with most of them.[31] In November 1981 a number of Unionist organisations combined to set up a steering committee to work out a formula for such a restoration.[32]

A return to a parliament at Stormont would attract the support of the Unionists and would at least ensure an elected body of Northern Irish representatives to attend to the problems of the province. It would also have the attraction (to the Unionists) of remaining within the UK and hence attracting Treasury funds.[33] The drawbacks to such a proposal are considerable. Without entrenched guarantees or some form of power-sharing it would be unacceptable to the Catholic minority. It is difficult to see what contribution it would make to ending sectarian strife or reducing the level of violence. It runs counter to the wishes of the British Government, the Irish Government and of interested international opinion, especially in the USA. It would satisfy a majority of those in the province, but no-one else. For that reason, it appears an unlikely prospect.

Integration with the UK

One proposal heard from some Unionist politicians is for the province to be fully integrated with the rest of the UK, with a status similar to that of Scotland and Wales. 'Legislation and political responsibility could rest at Westminster, and the local government of Northern Ireland could be taken over by institutions comparable to the major institutions of local government elsewhere in Britain.'[34] It would involve a Northern Ireland Secretary being in the Cabinet and an increase in the number of Northern Ireland MPs at Westminster. Integration would make the province even more 'British' than hitherto and make it less likely that the Westminster Government would wish to lose what had become an integral part of the UK. At the 1980 conference of the Official Unionists a number of speakers advocated integration and a MORI poll in 1981 found that the proposal was acceptable to 91 per cent of Protestant respondents.[35]

As with the proposal for a return to Stormont, integration finds little support outside of the Protestant community in the province. As John Whyte observed, 'such an arrangement would arouse fierce opposition, initially at least, from nationalists on both sides of the border. But the real objection is lack of support for it in mainland Britain. Neither elites nor masses show any wish to become more closely involved with Northern Ireland.'[36] The same MORI poll which found the proposal acceptable to Protestants found that it was unacceptable to 51 per cent of Catholics. Northern Ireland is often viewed by those in Britain as being alien, a feeling encouraged by the strife of the past decade. Reginald Maudling's comment about the Westminster pattern of government not being exportable has been seen as reinforcing this view.[37] It was also to find expression in the Prevention of Terrorism Act, under which it became possible to forbid entry to Britain of British subjects domiciled and born in Northern Ireland. The province is deemed to have problems which bear little relationship to those experienced by the other elements of the UK and hence a separate constitutional framework is deemed appropriate.

A power-sharing Assembly

Since the introduction of direct rule, the option favoured by successive British Governments has been that of an elected power-sharing Assembly. Once elected, politicians from the parties represented in the Assembly would enjoy some share in the governance of the province, be it through some form of committee system or through membership of an executive. It would constitute a solution designed to find acceptance with both communities as well as the British and Irish governments.

Within the province, it has found favour with the Alliance Party and, with some qualifications, with the Social Democratic and Labour Party. Opinion polls have revealed 'that . . . support for the idea is still powerful in the province'.[38] A poll in 1980 showed that 79 per cent of Catholics favoured the proposal (their first choice); though only 26 per cent of Protestants recorded it as their first preference, 67 per cent said they would work hard to make it work or give it a try.[39] Only 17 per cent of Protestants said that they would try to make it fail.[40] The 1981 MORI poll found that over 60 per cent of respondents 'strongly' approved or 'tended' to approve of power-sharing: 77 per cent of Catholics fell into this category as did a majority — 53 per cent — of Protestants.[41]

The primary drawback to power-sharing is the implacable opposition of many Unionists, especially the leaders of the Official Unionists. The Leader of the Official Unionist Party, James Molyneaux, has made it clear that he and his supporters are not prepared to share power with a minority which seeks its identity with the Republic of Ireland.[42] This attitude is shared by the Democratic Unionist Party of Mr Paisley: the party's 1979 election manifesto declared its opposition to power-sharing. In the conference convened by Mr Atkins in 1980, the DUP argued for an executive formed from the majority party, and the Official Unionists, who boycotted the proceedings, submitted a paper arguing for a similar Stormont-type structure.

Though power-sharing has found support among respondents in opinion polls, such polls are not definitive. In elections, be they to Westminster or to a Constitutional Convention or to the European Parliament, the Unionist candidates opposed to power-sharing are the ones who usually get elected. In the February 1974 general election, Unionist candidates favouring power-sharing (and the Sunningdale agreement on a Council of Ireland) were all defeated. A more recent complication has been added by the stance of the SDLP. In the wake of the Haughey—Thatcher discussions in 1980, 'it is unwilling to accept anything less than a settlement within this Irish dimension'.[43] To the Unionists the 'Irish dimension' is anathema. One thus has the position where the Unionists are not prepared to go anywhere along the road to power-sharing whereas the predominantly Catholic SDLP wants now to go much further. Any attempt to impose a power-sharing Assembly on the province would likely meet the same Protestant resistance as it did in 1974. For that reason the British Government prefers to persuade the Unionist parties to agree to it. There is little

if no evidence of any weakening of attitude on the part of Unionist
leaders. If anything, the reverse.

Unification with Eire

A united Ireland is favoured by many though not all Catholics in
Northern Ireland and is the only solution acceptable to the IRA.[44] It
constitutes the long-term aim of leaders in the Republic of Ireland and
of the SDLP in the North. It is a solution which appears to find some
favour in Britain as well.

Indeed, there are clear advantages to such a solution from a British
point of view. It would bring to an end the costly involvement in
Ulster, and close the centuries-old quarrel with Ireland. The strategic
and economic interests of Britain might be better protected by having a
friendly, because satisfied, government in Dublin than by relying on the
turbulent and endlessly suspicious unionists.[45]

Such a solution would doubtless be politically popular on the mainland:
it would be seen as removing not only a burden in terms of money
but also in terms of lives.

There is one major drawback to the integration of Northern Ireland
with the Republic. It is unacceptable to the Unionists. If it wasn't, they
would not be called Unionists. The 1981 MORI poll found the proposal
unacceptable to 91 per cent of Protestants (and, indeed, to 33 per cent
of Catholics). The Unionist position was made plain by Peter Robinson:

There will never, never, ever be a united Ireland. It's like saying Spain
should take over Portugal. Have you seen the kind of people they are
asking us to join? . . . We will stop at nothing if an attempt is made to
hand the Loyalists over to those whom we believe to be the enemies of
the country.[46]

Any hope that Unionists might be prepared to even contemplate a
union with the Republic rather than the United Kingdom is dashed by
the activities of the IRA. The point is well made by John Hume.

As it is now [he wrote in 1979] Unionists see themselves as a threatened
minority on the island of Ireland. If you ask a Unionist how real the
threat is, he or she will tell you of friends or relatives who have been
murdered or injured by the Provisional IRA. . . . The campaign of
violence of the Provisional IRA has, more than any recent development,

set back and distorted the cause of Irish nationalism in the eyes of Unionists, and of British and World opinion.[47]

Though one commentator believes the British Government is moving towards a 'Falkland Islands solution' — 'the commitment stays, people remain as British as they want, but are progressively nudged and prodded towards a closer relationship with the country which is their closest neighbour'[48] — Cabinet ministers are nonetheless reluctant to move too far and too overtly in favour of such a solution. For one thing, the Cabinet is committed to Northern Ireland remaining as part of the UK so long as the majority in the province so wish. It is clear that a majority so wish. (This was confirmed in a plebiscite in 1973 and there is statutory provision for another to be held in 1983 should the Government so wish.)[49] For another, the practical reality is that 'such a transfer would not be peacefully consummated'.[50] Though the IRA currently makes the running in achieving publicity and activities of violence, there are a number of Protestant paramilitary groups in Northern Ireland. In terms of manpower and firepower they are almost certainly superior to the IRA. In the event of any attempt to coerce the province to integrate with the Republic they would seek to defend the identify and territorial integrity of Northern Ireland. They would have the capacity to create political instability in the Republic given the latter's relatively small security forces. Violence and instability in Ireland would be neither to the advantage of the Republic nor to Great Britain. There would be the possibility of conflict spreading to Britain, especially cities such as Liverpool and Glasgow. As a result, both Irish and British Governments, while conscious of the need to acknowledge the 'Irish dimension' to the problem, are unwilling to contemplate coerced unification as a viable solution. If it is to come about, it must be a longer-term and, if possible, negotiated solution. For the moment, the classification by many politicians appears to be: desirable but not immediately attainable.

A federal Ireland

The proposal for a federal system of government in Ireland has found favour with some Catholics in Northern Ireland and in the Republic and has been advocated by Michael Sheane in *Ulster and the German Solution.*[51] It appears to find some favour now among the SDLP as a possible solution that might prove acceptable to Protestants following a withdrawal of the British guarantee (to maintain the border) and a realisation that independence was not a viable proposition. 'The hope would be that Protestants, faced with the unhappy choice between independence, a wholly united Ireland, or a federal arrangement, would choose the last as the least of many evils.'[52] From the Catholic standpoint a federal structure would be seen as a Republican institution, 'drawing Northern Ireland out of the United Kingdom rather than leading the South back to institutions it rejected after more than 700 years of British overlordship'.[53] Such a structure would appear to have the advantage of having certain attractions both for Catholics and Protestants, and the MORI poll found it to be acceptable to a majority of Catholic respondents.

Despite the fact that a federal structure would allow Ulster, or whatever territorial unit was formed, some measure of self-government, the proposal has not commended itself to a majority of Protestants. In the MORI poll it was rejected by 81 per cent of Protestant respondents. It is one of the few things on which they would appear to be in agreement with the IRA: that organisation will accept nothing less than a fully united Ireland. Were a federal structure to somehow be imposed, there would be the potential for conflict between the federal government in Dublin and the state government in, presumably, Belfast. The role of the Catholic Church would remain a sticking point with Protestants and a territorial unit based in Ulster – that is, incorporating the three Ulster counties not in Northern Ireland – would further intensify their fears. A confederal structure with provision for secession might prove somewhat more palatable to them, but would prove unacceptable to all the other parties involved.

Repartition

Given the concentration of Catholics in border areas, one proposal advanced by some commentators has been for Ireland to be repartitioned, that is, the border be redrawn. Those advocating such an option are not numerous and the only person of political substance associated with the idea is former Irish minister Dr Conor Cruise O'Brien. The advantages of a redrawn boundary would be that many Catholics would become citizens of the Republic while the majority of Protestants in Northern Ireland would not only become, proportionally, an even bigger majority but would also be rid of some of the areas which have witnessed the most serious expressions of violence and discontent.

The disadvantages to repartition are weighty. For one thing there would be the problem of deciding who was to redraw the boundary. 'Any British-imposed arrangement would lack legitimacy among nationalists; but, in view of the hostility to the whole operation which an Irish government would display, it is unlikely that an agreed outside arbitrator could be found.'[54] Even if the boundary was redrawn, it would solve little. 'First of all, it would create wrangles about what to do with Catholic or Protestant islands totally surrounded by areas of opposite persuasion. Second, repartition would not eliminate political minorities, but would simply alter their proportions.'[55] It would likely create what would amount to a refugee problem. 'That we should seriously suggest', said Liberal spokesman Stephen Ross, 'that 30,000 or more Protestants in Fermanagh and South Tyrone should face upheaval if they will not accept Dublin rule is totally unthinkable in the 1980s.'[56] It is one of the few options that brings a majority of Catholics and Protestants together: the 1981 MORI poll found it was rejected by a majority of both Protestant and Catholic respondents. It does not appear to be a too serious item on the political agenda.

Independence

The most radical option, at least the most radical in constitutional terms, is that Northern Ireland should become an independent nation. Such a suggestion has emanated from a few Protestants in the province and in 1981 attracted the support of former Labour Prime Minister James Callaghan.

The proposition that I wish to put [he told the House of Commons] is that Britain, from now on, should make it clear that we intend increasingly to regard the people of Northern Ireland as responsible for proposing and taking the initiatives to solve the problems of how they intend to live with one another. . . . The process that I envisage would take some years to complete and the final step would be that a new Northern Ireland would emerge as a broadly independent State.[57]

Mr Callaghan's proposal envisaged a rational, staged process. Others have contended that independence is more likely to be the product of a unilateral declaration by Protestants in the event of any attempt to coerce Northern Ireland into union with the Republic.

The attraction of an independent Northern Ireland is twofold. For one thing it would allow the province to sort out its own problems.

Concomitantly, it would free Britain of a responsibility it may prefer to be rid of. The drawbacks are considerable. It would rid the province of any mediating force in the sectarian conflict. Economically, it would not be viable. The province is small and lacking in natural resources. Over the past decade its economy has deteriorated steadily. It is heavily dependent upon support from the British taxpayer. In 1980 it was receiving a subvention more than ten times larger than required in 1968–9. Its problems would likely be exacerbated by emigration. It would not be acceptable to the Republic or to the Catholics in the province. The MORI poll in 1981 found that it was unacceptable also to a majority of Protestants. This point was reinforced shortly afterwards by Robert Bradford in the House of Commons. 'Independence', he declared, 'is not an option for Northern Ireland, for one basic reason. The people of Northern Ireland do not want independence. It is as simple as that. We shall not be disinherited.'[58] As he went on to observe, pressure from the EC and the USA would make independence untenable. Ironically, the reaction of some Protestants to Mr Bradford's assassination 4 months later suggested that they may be prepared to create conditions that might make a unilateral declaration more likely. Otherwise, it is not considered an acceptable option by all interested parties.

Withdrawal of British troops

The final option that can be identified is not one that stipulates a specific structure of government for the province. It does, though, entail a significant shift in the relationship between the Westminster Government and the citizens of Northern Ireland, and has profound implications for the future government of the province. It is the option to withdraw troops from the province. It has found expression in various places, including in the *Daily Mirror*, and would appear to be popular with many people in Britain. Mr Tony Benn has suggested that troops be withdrawn and the problem of Northern Ireland handed over to be dealt with by an international body.

There are a number of advantages, from Britain's point of view, in pursuing such an option. It would bring to an end an involvement which has been costly, most especially in terms of lives but also in terms of prestige. If a date was stipulated for withdrawal with sovereignty being handed over to whatever power had emerged as dominant, it would also relieve Britain of a heavy financial burden.[59] The effect of withdrawal, and a troop withdrawal would be tantamount to the British Government washing its hands of the whole problem, would be to transfer that burden to others. It would likely be a popular move with opinion on the British mainland.

The drawbacks to withdrawing troops are considerable. The British Government would be viewed as abdicating its responsibilities. The absence of troops could result in civil war. Knowledge that troops were to be withdrawn would encourage paramilitary groups to fight, literally, for a dominant position in the province, ready to take over after the British presence was ended. Likely quiescence by the RUC and the Ulster Defence Regiment in the activities of the Loyalist paramilitary groups would increase the chances of the Republic and its security forces being sucked into the fray.[60] Island-wide trouble could spread to Britain, in cities such as Liverpool and Glasgow, possibly complicated by the problem of refugees fleeing across St George's Channel. 'British prestige would suffer abroad and there might be a stream of refugees to look after. Thus, apart from humanitarian considerations, even from the point of view of British self-interest withdrawal has less to offer than appears at first sight.'[61] As yet there is no indication that such an option is among those that Mrs Thatcher's Government is prepared seriously to consider.

CONCLUSIONS

On occasion, a seemingly insoluble problem is resolved by pursuing an option that appears to have no chance of success and previously has not been much on the agenda of political debate. Some politicians, such as Mr Neil Blaney in the Irish Republic, apparently have argued that British withdrawal from Northern Ireland might fall into such a category. The risks of withdrawal, they contend, are not as great as has been feared.[62] Nonetheless, on the basis of past history and the information available, there is little reason to disagree with Richard Rose's comment on the problem of Northern Ireland. 'The problem is that there is no solution — at least no solution recognizable in those more fortunate parts of the Anglo—American world that are governed with consensus.'[63] Of the possible options delineated above, none appears to provide the likelihood of creating 'civil government that can work without full consensus'. In terms of opinion within the province, the one that comes — or did come — closest is that of power-sharing. However, it failed when tried in 1974 and the worsening of conditions in the province in late 1981 and the positions taken by the different parties were such as to make it unlikely that it would be a viable option, at least for the moment.

The problem of Northern Ireland is one not only of conflict but also of paradox. The point was well put by Conservative MP, Dr Brian Mawhinney, in the House of Commons in July 1981 when commenting upon Mr Callaghan's previous actions as Prime Minister:

On the one hand, he kept telling the country that Ulster politicians and the Ulster people must solve their own constitutional problems. On the other hand, he kept telling us that this House must govern and take the ultimate decisions. I would submit that this paradox is still at the centre of the difficulty that we, as a House, face in terms of our relationship with Northern Ireland. [64]

The British Government and the House of Commons are or have been unwilling to take decisive action, not for reasosn of cowardice but simply because they do not know what to do. Given the problems associated with the options we have identified, this is none too surprising. Instead, emphasis is placed upon politicians and the people in the province, with the British Government attempting to persuade politicians to gather round a conference table to resolve their differences. The problem is that these differences are irreconcilable. As Dr Mawhinney recognised: 'No agreement between the political parties in Northern Ireland is possible, I would submit, almost by definition. Different political parties have got different ends. It is not realistic to sit them around a table and expect them to reach agreement.'[65] Indeed, the problems which give rise to the paradox appear to be becoming greater rather than less at the time of writing. In Northern Ireland, the hunger strike in the first half of 1981 pushed a great many Catholics into unwilling alliance with the IRA and its sympathisers, the murder of Unionist MP Robert Bradford in November enraged Unionists, with the Rev Ian Paisley threatening to make the province 'ungovernable'. In Britain the main political parties appeared to be finding greater difficulty in maintaining a bi-partisan approach.[66] In his speech, Dr Mawhinney argued that the people of Northern Ireland, while not able to agree among themselves, may nonetheless acquiesce in a governmental framework imposed by the British Government.[67] In 1982 such an assumption as to the attitudes in the province appears to fall in the realms of optimism. The Northern Ireland Secretary, James Prior, appears ready to institute an 80-member Assembly elected by proportional representation[68] — coupled with some moves to strengthen the province's economic position — but whether such a development will serve to reconcile the irreconcilable must remain extremely doubtful. If there is a solution to the problems of Northern Ireland, it is far from obvious.

NOTES

1   Richard Rose, *Northern Ireland: A Time of Choice* (American Enterprise Institute, 1976), p. 142.
2   By far the best work on the subject is R. Rose, *Governing without Consensus* (Faber, 1971).
3   J. Magee, *Northern Ireland: Crisis and Conflict* (Routledge & Kegan Paul, 1974), p. 4.
4   Anthony H. Birch, *Political Integration and Disintegration in the British Isles* (Allen & Unwin, 1977), p. 90.
5   See Philip Norton, *Conservative Dissidents* (Temple Smith, 1978), p. 49.
6   *The Economist*, 4 March 1972, p. 24.
7   *HC Deb.*, 833, c. 1860.
8   See Philip Norton, *Dissension in the House of Commons 1945–74* (Macmillan, 1975), pp. 523–4.
9   R. Maudling, *Memoirs*, quoted in R. Rose, *Understanding the United Kingdom* (Longman, forthcoming 1982).
10 John Hume, 'The Irish Question: A British Problem', *Foreign Affairs*, 58 (2), Winter 1979/80, p. 303.
11 Those Unionists who supported power-sharing, followers of Brian Faulkner, had broken away in 1974 to form the Unionist Party of Northern Ireland.
12 See Derek Birrell, 'A Government of Northern Ireland and the Obstacle of Power-Sharing', *Political Quarterly*, 52 (2), April 1981, pp. 188–90.
13 See 'Northern Ireland', *Politics Today*, No. 14, 28 July 1980, p. 235 (Cons. Research Dept.).
14 *Ibid.*, p. 193.
15 *HC Deb.*, 6th series, 7, c. 1029–32.
16 *HC Deb.*, 7, c. 1050.
17 T.E. Utley, 'Simple Guide through the Irish Mists', *Sunday Telegraph* 5 July 1981.
18 *Daily Telegraph*, 7 November 1981. *HC Deb.*, 12, c. 421–2.
19 *Daily Express*, 7 November 1981.
20 See *HC Deb.*, 12, c. 421 and c. 543–4.
21 *HC Deb.*, 7, c. 1026.
22 *Ibid.*
23 Merlyn Rees, 'Direct Rule in Practice', in *Policy and Practice: The Experience of Government* (RIPA, 1980), p. 55.
24 *HC Deb.*, 7, c. 1029.
25 Rose, *Northern Ireland: A Time of Choice*, p. 154.
26 Rees, *loc. cit.*, p. 53.

27 *HC Deb.*, 7, c. 1060.
28 *HC Deb.*, 7, c. 1056.
29 *Ibid.*
30 Birrell, *loc. cit.*, p. 197.
31 *The Sunday Times*, 28 June 1981.
32 *The Sunday Times*, 22 November 1981.
33 Rose, *Northern Ireland: A Time of Choice*, p. 144.
34 *Ibid.*, p. 155.
35 *The Sunday Times*, 28 June 1981.
36 John Whyte, 'Why is the Northern Ireland Problem so Intractable?' *Parliamentary Affairs*, 34 (4), Autumn 1981, p. 432.
37 R. Rose, *Understanding the United Kingdom*, (forthcoming).
38 *The Sunday Times*, 28 June 1981.
39 Fortnight/RTE poll, as reported in Birrell, *loc. cit.*, p. 199.
40 *Ibid.*
41 *The Sunday Times*, 28 June 1981.
42 E.g. James Molyneaux to Peter G. French, interview.
43 *The Sunday Times*, 28 June 1981.
44 *Ireland Socialist Review*, No. 2, Summer 1978, p. 7.
45 Whyte, *loc. cit.*, p. 433.
46 *The Sunday Times*, 28 June 1981.
47 Hume, *loc. cit.*, p. 306.
48 Ivan Rowan, 'Ministers Move Towards a 'Falklands' Plan for Ulster', *Sunday Telegraph*, 11 Oct. 1981.
49 In 1973, 99 per cent of those voting — 58 per cent of the total elctorate — voted to retain the Union.
50 Rose, *Northern Ireland: A Time of Choice*, p. 159.
51 Highfield, 1978. He proposed a division based on Ulster, Leinster, Munster and Connaught, with a state government in each.
52 *The Sunday Times*, 28 June 1981.
53 Rose, *Northern Ireland: A Time of Choice*, p. 158.
54 Whyte, *loc. cit.*, p. 432.
55 Rose, *Northern Ireland: A Time of Choice*, p. 162.
56 *HC Deb.*, 7, c. 1065.
57 *HC Deb.*, 7, c. 1049–50.
58 *HC Deb.*, 7, c. 1054.
59 Whyte, *loc. cit.*, p. 430.
60 *Ibid.*, p. 431.
61 *Ibid.*, p. 431.
62 *Ibid.*, p. 431.
63 R. Rose, *Northern Ireland: A Time of Choice*, p. 139.
64 *HC Deb.*, 7, c. 1075.
65 *Ibid.*
66 'Northern Ireland', *Politics Today*, 14, 28 July 1980 (Cons. Res. Dept., 1980), p. 238. At its 1981 Conference the Labour Party expressed support for a United Ireland.
67 *Ibid.*
68 *The Sunday Times*, 13 Dec. 1981.

11

Referendums

Who decides?

A referendum may be defined as the holding of a ballot in which electors are called upon, not to elect, but to pass judgement on a particular question. Advocacy of referendums in Britain is far from new. A referendum was advocated by Liberal Unionists in the 1890s on the issue of Irish home rule. One was recommended shortly after the turn of the century by Joseph Chamberlain on the issue of tariff reform. The Conservative Party (then known as the Unionist Party) committed itself in 1910 to a referendum as a means of resolving major constitutional issues and actually fought an election on the basis of support for such a device. Stanley Baldwin in 1930 briefly advocated a referendum on protection and Winston Churchill in 1945 raised the possibility of a referendum on the question of whether or not the parties should continue in coalition until the war with Japan was brought to a conclusion. More recently the use of referendums has been advocated by disparate elements within all three main parties as well as by the Scottish National Party, the only party to remain committed consistently to their use. Indeed, referendums have actually been sanctioned by Parliament for use in certain localities on specific issues, such as whether or not public houses should remain closed on Sundays in Wales. Local option polls, as they are often known, are not new in British law.

However, prior to the 1970s, the use of referendums on a country or UK basis was unknown. Within a decade such usage was far from unknown. In 1973 a referendum was held in Northern Ireland on the question of whether or not the people of the province wished to remain within the United Kingdom. (The referendum itself was best described as a plebiscite, one in which electors were asked to confirm their judgement, a judgement which was well known and predictable, rather than to resolve a question on which their views were not well known.) 591,820 people, an absolute majority of the Northern Ireland electorate, voted to remain within the UK. Only 6463 voted against. In 1975 came the first and so far only referendum held on a UK basis. As a means of maintaining some semblance of party unity on an issue on which it was badly divided, the Labour Party had committed itself to renegotiating the terms of Britain's membership of the EC and to committing the new terms to the judgement of the people. Given what was claimed to be the uniqueness of the issue, it was considered that a referendum was the most appropriate way to ascertain that judgement. On 5 June 1975 the British electorate went to the polls in order to vote 'yes' or 'no' to the question: 'Do you think that the United Kingdom should stay in the European Community (the Common Market)?' 17,378,581 electors voted 'yes', 8,470,073 voted 'no'.[1] In 1977 the Labour Government sought to maintain a parliamentary majority for its legislation on devolution by agreeing to backbench demands for referendums to be held in Scotland and Wales on the proposals for elected assemblies in Edinburgh and Cardiff. In January 1978 an amendment to the Scotland Bill was carried against government advice stipulating that if 40 per cent of eligible voters did not vote 'yes' in Scotland, the Secretary of State would lay an order for the repeal of the Act.[2] A similar amendment to the Wales Bill was carried, also against the Government's wishes.[3] On 1 March 1979 the voters of Scotland and Wales went to the polling stations to vote aye or nay to the Government's devolution proposals. In Wales there was a decisive vote against: 956,330 people voted 'no' and 243,048 voted 'yes'. More than 40 per cent of the eligible electorate had voted 'no'. In Scotland, the result was less decisive: 1,230,937 people voted 'yes', estimated to constitute 32.85 per cent of the eligible electorate, and 1,153,502 (30.78 per cent of those eligible to vote) cast a 'no' vote. The 40 per cent threshold requirement was not met. The Government laid motions for the repeal of both Acts. A combination of backbench dissent and lack of enthusiasm expressed through the medium of referendums had put an end, temporarily or otherwise, to proposals for devolved Assemblies.

The use of referendums encouraged a number of politicians and academics to consider their use on other occasions. Reflecting on the experience of 1975 and 1979, George Cunningham MP commented: 'I do not say that referendums will become a regular part of our behaviour, but there is certainly a greater chance of that now than there was before and there are far more people who feel that a referendum is a useful tool in particular circumstances.'[4] As Leader of the Opposition Mrs Thatcher mused about the possibility of using referendums on issues affecting trade unions. The group Conservative Action for Electoral

Reform (CAER) expressed an interest 'in exploring the future use of referenda'[5] and came to see it as one of a number of desirable constitutional reforms: 'An elected Upper Chamber with real and usable powers, the proper use of referenda, a Bill of Rights and in a more limited sphere, P.R. for Local Government elections are all tributaries of the same river and the success of one will contribute to the success of all.'[6] In 1978 a Conservative Committee on the Referendum, chaired by Nicholas Edwards, recommended the introduction of a Constitution (Fundamental Provisions) Bill 'which would provide for a referendum before any fundamental change in the Constitution occurs'.[7] In 1981 the Secretary of State for the Environment, Michael Heseltine, sought to use referendums as a political weapon. As part of his Local Government Finance Bill of that year, he proposed that any local authority which wished to levy a Supplementary Rate would have to submit such a proposal to a referendum of domestic ratepayers. (However, support for referendums was not widespread among Conservative MPs and, following persistent criticism from backbenchers, the Government made known on 25 November 1981 that it would not proceed with the proposal.) On 14 December 1981 the House of Lords gave a second reading to a Constitutional Referendum Bill introduced by Conservative peer Lord Alport. The bill, explained Lord Alport, would make obligatory the holding of a referendum before a bill containing provisions to abolish the House of Lords or to diminish its legislative powers could proceed beyond third reading in the House of Commons. For the Government, Baroness Young opposed the bill. Such a matter was not best left to a Private Members' Bill, she said. Such a measure would need to be based on some agreement between the parties. At that time, she said, there was no sign of such agreement.[8]

Though the use of referendums — and their proposed use in 1981 — has been viewed as based on political expediency, a number of politicians have argued the case for referendums *qua* referendums. Among those who have advocated referendums on principle have been Conservative MP Philip Goodhart,[9] Liberal MP Jo Grimond (whose advocacy led him to support the referendum on the EEC), and Labour Member Tony Benn.[10] The most persuasive and recent support has been that emanting from an academic, Vernon Bogdanor. In his book *The People and the Party System*, he argues the case of the wider use of referendums. Such use, he contends, 'could offer real benefits in the operation of British politics'.[11] It would act as a powerful weapon against what Lord Hailsham categorised as an 'elective dictatorship': major changes would be impossible unless there was a popular consensus for them. 'In doing this, the referendum could improve the quality of the relationship between government and people; and that constitutes the central argument in favour of its wider use.'[12] Such enthusiasm is not universally shared.

Opposition to the use of referendums has been variously expressed. Members of Parliament, on the whole, are none too keen, including many who reluctantly acquiesced in that held on the question of continued EC membership (Harold Wilson being among them). In her first speech as Leader of the Opposition Mrs Thatcher argued forcefully against them, though her later musings suggest some modification in her approach. One of the leaders of the Social Democratic Party, Roy Jenkins, has been a consistent opponent, having resigned as deputy leader of the Labour Party in 1972 on the issue of Labour's support for an EC referendum. One of the most forceful opponents of a referendum in 1975 was Labour academic and MP John Mackintosh. Many Conservative MPs were vehement in their opposition to Mr Heseltine's proposal in 1981 for local referendums.

Given the disagreement on the value of referendums, a disagreement which appears to run through rather than between parties, what constitute the essential arguments for and against the more regular use of such devices?

THE ARGUMENTS FOR

The arguments for the more regular use of referendums are various. The referendum, it is argued, can be to the benefit of the people both as a participatory and an educative device; it serves to enhance consent. It can provide a clear answer on a single issue in a way that a general election cannot. It could well serve to strengthen, not weaken, the position of the House of Commons. It could serve to improve the quality and the legitimacy of the major measures of government. Also, its wider utilisation would not be incompatible with the British Constitution. Rather, it would be incompatible with an over-rigid party system, some of the defects of which it seeks to overcome.

A referendum campaign could serve to educate the public on the issue in question. In the debate on the EC referendum in 1975, voters were circulated with leaflets detailing the case for a 'yes' vote and for a 'no' vote. In the devolution referendums in Scotland and Wales 'many voters seem to have made up their minds how to vote upon the basis of a careful appraisal of the legislation offered to them, ignoring party cues and the interests of the parties which they supported'.[13] Such debate could also encourage some public spirit, as might be argued in the instance of the EC referendum. A referendum, as Dicey himself noted, 'would bring men to the ballot box who now hardly vote at all'.[14] Encouraging popular interest and allowing the electors to pass judgement could not only encourage a greater awareness of the issues in question but also reinforce consent for the political system.

The issues raised during a general election campaign are often many and varied. Though an elected government may claim a mandate for whatever programme was embodied in its election manifesto, it cannot demonstrate definitively overwhelming popular support for any one particular proposal. A referendum would permit such support to be expressed. 'The difference between an election and a referendum', wrote Alderson, 'is between voting on a muddle of issues and on a clear one.'[15] A government may be especially keen to seek such support if its own ranks are divided. This point was emphasised during debate on the proposed EC referendum in 1975. In the Commons' debate on the Government's proposal, the Lord President of the Council and Leader of the House, Edward Short, declared: 'That is the essence of the case for having a referendum. Only by means of a referendum can we find out whether the British people do or do not consent to our continued membership. A General Election could not give us this answer, because this is an issue within the parties, not between them.'[16] By putting a single and, as far as possible, unambiguous question to a referendum, one can obtain the judgement of the electors on that issue. In so far as one can isolate one issue from others, a referendum allows such isolation.

It has been argued that a referendum, far from weakening the House of Commons, could actually strengthen it. As far as the constitutional position is concerned it has been contended that so long as referendums remain advisory rather than binding, they do not undermine the concept of parliamentary sovereignty.

One of the characteristics of this Parliament [said Mr Short in 1975] is that it can never divest itself of its sovereignty. The referendum itself cannot be held without parliamentary approval of the necessary legislation. Nor, if the decision is to come out of the Community, could that decision be made effective without further legislation.[17]

Even if legislation were passed providing for a referendum to be binding, Parliament would retain the power to repeal that legislation. Furthermore, the use of referendums could prove to be a backbenchers' weapon. Vernon Bogdanor has argued that backbenchers could insist upon the introduction of a referendum clause as a condition for supporting a particular measure, as happened in the instance of devolution. 'In such circumstances, the referendum can prove an important addition to backbench power, enabling MPs to propose a popular veto on legislation without endangering the survival of the government which in general they support.'[18]

A referendum could serve also to improve the quality and legitimacy of major government measures, while at the same time serving to limit an otherwise unrestrained Government. Knowing that a measure may be submitted to the judgement of the electors may encourage Government to be more sensitive to the provisions of the measure. Backbenchers may stand a greater chance of getting amendments accepted: 'the government will have an incentive to accept reasonable amendments if they increase the likelihood of the legislation gaining public endorsement'.[19] Furthermore, the measures themselves will carry greater legitimacy in the eyes of the electors, given that they themselves have given express and direct assent to those measures. Referendums would overcome Rousseau's objection, expressed in *The Social Contract*: 'Every law the people have not ratified in person is null and void – is, in fact, now a law.' Referendums constitute now the only manageable means of obtaining such ratification.

Perhaps the most heavily emphasised argument for referendums in recent debate has been that they constitute a potential check upon an over-mighty single-party government, an argument most cogently argued by Vernon Bogdanor. As he contends, referendums would provide not so much a spear but rather a shield. The people would be called upon not to initiate a proposal but to assent to a proposal put before them on the authority of Parliament:

It is clear that the referendum, as hitherto used in Britain, must be a conservative device; for it provides an extra check against government, an additional protection to that given by Parliament. . . . Thus the role of the electorate is essentially negative. The referendum is an instrument of protection and not of change.[20]

A referendum has the effect of limiting government by effectively disjoining executive and legislative functions: the government ceases to have unfettered control of the latter. Referendums would provide a form of security which in other countries is provided by a written constitution. They could be used, in effect, to entrench particular parts of the Constitution against parliamentary majorities. This point was realised and developed by the Conservative Party Committee on the Referendum in 1978. At an early stage, the Committee 'reached the unanimous conclusion that it was as a constitutional safeguard that the referendum was most urgently needed':[21] it recommended the introduction of a Constitutional (Fundamental Provisions) Bill which would provide for a referendum before any fundamental change in the Constitution occurred. And Vernon Bogdanor brings the argument full circle to emphasise the relationship of this point to that of maintaining consent:

To the extent that the referendum is an entrenching device, it acts as a deterrent to government, a disincentive to legislate in the particular area in which it protects. . . . It then becomes clear that by ensuring that legislation cannot be passed against the will of the electorate, the referendum can be an instrument for securing consensus. . . . Thus a government, however large a majority it may enjoy, is prevented from carrying legislation which arouses the active disapproval of the electorate. In such a situation the referendum serves to encourage the politics of agreement.[22]

Thus, far from doing violence to the British Constitution, referendums would serve to restore to it the balance previously provided by a House of Commons not dominated by party government and a House of Lords untrammelled by the provisions of the 1911 and 1949 Parliament Acts. The Constitution would be restored, not destroyed, and the consent of the population maintained.

ARGUMENTS AGAINST

The case for the more regular use of referendums has been variously assailed. The arguments employed against it have been many and varied, and they may usefully be categorised under three headings: constitutional, practical, and political. Referendums have been attacked for running contrary to certain principles of the Constitution, for being expensive devices which fail to achieve their purpose, and for constituting means for pursuing potentially illiberal causes.

The most sustained opposition to referendums on constitutional grounds was that expressed by Mrs Thatcher in her first major parliamentary speech as Leader of the Opposition. She marshalled her attack under four heads: first, parliamentary sovereignty; second, collective responsibility; third, representative Parliament; and, fourth, the consequences for treaty obligations which have already been assumed.[23] In so doing, she brought together the main criticisms levelled at referendums by other opponents.

Mrs Thatcher observed that there was no power under the British Constitution which could come into rivalry with the legislative sovereignty of Parliament. 'To subject laws retrospectively to a popular vote suggests a serious breach of this principle.'[24] And, as she went on to observe, to subject laws prospectively before the final assent of the popular vote suggests the use of a different rule to validate laws. To have a number of referendums would create a new rule. 'We should be saying that some proposals require popular ratification and others do not. Without a written constitution one might ask: which proposals and what kind of measures?'[25]

The problem of determining the criteria by which to assess whether or not a measure should be subjected to a referendum is one which has plagued the advocates of referendums. In 1911 the Unionists sought to distinguish between 'ordinary' and 'constitutional' legislation,[26] a distinction which the Party Committee on the Referendum in 1978 also sought to establish.[27] 'Constitutional' measures should be subject to a referendum, ordinary legislation should not. The problems with seeking to draw such a distinction have been conceded by Vernon Bogdanor. He noted that it would be difficult for an authoritative list of constitutional issues to be drawn up which enjoyed the allegiance of diverse political viewpoints: a list drawn up by one government would offer a standing invitation to be amended by a subsequent government of a different political hue. The basic problem, as he admitted, was that the attempt to codify rules is essentially prescriptive; it cannot be neutral between different political viewpoints.[28] Furthermore, 'in Britain constitutional issues can easily arise out of seemingly non-constitutional legislation'.[29] A good recent example would be the attempt by Mr Heseltine to provide for local referendums under the provisions of his 1981 Local Government Finance Bill: opposition to the proposal was based essentially on constitutional points. Given this problem, Bogdanor rather cavalierly suggests that there is no need for *a priori* rules for determining when a referendum is to be held. The same point is made in a report emanating from a Hansard Society conference on the subject. Potential referendum subjects being so varied and controversial, 'it would be neither prudent nor practicable in a general enabling law to specify the categories of bills that either were open to referendum or had to be subject to referendum. The categories could not be defined in a simple way that would preclude argument.'[30]

The problem with failing to determine in advance the criteria by which referendums may or may not be held is that the decision as to their use will be taken on an *ad hoc* basis, the primary criterion being that of political expediency. Absent clear authoritative criteria as to what may be submitted to a referendum, there is the danger that important legislation which imposes some burden upon politically or economically powerful groups may not be regarded as legitimate by those at whom it is directed, unless first approved by the people in a referendum. The argument employed to defend the EC referendum as a 'once only' referendum on the grounds that it was being held on a 'unique' issue was quickly shattered, both in argument — 'In a real sense every political issue and, indeed, every individual member of our society is unique'[31] — and in practice, with the holding of the referendums on devolution in 1979. The use of referendums has entered British constitutional practice but with no clear and certainly no definitive delineation as to when they may or may not be employed. Should proposed reform of the House of Lords be submitted to a referendum? Should a proposed withdrawal from the EC be so submitted? Should a measure which is deemed to infringe civil liberties be subjected to the judgement of the people in the same way? If so, why? And who is to decide?

In the debate on the EC referendum in 1975, Mrs Thatcher also detected an inconsistency in the claims of referendum supporters. She observed that the Lord President of the Council, Mr Short, had said that the people must have 'the final say'. That, she said

is inconsistent with his earlier remark that the referendum did not derogate from parliamentary sovereignty. If it does not derogate from parliamentary sovereignty, it is Parliament which has the final say. He said that his pledge was that the British people should have the final say. That shows our constitutional difficulty in discussing this subject and in taking decisions before we have thought about them properly and considered all the consequences.[32]

The point was a well made one.

Mrs Thatcher's second point concerned the convention of collective ministerial responsibility. In the EC referendum the convention had been suspended in order that a number of Cabinet Ministers could

campaign for a 'no' vote. No Government, argued Mrs Thatcher, could
be properly accountable to Parliament unless it acknowledged a collective responsibility with regard to main matters of policy. 'We now face
a new system. If the Government cannot agree, gone is the discipline of
resignation, gone is the principle of accountability to Parliament. The
new doctrine is to pass the buck to the people.'[33] In so far as referendums
may be resorted to by Government to resolve internal disagreements,
the convention of collective ministerial responsibility – central to the
relationship between Government and Parliament (see above, Chapter
2) – is dispensed with.

This point leads on to Mrs Thatcher's third point: the effect of
referendums on representative government. Parliament comprised a
body of elected representatives, chosen by the people to discuss and
deliberate on Government proposals. Members of Parliament, Mrs
Thatcher argued, could consider the interests of minorities and see how
separate measures fitted into the whole. Referendums would undermine Parliament's position.

This point was developed even more forcefully by Labour MP and
academic, John Mackintosh. 'The fundamental assumption behind the
referendum', he declared, 'is that this House does not adequately
represent the feelings of this country.'[34] Hence, decisions were referred
to the decision of the people. A referendum on one important issue
made it difficult to deny one on another. Furthermore, a referendum
would perpetuate a confusion between government by debate, thought,
reflection and decision in the House of Commons with a head count of
the people.[35] Reasoned debate in an informed House would give way to
a national vote, based on a national campaign which would not enjoy
the same advantages.

Members of Parliament would, as Paul Rose argued, be asked to
abdicate their responsibilities,[36] an abdication for which a number of
Members failed to detect much support among their constituents. 'There
are many people in my constituency', declared one, 'who are bewildered
by the issues and would prefer the guidance of Parliament. That has not
been sufficiently stressed in the debate.'[37] According to Julian Critchley,
far from strengthening backbenchers, referendums would 'only acceler-
ate the decline in standing and influence of Members of Parliament and
of the House of Commons'.[38] By transferring the 'final say', *de facto*
if not *de jure*, to the people, Parliament would effectively lose its most
long-standing function, that of legitimisation.[39] The net effect of what
Mackintosh characterised as a drift towards a plebiscitary approach to

political decision-making would be an undermining of the concept of representative democracy and decision-making in a representative chamber.[40] It was, declared Mackintosh in 1975, 'a defeat for the parliamentary system of government'.[41]

Mrs Thatcher's fourth point concerned treaty obligations. It was a point specific to the EC referendum. She knew of no country in the Western world, she said, in which a referendum could be used to override a treaty obligation. 'Such a step would have a damaging effect on Britain's standing in the world.'[42] John Mackintosh made a related point which had a wider relevance. If a referendum affecting a treaty obligation went against the advice of the Government, the result being accepted by the Government, ministers could find themselves pursuing a policy in dealings with other countries which earlier they said was inadvisable. 'That', declared Mackintosh, 'would be utterly irresponsible in the technical sense of the word because they would be carrying on a policy for which not they but the referendum device was responsible.'[43]

The arguments employed against referendums on constitutional grounds are thus not inconsiderable. To these must be added a number of practical objections. For one thing there is the difficulty of posing a fair question, as well as the problem of isolating that question from others that may impinge upon the minds of voters. As Geoffrey Rippon pointed out in opposing a referendum on EC entry in 1972, a simple referendum would not necessarily provide an accurate reflection of electors' views on British membership: there would be those who were for entry on the terms negotiated, those who were for entry after renegotiation, and those who were against on any terms.[44] (There would presumably also be those who were for entry virtually regardless of the terms negotiated.) Similar problems arose in the devolution referendum in Scotland in 1979. Did the result demonstrate that Scottish voters were narrowly divided on the Government's specific devolution proposals or on the principle of devolution? And how were the abstentions (given the 40 per cent threshold requirement) to be interpreted? The dispute surrounding the ballot for the 1975 EC referendum demonstrated some of the serious problems associated with devising a question acceptable to the different parties involved.[45]

Other practical objections advanced against referendums include the cost of holding them (the administrative costs of the EC referendum totalled £5 million), a cost seen as not justified by the likely limited impact of such devices and the fact that the binding decision *de jure* has to and should be made by another body, Parliament. Furthermore,

a problem conceded by proponents of referendums is that of determining criteria to ensure a fair campaign between the two sides involved.
As early as 1911, Clifford Sharp drew attention to the fact that opinion
could be swayed by those with wealth and control of the media. 'For it
is clear', he wrote, 'that wealthy vested interests that can control the
Press must always be able to influence the electors far more easily than
they can influence any reasonably honest and public-spirited representative assembly.'[46] In the 1975 referendum the advocates of a 'yes'
vote included, according to Tony Benn, 'all but one of our national
newspapers and the entire business community'.[47] The income and
expenditure of the EC supporters greatly exceeded that of the anti-EC
campaigners.[48]

The two most weighty practical arguments that can be employed
against referendums are two that have been conceded by Vernon
Bogdanor. For one thing, a referendum will not necessarily determine
a question once and for all, any more than a vote in the Commons is
likely to. This is borne out by the referendums actually held to date.
British membership of the European Communities remains an issue on
the political agenda (see above, Chapter 8). Referendums failed to
resolve the issue of devolution (Chapter 9) and that of the constitutional
position of Northern Ireland (Chapter 10). Given this, the argument for
referendums as entrenching devices is undermined. Measures may be
entrenched against the whims of party government but not against the
transient whims of the electorate. For another thing, though referendums
may serve to enhance consent, they do little to contribute to resolving
the country's problems. As Bogdanor himself readily conceded, a referendum 'cannot do much to solve the social and economic problems
which are central to this country's failure as an industrial nation'.[49]
Any impression given to electors that referendums could serve such a
purpose would serve ultimately to undermine the value of such devices
for enhancing consent.

Over and above constitutional and practical arguments, there are a
number of political objections that have been expressed to the use of
referendums. These were expressed most succinctly by Roy Jenkins in
1972 when he resigned as deputy leader of the Labour Party on the
issue. 'Once the principle of the referendum has been introduced into
British politics', he wrote, 'it will not rest with any one party to put a
convenient limit to its use.'[50] Referendums could be used against the
progressive causes – such as abolition of capital punishment – for
which the Labour Party stood. Indeed, this objection leads on to one

of constitutional significance: referendums could be used against minorities. This point was recognised by Mrs Thatcher. 'I believe', she said, 'that if we have a referendum system, minorities would not receive anything like such a fair deal as they have under the existing system.'[51] The tyranny of an 'elective dictatorship' could give way to the tyranny of the electoral majority. Many opponents of referendums would prefer to trust to the House of Commons — or to some other safeguard, such as a Bill of Rights — the protection of minority rights. Far from protecting such rights, referendums could constitute a threat to them.

CONCLUSION

Advocacy of the regular use of referendums will ensure that the subject does not disappear from political and academic debate. Few important political bodies, least of all the main political parties, have been won over to favour with any enthusiasm the principle of referendums. Nonetheless, failure to win the intellectual argument will not necessarily act as a conclusive bar to the future employment of referendums. A referendum may yet again be the product of political expediency, chosen by the Government as the least objectionable means of achieving a particular goal. From the perspective of British constitutional history, such a development would have few claims to novelty.

NOTES

1   See, especially, David Butler and Uwe Kitzinger, *The 1975 Referendum* (Macmillan, 1976) and Anthony King, *Britain Says Yes* (AEI, 1977).
2   *HC Deb.*, 942, c. 1541—8. See also *HC Deb.*, 944, c. 597—606.
3   *HC Deb.*, 948, c. 619—24.
4   *HC Deb.* 6th series, 2, c. 1254.
5   *CAER: Aims and Structure* (CAER, n.d.).
6   Anthony Wigram, *Constitutional Reform Now* (CAER, n.d.).
7   *The Referendum and the Constitution*, Old Queen Street Paper, *Politics Today*, 16, 12 Sept. 1978 (Cons. Res. Dept, 1978), p. 299.
8   *The Times*, 15 Dec. 1981.
9   See P. Goodhart, *Referendum* (Tom Stacey, 1971).
10 For his early advocacy, see *Speeches by Tony Benn* (Spokesman Books, 1974), pp. 95—113, 119—30.
11 V. Bogdanor, *The People and the Party System* (Cambridge University Press, 1981), p. 93.
12 *Ibid.*

13   *Ibid.*, p. 84.
14   Quoted in S. Alderson, *Yea or Nay? Referenda in the United Kingdom* (Cassell, 1975), p. 1.
15   Alderson, *op. cit.*, p. 63.
16   *HC Deb.*, 888, c. 292.
17   *HC Deb.*, 888, c. 293.
18   Bogdanor, *op. cit.*, p. 76.
19   *Ibid.*, p. 81.
20   *Ibid.*, p. 69.
21   *The Referendum and the Constitution*, pp. 288–9.
22   Bogdanor, *op. cit.*, p. 71.
23   *HC Deb.*, 888, c. 310.
24   *Ibid.*
25   *Ibid.*
26   See Goodhart, *op. cit.*, p. 37, and Bogdanor, *op. cit.*, pp. 27–8.
27   *The Referendum and the Constitution*, pp. 288–92.
28   Bogdanor, *op. cit.*, pp. 73–4.
29   *Ibid.*, p. 73.
30   *Referendums: Guidelines for the Future* (Hansard Society, 1981), p. 7.
31   Richard Wood MP, *HC Deb.*, 888, c. 332.
32   *HC Deb.*, 888, c. 305.
33   *HC Deb.*, 888, c. 311.
34   *HC Deb.*, 888, c. 414.
35   *HC Deb.*, 888, c. 414.
36   *HC Deb.*, 888, c. 336.
37   Miss Janet Fookes MP, *HC Deb.*, 888, c. 417. See also c. 336.
38   *HC Deb.*, 888, c. 408.
39   See Philip Norton, 'The House of Commons and the Constitution: The Challenges of the 1970s', *Parliamentary Affairs*, 34 (3) Summer 1981, p. 259.
40   John Mackintosh, 'Attitudes to the Representative Role of Parliament', in John P. Mackintosh (ed.), *People and Parliament* (Saxon House, 1978), p. 3.
41   *HC Deb.*, 888, c. 417.
42   *HC Deb.*, 888, c. 314.
43   *HC Deb.*, 888, c. 416.
44   *HC Deb.*, 835, c. 277.
45   See Butler and Kitzinger, *op. cit.*
46   *The Case Against the Referendum* (Fabian Tract 155, 1911), quoted in Goodhart, *op. cit.*, p. 53.
47   Tony Benn, *Arguments for Socialism* (Penguin, 1980), p. 105.
48   See *The Financial Times*, 8 Oct. 1975.
49   Bogdanor, *op. cit.*, p. 92.
50   *The Times*, 11 Apr. 1972.
51   *HC Deb.*, 888, c. 314.

12

Electoral Reform

Adversary politics and natural justice?

The Constitution is sometimes viewed as being the product of some natural or evolutionary process, fashioned by dispassionate minds free of the pressure of sordid day-to-day politics. This, as we have seen, is not the case. Similar observations could be made about the electoral system. Though in the 1950s and 1960s there was a tendency to view the parliamentary election process as a 'settled' one, based on principles on which all could agree, the historical reality is that the rules governing who votes, how and where, have been subject to piecemeal and sometimes abrupt change, that change not uncommonly being the outcome of partisan political pressure. The franchise was variously extended because of demands for the vote from those denied it. Disraeli's 1867 Reform Bill was the product of political calculation rather than the inspired outgrowth of democratic ideals. The 1918 Representation of the People Act can be seen as a consequence of a reaction to the national sacrifice in the First World War: men and women who had worked and fought for their country could hardly be denied any longer the right to vote. (Indeed, Lloyd George took the opportunity to ensure that 19-year-old servicemen were included in the measure, an attempt to exploit as much support as possible in the 'coupon election' of that year.[1]) In 1968 a Speaker's Conference on Electoral Law recommended that the voting age be lowered from 21 to 20 years. A Cabinet Committee set up to consider the matter decided to support the recommendation, rather than an alternative proposal for the age to be 18 years, for sheer partisan reasons: it feared that to lower the voting age to 18 would increase the number of votes received by the Nationalist movements in Scotland and Wales.[2] (In the event, it was decided to lower it to 18 because of a precipitate statement by the Lord Chancellor, Lord Gardiner.[3]) These examples are selective but serve to make the point.

Similar observations could be made about the how and where of elections. The redrawing of electoral boundaries has rarely been free of dispute. Post-war boundary changes recommended by the Boundary Commissioners have for one reason or another incurred the criticism of parties, both locally and nationally.[4] The most contentious revision was that recommended by the Commissioners in 1969, the result of which would reduce the number of city-centre seats. Given that such a change would not be to the advantage of the Labour Party, the Labour Home Secretary James Callaghan introduced a bill to provide that the recommendations be implemented only in the case of Greater London and a few cases of gross over-representation. (The pretext employed was that the redistribution should await the redrawing of local government boundaries.) The bill was emasculated in the House of Lords and then abandoned. Instead, Mr Callaghan laid the recommendations of the Commissioners before Parliament, as he was required to do, but then advised Labour MPs to vote against them, which they did.[5] The recommendations were not approved until the next Parliament. More recently the 1981 recommendations of the Boundary Commissioners have proved also a point of political contention.

Of especial importance for our purposes, the use of the so-called 'first-past-the-post' method of election in single-Member constituencies has not been universal either in its acceptance or its application. The use of such a method in single-Member seats became the rule as a result of the 1885 Reform Act. It was, as Michael Steed noted, 'the product of inter-party bargaining',[6] reflecting the balance of interests at that time. Prior to that time, two- or three-Member seats had been common. Though reduced significantly in number in 1885, they did not disappear completely: a number of double-Member seats survived (e.g. Blackburn) until the 1950 general election. Likewise, the method of election. The first-past-the-post method became the rule but was not employed in all seats until 1950. Until then, the single transferable vote was employed in elections for University seats. With the abolition of the University seats this method of election disappeared from the electoral system at the parliamentary level. However, pressure for some new method of voting to replace the 'first-past-the-post' system has been a feature of the political landscape for some time. Various proposals for reform were advanced in the nineteenth century and again in this. A Royal Commission on Electoral Systems in 1910 recommended the use of the alternative vote and a Speaker's Conference in 1918 recommended the alternative vote in most seats and the use of the single transferable vote in boroughs returning three or more Members. Disagreement between the two Houses, plus Cabinet caution, was largely responsible for a failure to implement the Conference's recommendations.[7] To meet a commitment to the Liberal Party, the minority Labour Government in 1931 introduced a bill to provide for the alternative vote. The bill failed in the House of Lords and the 1931 election then intervened. The bill and its fate reflected prevailing party political considerations and strengths. The Liberals favoured the introduction of the single-transferable vote while Labour favoured no change at all; a compromise was the use of the alternative vote. The Conservatives opposed any change and, not being beholden to the Liberals, were able to use their majority in the Lords to reject it.[8] Since then, most Labour and Conservative politicians have not favoured a change in the electoral system. As the beneficiaries of the existing method of election, they have seen little need to do so. Liberals, by contrast, have been staunch advocates of electoral reform.

After 1950 many may have been forgiven for thinking that the electoral system had reached a settled position. The principle of 'one man, one vote' had been finally achieved (plural voting and University seats having been abolished), the Boundary Commissioners had the duty to recommend seats with roughly-equal electorates, and all adults with certain limited exceptions enjoyed the right to vote. The Liberals may have preferred a different system, but they were considered to be politically insignificant, an insignificance enhanced by the existing electoral system. Furthermore, many perceived the first-past-the-post method of election as having desirable consequences: it encouraged the return of a Government with an overall majority. It was thus central to the Westminster model of government (see Chapter 5), a model in favour both in Britain and abroad.[9]

The 1950s constituted a period of relative prosperity for Britain. Living standards were rising and more and more people were obtaining houses and consumer goods previously considered luxuries. The constitutional framework of Britain could not be considered responsible for such developments, but so long as people were content there was little incentive to criticise the form of government that was Britain's lot.[10] In the late 1960s and the 1970s this was to change. Britain began to experience economic and political difficulties. Increasingly, the existing parties and government seemed unable to cope adequately with the problems now facing the country. More and more electors began to look to other parties or a change in the form of government, or both, to effect some remedy. The electoral system became caught up in this process. Increased support for minor parties at the two general elections of 1974 demonstrated that the existing electoral system did not guarantee majority government: the results served also to highlight the disparity between the votes cast for a third party and the number of seats won. Pressure for electoral reform began to increase. The traditional Liberal argument in favour of a system based on proportional representation (PR) was to be joined by one derived from the analysis of the existing system as encouraging 'adversary politics'. Whereas the former argument was directed primarily to the question of consent, the latter was directed both to consent and the efficiency of government.

Prior to the 1970s there were two long-standing bodies which favoured electoral reform: the Liberal Party and the Electoral Reform Society.[11] In the 1970s these were to be joined by a number of newly formed organisations. In May 1974 a body called Conservative Action for Electoral Reform (CAER) was founded by Mr Anthony Wigram and in 1976 a Labour Study Group on Electoral Reform came into being. Also formed in 1976 was a National Committee for Electoral Reform (NCER) to co-ordinate the campaign of the party groups and also to act as a force for reform on its own account, both in and out of Parliament. A Student Campaign for Electoral Reform was also formed, operating under the auspices of the NCER. Whereas the Electoral Reform Society had been notable for the dearth of Conservative MPs (none) and Labour MPs (one) among its leaders,[12] MPs were prominent in the new organisations. Both Vice-Presidents of CAER are MPs and the organisation has its own parliamentary group; in its most recent literature it claims to have 37 Conservative MPs as members.[13] Though advocating reform on grounds of fairness and as a means of ending the effects of 'adversary politics', the literature emanating from these bodies is not silent on the partisan implications. 'The present electoral system', declared Anthony Wigram, 'could easily give power to a Socialist Party controlled by an extreme left wing group. . . . We have the power to extinguish the possibility of extreme left wing Government indefinitely [i.e. by PR] – we must make full use of this opportunity.'[14] A tract by Austin Mitchell MP for the Labour Campaign for Electoral Reform was directed explicitly to demonstrating that 'Electoral Reform is Right for Labour': Labour, he argued, gained least from the existing system.[15] The Liberals and the new Social Democratic Party are both committed to electoral reform, aware that it provides them with a much greater opportunity than the existing system to form, in alliance, a lasting government. Although such perspectives may appear unusual to those weaned on the post-war Westminster model, they are not surprising when viewed in historical perspective.

THE CASE FOR REFORM

The argument for a reform of the electoral system, primarily the introduction of PR, is two-fold: first a system of PR would be fairer than the existing one; second, it would put an end to 'adversary politics' and the iniquities that currently flow from that. An electoral system based on PR would likely encourage greater participation in the political system and would help encourage greater efficiency in allocating resources through producing a centre-coalition government enjoying popular support.

The argument based on fairness has been advanced for some time by the Liberal Party and by the Electoral Reform Society. The existing method of election, coupled with the distribution of party support in the country, favours disproportionately the two major parties. It produces only a very rough correlation between the proportion of votes cast in the country for a party and the proportion of seats received by that party in the House of Commons. A third party whose candidates obtain several thousand votes in each of the constituencies that it contests without coming top of the poll in any, can amass a national vote numbering in the millions without winning any seats at all. This is virtually the position in which the Liberal Party has found itself since its demise as a major party in the 1920s. In the February 1974 general election, the Liberals garnered 19.3 per cent of the national vote but achieved only 2.2 per cent of the seats in the Commons. A similar disparity occurred in the general elections of October 1974 and May 1979. By contrast the Labour Party in the October 1974 election obtained the votes of 39.2 per cent of voters but achieved an overall majority of seats. In May 1979 a Conservative Government was returned with the votes of 43.9 per cent of those going to the polls, Mrs Thatcher enjoying an overall majority of more than 40 in the House.[16] The distribution of party support nationally and as between constituencies can, under the existing electoral system, result in the votes of most electors being cast for losing candidates (as is clear from the foregoing figures and has been the case since the 1930s), in one party obtaining fewer votes than another, yet receiving more seats, as happened in 1951 and Februrary 1974, and in the phenomenon of the 'wasted votes'. Votes cast for Liberal candidates in contests in which the contest is effectively between the Conservative and Labour candidates, and for a losing candidate in a safe seat, are often termed as wasted: they not only do not affect the outcome of the election, it is well known that they will not affect the outcome. It is contended that such consequences are not only unfair to minor parties (and to major parties if getting a plurality of votes but not seats nationally) as well as to those casting 'wasted' votes, but also undermine consent for the political process. Knowing that votes cast for the candidates of their choice will have no effect, many on the electoral roll become disenchanted or apathetic. The 1970s witnessed a growing number of electors staying away from the polling booths.[17] Recognition of the unfairness of the electoral system raises doubts as to the legitimacy of the process as well as encouraging one to ask what the purpose of elections is, a fundamental question often previously ignored. If the method by which MPs are returned is considered to be of dubious legitimacy, then the legitimacy of the House itself may be questioned and hence its output of legislation. 'Since our electoral system produces unrepresentative MPs and an unrepresentative parliament, it is hardly surprising when laws are passed that most of us heartily dislike.'[18]

The answer to this problem is deemed to rest in a new electoral system based on PR. The argument is that it would be a fairer method of election, ensuring that parties achieved parliamentary seats in proportion to the number of votes cast. By being seen to be a fair method, it would increase public confidence in the electoral process. Since no votes would be 'wasted' votes (at least under the single transferable vote system), it would encourage those on the electoral register to go to the polls. And by producing a fairer electoral system it would strengthen support for the political system as a whole. Anticipating criticisms of PR, its proponents point out that it would not necessarily entail a larger House of Commons nor, if the mixed or Additional Member method of election (single-Member constituencies as at present plus a regional list system) was employed, would it put an end to the close relationship between a Member and his constituency. In short, the benefits of the existing system would be retained while dispensing with its deficiencies. 'The whole thing', declared the Electoral Reform Society, 'would be a lot fairer to all parties and to all voters.'[19]

To this argument has been added one that can be subsumed under the heading of the 'adversary politics' thesis. This thesis gained ground in the mid-1970s and was developed by a number of academics, notably Professor S.E. Finer and S.A. Walkland.[20] They diagnosed Britain's political malaise and its economic problems as being in part the result of a dysfunctional party and electoral system. Under the existing system the two main parties fought for the all-or-nothing spoils of a general election, with the successful party once in office governing with an eye to the next election. In office, an overall majority in the House of Commons ensured that the government could do virtually what it wished. However, with only a small shift of votes at the next election it could find itself in the political wilderness. The result, according to Professor Finer, was a combative relationship between the parties, which he styled adversary politics, and policy discontinuity as a consequence of changes of government. In office, 'each party has to reach some compromise between its left and right wings, in order to preserve its unity in the face of the Opposition',[21] the compromise falling between the two extremes in each party. Hence, the consensus position in the Labour Party could be described as being on the centre-left of the political spectrum and that in the Conservative Party as being on the centre-right; neither falls in the centre of the political spectrum, which would appear to be located at some mid point between the attitudes of the two parties.[22] When in office, a party thus pursues 'off-centre' policies. At the next or a subsequent general election the other party is returned to office and proceeds to reverse the measures of its predecessor, pursuing instead off-centre policies from the other side of the political spectrum. Such shifts from one party in office to another, with consequent changes of policies, produce uncertainty in economic management and industrial policy, uncertainty that undermines the confidence of investors and makes it difficult for industrialists to plan ahead. In the words of one industrialist, Viscount Caldecote:

Changes in markets and technology come relatively slowly and can usually be anticipated by efficient forecasting, and plans made accordingly. But changes in Government policy, stemming from a new party coming into power after a general election, are unpredictable until the result of the election is known, and cannot therefore be included in any logical planning process. Since such changes are unrelated to the basic market and technological factors they interfere with the task of industry in creating real wealth and prosperity for the community.[23]

The adversary relationship between the parties and the changes of power may make for 'exciting politics', according to one critic, but they produce 'low-credibility government strategies, whichever party is in power'.[24] The position was exacerbated in the 1970s, when the reformers argued that the parties were becoming even more polarised than before as well as electorally less relevant. A minority Labour Government

pursued vigorously a programme well to the left of the political con-
tinuum, reversing many of the policies of the previous Heath Government. The Thatcher Government returned in 1979 was seen to be
pursuing a rigid monetarist policy, rejecting the approach and the
measures of its predecessors. A future Labour Government was seen
as likely to pursue a clearly left-wing programme, one that could be
described as well off-centre. All this was made possible by the existing
electoral system, despite the fact that no party since 1935 has received
an overall majority of votes cast at a general election.

Proportional representation was seen as providing an answer to this
problem. Not only would it be a fairer method of election (the adversary
politics school is in accord with the Liberals on this) but it would help
also to ensure continuity in policy as well as producing a more effective
House of Commons. This would result from the fact that, on current
voting patterns, no party would obtain an overall majority of parliamentary seats. Hence a coalition would be necessary to form a government commanding a majority in the Commons. Furthermore, as one of
the main parties would 'have to co-operate with a party or parties taking
a more central political stance' in order to arrive at such a coalition,
'there would be a greater moderation in policy'.[25] The result would be
a moderate-coalition government, responsive to the centrist views of
the electorate, and one able to ensure continuity in policy given that it
would be less likely to be turned out of office at an election; as Professor
Finer has noted, a swing of 1 per cent under a system of PR would
result in the loss of only about six seats. So, a stable and moderate
government would be Britain's lot. Furthermore, the undermining of
the strong party hold of the electoral system would free candidates of
the power of the party electorates. By preference voting, electors could
choose between different candidates adhering to the same party label.
'Voters . . . can elect a more independent or "rebel" member of a party
if they wish. So no party machine can "discipline" any Member by
depriving him of his seat. Distinguished independents have a much better
chance of election.'[26] This would allow Members greater freedom of
action in the Commons itself, putting them in a better position to call
government to account and to engage in more rational meaningful
debate on Britain's problems. Not only would the House be enabled to
fulfil a more effective role in relation to the executive, it would also
derive greater moral authority by virtue of the fairer means by which
it was returned. Though not suggesting that the introduction of PR
would solve Britain's economic ills or all the defects attributed to the

House of Commons, the reformers nonetheless argued that it would at least help. 'I certainly don't believe that a change to PR would solve industry's problems overnight', wrote Lord Caldecote, 'but at least we would have a chance of solving those problems by a process of progressive change in a much more stable and receptive political environment than at present.'[27]

The case for electoral reform built up during the latter half of the 1970s and as can be seen acquired a formidable line of argument in its favour. Opinion polls suggested that a majority of electors considered the existing system to be unfair.[28] The Liberal Party found allies in the newly formed Social Democratic Party in 1981. Both committed themselves to electoral reform in the event of their forming a government or, in the event of a hung Parliament, to making its implementation a condition of supporting one of the other parties. The issue was clearly one of importance on the political agenda. However, electoral reform by no means commanded unqualified support and certainly not among the two main parties.

THE CASE AGAINST

The arguments in support of electoral reform have been countered on a number of grounds. The fairness argument has been countered with the contention that PR would have consequences which are far from fair. Also, it would produce a form of government inimical to the interests of effective government. The adversary politics thesis has been attacked on the grounds that it is unproven, in part inconsistent and in part empirically unsound.[29] PR would not have the effect its proponents claim.

The fairness argument has been countered at two levels. First of all, PR would facilitate the election of the least objectionable candidate rather than the one most strongly preferred by a plurality of voters. As Ferdinand Mount expressed the point:

PR transfers the power of making and unmaking governments from the most committed to the least committed voters; a candidate who gets the most first preferences may be dethroned in favour of a candidate who gets the most second and subsequent preferences; the most-desired is to be defeated by the least-objected-to. Is that really fairer and is it always advantageous?[30]

While conceding that PR would likely have such an effect, advocates of reform would counter that the result was indeed fair and that under the existing electoral system it is the least committed voters who make the difference at an election.

Second, and perhaps more substantially, it has been argued that the effect of PR would be to put a disproportionate amount of power into the hands of one or more minor parties and produce a government not knowingly chosen by the electorate. To form a government, as Professor Finer conceded, a major party would have to combine with another party to achieve a parliamentary majority. Opponents of PR contend that dependence on this partner would give it a position in policy-making not justified by its size. The point has been argued succinctly by George Cunningham:

I do not see . . . that it is more democratic to give to the small party or parties in the Centre a predominance of political power than it is to give it to the larger parties to the Left and Right of them. . . . If we were to have PR there would be a large Labour Party and a large Conservative Party and a small — though larger than now — Liberal Party. The Liberal Party would sell its support to whichever of the other two parties it wanted to see in Government. The Labour and Conservative Parties might alternate as they do now, but the Liberals would always be there. A Liberal can be forgiven for wanting that to happen, but let him not say that it is democratic when the middle of the see-saw is always in power simply because it is in the middle of the see-saw.[31]

As evidence to support this proposition, the influence wielded by the Liberal Party during the short-lived Lib—Lab Pact of March 1977 to May 1978 is cited. Though the influence wielded by the Liberal Parliamentary Party may not have been great relative to the power of the Government, many Labour MPs considered it disproportionate to the number of Liberal MPs; Tribune MPs in particular objected to the willingness of ministers to pay attention to Liberal MPs in preference to the Tribune Group.

Furthermore, a government could be produced as a result of bargaining between the parties after a general election. The result could be an alliance and policies not put before the electorate. Only in the event of an alliance formed before an election would the electors have the opportunity to express their wishes and the chances of such an alliance being formed with agreed policies are considered not great. The decision of the Liberal Party to agree to an alliance with the Social Democratic Party in 1981 pointed up some of the difficulties. The day after the

Liberal Party Assembly voted overwhelmingly to support such an alliance, delegates voted for a motion on defence which was at variance with SDP policy on the subject. What, then, would be the defence policy of a Liberal/SDP Government, assuming always that the alliance achieved an overall majority?

The traditional argument for proportional representation is also countered on the grounds that fairness alone should not be the sole criterion employed to determine the mode of election in Britain. This again raises the fundamental question as to the very purpose of holding elections. Defenders of the existing system incline to the view that it should attract the designation of being democratic inasmuch as it is based on the principle of 'one man, one vote', while working in favour of producing majority government. Strong single-party government is central to the Westminster model of government and adherents to that model are unwilling to jettison one of its mainstays. Given a choice between an allegedly fairer method of election and one that tends to encourage majority government, supporters of the Westminster model plump for the latter.

Other arguments employed against PR are that it would be difficult to understand and might destroy the intimate relationship in each constituency between electors and 'their' MP. The present system has the merit of being easy to comprehend and produces an MP with a responsibility for a specific constituency. Both these factors may be deemed to enhance support for the present method of election and hence the political system. Understanding and hence consent for the political process might be undermined if electors were faced with a complex voting system and (under the single transferable vote) with multi-Member constituencies. Advocates of the Additional Member method of election counter with the fact that their preferred method would retain the MP—constituency link. Opponents point out that the use of the regional list system would result in two classes of MPs (those elected by constituencies, those elected on the list) and that those chosen by the list system would find themselves chosen either on the basis of party patronage, thus strengthening the party machines, or on the basis of having failed to gain election in a constituency. While basically there would be nothing wrong with that, the stigma of being a constituency 'reject' would further encourage the perception of first- and second-class Members of Parliament.

As to the adversary politics thesis, the case expounded by its supporters has been subjected to various sometimes substantial criticism.

Professor Finer and others provide little empirical data to support the contention that the electorate is more centrist in opinion than parliamentary parties.[32] Furthermore, Finer would appear to confuse the distinction between what constitutes the 'ideological centre' and what constitutes 'common ground' among the electorate. The implication of what he writes is that what constitutes 'common ground' among electors can be equated with the 'centre ground' of British politics. However, as Ivor Crewe and Bo Sarlvik have pointed out, the 'centre ground' refers to a location along an ideological dimension, whereas the 'common ground' refers to the distribution of electors along that dimension. On certain issues, Crewe and Sarlvik found electors grouping to the right or left of the ideological centre: on what they termed populist—authoritarian (what would popularly be termed law and order) issues, their research revealed that 'the electorate clearly does stand on *common* ground: there is almost nothing to distinguish the views of the various electoral groups. But it is a ground far to the right of the ideological mid-point: the electoral centre does not coincide with the ideological centre.'[33] This distinction undermines an important part of the adversary politics argument.

The reformers' critique of the existing system of 'adversary politics' is also open to question. The instances of policy reversals instanced in Finer's work — a new Government coming in and reversing the policies of its predecessor — are clearly important but they are near-exhaustive in number, and exceptional. An important study by Professor Richard Rose has shown that party government in Britain is best characterised by the 'dynamics of a moving consensus'.[34] A party in Opposition usually opposes only a small proportion of the bills introduced by the Government. When it is returned to office, it accepts (that is, it does not seek to reverse) most of those measures which it opposed in Opposition. Indeed, it will itself often reintroduce measures introduced initially by its opponents, but left stranded because of the calling of the election. Such bills outweigh the number that a new Government seeks to repeal.[35]

Not only is the reformers' analysis of the existing political process a dubious one, so too is their contention as to the effect that PR would have. Indeed, there is a potential incompatibility between two of the likely effects that they postulate. On the one hand, it is argued that PR would facilitate a coalition government, one capable of ensuring policy continuity. On the other hand, part of the electoral reform argument is that PR would result in a loosening of party ties. Under the existing norms of party behaviour, MPs have displayed an occasional willingness to vote independently of their parties. At least one supporter of electoral reform has appreciated the consequences that more independent voting behaviour on the part of MPs could have. In consequence of PR, conceded Joe Rogaly, there would probably be 'shifting coalitions' of Members 'that would alter aspects of this or that law, or even decline to pass whole new laws, or introduce laws of their own'.[36] In many respects, no bad thing, but not something that augurs well for stable government and policy continuity, especially if Members are responsive to volatile public opinion.

Finally, looked at from the perspective of efficiency and consent, the reformers' argument can be undermined by speculation as to the form of government that PR would facilitate, extrapolating figures based on current voting behaviour. (Speculating on the basis of existing voting patterns is nonetheless an extremely questionable exercise; under a new electoral system, voting behaviour may well be very different.) Given that, on current voting patterns, no party would be returned to office with an overall majority, there are three possibilities. One is minority government, that is, one party assuming office without an overall majority. British experience of minority governments suggest that they are relatively weak and short-lived, as was the case in 1924, 1929 and 1974. The experience of the 1974–9 Labour Government was somewhat unusual and it could be described as something of a quasi-minority government: for much of the time it had the support of Nationalist MPs and for 1 year that of Liberal MPs. Nonetheless, it led something of a hand-to-mouth existence, unsure of what it could or could not get through the House and wondering where its majority was to come from in the next vote of confidence. A minority government would be unlikely to enhance support for the political system or be more efficient than governments formed via the existing electoral system.

The second possibility is a weak coalition government, weak because it comprises shifting partners or partners who have difficulty in reaching agreement. A feature of such a government could be a sense of insecurity and policy shifts. Again, it could hardly be argued that such a government would be more efficient or increase consent among the electorate.

The third possibility, the one apparently envisaged by many PR advocates, is that of strong coalition government, strong because the partners are committed to it and in agreement on policy. The danger here is that one could come close to permanent coalition government if the support enjoyed collectively by the partners to the coalition was well in excess of 50 per cent of the electorate. This point was well recognised by William Waldegrave.[37] Indeed, it would appear to be necessary to ensure policy continuity. One then has the danger not only of government taking its hold on office for granted but of a lessening of consent among those who support parties excluded from government. At present, 70 or 80 per cent of electors vote for one of the two main parties; at some stage these electors know that their party will form the government. The proportion of electors voting for parties standing little chance of forming a government is about 20–25 per cent. Under PR, it would be possible for two parties enjoying, say, 60 per cent of the vote to form a government and remain in government for the foreseeable future, assuming no major erosion in its voting support. The proportion of electors voting for parties not likely to hold office would be about 40 per cent, much higher than the proportion under the present system. Hence, consent might have to be sacrificed for the efficiency which adherents to the adversary politics thesis crave. And as to which of these three possibilities is likely in the event of the introduction of proportional representation, it is difficult to say. The experience of foreign countries, so often called in aid by supporters and opposers of reform, offers little guide. Much depends on the political culture. As the essays in *Adversary Politics and Electoral Reform* reveal, no clear conclusions emerge from practice abroad. PR works well in certain countries; not in others. 'Hitler . . . came to power under a very sensible PR system. Does that make PR responsible for Nazism and World War Two? Is the instability of Italian politics due to its system of PR, or not, or what?'[38] Foreign experience thus offers little guide; British experience of forms of PR (as utilised on occasion in Northern Ireland) is too slight to enable generalisations to be drawn. As Taylor and Johnston concisely conceded, 'We are literally working in the realms of speculation.'[39] So much, then, for the confident presumptions of electoral reformers.

CONCLUSIONS

The issue of electoral reform is one that has emerged on the political agenda in recent years and now stands as policy on the part of the Liberal and Social Democratic Parties. It is opposed by most Members of the two main parliamentary parties. That this should be so is not surprising. The Conservative and Labour Parties are the beneficiaries

of the existing system and it is unlikely that their MPs would wish to
vote themselves out of their own seats, which would be the effect in
some cases of voting for a bill to introduce proportional representation
for parliamentary elections. Fearing that if the principle is conceded
for other elections it will be more difficult to deny it for elections to
the Commons, MPs have voted down proposals for PR to be employed
in elections to the European Parliament and, under the ill-fated Scotland
and Wales Bill, to Assemblies in Scotland and Wales. At the moment,
there is no political will to achieve the goal of electoral reform,[40] at
least not on the part of those currently forming a majority in the House
of Commons.

The possibility of Britain attaining a new method of electing its MPs
is nonetheless far more likely to be achieved in the not too distant
future than was previously thought to be the case, including by this
writer. The formation of the Social Democratic Party, its apparent
support among electors, and its alliance with the Liberal Party has
greatly increased the chances of electoral reform being carried through
by a future Government. In the event of a Liberal/SDP alliance gaining
a parliamentary majority, a bill to introduce PR would be one of the
first that it would introduce. In the event of the SDP/Liberal alliance
holding the balance of power in a 'hung' Parliament, electoral reform
would be demanded in return for providing support and hence a parliamentary majority for one of the other parties. Changes of electoral
behaviour in recent years have in any event increased the likelihood of
hung Parliaments. Hence, the possibility of electoral reform is a serious
one. For some, that is good news. For others, it is bitterly unwelcome.

NOTES

1   Philip Norton, 'The Qualifying Age for Candidature in British
    Elections', *Public Law*, Spring 1980, p. 56.
2   Richard Crossman, *Diaries of a Cabinet Minister*, vol. III (Hamish
    Hamilton/Jonathan Cape, 1977), p. 92.
3   Norton, *loc. cit.*, pp. 58–9.
4   See G. Alderman, *British Elections* (Batsford, 1978), pp. 60–2.
    S.A. de Smith, *Constitutional and Administrative Law* (Penguin,
    1961), pp. 250–2.
5   Alderman, *op. cit.*, p. 62; de Smith, *op. cit.*, pp. 251–2.
6   M. Steed, 'The Evolution of the British Electoral System', in S.E.
    Finer (ed.), *Adversary Politics and Electoral Reform* (Wigram,
    1975), p. 40.
7   See Steed, *loc. cit.*, p. 46, and 48.

8   See *ibid.*, p. 49.

9   See Philip Norton, 'The US Congress in Comparative Perspective: The British Parliament', Paper presented to the APSA Conference, New York, Sept. 1981, pp. 9–10; L.D. Epstein, 'What happened to the British Party Model?', *American Political Science Review*, March 1980, 74 (1), p. 11.

10 See Norton, 'US Congress in Comparative Perspective', p. 9.

11 There were some short-lived groups also which advocated reform: e.g. the Anti-Socialist Front (1958) and the Labour Campaign for Local Election Reform (1968). See Steed, *loc. cit.*, p. 50, footnote 2.

12 The only non-Liberal MP serving as a Vice-President in 1965 was E. Lance Mallalieu, Labour MP for Brigg. See the officers as listed in *Memorandum to the 1965 Speaker's Conference on Electoral Reform from the Electoral Reform Society* (Electoral Reform Society, 1965). Significantly, Mr Mallalieu was a former Liberal MP.

13 CAER: *Aims and Structures* (CAER, n.d.).

14 *Constitutional Reform Now* (CAER, n.d.).

15 Austin Mitchell MP, *Labour and Electoral Reform* (Labour Campaign for Electoral Reform, Tract 2, Sept. 1980).

16 Figures derived from D. Butler and D. Kavanagh, *The British General Election of 1979* (Macmillan, 1980), pp. 353–4.

17 S.E. Finer, *The Changing British Party System 1945–1979* (American Enterprise Institute, 1980), pp. 58–9.

18 Student Campaign for Electoral Reform leaflet, *Get Your Politics in Proportion* (Student Campaign for Electoral Reform, n.d.). Note also the observations of H.M. Drucker, 'Two-Party Politics in the United Kingdom', *Parliamentary Affairs*, 32 (1), Winter 1979, p. 31.

19 'How to Get a Fair Deal with your Vote', *ER Leaflet No. 51* (Electoral Reform Society, n.d.).

20 S.E. Finer (ed.), *Adversary Politics and Electoral Reform* (Wigram, 1975); S.A. Walkland, 'Whither the Commons?', in S.A. Walkland and M. Ryle (eds), *The Commons in the Seventies* (Fontana, 1977), ch. 12; 'The Politics of Parliamentary Reform', *Parliamentary Affairs*, 29 (2), 1976, pp. 190–200; and 'Parliament and the Economy in Britain', *Parliamentary Affairs* 32 (1), Winter 1979, pp. 6–18.

21 Finer, *Adversary Politics and Electoral Reform*, p. 12.

22 See Finer, p. 13, for a diagrammatic representation of this point. Rose (ed.), *Studies in British Politics*, 3rd ed. (Macmillan, 1976), pp. 441–5.

23 Viscount Caldecote, *Industry needs Electoral Reform* (CAER, 1980).

24 Michael Shanks, *Planning and Politics* (PEP, 1977), p. 92. See also Walkland, 'Parliament and the Economy in Britain', *loc. cit.*, pp. 16–18.

25   Finer, *Adversary Politics and Electoral Reform*, pp. 30–1.
26   'Fair Voting is Safer', *ER Leaflet No. 40* (Electoral Reform Society, n.d.).
27   Caldecote, *op. cit.*
28   According to CAER, polls showed that 70 per cent of Conservative voters considered the present system unfair. CAER: *Aims and Structures.*
29   See Philip Norton, *The Commons in Perspective* (Martin Robertson, 1981), pp. 222–4.
30   Ferdinand Mount, 'Roy Stops the Clock', *Spectator*, 1 Dec. 1979, p. 4.
31   *HC Deb.*, 6th series, vol. 2, co. 1257.
32   See Norton, *The Commons in Perspective*, p. 223.
33   I. Crewe and B. Sarlvik, 'Popular Attitudes and Electoral Strategy', in Z. Layton-Henry (ed.), *Conservative Party Politics* (Macmillan, 1980), p. 258 (emphasis in original).
34   R. Rose, *Do Parties make a Difference?* (Macmillan, 1980), conclusions.
35   See Rose, *op. cit.*, table V.7.
36   J. Rogaly, *Parliament for the People* (Temple Smith, 1976), p. 5.
37   See W. Waldegrave, 'The Case Against', *Spectator*, 25 Oct. 1975.
38   Mount, *loc. cit.*
39   P.J. Taylor and J. Johnston, *Geography of Elections* (Penguin, 1979), p. 433.
40   Taylor and Johnston, *op. cit.*, p. 433.

13

A Bill of Rights

A Constitutional Catch-22?

Britain already has a Bill of Rights, that enacted in 1689. That measure effectively consolidated the Constitutional Settlement of 1688 and stipulated the relationship between the Crown and Parliament. Though it embodied references to what would be considered basic rights, it was not a 'Bill of Rights' in the sense in which the term has been used in contemporary debate. There is no agreed definition of the term, though the most sensible is probably that provided by Lord Lloyd of Hampstead. 'To my way of thinking', he wrote, 'a Bill of Rights is a document in the nature of a constitutional code of human rights which are enumerated comprehensively, though in a form which will be of necessity somewhat broad and generalised.'[1] So defined, Britain lacks a Bill of Rights. There is no enumerated code of human rights embodied, via statute, in British constitutional law.

In Britain the foundation of individual rights may be aptly described as negative. That is, an individual has the right or freedom to do whatever he or she likes, so long as it is not in violation of the law of the land. Individual liberty is secured by judicial decisions determining the rights of individuals in cases brought before the courts. It is the judges who have established the rule that 'everyone charged with a criminal offence shall have the right to be presumed innocent until proved guilty according to law', that no-one is 'to be compelled to testify against himself', and the rights of peaceful assembly, freedom of association and the right to a fair hearing.[2] 'Such human rights as the law of this country recognises', wrote F.A. Mann, 'are almost entirely judge-made and in many instances involve no more than a rebuttable presumption to the effect that Parliament is unlikely to have intended to interfere with or destroy them.'[3]

Under the doctrine of parliamentary sovereignty, Parliament could if it so wished interfere with or destroy such judge-made rights. Many writers have often ascribed to Parliament the function of protecting individual liberties, but there is nothing in constitutional law to prevent a majority of parliamentarians failing or refusing to fulfil such a function; some authorities do not even list it among the functions of Parliament.[4] It is the potential for Parliament to abrogate judge-made rights that underpins the current controversy.

In *The Power of Parliament*, Ronald Butt contended that it was MPs 'acting independently' that enabled the House of Commons still to act as guardian of the liberties of the subject.[5] But what if MPs cease or lose the ability to act independently? Does not the strength of party cohesion and executive dominance deny that independence? And given the pre-eminence of the Commons in the triumvirate of the Queen-in-Parliament, what is there to act as a counterweight to an executive-dominated Commons? With greater government intervention in economic and social matters, especially but not exclusively in the 1960s and 1970s, such fears began to find expression. Some pointed to certain Acts as evidence that such fears had been realised. A growing body of opinion began to assert that Parliament was no longer a reliable body for protecting (either by positive action or, more usually, by refusing to enroach upon) the liberties of the individual and that such protection must be provided by another means. A number of prominent individuals began to advocate a Bill of Rights, preferably with entrenched provisions, as the most effective and desirable way of defending fundamental human rights. Such a proposal was obviously of great constitutional import. If entrenched — its provisions being beyond amendment by ordinary legislative process (a plurality vote in both Houses and formal assent by the Crown) — the doctrine of parliamentary sovereignty would be at an end; indeed, to achieve entrenchment, the doctrine had to be circumvented and effectively dispensed with. Even without entrenchment, a Bill of Rights would create new opportunities for judges — more so than that provided by the 1972 European Communities Act — and would herald a new dimension to British Constitutional Law.

Advocacy of a Bill of Rights began to be heard in the latter half of the 1960s. Three pamphlets in particular helped bring the subject into the realms of political debate. Anthony Lester's Fabian Society Tract, *Democracy and Individual Rights*, appeared in 1968. It was followed, in 1969, by John MacDonald's Liberal Party pamphlet *A Bill of Rights* and Quintin Hogg's *New Charter* published by the Conservative Political Centre.[6] It also became a matter of some parliamentary attention: two 10-minute rule bills to introduce a Bill of Rights were brought before the Commons in 1969 (one by Conservative MP Lord Lambton, the

other by a Liberal, Emlyn Hooson) and the same year Liberal Lord
Wade initiated a debate in the House of Lords on the 'need for protection of human rights and fundamental freedoms'.[7] Pressure for a Bill of
Rights in Britain built up during the following decade and was most
apparent in the years from 1974 onwards. It gained prominence
especially as a result of the support expressed in lectures by two prominent jurists: Sir Leslie (now Lord) Scarman in his 1974 Hamlyn
Lectures[8] and Lord Hailsham (formerly Quintin Hogg) in the 1976
Dimbleby lecture, expressing slightly different views to those he had
expressed in earlier years: he now favoured a written constitution for
Britain as well as a Bill of Rights.[9] The subject became one of much
discussion in academic journals[10] and also began to attract the attention
of the House of Lords. Lord Wade introduced a Bill of Rights in the
Upper House in 1976[11] and another in 1977. Following introduction of
the latter Bill, the House established a Select Committee to investigate
the subject. The Committee presented a report which explained the
arguments for and against a Bill of Rights; six of its members favoured
such a bill; five did not. In the new Parliament returned in 1979, Lord
Wade again introduced his bill: despite opposition from some peers it
passed through all its stages without a division.[12] It made no progress in
the House of Commons. Lord Wade re-introduced his bill the following
session and again secured its passage through the House. This time it
had a little more fortune in the Commons: Liberal MP Alan Beith
introduced it as a Private Member's Bill. However, debated on a Friday
in a thinly-attended House, it was talked out.[13]

Support for the introduction of a Bill of Rights appears to be
strongest among constitutional lawyers and judges, members of the
House of Lords, and among Conservatives and Liberals. Such categories,
as will be apparent, are not mutually exclusive. Indeed, the concentration of Conservative and Liberal lawyers in the House of Lords provides
the most concentrated, structured and influential support for a Bill of
Rights. Opposition appears to be strongest on the left of the political
spectrum, though by no means confined to the Labour Party. A number
of Conservatives and some prominent lawyers are among opponents of
the measure as well. The current Government has adopted a somewhat
neutral position. It believes the subject to be one requiring all-party
discussion before any measures can be introduced,[14] but has not shown
much enthusiasm in initiating such discussion.

Such a line-up on this issue is not surprising. Constitutional lawyers
with their attachment to the rule of law view with increasing horror the

encroachment of government (via its parliamentary majority) upon rights they consider should be protected. Conservatives seek to limit what they perceive to the the Socialist threat of increasing government encroachment in the lives of citizens; and, from the perspective of the House of Lords, a Bill of Rights would serve as a limit upon government which the Upper House can no longer effectively provide. Labour politicians, though not unanimously,[15] oppose a Bill of Rights, seeing it as a device engineered by its opponents to limit the introduction and implementation of radical measures. Some Conservatives and a number of lawyers oppose it because they fear it could weaken the judiciary by bringing it into the political arena or because they adhere to the doctrine of parliamentary sovereignty. Others oppose it, quite simply, on practical grounds: they do not believe it would have the desired effect if implemented, assuming that such a measure could be implemented. The Government, for its part, is more concerned with other things, and as a Conservative Government sees little need for such a measure. Mrs Thatcher is reputed to have once expressed her view thus: When Labour is in power, a Bill of Rights would be ignored, when the Conservatives are in power such a bill would be unnecessary. Though fears about a future Labour Government may encourage many Conservatives to maintain their support for such a measure, it seems unlikely that action will be forthcoming, at least not with any enthusiasm or speed, at an official level in the immediate future.

THE CASE FOR

The case for a Bill of Rights has been variously expressed. The best known and perhaps most pungent argument has been that advanced by Lord Hailsham in his 'elective dictatorship' thesis. In Parliament, he contended, there was now one effective chamber, the Commons. That chamber was dominated increasingly by the government, and the government was controlled by the Cabinet, which itself was often dominated by a few of its members. The Cabinet had at its disposal the Civil Service, providing it with resources and information that could not be matched by Parliament. The consequence was an all-powerful Cabinet, introducing measures which Parliament did not and could not challenge or consider effectively.

So, the sovereignty of Parliament has increasingly become, in practice, the sovereignty of the Commons, and the sovereignty of the Commons has increasingly become the sovereignty of the government, which in addition to its influence in Parliament, controls the party whips, the party machine, and the Civil Service. This means that what has always been an *elective dictatorship* in theory, but one in which the component parts operated in practice to control one another, has become a machine in which one of those parts has come to exercise a predominant influence over the rest.[16]

The predominant influence of the Cabinet in the political process was perceived as being especially dangerous as a result of the pressures on government in the post-war years and as a result of the general elections of 1974. Government impinged increasingly upon rights previously perceived as inviolable. Legislation in the fields of town planning, race relations, immigration and the prevention of terrorism was variously cited. The 1974 elections demonstrated that a government could be formed with a minority of seats in the House of Commons and a small plurality of votes in the election, yet obtain the passage of measures without taking account of its lack of support in the country.

Again and again in Parliament [said Jo Grimond] MPs hear that the Government is entitled to push through some measure because it was in their election manifesto. Even if the Government had a majority, that would be questionable constitutionally, but as the Government represents only about 25 per cent of the electorate it is obvious non-sense.[17]

Some of the measures which the Government *did* introduce in the period from 1974 to 1979[18] fuelled anxieties as to what a future minority Government *could* introduce. The fact that a Parliament could not bind its successors was not seen as a sufficient safeguard. As former Home Secretary Lord Carr of Hadley observed in the Lords, a minority government could introduce fundamental changes which could prove irreversible.[19]

Furthermore, the encroachment on individual liberties was not seen as the exclusive preserve of Government as such. As Alan Beith commented in introducing his Private Member's Bill in 1981, 'Not all threats come from Governments; they also come from private individuals and outside organisations.'[20] In his 1968 pamphlet John Macdonald had drawn attention to threats to privacy from phone-tapping, industrial espionage and computers. The following year Lord Wade's motion debated in the Lords referred to the 'threat to personal privacy resulting from technological advance', and the point has been pursued since by his Liberal colleagues in both Houses. Conservatives have shown a tendency to draw attention to the power of trade unions, in particular to the effect of closed-shop agreements, while civil liberties groups have tended to emphasise the threat from public bodies such as the civil service and the police and from private organisations, particularly in the form of discrimination against minority groups.

Given this perceived real and potential threat to fundamental human rights in Britain, what can be done to protect them? The answer, according to Lord Scarman and those who think like him, is a Bill of Rights. It is not one universally agreed upon by those who share his analysis of the threat. Some, such as Lord Carr, see electoral reform as a potentially more effective solution to the problem, as they believe it would remove the potential for extreme minority governments.[21] For those who advocate a Bill of Rights, such a measure would have a number of advantages. It would act as a restraint on infringements of personal rights, not only legally but also morally. Even if not entrenched, Parliament would be hesitant to pass a measure which clearly contravened the Bill of Rights. Indeed, the element of moral restraint is sometimes cited as making unnecessary the need to try to entrench the bill, thus avoiding the crucial and constitutionally thorny problem of overcoming the doctrine of parliamentary sovereignty. This point was put by Paul Sieghart. The argument about formal entrenchment, he wrote, need not trouble us too much:

The ordinary citizen, to whose vote at election time Parliament owes not only its legitimacy but its very existence, takes little notice of scholastic disputes of this kind. Once Parliament has given its word that it will not do something, or will do it only in certain circumstances, he would treat that as a binding promise. And any candidate who has broken that pledge – or threatens to break it if elected – would have to contend with some very strong feelings from his electors.[22]

The means by which a bill could be given formal pre-eminence over other legislation without destroying the concept of parliamentary sovereignty we shall consider in a moment.

Not only would a Bill of Rights protect individual liberties, it would provide a means of doing so more speedily than existing machinery: at the moment one can appeal to Parliament, where political considerations are likely to be paramount, or to the European Court of Human Rights, where decisions are reached in a matter of years rather than months.

'The machinery is extremely ponderous. . . . It is clear that however dilatory English courts may sometimes be, they do not take so long to reach their decisions.'[23] A Bill of Rights would have the advantage also of bringing Britain in line with its international obligations. Britain is a signatory of the European Convention of Human Rights, yet has not incorporated the provisions of the Convention into English law. Under Article 13 of the Convention each member state is required to provide an effective remedy 'before a national authority' for 'everyone whose rights and freedoms as set forth in this Convention are violated'. Enactment of a Bill of Rights would also put an end to what amounts to the washing of Britain's dirty linen in the glare of international publicity when cases are taken to the European Commission on Human Rights. Given that, typically, such a bill would incorporate broad and general principles, it would prove a flexible and adaptable tool,[24] not the rigid one envisaged by some critics. Also, as the journal of the National Council for Civil Liberties observed, it would serve also to strengthen bodies which existed for the purpose of protecting human rights.[25]

As to the content and method of enactment of a Bill of Rights, various proposals have been put forward. Some advocates have recommended an entrenched Bill of Rights, its provisions to take precedence over Acts of Parliament, such Acts to be declared invalid if contrary to the provisions of the Bill of Rights. In other words, the doctrine of parliamentary sovereignty would have to be done away with. This in the eyes of some critics would be a desirable result; indeed, the doctrine is seen as responsible for the existing problem. Various means for entrenching a Bill of Rights have been suggested: a Constitutional Convention and/or a referendum to approve a Bill of Rights after Parliament has agreed to it and dissolved itself are among the most prominent suggestions.[26] More recently, Professor H.W.R. Wade has propounded the novel idea that entrenchment could be achieved by an attitudinal change on the part of judges and a simple amendment of the judicial oath.[27] Such entrenchment would, of course, bring about a fundamental change in the British Constitution: parliamentary sovereignty would disappear as the cornerstone of the Constitution, parliament being replaced by a document and the courts as the protector and ultimate delineator of the rights of citizens.

To avoid the problems associated with entrenchment — its effect as well as the difficulty of its attainment — various authorities have recommended the incorporation into English law of the European Convention on Human Rights,[28] * such a measure to enjoy precedence over other Acts in the same way that European Communities law enjoys precedence under the terms of the 1972 European Communities Act. Such incorporation would kill two birds with one stone: it would enact rights on which there is much general agreement and it would give those rights priority over other enactments without dispensing with the doctrine of parliamentary sovereignty. The arguments for the European Convention to provide the basis for a British Bill of Rights have been succinctly put by Emlyn Hooson. The Convention has existed for 30 years; 'if there were major flaws in its drafting they could have come to light by now'.[29] It has for years created international obligations for the UK; to incorporate it would remove the many uncertainties relating to its status in English law. Justice for complainants would be much swifter than the present haul through the Convention procedure. The judges would have a body of case law which could be incorporated, giving them a firm basis from which to work. And, broad though its provisions are, 'the Convention would safeguard civil liberties more surely than the often elusive protection afforded by our law'.[30]

The Bill of Rights incorporating the European Convention could be given precedence over other legislation by a provision similar to that enacted in Canada: legislation is deemed not to have intended to derogate from the Bill of Rights, unless Parliament provides expressly that it is to operate notwithstanding the bill. Such a provision has been variously advocated, as for example by Peter Wallington and Jeremy McBride.[31] Anthony Davies and Graham Zellick have suggested a stronger provision, one stipulating that repeal or amendment of the Bill of Rights would have to be express and not covered by a *non obstante* 'notwithstanding' clause.[32] Hence, the bill could achieve precedence

---

* The Convention forbids torture, slavery, and compulsory labour; decrees that everyone has 'the right to liberty and security of person' (no-one to be deprived of liberty save in accordance with a procedure prescribed by law in defined cases) and that everyone charged with a criminal offence shall be presumed innocent until proved guilty according to law; and decrees that everyone has the right to respect for his private and family life, his home and his correspondence; that everyone has the right to freedom of thought, conscience, religion, expression, peaceful assembly and freedom of association; all these rights to be secured without discrimination on any ground such as sex, race, colour, language, religion, national origin and the like. Many of these rights are subject to broad qualifications (e.g. 'No restrictions shall be placed on the exercise of these rights other than such as are prescribed by law and are necessary in a democratic society in the interests of national security or public safety . . .').

for fundamental rights, the courts having the responsibility for determining when other Acts conflict with such rights. Such formal precedence, as we have noted, would be reinforced by the moral weight carried by the Bill of Rights. A Government would not easily contemplate introducing a measure which clearly ran counter to the Bill of Rights.

As the foregoing implies, interpretation of the Bill of Rights would be a judicial function. As we have observed in an earlier chapter, it is not axiomatic that the courts should fulfil such a role.[33] Nonetheless, most advocates of a Bill of Rights attribute it to the courts. Anticipating criticism of the suitability of judges for such a task, various writers have sought to draw out the experience and the qualities of members of the judicial bench to protect basic rights. 'Now I would rather trust my life or my liberty to Lord Denning than to Mr Michael Foot', wrote one journalist in a rather partisan manner.[34] Lord Scarman put the case somewhat more judiciously, arguing the case for a Constitutional, or Supreme Court.[35] As Wallington and McBride argued, such a Court would have the advantage of providing a bench with a breadth of experience and would also serve to draw fire away from established courts; it would avoid the 'politicization' of the rest of the judicial system.[36] Other criticisms of the capacity of judges to interpret a Bill of Rights have been countered by Professor Zander. As he points out, interpretation of Bills of Rights or written constitutions is not unknown to English judges (on the Judicial Committee of Privy Council), judges to some extent are already 'politicized', and a Bill of Rights would provide judges with the opportunity to prove the view they tend to espouse, namely that they themselves constitute the citizens' chief bulwark against the state.[37] As evidence of the latter, some observers would cite the various cases decided by the higher judiciary in the 1960s and, especially, the 1970s, as detailed earlier in our consideration of the judiciary. In short, interpretation of the Bill of Rights is deemed to be a function aptly and probably safely attributed to the judiciary.

All in all, then, advocates of a Bill of Rights can claim a strong and well-argued case for their cause. It is one which would not only put an end to problems generated by the existing political system but also would create popular consent for the system resulting from the changed conditions. Individuals would know what their rights were, those rights would be protected, and popular support for the Bill of Rights would provide a restraint upon any government considering an infringement of its provisions. It is a change which would contribute to Lord Scarman's proposed 'constitutional settlement'.

THE CASE AGAINST

Despite the arguments advanced in favour of a Bill of Rights, it is not a proposal which enjoys unanimous approval. As we have observed, opposition has been expressed from the left of the political spectrum as well as by a number of Conservatives; it is a proposal on which successive governments have failed to take action. Some of the grounds for this opposition we have already touched upon briefly. They encompass points of principle as well as practical considerations.

The primary argument against a Bill of Rights is that it would, be it entrenched (with extraordinary provision for its amendment) or with provision for its contents to take precedence over other legislation, remove from Parliament a decision-making capacity which rightly belongs to Parliament. Disputes as to encroachment on fundamental rights are essentially political disputes and must be resolved politically, not judicially.

The fact of the matter [declared Lord Lloyd of Hampstead] is . . . that the law cannot be a substitute for politics. The political decisions must be taken by politicians. In a society like ours that means by people who are removable. . . . If what we fear is political tyranny, then we must seek to control that by political means.[38]

Those who adhere to the doctrine of parliamentary sovereignty do so not because of its longevity (a claim made by some Bill of Rights supporters) but because it is considered to be appropriate to a democratic society. From the writings of those who express support for the doctrine, it is clear that not only do they consider the existing constitutional procedure to be appropriate in its own right but also because of failings in the arguments of those who wish to dispense with it. A Bill of Rights would not provide much protection against the wishes of a determined majority and entrusting such a measure to the care of the judiciary could be harmful rather than beneficial to certain rights. If rights are to be protected, one must look instead to Parliament. If Parliament is seen as not providing the protection — though some would argue that it did fulfil that protective function in the period from 1974 to 1979[39] — then the answer is not to look elsewhere but rather, as Robert Kilroy-Silk perceived, to strengthen Parliament.[40]

The argument for a Bill of Rights has been contested on a number of practical grounds. The most important of these can be identified as the absence of any agreement on the rights to be protected. Indeed, this is where one could argue that the Bill of Rights argument falls foul of a Catch-22 position. Because of contemporary economic and political pressures, a party in Government encroaches upon certain rights perceived by the other parties as being fundamental rights which should not be touched. To protect such rights from becoming a political foot-ball, a Bill of Rights with some form of entrenchment provision is proposed. Yet to be an effective and lasting measure, such an important constitutional change requires some degree of all-party support; other-wise, it too will become a political football. Yet that all-party support is not, indeed cannot, be forthcoming since it is party disagreement which underpins the desire for the measure. One party emphasises certain rights to be fundamental; the other parties emphasise other rights. Certain rights may conflict with others; some politicians would contest what political opponents consider to be basic rights. This point was well recognised by a Committee of the Society of Conservative Lawyers.

Unfortunately [they noted] we see no prospect whatever of sufficient all-party support for a Bill of Rights that could provide any effective safeguard of the rights that Conservatives, and many Liberals, believe to be crucial to a free society. On the contrary, the range of rights on which there is fundamental disagreement is frighteningly wide.[41]

It is this disagreement which has prompted calls for a Bill of Rights; the same disagreement prevents such a measure being formulated and enacted.

Evidence of disagreement as to what should be contained in a Bill of Rights is clear from the proposals put forward by supporters of such a measure. Much of the argument in favour has revolved around the inclusion of civil and political rights. Stephen Pogany has argued the case for the inclusion of social and economic rights.[42] Various services provided by the welfare state, he argued, had increasingly been regarded as belonging to citizens as of right, and hence should be protected.[43] Such an argument is received more favourably by Labour than by Conservative advocates of a Bill of Rights. Lord Hailsham argued that under his formulation, a Bill of Rights would have resulted in the striking-down of trade union legislation introduced by the 1974–9 Labour Government. Sir Keith Joseph argued that such a measure should place 'a constitutional limit on taxation, that is taxation on

incomes and property, during life and death'.[44] Hardly proposals that
would endear themselves to Labour politicians. Even the European
Convention on Human Rights does not provide a list of rights around
which supporters of a Bill of Rights can unanimously gather. Even
those who favour the Convention as the basis for a British bill are not in
complete agreement as to whether or not it should be incorporated
almost lock, stock and barrel or more selectively. Emlyn (now Lord)
Hooson, for example, appeared content to skip and dip among the
Convention's provisions in recommending the contents of a British bill:
Article 5(1)(e) on vagrants 'should not be introduced into our law; it
places far too much arbitrary power into the hands of the executive';[45]
Article 17 could be used to censor unpopular views and should not be
included; as for Article 11 on trade unions, 'the safest conclusion might
be to leave the Convention as it is; but there is endless room for debate
on this point';[46] and some of the rights protected by Article 14 are
already well provided for in British law. Hardly a resounding vote of
confidence for the full incorporation of the Convention into British
law; and the tone indicates the room for disagreement on the desirability
of the Convention's various Articles.[47]

Incorporation of the European Convention into English law would
thus create difficulties. Furthermore, some have contended that it
would be unncessary. Given that Britain is already a signatory of the
European Convention and that various rights have been embodied in
statute or judge-made law, there is little need to incorporate the document. To do so would create wider problems not justified by the
limited effect it would have upon human rights. As Professor R.J.
Lawrence observed, 'I doubt whether a United Kingdom Bill of Rights
incorporating only the rights in the European Convention would enhance our rights and freedoms to any substantial extent. It would,
however, entail profound changes in Parliament and the courts and
probably mean some increase in bureaucracy and public expenditure.'[48]
Adding, 'A more comprehensive Bill of Rights containing some social
and economic guarantees and restraints on trade union power would be
unlikely to succeed.'[49]

The effect of a Bill of Rights upon the courts, as touched upon by
Professor Lawrence, is also used as an argument against the introduction of such a measure. Whether based on the European Convention or
not, a Bill of Rights would almost certainly stipulate rights in very
broad terms. The effect would be to bestow wide powers upon the
body or bodies empowered to interpret it; in this case, the courts.

Indeed, given the broad and general nature of the rights to be found in such measures, the power would extend beyond that of interpretation. As Lord Boston of Faversham observed, 'If we took the course proposed by those who wish to incorporate the Convention, we would be opening up a wide variety of legislative policies in a very general way and handing them over to the judiciary for detailed *development* (not just interpretation) on such subjects as, say, race relations, freedom of speech, freedom of the press, privacy, education, and forms of punishment.'[50] In short, it would provide a considerable increase in the role and powers of the judiciary, much greater than those created by virtue of the 1972 European Communities Act. Such a development is viewed as a negative rather than a positive one. In part this is because it would, as we have seen, remove a decision-making capacity from Parliament, a capacity which it is argued it should retain. As Lord Boston went on to say, 'these are matters which, under our constitution, have been the province of our legislature',[51] the implication was that they should remain such. In part, it is because such powers would create problems if vested in the courts. Many on the political left object to the effect that the courts could or would have on radical legislation and economic rights; some observers are concerned as to the effect that having such a power would have on the courts.

The argument against vesting the courts with such powers has been succinctly put elsewhere: 'This country's judges are drawn from a very narrow social base; they are generally conservative in their views; and it is feared that a Bill of Rights will allow them to strike down "progressive" legislation.'[52] To many Conservatives, this is no bad thing; indeed, it is what a number seek to achieve. However, to radical politicians it is perceived as a serious threat. Lawyers, declared John Griffith, 'are now the most conservative professional group in society'.[53] Could not judges use the right of free expression, asked Joe Jacob, as an excuse for declaring a closed shop in the press to be contrary to the Bill of Rights?[54] 'Do we really want to give them an invitation to declare the Government's Trade Union and Labour Relations Amendment Bill as invalid?'[55] Given such suspicion of the judiciary, investing them with power to interpret a broadly-written Bill of Rights would clearly not have the effect of enhancing general consent for the constitutional procedure for resolving disputes. In particular, it would have the effect of undermining the courts. This is the worry of a number of observers, such as Lord Lloyd. 'To try to bring the judiciary into this sort of contest', he said, 'can only have one effect, and that is to destroy the standing of the judiciary in the eyes of the people as a whole.'[56] Far from helping protect the courts and certain rights, enactment of a Bill of Rights would toss them to the centre of political controversy. By interpreting a right in a way clearly at variance with the wishes of Parliament and the populace in general the courts could serve to generate pressures on the political system with even more dire consequences than those being experienced at the moment. In Britain, trade unions have tended not to be overly responsive to decisions expressed via the ballot box; they have proved even less responsive to negative decisions handed down by judicial bodies.

In short, decisions as to rights, and the resolution of cases where rights prove mutually incompatible, should rest with Parliament, not the courts. Such decisions are political, not judicial. To enact a Bill of Rights would be to introduce broad rights, the delineation of which would rest with the courts. Such a power could be used to hold back social advance. It could even be used to bolster executive decisions. So broad are the provisions likely to be, they can be made to mean whatever the judges think they ought to mean. This is as true of the European Convention as of any other document on which a British bill might be based. (The Convention 'provides wide exceptions to most of the rights which it guarantees';[57] indeed, it includes provisions for derogation in the event of war or national emergency.) Recent experience in Britain has suggested that the higher judiciary has not been unwilling to provide politically controversial decisions, in some cases substituting the judgement of the bench for that of ministers. Even if provision for extraordinary means of amendment could not be attained – that is, effectively dispensing with an essential ingredient of parliamentary sovereignty – the courts would still fulfil a more central and controversial role in British politics; the Constitution would acquire a judicial dimension greater than that accorded by the 1972 European Communities Act. Though supporters of a Bill of Rights would favour this, opponents find it objectionable. It would threaten support for the courts and undermine the (changed) Constitution. Even in the United States, the decisions of the Supreme Court in cases of constitutional interpretation can be politically contentious (and damaging); and Britain lacks the features which have provided the Supreme Court with its popular support, or at least popular acceptance that it is the legitimate body to decide cases of constitutional dispute.[58] There is thus seen to be little case for having a Bill of Rights, and even less case for having one with the power of interpretation being vested in the courts.

If Britain suffers from the effects of an 'elective dictatorship' the remedy must come elsewhere than from a Bill of Rights.

NOTES

1   Lord Lloyd of Hampstead, 'Do We Need a Bill of Rights', *The Modern Law Review*, 39 (2), March 1976, p. 122.
2   F.A. Mann, 'Britain's Bill of Rights', *The Law Quarterly Review*, 94, Oct. 1978, pp. 514—15.
3   *Ibid.*, p. 514.
4   See e.g. P. Norton, *The Commons in Perspective* (Martin Robertson, 1981), ch. 4.
5   R. Butt, *The Power of Parliament* (Constable, 1967), p. 437.
6   See Michael Zander, *A Bill of Rights?* (Barry Rose, 1975), pp. 5—10.
7   *Ibid.*
8   Sir Leslie Scarman, *English Law — The New Dimension* (Stevens, 1974).
9   Lord Hailsham, *Elective Dictatorship* (BBC, 1976). See also his articles in *The Times*, 2, 16, 19 and 20 May 1975, and his book *The Dilemma of Democracy* (Collins, 1978), especially chs. 20 and 21.
10 In addition to articles cited below, see also: e.g. Ian W. Duncanson, 'Balloonists, Bills of Rights and Dinosaurs', *Public Law*, Winter 1978; Tom Harper, 'Note on the Question of a Bill of Rights', *New Law Journal*, 124, 12 Dec. 1974; Arthus S. Miller, 'A Bill of Rights to Protect our Liberties', *Political Quarterly*, 47, April 1976; A.J.M. Milne, 'Should we have a Bill of Rights', *Modern Law Review*, 40, July 1977; B. Smythe, 'The Case for a New Bill of Rights: Taking Stock', *The Solicitors Journal*, 120, 14 May 1976; Arthur S. Miller, 'Does Britain Need a Bill of Rights?' *Guardian*, 7 Nov. 1975. For bibliographical references, I have found Simon J. Wilson 'Should Britain have a Bill of Rights?', third-year underdraduate dissertation, University of Hull Politics Department, 1980, to be helpful. For a useful published bibliography (up to 1976) see Wallington and McBride, citation below, appendix 5.
11 Lord Arran had also introduced a similar bill in 1970. A number of bills were introduced also in the Commons: by Sam Silkin from the Labour benches in 1971; by James Kilfedder, an Ulster Unionist, and Alan Beith, a Liberal, in 1975; and by Sir Freddie Bennett, a Conservative, in 1979.
12 See especially *HL Deb.*, 402, c. 999—1071 and *HL Deb.*, 403, c. 287—311, 502—9. For details of the Wade Bill, see Lord Wade, 'A Bill of Rights for the United Kingdom', *The Parliamentarian*, 61 (2), April 1980, pp. 65—71.

13   *HC Deb.*, 6th series, Vol. 4, c. 419–57 (8 May 1981).
14   See speech of the Solicitor-General, Sir Ian Percival, *HC Deb.*, 4,
     c. 445–9. Note also *HL Deb.*, 403, c. 287.
15   See e.g. Peter Archer, *Human Rights*, Fabian Research Series
     Pamphlet 274 (Fabian Society, 1969), and the Labour Party
     Discussion document, *United Kingdom Charter of Human Rights*
     (Labour Party, 1976). Various Labour MPs are among the
     supporters of a Bill of Rights.
16   Hailsham, *Elective Dictatorship*, p. 8 (my emphasis).
17   Quoted in L. Neville Brown, 'A Bill of Rights for the United
     Kingdom?', *The Parliamentarian*, 58 (2), April 1977, p. 82.
18   E.g. Trade Union and Labour Relations Bill, Dock Work Regula-
     tion Bill and the Housing Finance (Special Provisions) Bill. See
     also the list contained in 'Bill of Rights: Code of Liberties or
     Constitutional Charter?', *The Economist*, 8 Nov. 1975.
19   *HL Deb.*, 402, c. 1014.
20   *HC Deb.*, 4, c. 422.
21   See Lord Carr of Hadley, *HL Deb.*, 402, c. 1015. Lord Hailsham
     takes a contrary view, *Elective Dictatorship*, p. 13.
22   Paul Sieghart, 'Problems of a Bill of Rights', *New Law Journal*, 11
     Dec. 1975, p. 1185.
23   Zander, *op. cit.*, p. 21.
24   This and the preceding points are to be found in *ibid.*, pp. 18–25.
25   'Do we need a Bill of Rights?' *Civil Liberty*, 42 (2), April 1976, p.
     2.
26   See, e.g. Hailsham, *Elective Dictatorship*, pp. 15–16; also note
     Nevil Johnson.
27   H.W.R. Wade, *Constitutional Fundamentals* (Stevens, 1980), pp.
     37–9.
28   As e.g. Mann, *loc. cit.*, Zander, *op. cit.*, Hooson, *op. cit.*, and
     Charles L. Black Jr, 'Is there already a British Bill of Rights?',
     The Law Quarterly Review, 89, April 1973, pp. 173–5. Lord
     Scarman has also added his support. *HL Deb.*, 402, c. 1033. Also
     see *The Times*, 19 April 1980.
29   Emlyn Hooson, *The Case for a Bill of Rights* (no publisher, c.
     1977/8). p. 27.
30   *Ibid.*
31   P. Wallington and J. McBride, *Civil Liberties and a Bill of Rights*
     (Cobden Trust, 1976).
32   A. Davies and G. Zellick, 'How to make a Bill of Rights Work',
     The New Law Journal 120, 16 April 1970, p. 372.
33   See above, ch. 7. The point was recognised by Jo Grimond, 'The
     Abuse of Power', *Spectator,* 13 Dec. 1980, pp. 13–14.
34   Anthony Shrimsley, 'Righting the Wrongs', *NOW!*, 28 Nov. 1980,
     p. 23.
35   Scarman, *op. cit.*
36   Wallington and McBride, *op. cit.*, especially ch. 5.
37   Zander, *op. cit.*, pp. 40–5.

38 *HL Deb.*, 402, c. 1026.
39 Most notably, for example, the Dock Work Regulation Bill was emasculated as a result of defeats in both Houses; and the Government was defeated in its attempt to remove the disqualification from the Clay Cross Councillors for their failure to implement the 1972 Housing Finance Act.
40 R. Kilroy-Silk, 'Wrongs of the Bill of Rights', *Guardian*, 4 Feb. 1977.
41 Committee of the Society of Conservative Lawyers, *Another Bill of Rights?* (CPC, 1976), p. 11.
42 See S.I. Pogany, 'The Content of a Bill of Rights', *The Juridicial Review*, 23 April 1978, pp. 12–32.
43 *Ibid.*, pp. 20–21.
44 Sir Keith Joseph, *Freedom under the Law* (CPC, 1975), pp. 11–12.
45 Hooson, *op. cit.*, p. 29.
46 *Ibid.*
47 Wallington and McBride, for example, recommend incorporation of all the Articles, bar No. 17; they include in their draft bill all the provisions of Article 5. See Wallington and McBride, *op. cit.*, pp. 123–9. For some other problems associated with incorporation, see J. Jaconelli, 'The European Convention of Human Rights – the text of a British Bill of Rights', *Public Law*, 1976, pp. 226–55.
48 R.J. Lawrence, 'Rights and Remedies', in Colin Campbell (ed.), *Do we need a Bill of Rights?* (Temple Smith, 1980), p. 15.
49 *Ibid.*
50 Lord Boston of Faversham, 'Arguments Against a Bill of Rights', in Campbell (ed.), *op. cit.*, p. 25 (emphasis in original).
51 *Ibid.*
52 *Civil Liberty*, 42 (2), April 1976, p. 2.
53 J.A.G. Griffith, 'Judges and a Bill of Rights', *New Statesman*, 10 Jan. 1975, p. 38. See also Griffith, *The Politics of the Judiciary* (Penguin, 1981) and above, ch. 7.
54 Joe Jacob, 'Say "No" to a Bill of Rights', *Tribune*, 6 Feb, 1976.
55 *Ibid.*
56 *HL Deb.*, 402, c. 1026.
57 *Civil Liberty*, 42 (2), April 1976, p. 2.
58 Britan lacks common acceptance of Lockean values, values which (coupled now with history – it is too late to argue that the Courts should not have the power of constitutional review) provide acceptance of political disputes as being resolvable by a judicial process. See Louis Hartz, *The Liberal Tradition in America* (Harcourt, Brace & World, 1955), p. 9.

Conclusion

Approaches to Constitutional Reform

The past 10 years or so have been remarkable for the number of constitutional issues that have come on to the agenda of political debate in Britain. What has also been remarkable, albeit understandable, is the lack of familiarity with the language of constitutional debate. Discussion on the issues covered in this volume has not been informed by a critical constitutional awareness. The arguments employed in debate on one issue have seemed to bear little logical or coherent relationship to arguments employed on other issues. It is thus possible to view the discussion on constitutional issues as an unconnected series of disputes with no common thread running through them. To do so, though, would be misleading. The arguments for constitutional changes have not taken place in a vacuum. As we have commented in the introduction, the constitution cannot be studied with 'the politics left out'. The positions taken in debate by proponents and opponents of constitutional change have been informed by coherent sets of political values. The sort of society posited by one set of values leads to advocacy of certain constitutional as well as political and social structures and relationships. The concentration on political and social goals in recent history has led to constitutional reform taking a low priority in politicians' considerations. Failure to articulate a coherent approach to constitutional reform nonetheless does not signify the absence of such an approach. As constitutional issues have come on to the political agenda, so political values can be seen to have helped motivate as well as shape responses to them. Indeed, it is possible to identify at least six separate approaches to constitutional reform that currently exist. These approaches are not well defined, at least not in their articulation, but they are discernible. A delineation of them serves both to give some shape to the constitutional debate of recent years (and, indeed, contribute to an understanding of contemporary and future debate) and to draw out the relationship between the constitution and the political environment in which it is nurtured and which it, in turn, helps to influence. These approaches can be categorised as those of High Tory, Socialist, Marxist, Group, liberal, and Traditionalist. The purpose of this chapter is to provide a brief sketch of each.

HIGH TORY

This approach, sometimes called Natural Conservatism, defends the existing constitutional framework, arguing for things to be left as they are. It contends that what exists should remain because it has been accommodated in a settled view of the world. Its most articulate exponent in this century has been Lord Hugh Cecil. In his book *Conservatism*, published in 1912, he wrote:

Why depart from the known which is safe to the unknown which may be dangerous? None would be so mad as to run the risk without much search and scrutiny. And this means perplexity, effort, confusion of mind, weariness. Why not let it alone? Why be weary instead of at rest? Why rush into danger instead of staying in safety?[1]

Such an approach could claim much support at a time when the British Constitution was much admired, both at home and abroad. Its strength was reflected not in its articulation but in the belief that there was no need to articulate it. Only at times when the constitution was under challenge was there a need to provide an explicit defence of it.

Today, with the constitution under challenge from disparate sources, the High Tory view finds a number of exponents within the Conservative Party. Its clearest and most recent expression was to be found in the motion tabled in the House of Commons by Conservative MP John Stokes in April 1981:

That this House believes in preserving the unity of the United Kingdom and all the great institutions of the realm, namely the Monarchy, the Church, the Houses of Parliament, the judiciary, the Armed Services of the Crown and of the police; and deplores the attacks on these institutions by those who ought to know better.[2]

In his speech Mr Stokes, while conceding somewhat the possibility of some change, more so than his motion would suggest, nonetheless argued that the constitution had evolved organically, requiring little if any mechanical tinkering.[3] The most pertinent observation of Mr Stokes' High Tory approach was that made by then Labour MP Eric Ogden. From reading the motion, he said, he was of the view that Mr Stokes 'was under the impression that our constitution and our institutions had the personal approval of the Lord God Almighty. . . . The impression that I gained was that it would not only be folly to oppose any changes in the constitution, but almost sinful to suggest them.'[4]

The High Tory approach assumes that most citizens in their attitude to the constitution are Natural Conservatives and that any radical change to the constitution would threaten the fabric and social unity of society, undermining the consent that exists for the known and the familiar, in other words the existing organs of government. Those who press for reform are advocating change the results of which can be no more than a matter of speculation. In the words of Cecil 'Why rush into danger instead of staying in safety?'

This approach has the strength of stipulating a very clear attitude towards constitutional change — namely, don't do it. However, it suffers now from having few adherents, from opposing change while claiming that the constitution is evolutionary (a problem inherent in Mr Stokes' speech), and from assuming a settled political society. Such a society does not now exist, any more than it did when Cecil was writing at the beginning of the century.[5] In the current debate on the constitution, the High Tory view is not prominent.

SOCIALIST

The Socialist approach (albeit not one enjoying the support of all those who profess to be Socialists) argues in part for some formal modification of the constitutional structure and, more importantly, seeks political change that will in effect ensure a shift in the exercise of power within the existing framework. It favours strong central government, party-dominated with adherence to (a) the concept of the mandate and (b) intra-party democracy. The latter is designed to create a 'bottom up' method of party control, one that will ensure that party leaders and MPs act in accordance with the party programme and the wishes of the membership.

Adherents to this view thus seek to effect changes that have constitutional import. Existing constitutional principles facilitate the 'top down' leadership exercised by party leaders when in government.

Change is sought to the formal powers of the Prime Minister, as delineated in Chapter 1. Further change is sought within the PLP, notably election of any Labour Cabinet, and in the relationship between party leaders, Labour MPs and constituency parties. Recent years have witnessed demands for Labour MPs to be subject to compulsory re-selection (that is, to go through a full selection procedure with other aspiring candidates at some point during the life of a Parliament), for the Labour leader and deputy leader to be elected by a wider franchise than that of the Parliamentary Labour Party,[6] and for the writing of the party manifesto to be the exclusive responsibility of the party's National Executive Committee. 1980 and 1981 witnessed notable successes for advocates of these changes, with the first two being achieved and the third only narrowly defeated. The party leader (and deputy leader) is now subject to election by an electoral college in which trade unions account for 40 per cent of the votes, the PLP 30 per cent and constituency parties 30 per cent.[7] Labour MPs are subject to compulsory re-selection and by the end of 1981 a small number had been denied re-selection.[8]

By creating a form of party control that ensures that leaders and MPs adhere to the party programme, Socialists believe that it will be possible to impose Socialist control of government and so create a strong, centralised government which can implement Socialist policies and concomitantly withstand attempts at obstruction by the City, by industrialists, by the capitalist-controlled mass media and by international financiers. The government would pursue a managed economy through implementation of planning agreements and by a programme of public ownership.[9] The management of the economy would be undertaken, in Tony Benn's words, 'in the interests of working people and their families'.[10]

The Socialist approach thus posits the maintenance of political authority, or rather the creation of new forms of political authority, in terms of both effectiveness and consent. Governmental effectiveness would be achieved by concentrating formal power in Parliament — indeed, by strengthening the powers of the House of Commons relative to those of ministers, officials and external bodies such as the nationalised industries — and by concentrating political power in the hands of party workers. Consent would be maintained by 'a wider and deeper accountability of power through greater democratic control by Parliament of government and of finance and industry',[11] through greater accountability and democratic control within the Labour Party

·itself, and through greater participation in industry and the trade unions by rank-and-file workers.

This approach has been best expressed by Geoff Hodgson. In his book *Labour at the Crossroads*, he argues that 'a democratic socialist transformation in Britain will come about as a dual strategy — combining electoral activity and legislation in Parliament, on the one hand, with a broad extra-parliamentary mobilisation for social change on the other'.[12] In short, a road to Socialism based on an interaction between parliamentary and extra-parliamentary action. 'It is recognised that both parliamentary legitimation and mass mobilisation are necessary conditions for socialist change. But neither, on its own, is sufficient.'[13]

This approach differs from the others in different ways. It differs from the High Tory approach in that it advocates radical change and, indeed, a radical transformation in terms of control of political institutions. It differs from the Marxist approach in its acceptance of the ability to achieve socialist goals through parliamentary means. It opposes the liberal approach because it deems it to be essentially anti-socialist, seeking to create barriers against the exercise of strong socialist government. Devices such as electoral reform would deny the likelihood of a socialist majority in Parliament; a Bill of Rights could deny a socialist government the right to legislate in areas in which it considers government intervention to be vital; and membership of the European Communities, as well as adherence to other international commitments, is viewed with distrust, such institutions being seen as essentially anti-socialist creations and hence opposed for that reason. Referendums, not strictly associated with the liberal view, could be used as a means for negating socialist goals (for instance, abolition of the House of Lords) and so generally fail to attract much support; such socialist support as there was for referendums largely dissolved in the wake of the 1975 referendum on the European Communities.

The Group approach is rejected because it tends to result in the incorporation of groups, or rather their leaders, into privileged and largely unaccountable positions, beyond the reach of the House of Commons. In the words of Mr Benn, 'we do not accept the present corporate structure of Government boards, Commissions and Agents, working secretly and not accountable to Parliament. The powers we want must be subjected to the House of Commons approval when they are exercised'.[14] Formal power must be concentrated in Parliament, not in unaccountable bodies.

The Socialist view clashes with the Traditional view not over the

formal powers to be exercised by the House of Commons — both seek
to defend the concept of parliamentary sovereignty — but over the
freedom of MPs to exercise their own judgements. The Traditional
approach tends to favour or rather accept the 'top down' method of
party and political leadership, with MPs having some degree of freedom
in determining their own voting behaviour. The Socialist emphasis on
the mandate and intra-party democracy favours MPs who are willing
and prepared to ensure the implementation of the party manifesto,
regardless of any persuasive murmurings favouring change on the part
of ministers who have been influenced by officials and outside
pressures. It is this division between the Traditional and Socialist views
which is at the heart of the current controversy within the Labour
Party. In his attitude towards the constitutional position of the House
of Commons and of Members of Parliament, Michael Foot is a
Traditionalist; Mr Benn and his supporters are, in terms of our specific
definition, Socialists. The so-called 'soft Left' of the Labour Party is
socialist in terms of policy goals but Traditionalists in terms of constitutional means; the 'hard Left' is Socialist in terms of both policy
goals and constitutional means. In short, Mr Foot belongs to the
former, Mr Benn to the latter. At the 1981 Labour Party Conference,
Mr Foot declared that the relationship between the PLP and the Party
Conference was the central question which he as party leader had to
resolve. He accepted that the PLP did not presume to dictate to the
Party Conference; conversely, 'the party conference does not presume
the right to dictate to the PLP'. He had a special duty, he said, to
protect the independence, judgement and experience of MPs. 'That
applies not only to me, but also to the whole range of those elected to
office inside the Labour Party.'[15] Intimidation of MPs did not only
come from Prime Ministers (a reference to Mr Benn's thesis, see
Chapter 1): 'intimidation can come from other places. And what we
want to see is proper toleration throughout the party'.[16] Since then,
Mr Foot has been under increasing pressure from within the PLP to
take more decisive action within the party to defend the independence
of Labour MPs and to root out those who seek to challenge it.

The Socialist approach is to be found most ardently expressed by a
section of the Labour Party, most especially at the constituency level.
It finds articulation at a national level most notably but not exclusively
by Mr Benn. It suffers, though, from a number of drawbacks. For one
thing, it does not enjoy majority support at the elite level within the
Labour Party. For another, there is a problem of nomenclature and

concomitantly of its alleged supporters. There are a number of politicians who ascribe to themselves the label of Socialist, but who do not share the approach that we have outlined.[17] On the right of the Labour Party are those who define the term somewhat differently than does Mr Benn and who in their approach to the constitution are essentially Traditionalists or liberals; a number of these, such as Mrs Shirley Williams and Dr David Owen, have left the Labour Party to found the Social Democratic Party. To the left of Mr Benn are various activists who overtly support his approach yet appear to come close (certainly in the eyes of critics) to rejecting the concept of parliamentary sovereignty, preferring to take over in order to destroy the existing constitutional framework rather than to utilise it for the purpose of achieving socialist goals. They take the view, as Eric Heffer well expressed it,

that fundamental change cannot be achieved because the forces of reaction, that is, the privileged classes, will not allow it to happen and, under certain circumstances, would resort to undemocratic means to stop a democratic socialist Government from carrying through its far-reaching policies.[18]

Hence a willingness to employ extra- *and anti*-parliamentary means to achieve socialist goals. A number of Mr Benn's supporters appear to fall, or are accused of falling, into this category; it was the alleged advocacy of essentially *anti*-parliamentary action that led to Peter Tatchell being repudiated in December 1981 as prospective Labour candidate for Bermondsey by Mr Foot. The support of such activists both undermines support for the Socialist approach by virtue of what might be termed 'guilt by association' and blurs the intentions posited by this approach. Mr Benn, Mr Heffer and others attract in consequence much of the criticism that is or should be directed at the next approach to be identified, the Marxist one. The distinction between the two approaches, in terms of popular perception, is not as clear as it might be.

MARXIST

The Marxist approach, expressed in very simple terms, is that the restructuring or extension of existing state institutions is largely irrelevant in terms of what is conceived to be the basic and inherent problems of capitalist society.

The analysis most commonly associated with this approach is that the institutions of state are, in Aaronovich's words, 'manned and controlled by finance capital'.[19] Far from being a neutral arbiter between competing group demands, government operates to maintain the interests of capital.[20] Whichever political party is in government is largely immaterial: finance capitalists remain the ruling class and any attempts to improve the economy remain attempts to improve a capitalist economy.

In short, no Labour Government can ever hope to achieve socialist goals because private capital will conspire to prevent it. The Treasury, the City, industrialists, the Civil Service and the mass media operate in order to constrain any government from straying too far from the paths of maintaining the interests of capital. Some concessions are permitted, but they are designed to diffuse or ameliorate rumblings of discontent among workers, a classic case of change in order to conserve.

A more sophisticated and complex Marxist view goes beyond this simple notion that Labour Governments are thwarted in their attempts to achieve socialist goals as a result of planned resistance by domestic bodies representing the interests of private capital. Rather, this view emphasises the importance of what Stuart Holland has termed the mesoeconomy,[21] the growing concentration of economic power in international, or multinational, corporations which can operate largely beyond the control of any one government. Governments require the co-operation of finance capital, of the increasingly important multi-national corporations, for the investment necessary to sustain economic growth. For that, governments have to maintain the confidence of such multinationals. Policies or conditions which run foul of their interests — high business taxes, unstable industrial relations or soaring wage demands for instance — may motivate them to transfer their investment elsewhere.[22] Governments are thus constrained in the policies they pursue. Regardless of how popular measures may be with the domestic electorate, regardless of the formal constitutional framework within which it operates, a government cannot afford to threaten the interests of finance capital.

This view has been developed further by writers such as David Coates. He has argued that not only has British Government been constrained by external elites but that such elites themselves have been increasingly unable to determine events.[23] As a result of the working out of what in conventional Marxist analysis constitutes the law of value, with decreasing profit rates in the mesoeconomy, elites have been forced to follow rather than determine events. 'The major role of elites, and that includes even the IMF, is much more that of *articulating* imperatives rather than *inventing* them'.[24] What is the major stumbling block to the achievement of radical socialist goals by any government is not capitalists, but capitalism. Operating within an international capitalist economy, no government can hope to overcome the crises and contradictions of that economy. Certain domestic features may exacerbate the problem for British capitalists, notably the strength of the labour movement, but it is the international environment that is crucial.

In this process, a Labour Government in Britain would be and was (in 1974–9) pulled into a particular role, that of embodying and articulating the interests of capital as a whole, if need be against sections of capital itself, and certainly against the labour movement. 'That is *par excellence* the job of the state in the middle of a period of capitalist crisis.'[25] It entails giving the state a crucial role in restructuring capital and in incorporating the working class by diffusing class militancy and accommodating union demands to the existing 'level of the possible' in the middle of a recession. It is a task for which Labour politicians, with a tendency to put 'nation' before 'class', are well suited. It also ensures that the Labour Party in power will not achieve its radical pretensions. Rather, what one is likely to witness is the growth of a corporatist relationship between the state and private industry, with parliamentary institutions increasingly being displaced by corporatist institutions as the dominant state apparatus.[26]

In terms of constitutional change, the more simple Marxist approach rejects the contemporary debate as largely irrelevant. The institutions of the state are run by the state elite and any change will be for their benefit. Effectiveness is achieved by their control of the central institutions and consent maintained by manipulation of the working class. Any attempt by a Labour Government to achieve radical programmes will be thwarted by the machinations of capital, the hegemony of which is not challenged but, if anything, enhanced by the constitutional reforms currently on the agenda of political debate (withdrawal from the European Communities being an exception). The more sophisticated Marxist approach advanced by Coates and others allows a greater degree of autonomy to government in its dealings with business. 'If there is a fit between Labour Government aspirations and business aspirations, then that is a consequence of a particular pattern of class forces surrounding the State, and not a consequence of any organic connection between the Labour Government and the business elite as such.'[27] Nonetheless, the crises and contradictions of capitalism at a time of what Dr Coates refers to as Late Capitalism draws government into fulfilling the role of articulating the interests of capital. Any constitutional change achieved through existing procedures is likely to be geared to pursuing that interest. Thus, though the analyses of Marxists differ, the conclusions reached are similar. In Britain, socialism is unlikely to be achieved by parliamentary means and any change in the constitutional framework is wrought in order to maintain the hegemony of finance capital. Current constitutional disputes are significant primarily as but one element in an analysis of the weakening and tensions within the international capitalist economy.

GROUP

The Group, or Functionalist, approach quite simply seeks to ensure the more formal incorporation or co-option of groups into the governmental decision-making process.

With government dominance of the legislature and with increasing involvement of government in the social and economic life of the nation, to a point where in 1976 government expenditure accounted for about 60 per cent of the Gross Domestic Product, government has become a focal point for group demands. Such demands may emanate from (to use the simplest and most common distinction) sectional interest groups, seeking to protect and further the interests of particular sections of society, or promotional groups, seeking to advance a particular cause or causes. Such groups seek to influence government in the allocation of scarce economic resources or in the introduction of particular legislation.

Sectional interest groups are of especial importance in the governmental decision-making process. Such groups may need the government in order to achieve certain of their aims but conversely the government is usually dependent upon such groups both for advice and co-operation. The more a sectional group's actual membership corresponds to its potential membership, the greater the likelihood of it enjoying a monopoly of expertise in its particular sector; government lacks the resources to match such expertise. Most sectional interest groups enjoy positions of some economic significance. they have the sanction of refusing to co-operate with government in the implementation of policies. Failure by groups to co-operate can result in the non-implementation or the failure of government policy. As a result, there is usually close contact between government and sectional interest groups. This contact is normally regular and direct. Promotional groups, by contrast, lack generally the economic clout enjoyed by sectional interest groups, usually but by no means always lack expertise which is valuable to government, and often are of a temporary nature. For achieving their goals, they rely primarily upon persuasion via public lobbying of government and of Parliament.

The interdependence of government and sectional interest groups has found recognition not only in the consultations which take place between the two but also in the occasional formal co-option of such groups into the governmental process. In a number of instances, certain groups participate in some aspect of this process not because a minister has exercised his or her discretion in seeking their advice but because they have been given a statutory right to be so involved. Some such statutory provisions are of long standing. For example, the 1924 National Health Insurance Act provided for the functional representation of specific interests on the various committees charged with administering the system of social insurance. Analogous provisions had appeared in the minimum wage legislation enacted in the Trade Board Acts of 1909 and 1918.[28] In its annual price review, the Ministry of Agriculture is required under the provisions of the 1947 Agriculture Act to consult 'such bodies of persons who appear . . . to represent the interests of producers in the agricultural industry'. (In practice, this has meant the National Farmers Union and, since 1978, the Farmers Union of Wales.) In recent years this formal co-option has been most apparent in the development of what has been termed tri-partism, a form of consultation between government, employers and unions, one in which, taken to its logical conclusion, all three in Edward Heath's terms 'share fully . . . the benefits and obligations of running the country'.[29] In practice this has taken two forms. There is the co-option of the representatives of trade unions and employers' organisations on to bodies concerned with detailed and specialised matters of administration and (in the case of ACAS) resolving specific disputes, and the more general negotiation between government, union and employers in the government's economic policy-making. Under the former heading comes the representation of unions and employers (and in some cases local authorities) on bodies such as the Metrication Council, the Coal Consumers Council, the Potato Marketing Board and, more recently and more importantly, the Manpower Services Commission, the Health and Safety Commission and the Arbitration and Conciliation Service (ACAS). Under the latter heading comes especially the National Economic Development Council, set up in 1962, bringing together ministers, trade unionists and employers (as well as representatives of nationalised industries and other bodies such as, now, the Manpower Services Commission) for formal and regular discussions. Over the years there has been an increasing awareness of less formal tripartite negotiations, conducted as and when deemed necessary, as well as (often more importantly and frequently) instances of bilateral negotiations. Such negotiations have variously impinged upon the exercise of the formal powers vested in other bodies. In 1976, for example, the Chancellor of the Exchequer, Denis Healey, made a 3 per cent reduction in income tax conditional upon the acceptance of pay restraint by the trade unions. It was viewed by some as a constitutional outrage, giving power to accept or reject taxation to a body outside Parliament.[30] Others defended it as a desirable action in order to achieve wage restraint: the country's economic health took precedence over disputed constitutional niceties.

The interdependence of groups and government has reached a stage where some commentators argue that government has ceased to be the authoritative allocator of values and resources, becoming instead 'merely one participant, albeit a powerful one, in a complex process of bargaining'.[31] Britain, according to some, is developing a form of societal corporatism. (Others, perceiving government to be in a more dominant position, have argued that a form of state corporatism is developing.)[32] There are those who argue that this should be given more formal recognition, with the more extensive co-option of groups into the official decision-making process. This, it is contended, would not only formalise the reality but would also enhance consent by giving groups a greater sense of legitimacy and involvement in decision-making and contribute to greater government effectiveness by virtue of a sense of responsibility on the part of groups: by being part of the policy-making process, officially so, groups would be more willing to accept the obligation to work for the success of policies decided upon.[33] Such involvement could also contribute to the *formulation* of more considered and workable policies, given that they would be the product of an even more regular and considered process of consultation.

Calls for the incorporation of groups into the formal governmental process are not new. They have been made at various times by Labour politicians as well as by Conservatives. On the left, Guild Socialism represented the most obvious force for a form of functional representation. G.D.H. Cole argued for the House of Commons to be replaced by a series of self-governing guilds, each based on a branch of industry.[34] Somewhat less radically, on the Conservative side Winston Churchill argued in 1930 for an Economic Sub-Parliament, comprising forty MPs, twenty peers and sixty others — businessmen, trade unionists and economists. Similar proposals emanated at the same period from other writers and politicians, including Lord Eustace Percy, R.D. Denman and W.G.S. Adams.[35] Such a form of functional representation also found favour with various Conservative politicians in the 1940s, most notably L.S. Amery, Harold Macmillan and Christopher Hollis,[36] and found later expression in a pamphlet in 1963 by a group of Conservative MPs.[37] Indeed, it finds expression in a particular strand of Conservative thought.[38] More recently, various sectional interest groups have appeared to favour a greater formal recognition of their role in the policy-making process.

Trade unions, in particular, appear keen to assert and acquire what amounts to a right to be consulted before decisions are reached affecting their interests; indeed, they would seem to be inclined to deny the legitimacy of any legislation passed which does not enjoy their prior assent. In some cases this appears to extend to denying even the right of Parliament to pass legislation on industrial relations.[39] Although somewhat wary of being too incorporated formally into the governmental process, and hence having to share responsibility for public policy, unions would appear to favour (along with other groups) recognition of their right to be consulted as enjoying the status of a constitutional convention. Sir Ivor Jennings accorded such a status in *The Law and the Constitution*, while admitting that 'the scope of the convention is still vague'.[40] Harold Wilson appeared to give some credence to this view in 1966 when he told the House of Commons that it was the government's *duty* to consult with the CBI, the TUC and others.[41] Nonetheless, governments generally have not been willing to accept Jennings' assertion, and the present Conservative Government very clearly has rejected it.

Trade unions are by no means alone in pressing for constitutional reform in order to formalise a degree of functional representation in the political process. In recent years various calls have been made for parliamentary reform in order to achieve such representation. As we have noted already (chapter 6), John Mackintosh argued the case for the House of Lords to be reformed in order to allow for a Second

Chamber based on functional representation.[42] In 1976 Conservative MP David Crouch, writing in support of Mr Healey's action referred to above, declared: 'I believe the public are ready for a major reform of Parliament to bring the unions into our parliamentary democracy and make them share their responsibilities with the people's ordinary elected representatives.'[43] In short, Mr Crouch wanted the unions to bear the weight of responsibility in addition to enjoying the (unavoidable) fruits of their power. Both MPs (Mackintosh and Crouch) favoured some reform of existing parliamentary structures in order to facilitate the integration of groups into the formal decision-making process. As we have seen, some others favour a formalised acknowledgement of the existing process of consultation between groups and government.

The emphasis, then, is on reform of existing structures and procedures. Of reforms advocated that would provide new dimensions to the constitution, the Group approach posits no comprehensive view. Referendums are opposed, especially by the trade unions, because they could be used as a counterweight to group influence (a possibility upon which Mrs Thatcher mused when Leader of the Opposition) and a Bill of Rights would be unacceptable inasmuch as it would incorporate rights that could restrict the free interplay between groups and government and the exercise of existing group powers. By contrast, electoral reform has enjoyed some support from employers on the grounds that it might help lead to greater continuity in government policy (see Chapter 12) and devolution finds favour with the Group approach inasmuch as it would allow for a greater degree of group influence at a sub-national level; in practice, however, groups were divided on the issue in the 1970s, and in any event the devolution favoured primarily by this approach is, of course, a functional rather than a geographical one. The Group approach thus generates no comprehensive response to the range of issues on the agenda of political debate.

The Group approach suffers from limited political support. It is opposed by the other approaches we have identified. The Socialist approach views it as a possible threat to the achievement of its own goals. The Marxist approach rejects the pluralist analysis on which it is based.[44] The liberal approach is, on the whole, vehemently opposed to it. Though some writers have sought to integrate Group and liberal theory,[45] the dominant liberal view is that groups pose a threat to the liberal concept of representation, with the ever-increasing power wielded by sectional interest groups in policy-making constituting a challenge to citizens in their capacities as individuals. Indeed, it is this perception which has motivated or reinforced several of the proposed constitutional reforms discussed in the preceding chapters. A Bill of Rights, in particular, has been advocated by a number of politicians as a means of restricting the influence wielded over government by groups, especially the trade unions.[46] Also opposed to the Group approach is the Traditional approach. While acknowledging the need for consultation by government with interested groups, Traditionalists reject any constitutional change that would threaten the position of Parliament.

Of those opposed to the Group approach, some argue that the integration of groups in the governmental process, far from enhancing consent, would undermine it. As David Steel expressed it: 'Parliament is answerable to the people. The TUC is responsible to about 20 per cent of the people, and less than half of the working population.'[47] Furthermore, many groups themselves lack developed democratic structures or extensive member participation.[48] Co-opting groups into the governmental process would constitute no more than extending power to an elite, one which would not be greatly accountable, either to group memberships or to the electorate. Given extensive public distrust of existing group influence, to formalise that position would undermine consent for the process by which public policy is determined. Hence, although groups are powerful in both economic and political terms (indeed, to a large extent, because of this) there is considerable opposition to any further constitutional change that would consolidate or enhance the position of such groups in the process of government.

LIBERAL

The liberal approach derives from traditional liberal theory and emphasises the centrality of what Giovanni Sartori in *Democratic Theory* succinctly terms 'the theory and practice of individual liberty, juridicial defence and the constitutional state'. It assumes that citizens exercise their political rights as individuals, choosing freely from rival candidates and preferred policies, and not as members of organised groups; that the state is or should be neutral in its attitudes towards conflicts within society; and hence that disputes can be resolved within established constitutional procedures. Absent any fundamental conflicts, society proceeds on the basis of consensus. Constitutional rules are not only the effect of consensual values but can also help shape them. A consensual society is best assured by allowing individuals the right to choose and participate in political decisions that will affect them and concomitantly by providing for limited government, one subject to the rule of law.

Whereas the liberal approach was initially a reforming one, it became essentially the accepted doctrine in the nineteenth century.[49] Government was limited: the sectors in which government was believed to have a right to be involved were limited (indeed, extending not much beyond raising revenue for the national defence) and arbitrary government was protected against by the constitutional balance within the Queen-in-Parliament, by an independent judiciary, and by the general acceptance that the government's role was a limited one. Individuals were granted political rights, with the concept of 'one man, one vote' (or rather, subsequently, 'one person, one vote') being conceded, albeit not fully until the twentieth century. The balance within the constitution served to prevent an electoral majority enjoying unfettered power to oppress individuals or minorities.

Today, the liberal approach is again a reforming one. Until the 1960s it was essentially allied with the Traditional view in accepting the existing mix of constitutional precepts and political circumstance embodied in the Westminster model of government. However, political events in the past decade or so have led to a divorce between the two approaches, the liberal one now being in the forefront in pressing for constitutional change.

The motivation for this advocacy of constitutional reform is clearly discernible. Increasingly, individual liberties have come under threat, not only from government as such but also from associated quasi-government bodies and from private organisations. Government by virtue of the constitution (parliamentary sovereignty) and political controls (party cohesion and the whips) is assured of hegemony in the formal decision-making process, and in its policy formulation has become overly influenced by group pressures. Functional representation has begun to outweigh the representation of individuals through Parliament. In the formulation of public policy, individuals are being isolated and ignored: decision-making is highly centralised, influenced by external pressures and by the advice of experts, and it is implemented by a somewhat remote bureaucracy. Such a divorce between citizens and the making and carrying out of public policy lessens consent for the political system and by lessening consent undermines governmental effectiveness. The balance within the Queen-in-Parliament has been lost and even the independence and neutrality of the courts have been challenged in some quarters. To restore the balance, to protect individual liberty, and to give back to the individual the ability to participate in decision-making, political and constitutional change is not only desirable but imperative.

Of the reforms detailed in the preceding chapters, especially in Part 2, the liberal approach may be seen as the moving force behind most of them. In particular, it favours a Bill of Rights, devolution (or rather a more comprehensive scheme of decentralisation), and electoral reform. Given the ability of government in effect to determine legislation and the increasing pressures on government which result in it utilising the powers at its disposal to intervene in spheres that impinge upon individual liberty, restraints upon government are necessary. Similar restraints are necessary upon other bodies which increasingly also impinge upon individual liberties. Whereas the Traditional view emphasises a revitalised Parliament as sufficient to provide the necessary limitations, the liberal approach prefers the more radical prescription of a Bill of Rights. The arguments surrounding this issue we have considered already in some detail.

Similarly, the emphasis upon the individual leads the liberal approach to favour decentralisation of decision-making. This would both limit the over-powerful central government and also allow greater opportunities for individuals to participate in the decision-making process. Greater participation is valuable not only for maintaining consent (as well as encouraging greater effectiveness through citizens' willingness for policies to work) but also contributes to better decision-making: individuals are as likely to be as or more fully aware or informed of problems affecting them as are the so-called experts on the subject. Decentralisation would be one step in the direction of moving back (or rather forward) to a system of participatory politics, with needs defined by consensus.[50]

Consensus could and should be facilitated also by a move away from the existing process of adversary politics. The mutually exclusive and divisive battle between political parties for the spoils of government contributes to public cynicism and government 'overload'. Governments cannot hope any more to allocate resources sufficient to meet the expectations raised by their own inflated promises. Attempts to overcome this process of adversary politics might be possible by political means within the existing constitutional framework, as suggested by the electoral success in by-elections of the consensus-seeking SDP/Liberal alliance. Nonetheless, the likelihood of success is militated against by the existing first-past-the-post method employed for parliamentary elections. The introduction of a system of proportional representation for such elections would enhance consent and facilitate consensus. By being seen to be a fairer method of election and by ridding the electoral process of so-called 'wasted votes', voters would be more likely to go to the polls. By reducing the likelihood of single-party government based on extravagant manifesto promises, substituting instead coalition government representing the wishes of the politically centrist electorate, consensus politics would be pursued. Again, the arguments on the issue have been considered already in some detail.

The liberal approach on the other two issues in Part 2 (excluding Northern Ireland) are less clear-cut. Most of those politicians whom one would associate with this approach are supporters of British membership of the European Communities. Though membership can be justified in terms of economic liberalism, at least to some extent,[51] it is less easy to justify on liberal grounds in terms of the decision-making structure involved. The Communities may proceed on the basis of consensus and exist within what amounts to a confederal structure, but decisions are taken at a supra-national level and mostly by officials. Hence it is not surprising that liberals have been among the keenest advocates of direct elections to the European Parliament. As to referendums, there are liberal arguments both for and against. On the one hand, referendums ensure that citizens express themselves on an issue, doing so without the mediation of politicians or groups, and can serve as an extra balancing element within the constitution. On the other hand, there is the classical liberal fear of an unrestrained majority acting without the benefit of educated debate. Referendums could be weapons to be used by the majority in pursuit of illiberal causes. If one concedes a referendum on one important issue, what is there to prevent having to concede referendums on other issues, such as capital punishment, immigration or withdrawal from the European Communities? It is the latter argument which has tended to predominate and as a result liberals have generally, but by no means unanimously, opposed the concept of referendums.

As for the existing constitutional structures, the liberal approach tends to support reform also, at least (and obviously) insofar as reform is compatible with its aims. If favours parliamentary reform designed to strengthen the House of Commons — liberals support the extension of select committee powers and activities – and reform of the House of Lords designed to provide a more legitimate counterweight to the Lower House. Such reforms would help contribute to restoring some element of balance in the relationship between Parliament and the executive. Support for a Bill of Rights and of resolution of disputes by independent arbiters leads to support for the maintenance and, if necessary, the strengthening of an independent judiciary. Conversely, scepticism of a secretive and 'expert' Civil Service leads to demands for more open government and greater accountability on the part of quasi-governmental agencies.

The liberal approach is thus a radical and extensive one. In effect it advocates a new constitutional framework for the UK. Hence the appearance of various tracts which advocate not isolated reforms but rather comprehensive schemes of constitutional change.[52]

Though exhibiting a high profile in the debate on constitutional issues, the liberal approach is not without its detractors. It differs from the other approaches covered in this chapter. The Socialist (and Marxist) approach emphasises the importance of class rather than individuals and seeks a strong, centralised government. The High Tory approach considers the reforms advocated to be unnecessary and largely un-British, likely to endanger rather than enhance consent. The Group approach obviously places the emphasis on the group rather than the individual. The Traditional view also displays a scepticism of the emphasis on the individual. Most citizens have interests other than those of public policy. Those that do participate in policy discussions tend not be socially typical. In planning decisions, for example, those who participate are generally middle-class, having both the time and the knowledge to be involved; the poor and the inarticulate tend not to be heard.[53] Those best placed to make decisions on behalf of citizens are MPs: through election they enjoy the support of their constituents and are in a position to reflect upon and influence public policy. Hence the focus should be upon Parliament and, in terms of constitutional change, reforming the existing structure. External constraints pose a threat to parliamentary sovereignty. Whereas the liberal approach deems this to be desirable, the Traditional one does not.

TRADITIONAL

Just as Tony Benn has claimed that Democratic Socialism in Britain is very much a 'home-grown' product,[54] so one could claim that the

Traditional approach is very much British not only in form but in content. It derives from no one clearly defined strand of thought, but rather draws from various strands of thought which have found expression in British history. It combines the prescriptive with the descriptive, blending the formal constitutional position with an acceptance of political circumstance. It finds its articulation in the Westminster model of British Government.

The Traditional approach draws from Old Tory theory in its emphasis upon the effective exercise of government. It draws to some extent from a modified Whig theory in its acceptance of an important role for Parliament. It bows to democratic theory in its acceptance of mass suffrage (albeit an acceptance based as much on pragmatism as on principle) and to some extent there is a nod in the direction of accepting, albeit ambiguously and rather tenuously, the Socialist belief in the doctrine of the mandate, an acceptance that has not gone much beyond a belief that a government has a moral duty (if that) to carry out promises embodied in its election manifesto.[55] These various elements are drawn upon in order to mould and justify the Westminster model.

This model posits a balanced constitution but one in which the balance favours government. However, government, though strong, must not be over-powerful. It must be subject to restraint by Parliament. Government must be allowed to govern, to negotiate, initiate and propose, but with Parliament fulfilling what Michael Mezey has characterised as the role of a 'reactive' legislature,[56] subjecting the measures and the actions of the executive to scrutiny and setting the limits within which government may govern. The House of Commons comprises the elected representatives of the citizenry and is the body best suited to expressing the national interest. Through its election and its deliberation the House can give authoritative assent to the government and to its measures. Party provides the vehicle by which the government of the day is usually assured the assent of the Commons; acceptance of the Commons as a 'representative' body, one that is elected by and acts for and on behalf of the electorate,[57] provides one of the supports of the political system. Hence, political authority is maintained: the former condition (assent for government) allows for government effectiveness; the latter (a representative House) helps maintain consent for government.

Strong government and the assent of the Commons is derived from the maintenance of a party majority in the House of Commons. This is facilitated by the existing first-past-the-post method of election and by the not unrelated existence of two dominant parties; though the need for two dominant parties to ensure a parliamentary majority is not axiomatic. Hence, the model combines constitutional precepts and structures with political circumstance to provide a view of the constitution which is part descriptive, part prescriptive. In recent years, as the model has ceased to accord with experience, so many who adhere to this view have begun to admit of the need for change; but a change which ensures that the prescription and the description fit more tightly, not a change that adheres to a different prescription.

How then does the Traditional approach differ from the other approaches we have identified? Who adheres to it? And just how unified an approach is it?

It differs from the liberal approach in its adherence to Parliament and the concept of parliamentary sovereignty. It is sceptical of the liberal belief in the rationality of the individual and in popular participation. The relationship between citizens and government should be mediated by MPs. Individuals have neither the time nor the interest to reflect continuously upon the affairs of the nation, let alone participate regularly in political activity. Rather, they look to MPs to deliberate and judge on their behalf. For the protection of individual rights one should look to Parliament, not to some document embodying some abstract higher law. If Parliament proves incapable of defending individual rights then, as Robert Kilroy-Silk recognised, that is an argument for strengthening Parliament, not weakening it.[58] Whereas the liberal approach puts the emphasis on the Rule of Law, the Traditional view retains the emphasis on parliamentary sovereignty, accepting to some extent Dicey's view as to the relationship between the two.[59] Hence a rejection of the case for a Bill of Rights. The acceptance of strong government leads also to a rejection of electoral reform, so favoured by the liberal approach.

The Traditional view differs from the Socialist in that it adheres to a belief in existing constitutional prerogatives and concomitantly a 'top down' process of party leadership. Government leaders must be allowed flexibility in responding to changing conditions. In implementing policies they must be allowed to give an authoritative lead with party serving as an important support. Party loyalty and the persuasive techniques of the whips will normally ensure that such support is forthcoming. If it is not, the government is forced to think again.

In this relationship, government and Members of Parliament are expected to be sensitive to, but not fettered by, public and party opinion. The theory of the mandate, so important in Socialist thought, is deemed to be persuasive only. A manifesto serves as a guide to a party's intentions if returned to office (one which in practice governments often manage to fulfil in large measure) but not a contract or binding document. And in responding to government proposals, MPs must be allowed to decide for themselves what is in the best interests of their constituents, their party and their country. Though democratic theory prevents acceptance of the view that MPs must deliberate in some form of political vacuum, they are nonetheless expected to deliberate free of undue outside pressures. This Whig element in the Traditional view has ensured the strong response to attempts by adherents to the Socialist view to ensure rigid adherence to a party programme via discipline imposed by the extra-parliamentary party in the Labour Party.

The Traditional view rejects also the other approaches identified. It rejects the Marxist approach with which it has little or nothing in common. There is a strong belief in the durability of political institutions in Britain, the Traditional view allowing for flexibility and a form of balance, both between constitutional and party norms and between liberal and democratic theory. Although some adherents to the Traditional view share the same ends as those of the High Tory persuasion, they reject the High Tory reasoning: the structures that exist are supported because there are rational and compelling reasons why those *particular* structures not only do but should exist rather than any other structure. Other Traditionalists have accepted a need for reform of existing institutions. Though the Traditional view accepts that there is an important role for interest groups and for experts in the political process, that role is deemed to be an advisory and extra- (but not un-) constitutional one. Government requires the advice and co-operation of groups in the formulation of measures. It needs the talents of experts at its disposal. However, at the end of the day formal legitimation of the government's measures has to be, and should only be, given by Parliament. Interest groups carry political weight already because of their economic clout. Effectively to co-opt them into the structure of government, or rather to co-opt them further, would undermine the position of the House of Commons. In so doing, political authority in the form of consent would be jeopardised. It would constitute giving groups a formal privileged position in the political process. Already, grave doubts exist in the public mind as to the influence exerted by interest groups: to formalise that influence would sow further the seeds of public disquiet.

The Traditional approach thus forms something of a balance between the other approaches. It is a balance born of a degree of scepticism. While accepting the need for functional and professional advice for government it exhibits a certain doubt towards the 'we know best' attitude implicit in the Socialist and Group approaches. While accepting the importance of individuals and democratic theory, it harbours a degree of scepticism as to liberal claims of the rationality and participatory interest of the individual. While rejecting the High Tory view that any constitutional change is to be resisted it nonetheless displays a healthy scenticism of the claims of other approaches that existing constitutional structures have contributed to Britain's current ills and that constitutional change would help alleviate or resolve some of those ills. Rather it views Britain's problems as essentially economic and social. The Westminster model can help facilitate the maintenance of political authority, but constitutional change will do little if anything to affect the roots of contemporary problems that impinge most upon citizens' lives. Electoral reform or frequent referendums will do nothing to ensure that blacks in Liverpool gets jobs, or that the harassed housewife can make ends meet in providing for her family. Claims of greater participation in the political process if liberal reforms are implemented, or of greater continuity in policy if the electoral system is reformed, are perceived as being of dubious validity and, in the latter case, in the outer reaches of speculation.

The Traditional view thus finds itself pitted against the other approaches. Yet just how unified an approach is it and how much support does it enjoy? Given the strands of thought from which it draws, it is perhaps not surprising that there is a degree of internal tension. On the one hand there is some difference between those who tend to stress the Tory emphasis on strong government and those who stress the importance of Parliament. The two are not altogether mutually exclusive, but the former tends to express doubt about extending parliamentary powers, the latter to favour such extension. On the other hand, there is some tension between those who believe that the prescriptive Westminster model corresponds to a sufficient degree with what currently exists to make change unnecessary (hence sharing the same ends as the High Tory approach) and those who believe that the prescription and the description diverge to a degree that makes change necessary. The former view was the predominant one in the 1950s, the two were pitted against one another in the 1960s,[60] and the latter view became the predominant but far from exclusive one in the 1970s.

As the 1960s progressed, and more especially during the 1970s, there was a widening realisation that in the balance between the House of Commons and that part of it which formed the government the scales were not only tipped in favour of government but tipped much too heavily in favour of government. So much so that the House of Commons not only was not performing effectively the tasks posited by the Westminster model but was increasingly being seen as not performing those tasks. The greater the public awareness of Parliament's ineffectiveness, the greater the threat to the maintenance of consent for political institutions and the measures assented to by Parliament. Hence a need for change to ensure that what was, matched what the Westminster model posited ought to be.

The parliamentary reformers of the 1960s, academics such as Bernard Crick, Victor Wiseman and Harry Hanson, did not fault the Westminster model. Rather than reformulate it, they sought to influence a change of conditions to fit it.[61] They argued for a relationship between government and the House of Commons in which the House subjected government measures to critical and informed scrutiny. They advocated improved pay and facilities for Members and, most importantly of all, the greater use of investigatory select committees. This attempt to change conditions to fit the model was to find practical expression in the reforms introduced in the 1966–70 Parliament by Richard Crossman as Leader of the House. However, the reforms implemented[62] represented something of a compromise — between those favouring strong government (hence various procedural changes to facilitate government business) and the more Whiggish advocates of a stronger House of Commons (improved pay, better facilities, experimentation with select committees). These reforms, coupled with others tried in the three Parliaments of the 1970s, failed to achieve a significant shift in the imbalance that existed between government and the House of Commons. Realisation of this fact had two important consequences. One was a split between adherents to the liberal view and those who continued to support the Westminster model of government; liberals came to the view that the existing constitutional structure no longer provided the necessary balance and protection that they expected, and so opted for advocacy of reforms that they believed would create that balance and the protection of individual rights. The other consequence was that those who maintained their adherence to the Traditional view realised that more radical (but internal) reforms were necessary if the imbalance between government and the Commons was to be redressed. There was thus much greater pressure for change. This mainly took the form of advocacy of more comprehensive and much stronger select committees; there were those who stressed also the need for an attitudinal change on the part of MPs as a prerequisite for effective structural changes.[63] Such changes were to be realised in the 1970s: an attitudinal change can be recognised as having occurred in the latter half of the 1970s (building on the experience of the 1970–4 Parliament)[64] and in 1979 came the creation of the departmentally related select committees. In the 1980s the adherents to the Traditional view hence tend to favour the growing influence of the select committees and the willingness of the House to assert itself on occasion against the Government. There is a strong and growing feeling also favouring greater parliamentary scrutiny and influence of one particular sector, namely public expenditure.[65] The emphasis remains upon the House of Commons.

The Traditional view has the advantage, albeit it one under strong challenge, of enjoying more support at the governmental and parliamentary level than any other approach. At the parliamentary level its supporters are most prominent on the backbenches on both sides of the House, though even party leaders adhere to it; the latter, though, are more inclined to voice support for strong government. The current Government falls most appropriately within the Traditional rubric. Although the Prime Minister, Mrs Thatcher, occasionally gives the impression of instinctively supporting the High Tory approach and in its economic approach the Government in principle favours limited government, the policies pursued by the Government have nonetheless necessitated the exercise of strong central government (primarily in the sphere of centre–local government relationships) and in its attitude towards Parliament the Government has paid lip service to, and acquiesced in the creation of, the strengthened select committees and the need for the supremacy of Parliament. The formal commitment found expression in the Conservative manifesto of 1979[66] and found practical expression in the Cabinet's (albeit reluctant) acceptance of the proposed select committees, along with subsequent procedural reforms, advocated by the then Leader of the House, Norman St John-Stevas, with strong backbench support.[67]

A somewhat more enthusiastic embrace of the Traditional view is to be found in the Government's rejection of, or unwillingness to embrace, the reforms advocated by supporters of the other approaches. The reforms advocated by Socialists (election of the Cabinet, limiting the constitutional prerogatives of the Prime Minister) and by adherents of the Group approach (co-option of groups into the governmental structure) are rejected outright. Those constitutional innovations favoured by liberals are not subject to such rejection but are nonetheless received with something less than enthusiasm. As we have seen, the only action taken on the issue of devolution resulted in some modification to the Standing Orders of the House of Commons. That, though, represented a greater degree of success than on any other of the innovations proposed. Indeed, the position of the Government was best expressed by Home Office Minister Timothy Raison in April 1981 in commenting upon the speeches made during debate on John Stokes' motion on the constitution. On the issue of the House of Lords, the Minister declared:

As hon. Members know, a number of views are held about the desirability of making some changes in the composition of the other place. That is something that the Government will continue to have in mind in the light of all the views that have been expressed. . . . Any proposals for changes in the composition of the other place would need to be given the most careful consideration by the Government of the day. Any Administration would be under a duty to consult widely about proposed constitutional changes. . . . One view that may find favour with many is that any measure of protection for the other place should be associated in some way with a reform of the Second Chamber. . . . The Government has not yet come to a firm view on that.[68]

Mr Raison was somewhat more definite in expressing the Government's view on electoral reform. 'Our belief is that our present simple majority system is most appropriate for elections to this House.'[69] And on the question of a Bill of Rights, he said:

The Government have no settled view on the merits of a Bill. We believe that important proposals for constitutional change of the type involved in any Bill of Rights should proceed as far as possible by agreement between the political parties. The Government have in mind to initiate talks at a suitable time. . . . The subject is important and needs fuller discussion before we can take any steps along that path.[70]

Similar comments have been made by Government spokesmen in responding to other parliamentary debates on topics such as referendums.[71] In short, the Government is not keen to adopt any of the reforms advanced by liberals, responding to pressure for change in classic 'Yes, Minister' style.[72] The attachment to the Wesminster model was best revealed by Mr Raison's peroration in which he declared that in the debate

we have seen a deep devotion to parliamentary democracy but a willingness on the part of some of us to say that all is not perfect. There is nothing more important than that we stick up for the system that we have inherited down the ages, and that still has so much to offer all the people of the country.[73]

It is a view not confined to the Conservative side of the House of Commons. For the moment, it appears to enjoy plurality support within the House.

SOME QUALIFICATIONS

Having identified these six broad approaches to constitutional change, three qualifications must now be recorded. First, the approaches themselves are not necessarily well defined or delineated in current debate. Second, the means proposed to achieve the desired ends are not necessarily mutually exclusive. And, third, the approaches do not correlate precisely with existing political parties.

That the approaches identified are not always well defined or clearly articulated in the debate on constitutional reform is not surprising. Though the conflicting values and philosophies from which they are derived are well established and have motivated the enunciation and carrying through of policies within the existing constitutional framework, their relationship to that framework has not been much considered. This is, in large measure, attributable to factors identified in the introduction. Until recently the constitution has not been the subject of considered, and certainly not of sustained, debate. There was a consensus sufficient to sustain the existing constitutional framework (comprising in essence the Traditional, liberal and High Tory approaches). If change was deemed necessary, the expectation was that it would take place incrementally, with little need to reflect upon the rationale of the constitution as a whole. As Professor Wade succinctly observed, though the functions and nature of government and the party system have changed beyond the dreams of earlier generations whose practices gave rise to our constitutional laws and conventions, there has never been any general review of the constitution as a whole.[74] As a result, we tend to lack the familiarity with the language of constitutional debate enjoyed in other countries, such as West Germany.[75] Only in recent years, with the policies pursued by successive governments failing to meet public expectations and with the general withering away of the consensus supporting the existing structures and relationships created by the constitution, has it proved possible or necessary for the various political values to be applied and considered in the context of the constitution and constitutional change. As the relationship between such values and the constitution are developed, the greater will be the intimacy with the language of constitutional debate and the greater the degree of sophistication in such debate. For the moment, though, it is possible only to identify the approaches in general and rather crude terms.

That the means to achieve desired ends are not mutually exclusive will be apparent from the brief summaries of the approaches. Not only are various approaches united in their opposition to certain constitutional changes, a number are in agreement on proposed reform. Whereas referendums would appear particularly unattractive to most approaches (at least on principle), the strengthening of select committees in the House of Commons attracts the support of at least three of the approaches: the Socialist, the liberal and the Traditional. Even some advocates of the Group approach may find such committees an attractive proposition as an additional conduit of group representations to Parliament and the executive. It is possible that one particular approach may enjoy such support at the mass or elite level that it can ensure the implementation of a certain reform. In other cases it is more likely that it will be necessary for supporters of two or more approaches to come together to ensure the implementation of a particular reform. In the case of the new select committee structure in the Commons, it was carried through as a result of overwhelming support from a combination of Socialist, liberal and Traditionalist MPs. Any analysis of the current debate on constitutional issues will thus have to take this point into account, considering not only the support for each approach but also the chemical-like change from issue to issue in terms of the coming together or disseveration of supporters of particular approaches. On certain proposed reforms, some of the approaches will be convergent, on others they will be divergent.

The third point is especially important for understanding the contemporary debate on constitutional issues. The approaches delineated above are not coterminous with the existing political parties. This point is easily demonstrated. Though most Liberals adhere to the liberal approach, not all adherents to the liberal approach are Liberals. (It is in order to distinguish between the two that we have referred consistently to the liberal approach with a small 'l'.) Adherents to the liberal approach are to be found within the Social Democratic Party as well as within the Conservative Party and (to a lesser extent) the Labour Party. The Conservative Party contains within its ranks some who adhere to the liberal approach (for example, Conservative Action for Electoral Reform, Lords Hailsham and Carr), some who are Traditionalists (the existing Government and probably a majority of the parliamentary party), some who are best placed in the Group approach (notably Edward Heath) and those who are High Tories (for instance, MPs John Stokes and Sir Marcus Kimball). The Labour Party comprises an array of Socialists (such as Tony Benn, Eric Heffer), Traditionalists (probably a plurality of Labour MPs), some who support liberal reforms (e.g. MP John Ryman on a Bill of Rights, Austin Mitchell on electoral reform, and a section of the party which continues to expound a belief in decentralisation), as well as some Marxists. A number of Labour MPs who have defected to the Social Democratic Party are probably best categorised as Traditionalists rather than liberals. The leading Traditionalist MP to have left the Labour Party (though at the time of writing not having joined the SDP) was and is George Cunningham. Some supporters of the Social Democratic Party exhibit some sympathy for the Group approach.[76]

The lack of a complete fit between approaches to constitutional reform and the existing political parties has important implications. In one respect it could contribute to constitutional change, given that governments prefer to commend constitutional measures to the House of Commons on the basis, if possible, of all- or cross-party support. On the other hand, and more likely, it discourages a government from pursuing with any enthusiasm a measure which does not have overwhelming support within its own ranks. Given this, and the orientation of their current leaders, the Conservative and Labour Parties tend not to display enthusiasm for comprehensive change; though both are subject to pressures from within their own ranks. By contrast, the liberal approach is the dominant though not exclusive view among leaders and led within the Liberal Party, and to a much lesser extent within the SDP, and a Liberal/SDP Alliance Government would be committed to the introduction of electoral reform. However, if the

SDP/Liberal Alliance was to hold the balance of power in a 'hung' Parliament and made electoral reform a condition of support for one of the other parties, there is no guarantee that the other party could deliver the necessary parliamentary votes. Attitudes to the constitution (Traditionalist) and personal survival (not wishing to vote oneself out of one's seat) may be sufficient for certain MPs to outweigh the pull of party loyalty.

Of these three features, the first is likely to change as further debate takes place and the greater the realisation of the constitutional implications of change, the more sophisticated the debate and the more well-defined and articulated will be the approaches to constitutional change. Nonetheless, the existence of different approaches and of the other two factors identified above ensures that divisions will remain and that the landscape of constitutional debate will be an uneven and complex one. Though constitutional debate may become more sophisticated, there is no guarantee that any comprehensive or rationally planned reform of the constitution will take place. Of the approaches identified, only two – the Socialist and the liberal – have what might be described as anything approaching blueprints for a reformulation of the constitution. The Socialist suffers from a lack of support and from the fact that it seeks largely to change relationships within the existing formal framework rather than reshape the framework itself. The liberal suffers from the difficulty entailed in trying to translate plans into action. Though various 'packages' of constitutional reform have been put forward, there is no clear and apparent means by which such a package may be implemented. The Liberal Party's Reform of Government panel in 1980 conceded that implementing the package it proposed would be 'a mammoth undertaking'[77] – 'The UK political system has shown how indigestible it finds constitutional change'[78] – and recommended 'reform over a period of time, say the lifetime of a Parliament'.[79] Nevil Johnson has also expressed support for a form of step-by-step approach, with the possibility of a series of measures being enacted, such measures being based on recommendations from a body of inquiry on fundamental constitutional questions, analogous in some respects to the Law Commission.[80] Nonetheless, an air of measured doubt pervades Johnson's conclusions. Though, as he recognises, a greater constitutional awareness favours the liberal approach, it is not sufficient to overcome the obstacles created by existing interests. The problem for the reformers is the very nature of the beast which they seek to change. The more radical and the more comprehensive the constitutional reformulation, the greater the pitfalls to its achievement. Radical proposals such as a Bill of Rights fall foul of the very principle of the constitution which they seek to do away with (parliamentary sovereignty). The more measures that constitute a comprehensive package of reforms, the greater the chances of one or more elements failing at one of the various hurdles which they have to overcome. The danger is one of ending up with a part-fulfilled package, producing a somewhat ragged constitutional reformulation. Such change may be more acceptable than no change at all, but for the liberal approach it reduces the chance of creating a set of consensus-building constitutional rules. The result, in short, is likely to be typically British, in essence piecemeal, albeit taking place at a more rapid rate than hitherto and based on a more critical constitutional awareness. What is not typically British is the fact that, so long as there is no clear consensus on the form of constitution and constitutional change for the United Kingdom, the debate on the constitution is likely to be with us for some time. It is important that the complexity of that debate, the arguments surrounding the reforms proposed, the political environment and the approaches to constitutional change, be understood. This work is designed to contribute to that understanding.

NOTES

1   Lord Hugh Cecil, *Conservatism* (Home University Library, 1912), p. 10.

2   *HC Deb.*, 6th series, Vol. 2, c. 1213.

3   *HC Deb.*, 2, c. 1213–19.

4   *HC Deb.*, 2, c. 1219.

5   See P. Norton and A. Aughey, *Conservatives and Conservatism* (Temple Smith, 1981), p. 22.

6   See e.g. Ken Coates, *Democracy in the Labour Party* (Spokesman, 1977).

7   See e.g. Donald R. Shell, 'The British Constitution in 1980', *Parliamentary Affairs*, 34 (2), Spring 1981, pp. 160–4, David Kogan and M. Kogan, *The Battle for the Labour Party* (Fontana, 1982).

8   By the spring of 1982, 7 Labour MPs had been denied re-selection.

9   See *The Labour Programme 1973* (Labour Party, 1973), Stuart Holland, *The Socialist Challenge* (Quartet, 1975), and the Labour Party NEC document, *The Socialist Alternative*, approved by the 1981 Labour Party Conference.

10   Tony Benn, *Arguments for Socialism* (Penguin, 1980), p. 52. See also *The Labour Programme 1973*, p. 7.

11 Benn, *op. cit.*, p. 147.
12 G. Hodgson, *Labour at the Crossroads* (Martin Robertson, 1981), p. 216.
13 *Ibid.*, pp. 216–17.
14 Benn, *op. cit.*, p. 51.
15 *Guardian*, 30 Sept. 1981.
16 *Ibid.*
17 This point is well made by Eric Heffer MP, 'Would our British System Allow *Real* Socialism?' *Daily Telegraph*, 12 June 1979.
18 *Ibid.*
19 Sam Aaronovich, *The Ruling Class* (Lawrence & Wishart, 1961), p. 134.
20 See Ralph Miliband, *The State in Capitalist Society* (Quartet, 1977).
21 Holland, *op. cit.*
22 This point is well summarised in Pippa Norris, 'Do the Capitalists Rule?', in H.J. Elcock (ed.), *What sort of Society?* (Martin Robertson, 1982).
23 David Coates, 'Capital and State in Britain: The Industrial Policy of the Labour Government 1974–1979', *Hull Papers in Politics No. 24* (Hull University Politics Department, 1981). See also, by the same author, *Labour in Power?* (Longman, 1980) and *The Labour Party and the Struggle for Socialism* (Cambridge University Press, 1975).
24 Coates, *op. cit.*, p. 17.
25 *Ibid.*, 26.
26 See e.g. Bob Jessop, 'Capitalism and Democracy: the best possible shell?' in G. Littlejohn (ed.), *Power and the State* (Croom Helm, 1978), pp. 10–51, especially pp. 44–5.
27 Coates, *op. cit.*, p. 26.
28 S.H. Beer, *Modern British Politics* (Faber, 1965 ed.), p. 78.
29 Quoted in J.J. Richardson and G. Jordan, *Governing Under Pressure* (Martin Robertson, 1979), p. 50.
30 See e.g. David Steel, 'Constitutional Outrage and a Recipe for Decline', *The Times*, April 1976.
31 Anthony King, 'Overload: Problems of Governing in the 1970s', *Political Studies*, 23, 1975, p. 295.
32 The distinction between societal and state corporatism is drawn by Philippe C. Schmitter, 'Still the Century of Corporatism?', *The Review of Politics*, 36 (1), Jan. 1974, pp. 85–131. On the perceived movement towards a form of state corporatism, see R. Pahl and J. Winkler, 'The Coming Corporatism', *New Society*, 10 Oct. 1974.
33 On the costs and gains to groups of more formal involvement in the decision-making process, see Johan P. Olsen, 'Public Policy-Making and Theories of Organisational Choice', *Scandinavian Political Studies*, 7, 1972, pp. 22–3.
34 See G.D.H. Cole, *Guild Socialism, A Plan for Economic Recovery*

(Fabian Tract 192, 1920). Also see A.W. Wright, *G.D.H. Cole and Socialist Democracy* (Clarendon Press, 1979), especially pp. 58–9.

35 Hansard Society, *Parliamentary Reform 1933–60*, 2nd revised ed. (Cassell, 1967), p. 31.

36 *Ibid.*, pp. 31 and 34; Beer, *op. cit.*, pp. 76–7.

37 *Change or Decay* (Conservative Political Centre, 1963). The MPs argued for the creation of 'Standing Economic Committees'.

38 Norton and Aughey, *op. cit.*, pp. 84–6.

39 See the comments of Gillian Peele, 'The Developing Constitution', in C. Cook and J. Ramsden (eds), *Trends in British Politics since 1945* (Macmillan, 1978), p. 9.

40 Sir Ivor Jennings, *The Law and the Constitution*, 5th ed. (University of London, 1959), p. 102.

41 Quoted in A.H. Hanson and M. Walles, *Governing Britain*, revised ed. (Fontana, 1975), p. 156.

42 See *Reshaping Britain* (PEP, 1974). See also Brendon Sewill, 'How to End the British Disease', *The Sunday Times*, 20 Aug. 1978.

43 Letter to *The Times*, 9 Apr. 1976.

44 See Norris, *loc. cit.*

45 See e.g. L.T. Hobhouse, *Liberalism* (Butterworth, 1911).

46 Other attempts to limit trade union power have been made. Professor Hayek, for example, has advocated the revocation of the privileges granted them by the 1906 Trade Disputes Act. Letter to *The Times*, 21 July 1977.

47 Steel, *loc. cit.*

48 See, e.g., Reginald J. Harrison, *Pluralism and Corporatism* (Allen & Unwin, 1980), ch. 5.

49 See A.H. Birch, *Representative and Responsible Government* (Allen & Unwin, 1964), ch. 4.

50 See Ivan Illich *et al.*, *Disabling Professions* (Marion Boyers, 1977) and Pippa Norris, 'Who Should Decide? The experts versus the public', in H.J. Elcock (ed.), *What Sort of Society?*, ch. 16.

51 Liberal supporters tend to stress the free trade area created within the Communities; liberal opponents, such as MPs Enoch Powell and Richard Body, tend to stress the restrictive and insular existence of the EC in a world context.

52 See, for instance, *A New Constitutional Settlement*, by the Liberal Party's Reform of Government panel (Liberal Publications Department, 1980); *The Economist*, 5 Nov. 1977; and Nevil Johnson, *In Search of the Constitution* (Methuen, 1980 ed.).

53 See e.g. Michael Fagence, *Citizen Participation in Planning* (Pergamon, 1977).

54 Benn, *op. cit.*, p. 146.

55 For a delineation of these theories, see Birch *op. cit.*, and Beer, *op. cit.*, Part 1.

56 Michael Mezey, *Comparative Legislatures* (Duke University Press, 1979). In the British context, though, 'legislature' is something of a misnomer.

57 See Philip Norton, *The Commons in Perspective* (Martin Robertson, 1981), ch. 4; also Hanna Pitkin, *The Concept of Representation* (University of California Press, 1967).

58 Robert Kilroy-Silk MP, 'Wrongs of a Bill of Rights', *Guardian*, 4 Feb. 1977.

59 See above, Introduction, pp. 16–17.

60 For example, Bernard Crick, *The Reform oj Parliament* (Weidenfeld & Nicolson, 1964) represented the latter view; Ronald Butt, *The Power of Parliament* (Constable, 1968) was the prime example of the former.

61 Philip Norton, 'The U.S. Congress in Comparative Perspective: The British Parliament', Paper presented at the American Political Science Association annual conference, New York, USA, 1981, pp. 11–12.

62 See Norton, *The Commons in Perspective*, pp. 204–6.

63 *Ibid.*, ch. 9.

64 See Philip Norton, *Conservative Dissidents* (Temple Smith, 1978).

65 See *First Report from the Select Committee on Procedure (Supply)* Vol. 1, HC 118–1 (HMSO, 1981). See also 'MPs call for state audit', *The Times*, 9 Dec. 1981, and *HC Deb.*, 13, c. 39–112.

66 *The Conservative Manifesto 1979* (Conservative Central Office, 1979), p. 21.

67 See Norton, *The Commons in Perspective*, pp. 231–2.

68 *HC Deb.*, 2, c. 1262–3.

69 *HC Deb.*, 2, c. 1263.

70 *HC Deb.*, 2, c. 1264.

71 *HL Deb.*, vol. 426, c. 52–6. See also *HC Deb.*, 4, c. 444–54.

72 A BBC television series in which the Permanent Secretary deftly fends off his Minister's insistence on action with responses such as 'In the fulness of time . . .', 'when circumstances permit . . . ,', 'It all depends, Minister . . .', and the like.

73 *HC Deb.*, 2, c. 1268.

74 H.W.R. Wade, *Constitutional Fundamentals* (Stevens, 1980), p. 2.

75 See e.g. Nevil Johnson, *Government in the Federal Republic of Germany* (Pergamon, 1973).

76 Indeed, a desire for social harmony, for consensus, has led to a certain ambiguity in the stance of the Social Democrats (and some liberals) towards the role of the State in economic planning. Note especially the comments of Hodgson, *op. cit.*

77 *A New Constitutional Settlement*, p. 13.

78 *Ibid.*

79 *Ibid.*

80 Johnson, *In Search of the Constitution*, pp. 231–2.

Select Reading List

For students wishing to read further on the topics covered in this volume, the following texts are recommended. Where possible I have opted for a few texts which are comprehensive and easily accessible.

THE CONSTITUTION

For general texts on the Constitution and Constitutional Law, see:
O. Hood Phillips' *Constitutional and Administrative Law*, 6th ed. by O. Hood Phillips and Paul Jackson (Sweet and Maxwell, 1978).
E.C.S. Wade and G. Godfrey Phillips, *Constitutional and Administrative Law*, 9th ed. by A.W. Bradley (Longman, 1977), much improved on the eighth edition; and
S.A. de Smith, *Constitutional and Administrative Law*, 4th ed. revised by H. Street and R. Brazier (Penguin, 1981).

Still extremely useful but now probably difficult to obtain is Geoffrey Marshall and Graeme C. Moodie, *Some Problems of the Constitution*, 4th revised ed. (Hutchinson, 1967). For constitutional theory see Geoffrey Marshall, *Constitutional Theory* (Oxford University Press, 1971).

For recent debate on constitutional developments, see:
Nevil Johnson, *In Search of the Constitution* (Methuen ed., 1980).
Max Beloff and Gillian Peele, *The Government of the United Kingdom* (Weidenfeld & Nicolson, 1980).
Sir Leslie Scarman, *English Law – The New Dimension* (Stevens, 1974).
H.W.R. Wade, *Constitutional Fundamentals* (Stevens, 1980).
Lord Hailsham, *The Dilemma of Democracy* (Collins, 1978).
Peter Bromhead, *Britain's Developing Constitution* (Allen & Unwin, 1974).

THE PRIME MINISTER

There is no shortage of texts which deal wholly or in part (usually the latter) with the office and behaviour of the Prime Minister. See especially Anthony King (ed.), *The British Prime Minister* (Macmillan, 1969) which comprises a collection of now dated essays by, among others, Richard Crossman, G.W. Jones, D.J. Heasman and John Mackintosh. For a short essay on the history of the office see Lord Blake, *The Office of Prime Minister* (Oxford University Press, 1975).

Also see John P. Mackintosh, *The British Cabinet*, 3rd ed. (Stevens, 1977); Harold Wilson, *The Governance of Britain* (Sphere Books, 1977); P. Gordon Walker, *The Cabinet*, revised ed. (Fontana, 1972); Brian Sedgemore, *The Secret Constitution* (Hodder & Stoughton, 1980); Richard Crossman, *The Diaries of a Cabinet Minister*, vol I, II, and III (Hamish Hamilton/Jonathan Cape, 1975, 1976 and 1977); Richard Crossman, *Inside View* (Jonathan Cape, 1972); and Tony Benn, 'The Case for a Constitutional Premiership', *Parliamentary Affairs*, 33 (1), Winter 1980, pp. 7–22.

INDIVIDUAL AND COLLECTIVE MINISTERIAL RESPONSIBILITY

See the works cited above by Marshall and Moodie, O. Hood Phillips, Wade and Phillips, S.A. de Smith, Nevil Johnson, and Brian Sedgemore (ch. 9), as well as the article by Tony Benn. See also Edmund Dell, 'Collective Responsibility: Fact, Fiction or Facade?" in *Policy and Practice: The Experience of Government* (Royal Institute of Public Administration, 1980), pp. 27–48.

THE MACHINERY OF GOVERNMENT

The Reorganisation of Central Government, Cmnd. 4506 (HMSO, 1968).

Sir Richard Clarke, 'The Machinery of Government', in W. Thornhill (ed.), *The Modernization of British Government* (Pitman, 1975).

Edward Heath and Anthony Barker, 'Heath on Whitehall Reform', *Parliamentary Affairs*, 31 (4), Autumn 1978, pp. 363–90.

J.M. Lee, 'The Machinery of Government under Mrs Thatcher's Administration', *Parliamentary Affairs*, 33 (4), Autumn 1980, pp. 434–47.

THE CIVIL SERVICE

Like the Prime Minister, much has been written about the Civil Service. See especially *The Report of the Committee on the Civil Service* (the Fulton Report), Cmnd. 3638 (HMSO, 1968) and *The Eleventh Report from the Expenditure Committee*, HC 535 (HMSO, 1977).

Useful books to consult are Lord Crowther-Hunt and Peter Kellner, *The Civil Servants* (Macdonald Futura, 1980), John Garrett, *Managing*

the Civil Service (Heinemann, 1980) – the latter more concerned with
management functions in the service – and the diaries of Richard
Crossman, cited above, and of Barbara Castle, *The Castle Diaries 1974–
76* (Weidenfeld & Nicolson, 1980).

Useful chapters and articles to consult are Bruce Headey, 'Cabinet
Ministers and Senior Civil Servants', in V. Herman and J. Alt (eds),
Cabinet Studies: A Reader (Macmillan, 1975); Maurice Wright,
'Ministers and Civil Servants: Relations and Responsibilities', *Parliamentary Affairs*, 30 (3), Summer 1977, pp. 293–313; Richard Wilding,
'The Civil Servant as Policy Adviser and Manager', *Public Administration
Bulletin*, 32, April 1980, pp. 34–49; and the articles by Finer,
Crowther-Hunt, Summerton and Lewis in the special issue of *Parliamentary Affairs* ('Government and Public Servants'), 33 (4), Autumn 1980.

THE HOUSE OF COMMONS

Philip Norton, *The Commons in Perspective* (Martin Robertson, 1981).
S.A. Walkland and M. Ryle (eds), *The Commons Today* (Fontana, 1981).
Philip Norton, 'The House of Commons and the Constitution: The
Challenges of the 1970s', *Parliamentary Affairs*, 34 (3), Summer
1981, pp. 253–71.
And, for library consultation, S.A. Walkland (ed.), *The House of Commons in the Twentieth Century* (Oxford University Press, 1979).

THE HOUSE OF LORDS

House of Lords Information Office, *House of Lords Reform 1850–
1970*, 2nd ed. Factsheet No. 1 (House of Lords Information Office,
1978).
Janet Morgan, 'The House of Lords in the 1980s', *The Parliamentarian*,
62 (1), Jan. 1981, pp. 18–26.
The House of Lords: Report of the Conservative Review Committee
(Conservative Central Office, 1978).
Lord Chalfont, 'Reform of the House of Lords', *The Parliamentarian*,
58 (4), pp. 233–39.
Lord Boyd-Carpenter, 'Reform of the House of Lords – Another View',
The Parliamentarian, 59 (2), April 1978, pp. 90–93.

THE JUDICIARY

See the works cited under 'The Constitution'. Also see J.A.G. Griffith,
The Politics of the Judiciary, 2nd ed. (Fontana, 1981).

THE EUROPEAN COMMUNITIES

There are multiple texts dealing with the European Communities in one form or another. On British applications for membership, see Robert J. Lieber, *British Politics and European Unity* (University of California Press, 1970) and Uwe Kitzinger, *Diplomacy and Persuasion* (Thames & Hudson, 1973). On the 1975 Referendum, see David Butler and Uwe Kitzinger, *The 1975 Referendum* (Macmillan, 1976) and Anthony King, *Britain Says Yes* (American Enterprise Institute, 1977). On Britain and the Communities, see especially William Wallace (ed.), *Britain in Europe* (Heinemann, 1980), a very useful book which came to my attention too late to be fully incorporated in this volume.

On the EC and the European Parliament, see Robert Jackson, *The Powers of the European Parliament* (Conservative Group for Europe, n.d.), and, by David Coombes, *The Future of the European Parliament* (Policy Studies Institute, n.d.) and *The Political Significance of the EEC* (Macmillan, 1982).

DEVOLUTION

The Royal Commission on the Constitution, Vol. 1: Report. Cmnd. 5460 (HMSO, 1973).

A.H. Birch, *Political Integration and Disintegration in the British Isles* (Allen & Unwin, 1977).

H.M. Drucker and Gordon Brown, *The Politics of Nationalism and Devolution* (Longman, 1980).

Tam Dalyell, *Devolution: The End of Britain* (Jonathan Cape, 1977).

Vernon Bogdanor, *Devolution* (Oxford University Press, 1979).

Dr David Owen, *Face the Future* (Oxford University Press, 1981).

Richard Rose, *Understanding the United Kingdom* (Longman, 1982).

NORTHERN IRELAND

Richard Rose, *Governing Without Consensus* (Faber, 1971).

A.H. Birch, as cited under 'Devolution'.

John Whyte, 'Why is the Northern Ireland Problem so Intractable?', *Parliamentary Affairs*, 34 (4), Autumn 1981, pp. 422–35.

Richard Rose, *Northern Ireland: A Time of Choice* (American Enterprise Institute, 1976).

R.J. Lawrence, 'Northern Ireland', in W. Thornhill (ed.), as cited above under 'Machinery of Government'.

D.C. Watt, *The Constitution of Northern Ireland* (Heinemann, 1981).

REFERENDUMS

Vernon Bogdanor, *The People and the Party System* (Cambridge University Press, 1981).
Philip Goodhart, *Referendum* (Tom Stacey, 1971).
S. Alderson, *Yea or Nay?* (Cassell, 1975).
See also Anthony King, *Britain Says Yes*, and David Butler and Uwe Kitzinger, *The 1975 Referendum*, as cited above under 'The European Communities'.

ELECTORAL REFORM

Vernon Bogdanor, as cited above under 'Referendums'.
S.E. Finer (ed.), *Adversary Politics and Electoral Reform* (Wigram, 1975).
Joe Rogaly, *Parliament for the People* (Temple Smith, 1976).
Sir Angus Maude and John Szemerey, *Why Electoral Change?* (Conservative Political Centre, 1982).
J.A. Chandler, 'The Plurality Vote: A Reappraisal', *Political Studies*, 30 (1), March 1982, pp. 87–94.
William Waldegrave, 'Electoral Reform – The Case Against', *Spectator*, 25 Oct. 1975.

BILL OF RIGHTS

P. Wallington and J. McBride, *Civil Liberties and a Bill of Rights* (Cobden Trust, 1976).
Lord Hailsham, *The Dilemma of Democracy*, as cited above; also Scarman, H.W.R. Wade and Nevil Johnson, all cited under 'The Constitution'.
Michael Zander, *A Bill of Rights?* (Barry Rose, 1975).
Lord Wade, 'A Bill of Rights for the United Kingdom', *The Parliamentarian*, 61 (2), 1980, pp. 65–71.
L. Neville Brown, 'A Bill of Rights for the United Kingdom', *The Parliamentarian*, 58 (2), April 1977, pp. 79–88.
Committee of the Society for Conservative Lawyers, *Another Bill of Rights?* (Conservative Political Centre, 1976).

APPROACHES TO CONSTITUTIONAL REFORM

For the High Tory approach see Lord Hugh Cecil, *Conservatism* (Home University Library, 1912). For the Socialist approach see Tony Benn,

Arguments for Socialism (Penguin, 1980). For the Marxist approach see Ralph Miliband, *The State in Capitalist Society* (Quartet, 1977) and David Coates, 'Capital and State in Britain: The Industrial Policy of the Labour Government 1974–1979', *Hull Papers in Politics No. 24* (Hull University Politics Department, 1981). For the group approach see J.J. Richardson and A.G. Jordan, *Governing Under Pressure* (Martin Robertson, 1979). For the liberal approach, see especially A.H. Birch, *Representative and Responsibile Government* (Allen & Unwin, 1964) and the works cited above by Nevil Johnson and David Owen. No one recent work details the Traditional approach, though see Leon D. Epstein, 'What Happened to the British Party Model?', *American Political Science Review*, 74 (1), March 1980, pp. 9–22. All of the foregoing should be read within the context of the concluding chapter to this volume.

Index

St John Stevas, Norman   80,
113, 120, 130, 285
Salisbury, Marquess of   23, 117
Sands, Bobby   198
Sarlvik, Bo   238
Sartori, Giovanni   275
Scarman, Lord   109, 135, 137,
145, 148, 246, 252, 253
Scotland   18, 28, 30, 102, 123,
142, 144, 153, 201, 214,
216, 223, 227, 241
Act of Union with   6
Scotland Act   30, 144, 186
Scotland and Wales Bill (1976)
64, 179–80, 241
Scotland Bill   180, 182, 183,
185, 186
Scotland, Secretary of State for
46, 144, 182, 214
Scottish Development Authority
181
Scottish Grand Committee,
House of Commons   181
Scottish Labour Party   183
Scottish National Party (SNP)
161, 175–85, 213
Scottish Office   175, 181
Secret Constitution, The   45
Sedgemore, Brian   43, 45, 46,
65, 83
Settlement, Act of (1701)   5, 6
Sharp, Clifford   224
Sheane, Michael   205
Shell, Donald   66
Short, Edward   217, 221
Sieghart, Paul   249
Silkin, John   91
Silkin, Sam   139
Sillars, James   183
Simon, Lord   137
Smith, Brian C.   58
Social Contract, The   218
Social Democratic and Labour
Party (SDLP) (NI)   161,
196–7, 203, 204, 205
Social Democratic Party   109,
123, 130, 171, 174, 186,
187–8, 216, 235, 236, 240,

241, 267, 289
alliance with Liberal Party
109, 131, 188, 236–7,
241, 278, 289, 290
Social Services, Secretary of State
for   60, 62, 79
Society of Conservative Lawyers
Bill of Rights Committee   254
Constitutional Reform
Committee   122, 124–7
South Africa   139
Sovereign, *see* under 'Crown'
Spain   204
Speaker's Conference on Electoral
Law   227, 228–9
Stacey, Frank   77
Standing Committees, House of
Commons   112
Stanyer, Jeffrey   58
Statute Law   5–6, 7, 8, 9, 18
Steed, Michael   228
Steel, David   186, 275
Stockdale v. Hansard   7
Stokes, John   2, 24, 148–9,
262–3, 286, 289
Supply, Ministry of   73
Sweden   93, 166
Switzerland   166

Tameside   138
Tatchell, Peter   267
Taylor, P.J.   240
Technology, Ministry of   75
Thatcher, Mrs Margaret   8, 42,
47, 48, 65, 83, 102, 141,
162, 170, 198–9, 203, 209,
214, 216, 219–23, 225,
231, 234, 247, 274, 285
Thorneycroft, Lord   65
Thurlow, Lord Chancellor   61
Trade and Industry, Department
of   59, 75
Trade Board Act (1909)   271
(1918)   271
Trade, Board of   75
Trade, Department of   59, 139
Trade Union and Labour